SIEGE CITY

The Story of
Derry and Londonderry

Brian Lacy

THE
BLACKSTAFF PRESS
BELFAST

ACKNOWLEDGEMENTS

Grateful acknowledgement is made to: Collins Publishers for permission to quote from *A House Divided: The Dilemma of Northern Ireland* (1973) by James Callaghan; the Controller of Her Majesty's Stationery Office for permission to reproduce material from the Historic Monuments and Buildings Branch, Department of the Environment for Northern Ireland, Crown copyright; André Deutsch and Observer Books and Features Limited for permission to quote from *The Price of my Soul* (1969) by Bernadette Devlin; Gill and Macmillan for permission to quote from *Derry: Countdown to Disaster* (1986) by Frank Curran; Pluto Press and Eamonn McCann for permission to quote from *War and an Irish Town* (1984); and Ward River Press for permission to quote from *The Road to Bloody Sunday* (1983) by Raymond McClean.

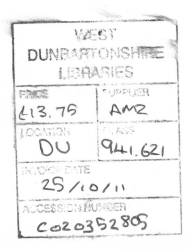

First published in 1990 by
The Blackstaff Press Limited
3 Galway Park, Dundonald, Belfast BT16 0AN, Northern Ireland

This book has received financial assistance under the
Cultural Traditions Programme which aims to encourage
acceptance and understanding of cultural diversity.

Printed in Northern Ireland by
The Universities Press Limited

British Library Cataloguing in Publication Data
Lacy, Brian
Siege city: the story of Derry and Londonderry.
1. Derry (District). Londonderry, history
I. Title
941.623
ISBN 0-85640-443-8

to my mother and father
Nora and Tommy Lacey

CONTENTS

PREFACE

Derry is one of the longest, continually inhabited places in Ireland. Like a number of similar settlements throughout the world with a parallel dramatic history of colonisation and exodus, siege and deliverance, it is, in some ways, a 'holy' city – a place of special (even mythical) meaning for the Protestant and Catholic communities which claim an attachment to it. For almost seventy years Derry has been a border city, and in earlier times it was often a frontier settlement, the control of which was frequently contested between opposing social and political groups. Indeed, the history of the city is as complicated as it is ancient.

Although parts of this book are based mainly on my own research, some sections owe a great deal to other authors. I am also indebted to a number of people and institutions who have assisted me. I must thank my former colleagues and students at Magee College, especially Frank D'Arcy and Bob Hunter, and the staff of the Magee Library, particularly Alan Roberts, Lewis Childes and Patrick Tesky. Staff at the Central Library in Derry have been of great assistance, especially Carmel Doherty, Joe McGuigan and Gerry Quinn. Colleagues at Derry City Council have assisted me in a variety of ways. Many individuals have helped also, in particular: Nick Brannon; Harry Bryson; Ian Fisher; David Gilliland; Pat Hodgson; John Hume MP, MEP; John Kelnhauser; Annsley Malley; Eamonn McCann; Mitchel McLoughlin; Sean MacMahon; Michael McGuinness; Jim Mullan; Professor Maurice O'Connell; the Very Reverend Cecil Orr, dean of Derry; Pauline Ross; and Eileen Schlindwein. As in many areas of my work, Dermot Francis has been of immense practical help particularly in the production of all the new drawings in this book. My special gratitude is due to the staff of The Blackstaff Press. Finally I must acknowledge the continuous support of Michael McLaughlin throughout the writing of this book.

BRIAN LACY

OCTOBER 1990

1

'IF STONES COULD SPEAK'

Derry is built on hills. It is a city of steep streets, of steps and wonderful panoramas. It is a city of perspectives, historical and political as well as topographical. Most people who visit Derry for the first time are struck by its beautiful location and it is often claimed that it has the finest situation of any Irish city, with its position on a lovely curve of the River Foyle and the mountains of Inishowen forming a dramatic backdrop.

THE 'MANNER OF AN ILAND'

The ancient monastic settlement of Derry and the walled plantation city of Londonderry were established on a hill on the west side of the River Foyle. The modern city has spread well beyond this original area and now covers the surrounding hills and valleys on both sides of the river. Five thousand to six thousand years ago, when sea level was about thirty feet higher than it is today, the river flowed around each side of the hill of Derry, making it an island. Gradually the water level dropped and by the time the monastery was founded in the sixth century AD the channel on the west side of the hill was above river level, but its floor was still wet and boggy. Although causeways had been built across this bog, the hill was sufficiently cut off for the Elizabethan soldiers who captured Derry in May 1600 to describe it as being in the 'manner of an iland'. It continued to be referred to as the 'island of the Derrie' by the first plantation settlers who came there at the beginning of the seventeenth century. The marshy valley which separated the island from the high ground to the west was later reclaimed and built over as a suburb. In the late 1960s this area became known all over the world as the Bogside, a name reflecting its ancient origins as a marsh.

The island of Derry is a roughly wedge-shaped hill, which covers 200 acres and rises to 120 feet above sea level. The River Foyle, which is still tidal at this point, is fast flowing, about forty feet in depth at high tide and a little over one thousand feet wide. Until 1790, when a bridge was built connecting the city to the east bank, the only means of crossing the river was by ferry.

Derry is located at the eastern end of a small range of hills which occupy an important position between the Swilly and Foyle valleys. To the north, the range is cut off from the Inishowen Peninsula by a valley, sometimes referred to as the Pennyburn Depression. Most of the floor

Opposite
Nailor's Row by John [illegible] Hunter (1893–1951) (Courtesy of St Colun[illegible] Cathedral)

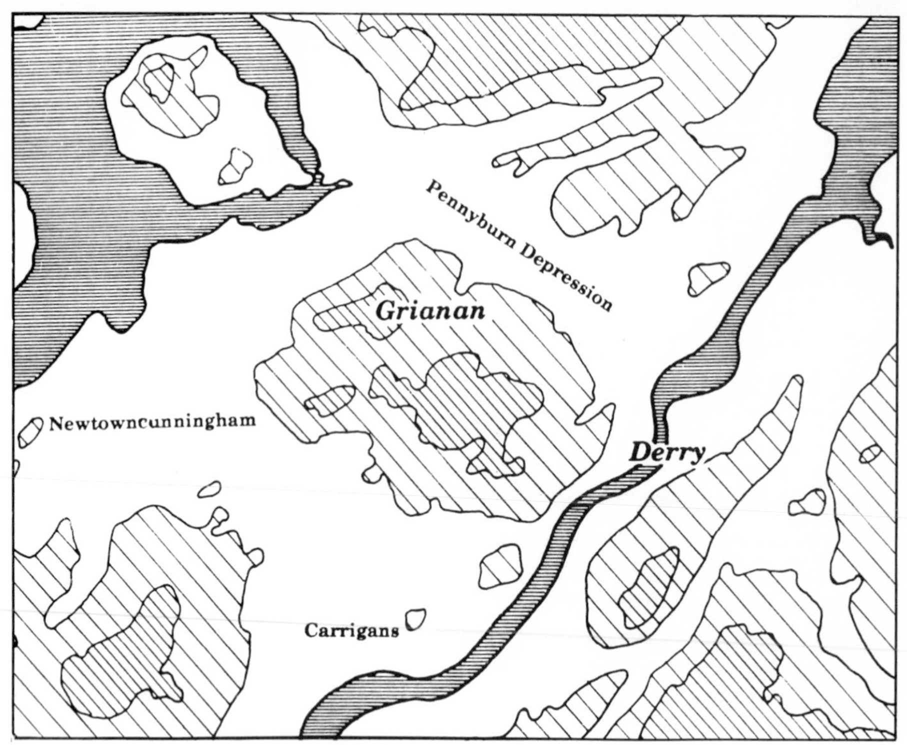

The area of high ground between Derry and the Grianan of Aileach, isolated to the north and south by low-lying, boggy valleys

of this valley has been reclaimed, but until quite recently, it too was wet and boggy. Similarly to the south, another low-lying marshy valley between the present-day County Donegal villages of Carrigans and Newtowncunningham helps to further isolate the range. In ancient times it was possible to cross these wet areas at only one or two places. At the western, or Lough Swilly, side the range ends at Greenan Mountain, four and a half miles from the city, and the ancient fortifications of the Grianan of Aileach, which dominate its summit, indicate the importance of this range of hills as a pivot around which the early history of the north-west of Ireland turned.

LAYERS OF STONE

Derry's famous walls and many of its older buildings were built with a

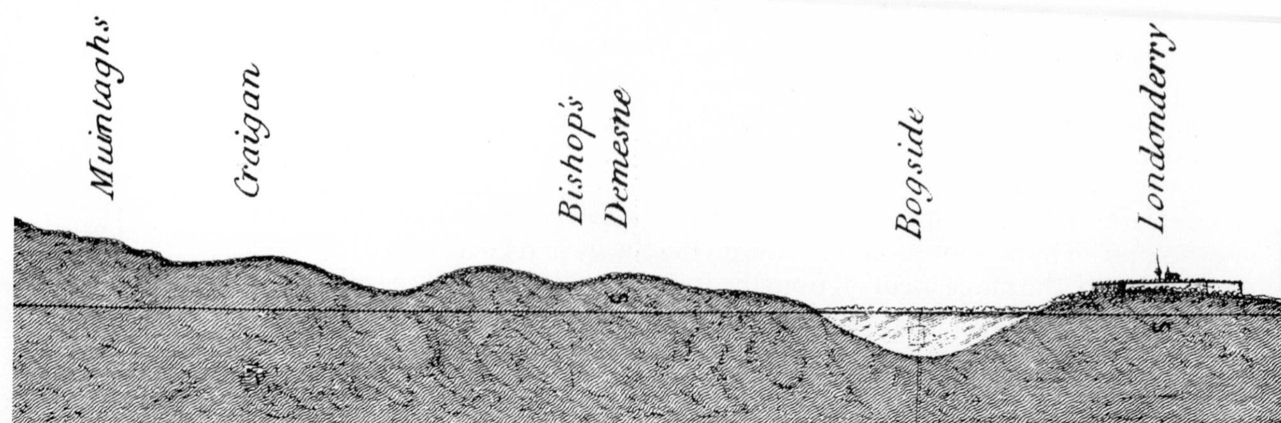

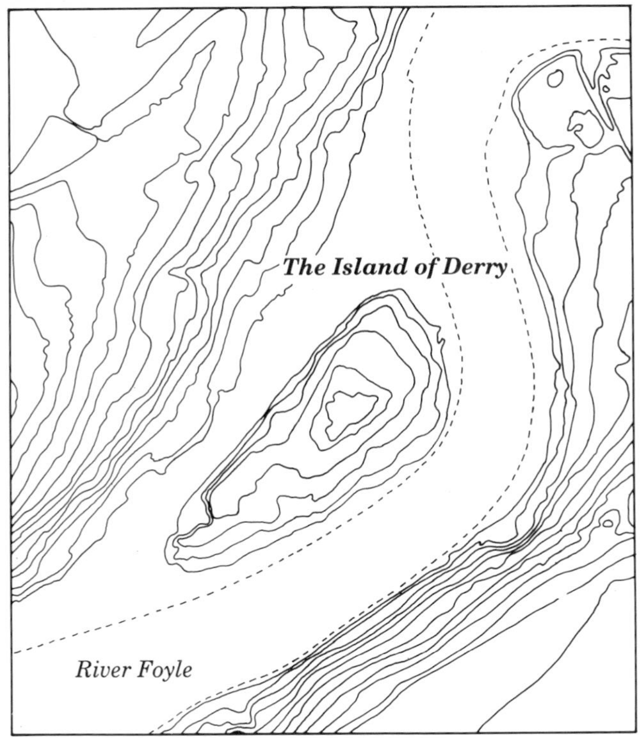

The 'island' of Derry, showing the modern river course and contours at twenty-foot intervals

distinctive type of stone, a local variety of schist, and the hills on which the city itself is built are also formed from the same material. Schist was quarried on the island until well into the twentieth century, linking the homes and workplaces of the citizens with the remote geological events that shaped the topography of the later city. The geology of the area around Derry is extremely simple. Indeed, it is one of the more ironic aspects of a study of the city's past that the least complicated part of it is its geology.

The rock beneath the city is essentially formed of just one geological layer that came into existence five hundred million years ago. At that time, sands and clays which were washed down onto the floor of what might be described as an ancestor of the Atlantic Ocean solidified into schist. Four hundred and fifty million years ago this layer was lifted and violently folded into a series of north–east/south–west parallel hills and

Cross-section through the landscape to illustrate the original 'island' nature of Derry, from George Vaughan Sampson's chart of County Londonderry (1813)

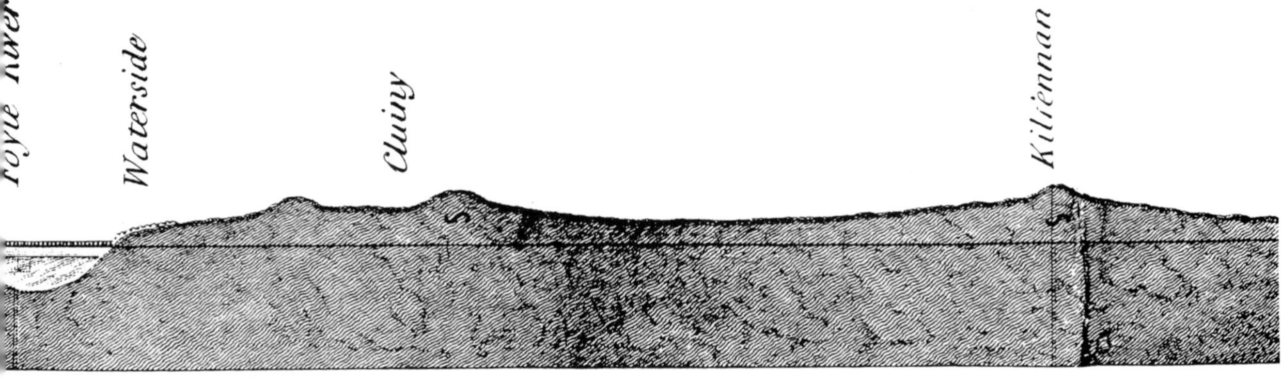

valleys as part of the widespread geological event known as the Caledonian Upheaval. The hills and valleys around Derry, including the island itself, are aligned according to this pattern. Even the River Foyle follows this trend, flowing in a downfold in the rocks. While subsequent geological processes continued to affect Ireland, the rocks formed at later stages were almost all eroded away again in the vicinity of Derry. Some traces of these later formations can still be detected on the landscape, particularly in the east–west routes of the smaller rivers which flow into the Foyle. However, it is the folded layer of schist that forms the underlying skeleton of the beautiful topography and scenery of the city and its surroundings.

THE EFFECTS OF THE ICE AGE

In 1924, J. Kaye Charlesworth, Professor of Geology at Queen's University Belfast, published his research into the effect of the Ice Age influences on the north-west of Ireland. According to Professor Charlesworth, a huge ice mass was formed in the Highlands of Scotland during the Munsterian Cold Stage (175,000–100,000 BC). This spread as far west as Lough Swilly and Inishowen in County Donegal, stopping immediately north of Derry in the Pennyburn Depression. At its edge, sand and gravel would have been washed out by the melting waters and this is probably the origin of the gravel and reddish sands which can be found overlying the schist on the island of Derry itself. Pits for the extraction of these deposits existed in the centre of the city up to the twentieth century. The Scottish ice also blocked off the Lough Foyle exit to the ocean. The river had to find an alternative outlet to the sea along

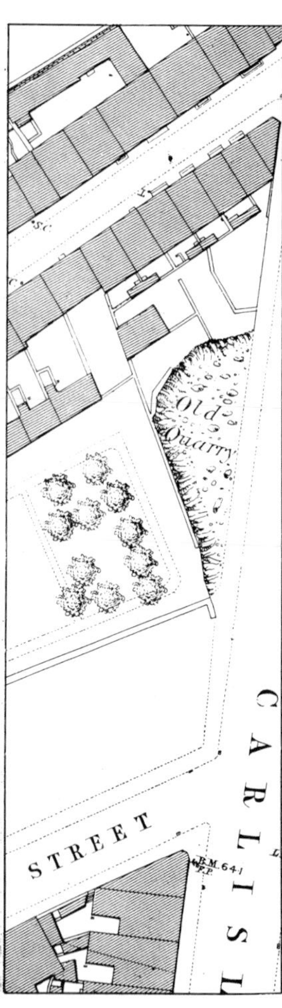

A schist quarry at Carlisle Road, near the city centre, as shown on an Ordnance Survey map of 1873

Aerial view of Eglinton Airport, which is built on the level terrain on the eastern side of Lough Foyle (Seamus Devine)

the existing preglacial valley between Carrigans and Newtowncunningham. This area was later left as low-lying, wet and marshy country when the river returned to its normal route. It proved an effective barrier in later prehistoric and early historic times.

About 20,000 BC, during the Midlandian Cold Stage, glaciers began to form in the Bluestack Mountains in south Donegal. The ice spread northwards, reaching Lough Swilly, and passed over the low hills which lie to the north of Derry (on which many of the newer suburbs of the city are built), giving them their smooth convex appearance. Sands and gravels were also washed out of its melting edge and this is probably the origin of some of the level terraces of gravels which lie along the southern and eastern side of Lough Foyle. Some of these terraces lay a little above the present water line but others have been artificially drained, with Dutch-like dykes built along their edge. These gravels make for excellent farmland but they also have a strategic importance; for example, during the Second World War four separate aerodromes were built on the level terrain. One abandoned airfield is now the site of the Du Pont industrial complex, and another serves as the city's municipal Eglinton Airport.

Towards the end of the cold phase there seems to have been a readvance of the Scottish glacier, which blocked the exit of Lough Foyle for a second time. Again the river had to find an alternative outlet through Lough Swilly and this time the route was along the Pennyburn Depression. When the Scottish ice withdrew and the river returned to its normal course, the abandoned channel was also left as a low-lying, marshy and boggy valley, prey to the rising sea levels of the post-glacial period and an obstacle to communication until reclaimed in modern times.

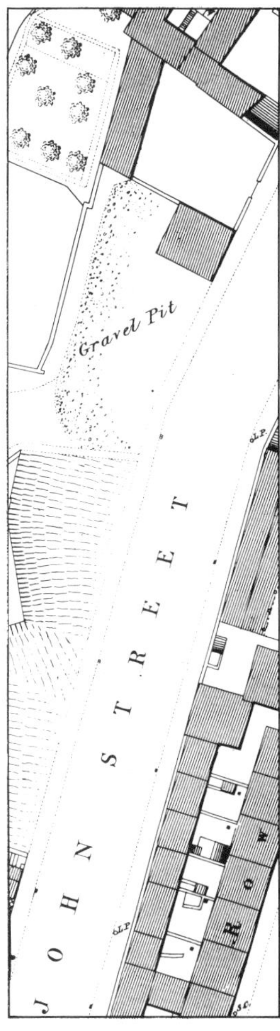

A gravel pit at John Street, near the city centre, as shown on an Ordnance Survey map of 1873

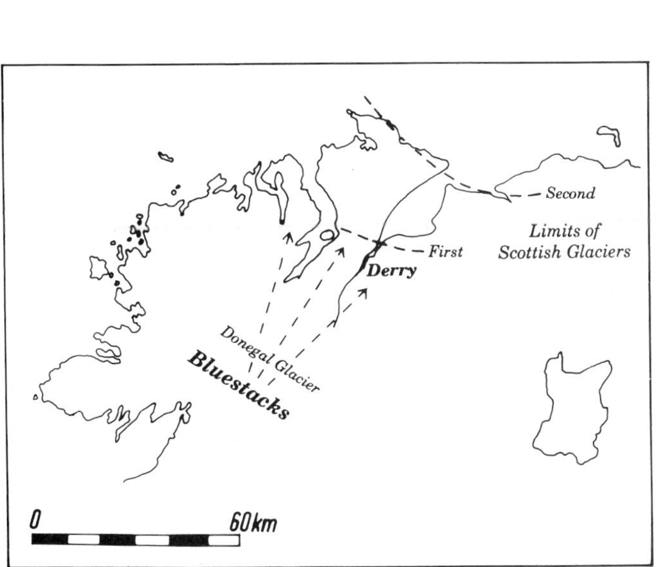

Simplified movements of glaciers in the Derry area during the Ice Age

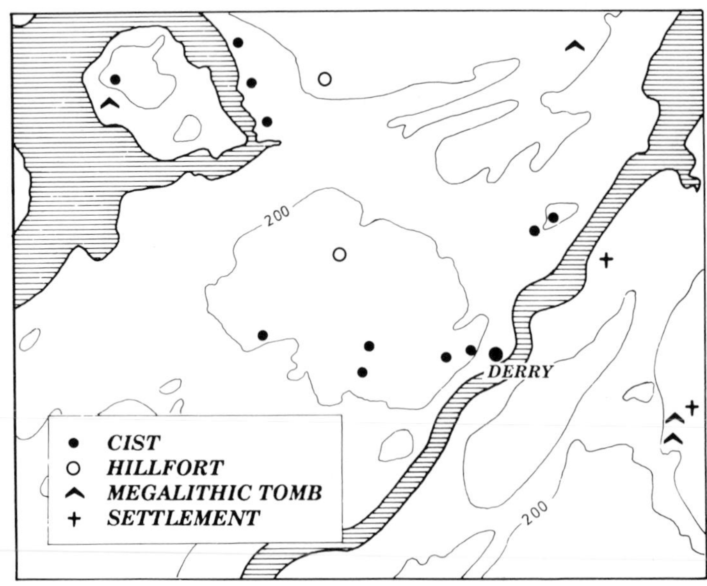

Map showing some sites of the Neolithic and Bronze Age in the vicinity of Derry

THE ARRIVAL OF HUMAN BEINGS

After the ice withdrew, about 15,000 BC, and the climate improved, the former arctic terrain began to be colonised with flora and fauna. A natural sequence of simple plants succeeded by scrublands and later by forests was set in motion. Animals quickly followed, and by about 7,000 BC humans, too, had established themselves in Ireland, coming across from the northern parts of Britain. The most impressive evidence found in Ireland for these Mesolithic (Middle Stone Age) people comes from Mount Sandel near Coleraine in County Derry. There, in a forest clearing, a small community lived in dome-shaped huts for most of the year. They ate a variety of local fish and plant foods and hunted small animals with their flint and stone implements. The discovery of similar tools and weapons elsewhere shows that Mesolithic people travelled inland on the River Foyle and its tributaries. Their boats, possibly similar to the currachs which still are used in the west of Ireland, would have been a common sight on the river near where, thousands of years later, the city of Derry would be built.

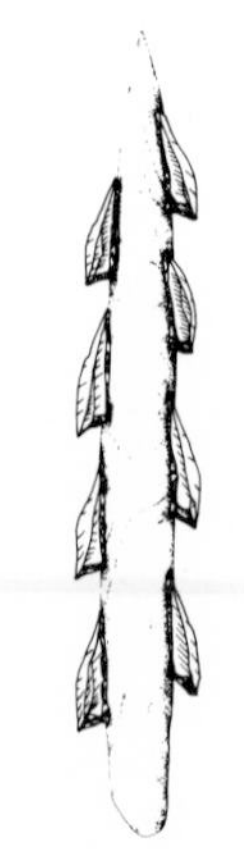

Reconstruction of a Mesolithic flint implement, based on finds from Mount Sandel, County Derry (Historic Monuments and Buildings Branch, Department of Environment for Northern Ireland)

Around 4,000 BC new kinds of settlers were making an appearance in Ireland. These were the first people to practise agriculture, Ireland's first farmers. With their stone axes they had to clear sections of the extensive forests which were by then widespread. Their houses were usually rectangular in shape and they made distinctive types of pottery which, as well as being used for domestic purposes, were also sometimes buried in the elaborate tombs they built to house their dead. Many of these tombs of the Neolithic and early Bronze Age periods, called megaliths because they are usually made of large stones, can be found in the hinterland of Derry, as can the ancient field enclosures buried deep under later growths of peat bog, such as those at Ballygroll, a few miles east of the city. These are the remains of the Neolithic farms.

There is direct evidence that people were living within the limits of the modern city during the Bronze Age. This was the age during which the mysterious properties of metals were first discovered and exploited. Most of the people continued to live by farming but some highly skilled craftsmen began to emerge, making a wonderful range of bronze and gold ornaments, weapons and tools. A small excavation at Rough Island in Enagh Lough, three miles north-east of Derry, turned up a looped-and-socketed bronze spear-head and some pottery, upon which impressions of wheat, barley and oat grains had accidentally been stamped into the soft clay while the pot was waiting to be fired. In March 1988 a small cist-burial or stone grave was discovered in Shantallow on the northern outskirts of Derry and others have been found near the city on previous occasions, such as in the Creggan area and at Pennyburn. The Shantallow grave contained the skeletal remains of an adult male who, typically, had been buried with a decorated funerary pot known as a Food Vessel. The man had died within a few centuries after 2,000 BC and the pot probably originally contained a quantity of food to sustain him on his journey to the 'kingdom of the dead'.

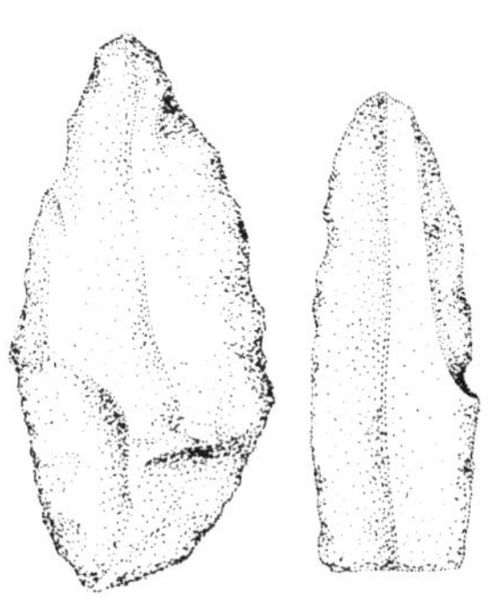

Mesolithic flint implements found on the shore of River Foyle at Shantallow, Derry

As human colonisation of Ireland was becoming more extensive, a further natural drama had been taking place imperceptibly. The end of the Ice Age set in motion a complex series of changes in the relative levels of land and sea. First the land level rose, relieved of the immense weight of the glaciers. However, as the ice in turn melted, the lower ground was drowned by the flooded seas to well above the present water line. This resulted in the characteristic abandoned raised beaches which can be seen in many places near Derry. The point when the sea rose to its highest level vis-à-vis the land took place a little over five thousand years ago. One effect of this was that much of the low-lying land around the present city was drowned and the Bogside valley was partially under water. The hill of Derry would have been a true island. About the same time, the trees which were to be so important in the history of that island would have taken root. The oaks of Derry had arrived.

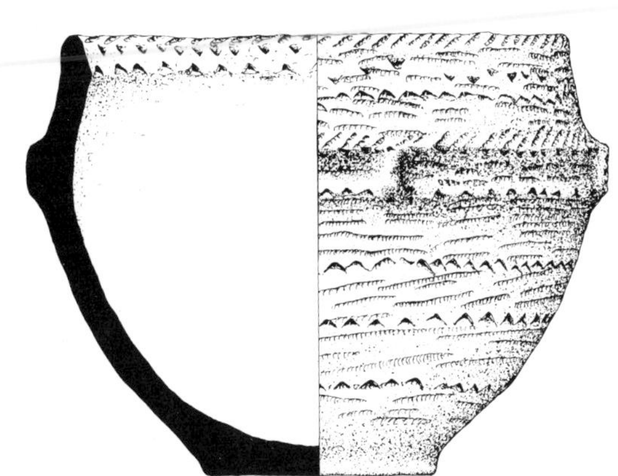

Food Vessel found in Bronze Age cist-burial at Shantallow, Derry, in 1988 (Historic Monuments and Buildings Branch, Department of Environment for Northern Ireland)

THE OAKS

Derry, from the old Irish *daire*, modern Irish, *doire*, means 'oakwood' or 'oakgrove'. From the beginning of recorded history this word, in a variety of versions and associations, has been used as the name of the hill on which the centre of the modern city is built. The placename element 'derry' is very common in Ireland, recalling the widespread oakwoods of ancient times. There are over a thousand townlands throughout Ireland which have this word in some combination. Frequently, it was used to denote an island of high, dry land totally or partly surrounded by peat bog. Derrynaflan in County Tipperary, where a magnificent eighth-century chalice and a hoard of ecclesiastical objects were found, was an early Christian monastery situated on one of these islands. In the early Christian period Derry was a similar kind of island.

Acorn and leaf of English oak (*Quercus robur*)

Oak trees first made their appearance in Ireland about 5,000 or 6,000 BC. They spread fairly rapidly and within a few thousand years had become a dominant feature of the Irish landscape. They remained one of the most common elements in the Irish woodlands until the great forests, such as Killetra and Glenconkeyne near Lough Neagh and the River Bann, were systematically cut down, beginning in the early seventeenth century. Tragic clearances like these have been commemorated by the Gaelic poets of the time:

> Now, what will we do without timber,
> The last of the woods are all felled.

Leaf of sessile oak (*Quercus petraea*)

Two kinds of oak are native to Ireland. The English oak (*Quercus robur*) is the well-known large tree with a thick trunk and low, twisting branches. It produces large crops of acorns, which were a favourite food for both wild and domesticated pigs in ancient times. The sessile oak (*Quercus petraea*), on the other hand, has a tall slender trunk with branches which start much higher up. The timber from each type of tree is suitable for different kinds of carpentry and in folklore and mythology

English oak (*Quercus robur*)

Sessile oak (*Quercus petraea*)

each species had different associations. Around AD 700 Adomnan, abbot of the monastery on Iona in Scotland, translated the Irish name for Derry, Daire Calgach, into the Latin form Roboretum Calgachi. His use of *roboretum* might suggest that the original trees of Derry were principally the English oak.

The oak was imbued with a great deal of symbolism by the Iron Age Celtic people throughout Europe, who incorporated it into their religious beliefs and practices. Celtic religious ideas and rituals were elaborated from the cycles of the natural world. Individual trees, particular species of trees and impressive woods or clusters were infused with supernatural associations. The Roman poet Lucan gives an unsympathetic description of a sacred Celtic wood near Marseilles:

> A grove there was, untouched by men's hands from ancient times, whose interlacing boughs enclosed a space of darkness and cold shade, and banished sunlight from above. No rural Pan dwelt there, nor Silvanus, ruler of the woods, no Nymphs; but gods were worshipped there with savage rites, the altars were heaped with hideous offerings, and every tree was sprinkled with human gore. On these boughs . . . birds feared to perch; in those coverts wild beasts would not lie down . . . the trees, even when they spread their leaves to no breeze, rustled among themselves.

There is no direct evidence that the oakgrove of Derry had a particular ritual significance. The pagan period when this could have been the case came before the introduction of writing and the beginning of recorded history. However, a Life of Saint Colmcille, written at the beginning of the sixteenth century, demonstrates that a number of supernatural traditions and superstitions about the trees of Derry survived until that late date. Although these are given a Christian explanation by association with the saint, it is clear that this is merely a veneer. The true significance of the trees in these stories derives from the pagan beliefs of pre-Christian times.

On two separate occasions in the twelfth century, medieval chroniclers recorded the destruction of sections of mature wood in Derry by particularly violent winds:

> A great wind storm occurred on the third day of December [1146] which caused a great destruction of woods throughout Ireland; it prostrated sixty trees at Derry of Colmcille and killed and smothered many persons in a church.

And again in 1178: 'A wonderful violent wind. It prostrated also six score oaks or a little more in Derry of Colmcille.' The total of nearly two hundred trees destroyed in this thirty-year period gives us some indication of the size of what must have been an impressive wood. The fact that the annalists recorded the destruction of the trees is also indicative of how greatly they were prized. There is also a very strange entry in the Annals of the Four Masters for the year 1188, which records that a Donegal aristocrat, Domnall hUa Canannain, injured his foot with his own axe while cutting firewood in Derry. He died 'through a miracle of Colmcille'. It appears that Domnall had violated one of the important taboos which protected the trees of Derry. He was accordingly punished through the intervention of their holy protector.

DAIRE CALGACH

Calgach, the second part of the original Irish name for Derry, is a comparatively rare personal name which means 'fierce' or 'sharp'. There is no way of ascertaining who Calgach was, but he must have been an important person who either owned, or was in some way particularly associated with, Derry in the late prehistoric period. Dr John Keys O'Doherty, an antiquarian writer and Catholic bishop of Derry from 1889 until his death in 1907, tried to identify the elusive Calgach as the Scottish warrior Galgachus, who fiercely opposed the Roman military leader Agricola. According to the first-century Roman writer Tacitus, as Agricola's campaign in Scotland got under way,

> upwards of thirty thousand men appeared in arms, and their force was increasing every day. The youth of the country poured in from all quarters, and even the men in years, whose vigour was still unbroken, repaired to the army, proud of their past exploits, and the ensigns of honour which they had gained by their martial spirit. Among the

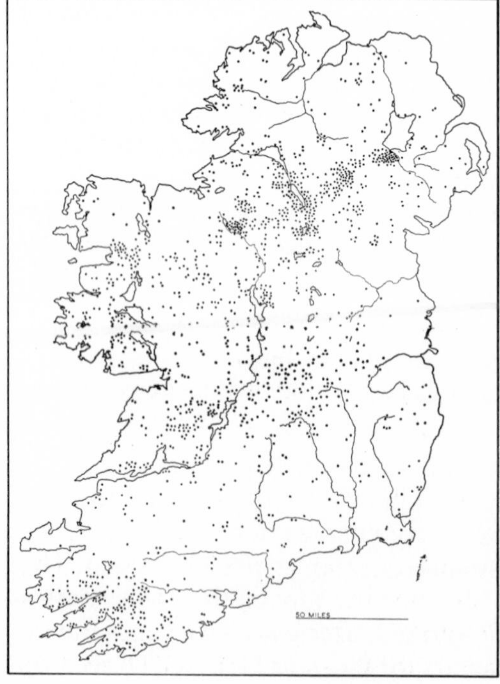

Map of Ireland showing distribution of townland names incorporating the word 'derry' (from Eileen McCracken, *Irish Woods since Tudor Times*)

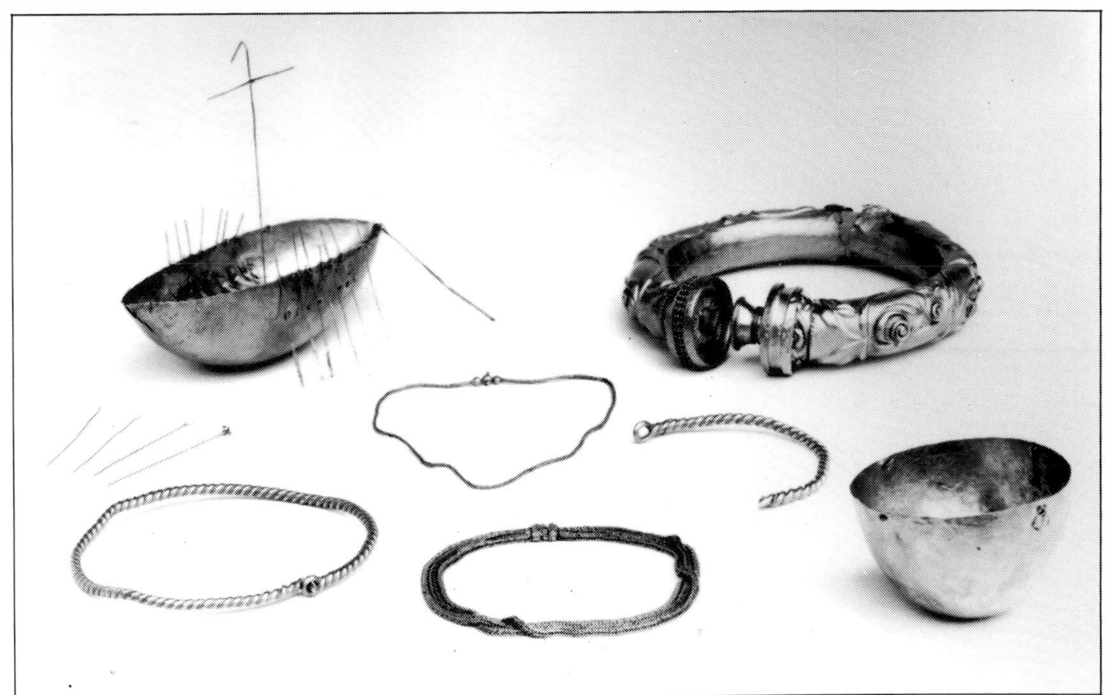

Gold objects from the Broighter Hoard, including a model boat and a torc or neck-ring. The hoard was found in the late nineteenth century near Limavady, County Derry, during ploughing and became the subject of a celebrated treasure-trove inquiry. It was probably deposited originally as a votive offering to the Celtic sea god Manannan mac Lir. (National Museum of Ireland)

> chieftains, distinguished by their birth and valour, the most renowned was Galgachus. The multitude gathered round him, eager for action, and burning with uncommon ardour.

But there is no strong reason for accepting Dr O'Doherty's identification and Calgach of Derry remains unidentified.

THE IRON AGE CELTS

Virtually nothing is known about what was happening at Derry during the Iron Age, immediately prior to the foundation of the monastery. However, the countryside and landscape near the city, in particular Greenan Mountain and Lough Foyle, figure prominently in the mythological stories of this period which belonged to the oral tradition of the Celtic people living in the area. Many stories claim to explain the origins of particular topographical features or the background as to how places in the district came to be named. Some of them concern the activities of the Celtic god Manannan mac Lir, whose underwater kindgom could be entered by way of Lough Foyle. The beautiful hoard of gold objects found at Broighter near Limavady in County Derry, on the eastern shore of the lough, was probably deposited there as a ritual offering to this powerful god. In one of the stories Manannan appears with the name Mongan and meets Saint Colmcille at Lough Foyle. The saint eventually converts Mongan to Christianity and ever afterwards the former pagan deity is obedient to the true God.

The Grianan of Aileach also figures in these mythological stories. Although generally believed to be a royal fortification, the stories show that in origin the Grianan was a burial monument. The principal story tells how Aed, the son of The Dagda, chief god of the Tuatha Dé Dannan (the otherworld gods of the Celtic Irish), is killed in revenge by a man called Corgend. Aed had made love secretly to Corgend's wife while she was on a visit to Tara, the principal home of the gods. Although everyone advises The Dagda to punish Corgend with death, instead the killer is condemned

> To carry the slain man on his back
> Till he finds a stone fit for the burial covering.

Carved stone head, of probable Iron Age date, from near Claudy, County Derry

Corgend, with Aed's corpse on his back, is forced to wander through Ireland until he comes to the district of Lough Foyle, where he finds the gravestone of Febal (after whom Lough Foyle is named). Corgend carries the stone and the dead Aed to the top of Greenan Mountain but dies himself from the strain. The Dagda then orders an enclosure to be built around the tomb and, playing on the meaning of words, says:

> The place shall be named from the stone [*ailigh*],
> Aileach will be the name of this residence of Banba [Ireland].

Interestingly, in the early nineteenth century, when the Grianan was inspected during the first Ordnance Survey of Ireland, the remains of a 'tumulus' or ancient tomb were still visible inside the great enclosure. However, the tomb no longer survives.

The Celts had a particular religious interest in the human head and employed it widely as an art motif. Stylised stone models of heads, sometimes having two or three faces, have been found throughout the Celtic world. Two collections of these heads have been found near Derry, one to the south of the city in the Laggan area of County Donegal and another near the village of Claudy, County Derry, on the eastern side of the Foyle.

THE NORTHERN UÍ NÉILL

According to legend, before becoming a monastery, Derry was a fortress of the local Cenél Conaill kings, whose territory stretched over most of modern County Donegal except for the Inishowen Peninsula. They, with their relatives the Cenél Eóghain, who gave their name to Inishowen (Inis Eóghain) and later Tyrone (Tír Eóghain), formed an aristocratic kin-group known as the northern Uí Néill. The two dynasties were said to have descended from Conall and Eóghan, allegedly sons of the legendary Nial of the Nine Hostages. By the end of the fifth century, emerging from the shadowy mists of prehistory, these dynasties were in effective control of the north-west of Ireland. The northern Uí Néill were closely related to the southern Uí Néill, also said to descend from the legendary Nial, who occupied the present-day counties of Meath and Westmeath. During the early Christian period the northern and southern groups shared, and alternately occupied, the most prestigious office in the country, the high-kingship of Tara.

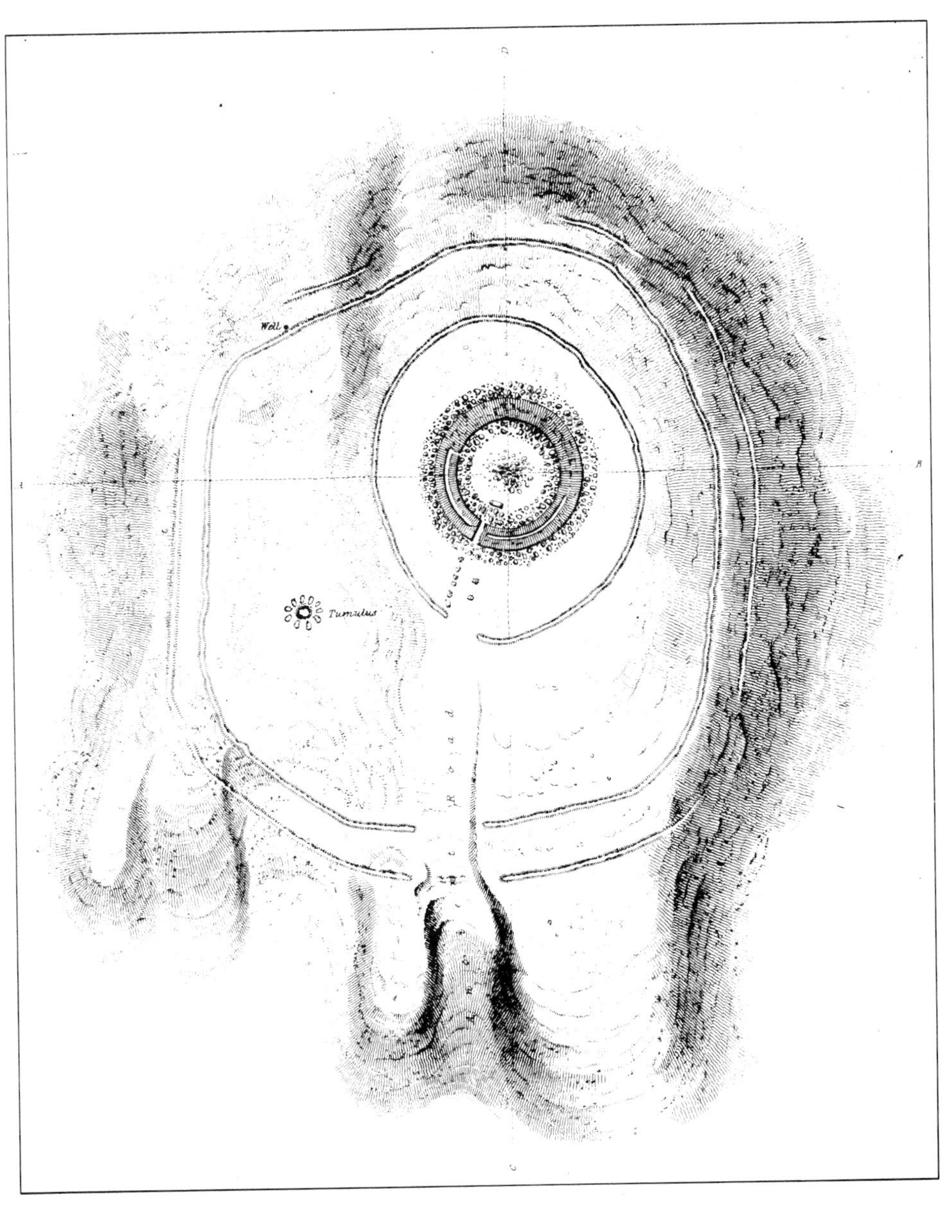

Ordnance Survey (*c.* 1830) plan of the Grianan of Aileach, showing the ancient tomb (tumulus), roadway, hillfort, holy well and central cashel

The developing rivalry between the Cenél Conaill and the Cenél Eóghain was to be one of the most abiding features of the story of Gaelic Ulster and the medieval history of Derry. This feud, which lasted one thousand years, was finally brought to an end in the sixteenth century with a truce necessitated by the advancing English forces of Elizabeth I. By that time the two groups were represented respectively by the O'Donnell and O'Neill families. In the sixth, seventh and eighth centuries the two dynasties had contested for the kingship of Aileach, the large overkingdom comprising the modern counties of Donegal, Derry and Tyrone, as well as other adjacent territories. In 789 the Cenél Eóghain captured the supremacy over Aileach outright but before this, the Cenél Conaill had frequently held this important kingship.

No trace of a Cenél Conaill fortification at Derry has been found although defences of the same period are known in the surrounding

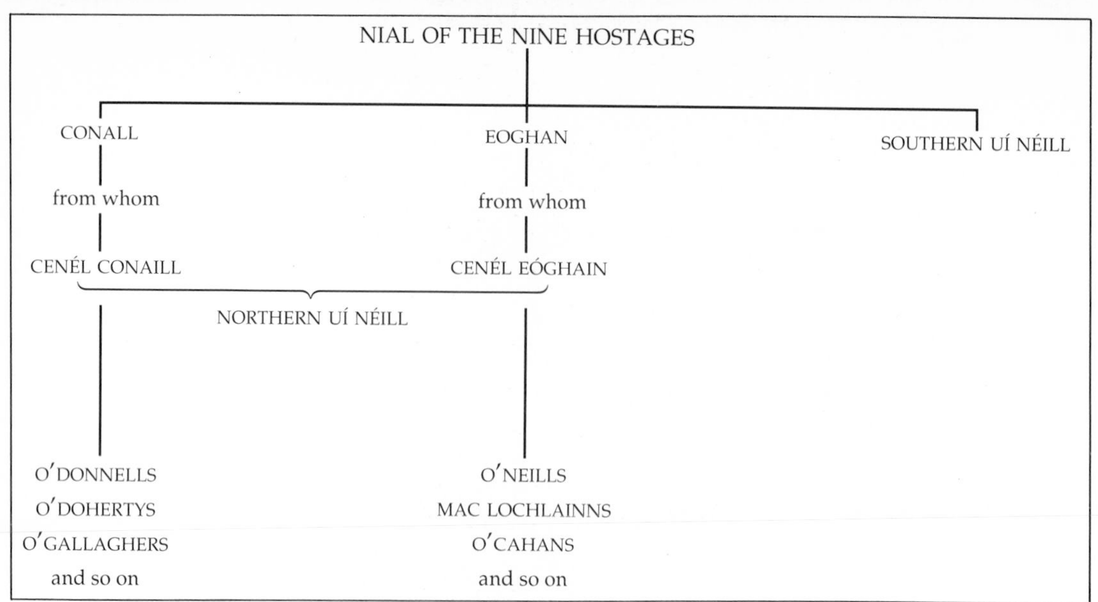

The Uí Néill dynasties

area. The top of Greenan Mountain is enclosed by a huge double-banked earthwork which must date to the late Bronze Age or early Iron Age. This was possibly a large tribal assembly place where public ceremonies and other formal business took place. Inside the hillfort is the stone cashel known as the Grianan of Aileach, which may have been built about the same time that the monastery was being founded at Derry. There are other unusual hilltop fortifications near the city, which probably belong to the late prehistoric period.

Writing, as we know it, first came to Ireland as part of the package of cultural changes that coincided with the spread of Christianity, which is 'a religion of a book' and is not possible institutionally unless accompanied by a knowledge of reading and writing. The Christian religion had already filtered into Ireland by the year 431 when, according to the Chronicle of Prosper of Aquitaine, *'ad Scottos in Christum credentes ordinatus a papa Caelestino Palladius primus episcopus mittitur'* (Palladius, ordained by Pope Celestine, is sent as first bishop to the Irish already believing in Christ). The work of Saint Patrick, probably in the second half of the fifth century, is best known, but it is clear that many missionaries were involved in the introduction of Christianity to Ireland. By the early sixth century the new religion was widespread throughout the country but it would take many more centuries to eradicate paganism entirely.

From the beginning, Christianity in Ireland acquired distinctive characteristics, foremost of which was the importance of monasticism and learning, including the contemporary recording of important events. The monasteries associated with Saint Colmcille played a leading role in the development of this branch of historical study and in the evolution of the documents known as the annals, in which the earliest real evidence for Irish history is preserved. In many instances discrepancies occur between the stories that are found in the ancient legends and the more factual versions in the annals. As we shall see, this is the case in the accounts of the foundation of the monastery of Derry.

Saint Columba (Colmcille) in the oakgrove of Derry (Stained-glass window, Guildhall, Derry)

2

THE FOUNDATION OF THE MONASTERY

Although tradition credits Saint Colmcille (Columba) with the founding of the monastery of Derry, a major conflict exists between the legendary accounts found in two medieval Irish texts which purport to be Lives of the saint and the contemporary historical sources. The earliest of the legendary accounts occurs in the Old Irish Life, written in Derry between 1150 and 1182. The second is a larger work, written in 1532 by Manus O'Donnell at his castle near Lifford, County Donegal.

THE LEGEND

According to both Lives, Colmcille was a student of Saint Mobhi at the monastery of Glasnevin, now on the outskirts of Dublin, when the plague known as the Buidhe Conaill broke out. As a precaution against contracting the plague, the students were dispersed to their home

Glasnevin, Dublin, site of the ancient monastery where Colmcille was a student (Bord Fáilte)

territories and Colmcille went to Daire Calgach in the territory of the Cenél Conaill, his own people. There the king, Aed mac Ainmire, a cousin of Colmcille's, had his fort, which he offered to Colmcille as a location for a church, but the young monk refused it. Soon afterwards, however, Colmcille got a mysterious sign from Saint Mobhi, who had recently died, that he should take the site. Colmcille then accepted the gift but curiously set fire to the whole place to erase 'the works of worldly men that he might consecrate it to God and to himself'. Aed was furious at this destruction but Colmcille assured him that there would never be any scarcity in Derry. At one point the fire became so large that it threatened to engulf the grove of trees from which the place was named. Seeing this, Colmcille pronounced the Latin prayer *Noli Pater Indulgere* as a protection for the trees. The fire obediently subsided and the prayer 'is said against all fires and thunders from that day to this, and if a man pronounces it on lying down and on getting up, it will protect any nine persons whom he chooses from fire and thunder and lightning'. It is difficult not to see in this story an echo of a belief in the sacred or magical properties of the trees of Derry and a hint of some sort of rite of exorcism before the place could be taken over as the location for a Christian monastery.

Recounting the story about the building of the first church in Derry, Manus O'Donnell further hints at the ritual importance of its trees:

> Here we can see how greatly Colmcille loved Derry, and how loth he was to cut or fell the grove of trees there . . . He ordered his successors to chop no tree that fell of itself or that was blown down by the wind till the end of nine days, and then to divide it among all the folk of the place, good and bad.

To save some of the trees from being cut down, the church was built running north–south, instead of in the customary east–west way. According to O'Donnell, this was the situation in his own time, although the original monastic church must have been replaced at least once, if not more often, by then. Adding to the sense of taboo about interfering with the trees, Manus has Colmcille say:

> Though truly I'm afraid
> Of death itself and Hell,
> I'm frankly more afraid
> Of an axe-sound, west in Derry.

One of the most important trees in Derry in medieval times was the special 'Yew of the Saints'. In the early sixteenth century this stood on the left-hand side of the entrance to the Black Church, the best known of Derry's medieval churches. It was popularly thought of as the resting place of 'a thousand angels'. More numerous even than the leaves on the trees were the numbers of these spirits who were believed to hover above the monastery and 'nine waves distant therefrom', so that a medieval poet could speak of 'angel-haunted Derry'.

The purpose of these stories was to show that Colmcille was particularly favoured by God. One story in the O'Donnell Life has Jesus, in the guise of a beggar, appearing to the saint in Derry at a place called *'an t-impodh deisiul'* (the right turn), near the location of the present Long Tower Church. Other stories are introduced in order to explain certain physical features as they were at the time the Life was written. The existence of St Colmcille's Well in the Bogside, marked now by a nineteenth-century cast-iron pump, which is still popularly venerated and decorated on the saint's feast day, 9 June, is explained by a story of the saint miraculously bringing water from a rock in order to baptise a child. The Lives claim to give a comprehensive account of the foundation of the monastery but they were written many centuries after Colmcille's death. They are not an accurate reflection of the events of the sixth century and their real value is as an indication of the state of the cult of the saint at the time when they were written.

Saint Columba's (Colmcille's) Well, Bogside, Derry (Eason and Son)

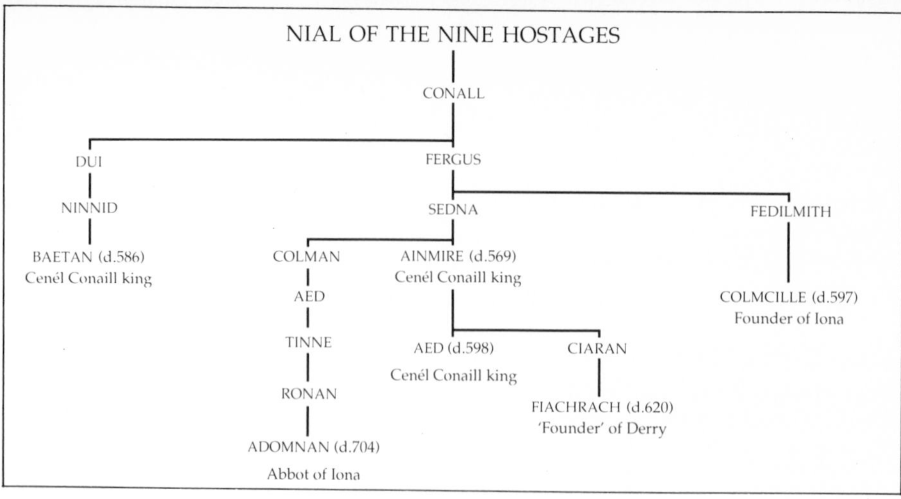

Genealogical table showing family relationships between Saint Colmcille, Fiachr ('the other founder of Derry'), Adomnan (abb of Iona) and the three Cenél Conaill kings – Ainmire mac Sedna, Ae mac Ainmire and Baeta mac Ninnid. According the medieval Book of Fenagh, each of the thre kings in turn is said to have had his fortress at Derry before it 'fell to Colmcille'. Dates of deaths are given in brackets.

THE HISTORICAL VERSION

The Annals of the Four Masters, composed in the early 1600s, tells us that Colmcille founded Derry in 535. As evidence, however, this is as doubtful as the account in the Lives. Contemporary historical records give a different picture. Adomnan, a relative of Colmcille's and an abbot of Iona in Scotland, mentions Derry on a number of occasions in his Life of the saint, written in Latin about AD 700. However, he does not say, nor does he imply, that the church there was founded by Colmcille. The Annals of Ulster, usually the best source of information for early Irish history, says that 'Daire Cholmcille was founded' in 546 but does not name the founder. The use of 'Daire Cholmcille' raises a suspicion that the entry is not a contemporary record as it does not occur again in the annals until 1121, suggesting that the 546 reference was probably inserted at the end of the twelfth century when the annals were being kept and added to in the monastery of Derry. The year 546 was probably chosen to link the foundation with the death in 545 of Saint Mobhi.

Remains of the medieval monastery on Iona, where Colmcille founded a monastery *c.*561

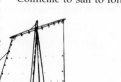

The death in 620 of a man called Fiachrach mac Ciarain mac Ainmire mac Setna is recorded in many of the Irish annals, but not all versions give us the same amount of information. Only the Annals of Tigernach and the Chronicon Scottorum, both compiled at the monastery of Clonmacnoise, County Offaly, in the twelfth century by copying from older documents, tell us that Fiachrach was 'the other founder of Derry'. The compiler of the relevant entry in the Annals of Ulster must have been disconcerted by this identification because he did not copy it. The southern annalists would have had no reason for inventing such a claim had they not seen it in an older document. A number of other important Ulster texts which might be expected to mention Fiachrach are also silent about him. The monks who wrote the Annals of the Four Masters compiled a set of genealogies of the saints of Ireland, where most of the entries refer to saints of their own people, the Cenél Conaill, including a number of very minor figures. Fiachrach belonged to the Cenél Conaill and surely merited inclusion; suspiciously, the document ignores him. Either Fiachrach was the joint founder of Derry along with Colmcille or there was an alternative tradition that he was the sole founder. Whichever, Fiachrach was an important man in the history of

Reconstruction of the type of boat that might have been used by Colmcille to sail to Iona

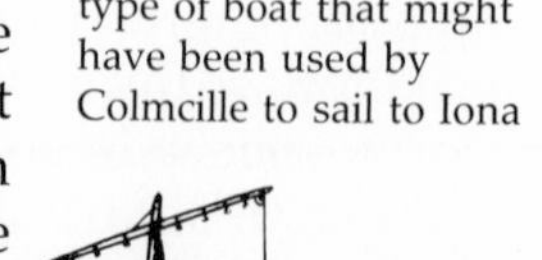

Derry, yet he was ignored by everyone who wrote about the foundation of the monastery. It is difficult to resist the conclusion that the medieval chroniclers did not want a memory of Fiachrach's role in the foundation of Derry to survive.

Aed mac Ainmire, who in the legendary accounts is said to have given the site for the monastery, would not have succeeded to the kingship, or been in the position to grant away Derry, until after the death of his predecessor, Baetan, in 586. By that time Colmcille had been in Iona for twenty-five years, although all the legends maintain that he founded Derry before he left Ireland. On the other hand, Aed was Fiachrach's uncle, and if there is any truth in the tradition that he was the benefactor who gave the land for the monastery of Derry, then the timing makes it more likely that the donation was to his nephew Fiachrach rather than to Colmcille. Colmcille, of course, could have played some kind of secondary, supportive role.

Despite a very strong medieval and modern tradition that the monastery of Derry was founded by Colmcille, no historical documentation supports this view. On the contrary, contemporary records suggest that the foundation was made by Fiachrach. As one of the city's present-day thaumaturges, Paddy 'Bogside' Doherty, has wryly remarked, 'This wouldn't be the only instance in the history of the city when someone got the credit for a job they didn't do.' The Columban tradition was fostered, if not actually invented, at a much later period than the sixth century. The reasons why this was done will be examined when we come to look at developments in Derry in the twelfth century.

However, the monastery of Derry was probably established during the reign of Aed mac Ainmire (586–98) and before the death of Colmcille in 597, and was certainly part of the *Paruchia* of Colmcille, the confederation of churches in Ireland and Britain that looked upon the saint as their founder and spiritual leader. According to Adomnan, before Colmcille's death in 597 he prophesied that certain events would occur in Derry, so clearly the saint knew of the existence of the monastery there. He had other connections with Derry also: Daire Calgach is mentioned by Adomnan in circumstances which show that it was in close connection by sea with Iona and various other parts of Britain during the lifetime of Colmcille. Also, a list of Colmcille's relatives, compiled about sixty years after the saint's death, tells us that Bran his nephew was buried in Derry.

Saint Colmcille's Cross, Moone, County Kildare. Moone was one of the principal monasteries associated with Colmcille.

THE CENÉL CONAILL

From the start and for the next five hundred years, the monastery at Derry was a Cenél Conaill foundation. Early Irish society was tribal and dynastic in nature and the Christian church was forced to accommodate to this. Monasteries were closely associated with particular kin-groups and virtually became 'family businesses'. For instance, almost all the abbots of Iona (the most important Columban monastery) down to the ninth in succession and beyond belonged to Colmcille's own family group. Despite the uncertainty about its origins, it is clear that the monastery of Derry was founded by and for the Cenél Conaill and it retained that link until the twelfth century.

For many centuries the Grianan of Aileach, the royal fortification four and a half miles west of Derry, was the symbolic headquarters of the northern Uí Néill, and control alternated initially between the Cenél Conaill and the Cenél Eóghain. Although located at the centre of a much older, but now largely eroded, complex of prehistoric enclosures and burial monuments, the imposing stone cashel which still survives at the Grianan was probably built about the sixth or seventh century, perhaps coinciding with the foundation of the monastery at Derry.

Although outright control of the surrounding area and the Grianan passed to the Cenél Eóghain from the late eighth century onwards, Derry continued to belong to the Cenél Conaill until the end of the eleventh century. Almost every identifiable person whose name is connected with Derry in this period can be shown to have Cenél Conaill associations. However, from the ninth century, Derry became an island of Cenél Conaill influence entirely surrounded by the territory of the Cenél Eóghain, who must have looked on the monastery with greedy eyes.

THE NEIGHBOURING PEOPLE

From the late seventh century onwards the Cenél Eóghain were also in control of the territory on the eastern side of the River Foyle, where the

The Grianan of Aileach, four and a half miles to the west of Derry

Waterside district is now located. The inhabitants were a small and relatively insignificant tribe known as the Uí Meic Cairthinn of Lough Foyle, who belonged to a larger group of equally insignificant subject tribal kingdoms collectively known as the Airgialla, who inhabited the centre of Ulster in the first millennium AD. The territory of the Uí Meic Cairthinn stretched alongside the Foyle from near Ballykelly in the north to near Strabane in the south and inland to near the present-day village of Claudy. In 675 the king of the tribe, Dunchad mac Ultan, was killed by the king of Aileach, Maelduin mac Maelfithrich, at a place called Dún Forgo, possibly the crannog at Dungorkin near Claudy. Maelduin belonged to the Cenél Eóghain and it is likely that Dunchad's death signalled the beginning of their control in this area. To the north of the Uí Meic Cairthinn was the similarly unimportant subject tribe, the Ciannachta Glen Geimhinn, who inhabited the valley of the River Roe from Dungiven to the estuary at Lough Foyle. The Rough Fort, situated between Ballykelly and Limavady, would have been the dwelling place of some of the more important members of this tribe.

There are several dwelling sites of this period in the hinterland of Derry. A few miles north of the city, on the eastern side of the river, the overgrown remains of a crannog can be seen in Enagh Lough and other crannogs have also been noted nearby. In the middle of the Creggan

On the left, the Cropie Fort, or The Rath, Creggan, in the late 1940s; to the right, building is just starting on the Creggan housing estate. (Michael McGuinness)

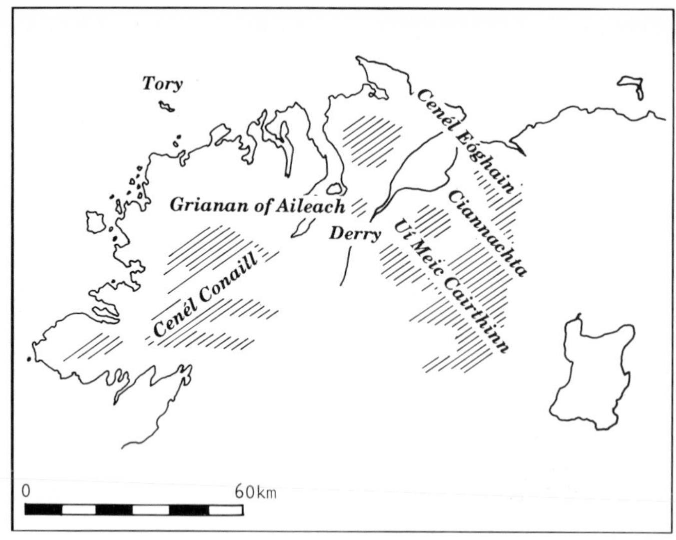

Political geography in the vicinity of Derry *c.* 700

Estate on the western edge of the city there is a large circular earthwork known as the Cropie Fort or The Rath, which sits in the middle of a road roundabout. We do not know the exact nature of this earthwork nor can it be dated. However, it lies on the direct route over the hills from Derry to Aileach and it could possibly be the Rath of the Banquets mentioned by Manus O'Donnell, where, somewhere along this route, Colmcille entertained a band of poets.

THE SOCIETY OF THE TIME

At the time that the monastery of Derry was founded, society in Ireland was undergoing great change. Christianity was spreading and altering many ancient pagan practices and major political innovations were also taking place. Powerful new dynasties, such as the various sections of the Uí Néill, were emerging to dominate the smaller tribal kingdoms or *tuath*s, all of which, in theory at least, were sovereign. Each *tuath* had its tribal legends, symbols and assembly places, and its king or *rí*. These tribes would have been grouped together into larger units by particularly powerful local kings and these in turn would have been welded into provincial kingdoms under national figures like the Uí Néill chieftains. The twelfth-century writer Giraldus Cambrensis, who accompanied the Normans to Ireland, sparing, as he says, 'neither truth nor modesty', gives an interesting if unsympathetic account of the inauguration ceremony of the king of the Cenél Conaill:

> In Cenél Conaill, the northern and remotest part of Ulster, there is a group of people accustomed to consecrate their king with an abominable and awful rite. When all the people of that place have gathered together, a white mare is brought into the centre of the assembly. The man about to be inaugurated, not as a chieftain, but as a beast, not as king, but as an outlaw, publicly embraces the animal, declaring himself a beast also. The mare is then killed, cut in pieces, and boiled in water. Afterwards a bath is prepared for the man in this water. Surrounded by his people, he sits in

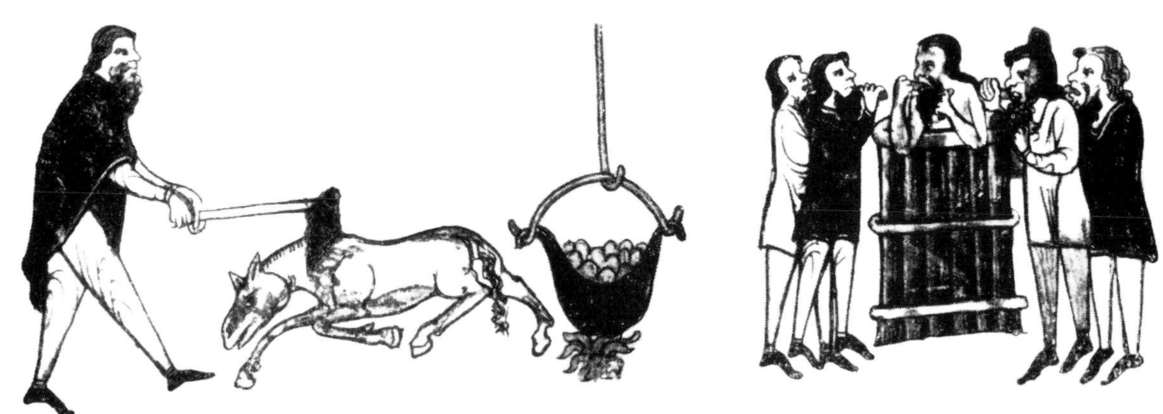

Inauguration ceremony of the kings of the Cenél Conaill from a twelfth-century copy of the *Topography of Ireland* by Giraldus Cambrensis (National Library of Ireland)

> the bath, and everyone, he and they, eat the meat of the mare which is given to them. He drinks the broth in which he is bathing, not with a cup, or by using his hand, but just by dipping his mouth into what is round about him. By this dreadful ceremony the man is conferred with his authority and kingship.

Giraldus did not witness this ceremony himself and it is very unlikely that the practice of what is clearly a pagan fertility rite survived in such a pure form as late as the twelfth century. Nevertheless, the description can be compared with a number of stories in Irish mythological literature and with practices in many other parts of the ancient Indo-European world. Early Irish kings were inaugurated in a 'marriage' ceremony through which they were united with the 'female' territory over which they were to reign, guaranteeing its fertility and fruitfulness. The account by Giraldus may be several centuries out of date but it probably reflects the kind of ceremony by which Cenél Conaill kings were installed in an earlier period.

While there were a small number of slaves at this time, the ordinary people were predominantly independent farmers, living in extended family groups who owned their own land. Their wealth, indeed their whole system of reckoning value, was assessed in terms of their cattle – they did not use money. Most of them lived inside earthen enclosures called ringforts or raths. In the more rocky areas stone cashels were built instead. Sometimes underground passages and chambers were built and these souterrains would have served as stores but, more importantly, as refuges for the people in the event of their homes coming under attack. Battles and warfare between kingdoms, tribes and dynasties were endemic but small-scale. Fighting rarely lasted for more than a day and even one or two deaths shocked those who recorded the events. Early Irish warfare could be compared, to some extent, to a modern-day riot.

This was a 'man's world' where polygamy was practised and at the one time a man might have several wives, each in a different legal relationship to him. However, such women had certain rights whereby they could divorce their husbands and take away with them any property which they had brought to the marriage.

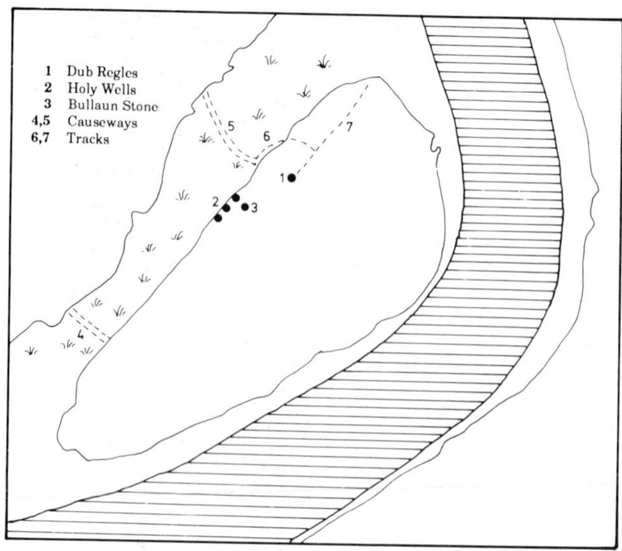

The 'island' of Derry showing the location of the Dub Regles

Apart from years of famine and plague, the impression of life at this time is that everyone was reasonably comfortable without being overly rich. Social relations were to a great extent governed by genealogical considerations. There existed a detailed and elaborate social code, now popularly known as the Brehon Laws. The Brehons were the jurists who adjudicated on legal matters. They had close traditional associations with the poets or *filí*, the direct descendants of the druids of pre-Christian times and the officials responsible for keeping the collective cultural lore. The *filí* preserved remnants of the old pagan religion and occasionally there were unsuccessful attempts to abolish the *filí* altogether. Colmcille himself is said to have become involved in their defence at the Convention of Drumceat, held in the territory of the Ciannachta, near present-day Limavady, in AD 575.

THE DUB REGLES

The early monasteries must have looked very similar to many of the secular dwelling places of the time. The main difference would have been the presence of a church building within the enclosure. By the middle of the twelfth century there were at least three churches in Derry. The tradition that one of these, the Dub Regles or Black Church, was the original Columban foundation was very strong. One entry in the annals for the year 1166 implies that this church, even by that time, was already a very old establishment: 'Daire Cholmcille for the greater part was burned and the Dub Regles was burned, something which had not been heard of from ancient times.'

By the middle of the thirteenth century the monks of the Black Church had adopted the Rule of Saint Augustine. The monastery survived in this manner until its dissolution at the end of the Middle Ages. The abbey church was ultimately taken over for use by the first plantation settlers in the seventeenth century. Clearly, the building still standing at that time was not the same as that erected at the foundation of the monastery in the late sixth century. Nevertheless, throughout the

St Augustine's chapel-of-ease, which takes its name from the Augustinian monastery located on this site from the thirteenth to the sixteenth centuries. This in turn evolved from, and was located at the site of, the ancient Dub Regles church of the Columban monastery of Derry established in the sixth century.

Middle Ages it was believed that this was at least the site of the original monastic church. The site has continued to be used for ecclesiastical purposes to the present day. Two separate Church of Ireland St Augustine's chapels-of-ease have succeeded each other there since the medieval building disappeared, about the middle of the eighteenth century. Although the present church building is comparatively modern, the site itself has been in ecclesiastical hands for about 1,400 years.

It is popularly believed in Derry, with no historical justification, that the original monastic site was where St Columba's Long Tower Church stands today. One of the most enthusiastic advocates of the traditional Columban association with Derry, and the identification of the site of the Dub Regles with the Long Tower Church, was Father William Doherty, a controversial priest and later the administrator of that church at the start of the twentieth century. Father Doherty masterminded the celebrations in Derry in 1897 for the thirteen-hundredth anniversary of the death of Colmcille. Father Doherty had a strong personal devotion to the saint and a firm belief that the Long Tower Church was the site of the original monastery. Between 1907 and 1909 he made extensive alterations to the church and the finished building was in effect a translation into architecture and art of the ancient legend. Elaborate stained-glass windows, paintings, sculpture and mosaic were used throughout the building to tell the familiar legendary stories. He transformed the church into a monument to Saint Colmcille and to the traditional account of the foundation of the original monastery of Derry. According to one history of the church, Father Doherty took the opportunity of rebuilding to investigate the location of the monastery.

The controversial priest, Father William Doherty, who strongly believed that the Long Tower Church was the site of the original Columban monastery at Derry (from *The Story of the Long Tower Church 546–1946*)

The exact position of the Dub Regles was

> fixed beyond yea or nay by the discovery of the foundations during excavations preparatory to the erection of the present church. Father William Doherty made a careful examination of the remains and, after comparing them with the seventeenth-century manuscript maps, and [Manus] O'Donnell's description, was able to define the original outline.

The results of Father Doherty's investigations were immortalised in a series of inscribed plaques inserted into the floor of the church and the surrounding churchyard. Unfortunately, he has left us no record of the foundations which he discovered. He was almost certainly mistaken in his identification, but no doubt great zeal on the part of this enthusiastic priest was responsible for his strongly held views. However, the possibility cannot be overlooked, given the prevailing divisive atmosphere at the beginning of the twentieth century, that Derry Catholics would have found it very difficult to accept the fact that the location of the original Columban monastery was in modern times occupied by a Protestant church.

THE MONASTERY

The monastery of Derry must have been a fairly small institution for the first few centuries of its existence. Part of the island would have been good agricultural land and would have been farmed by the monks. When Englishman Henry Docwra came to Derry in the year 1600 he

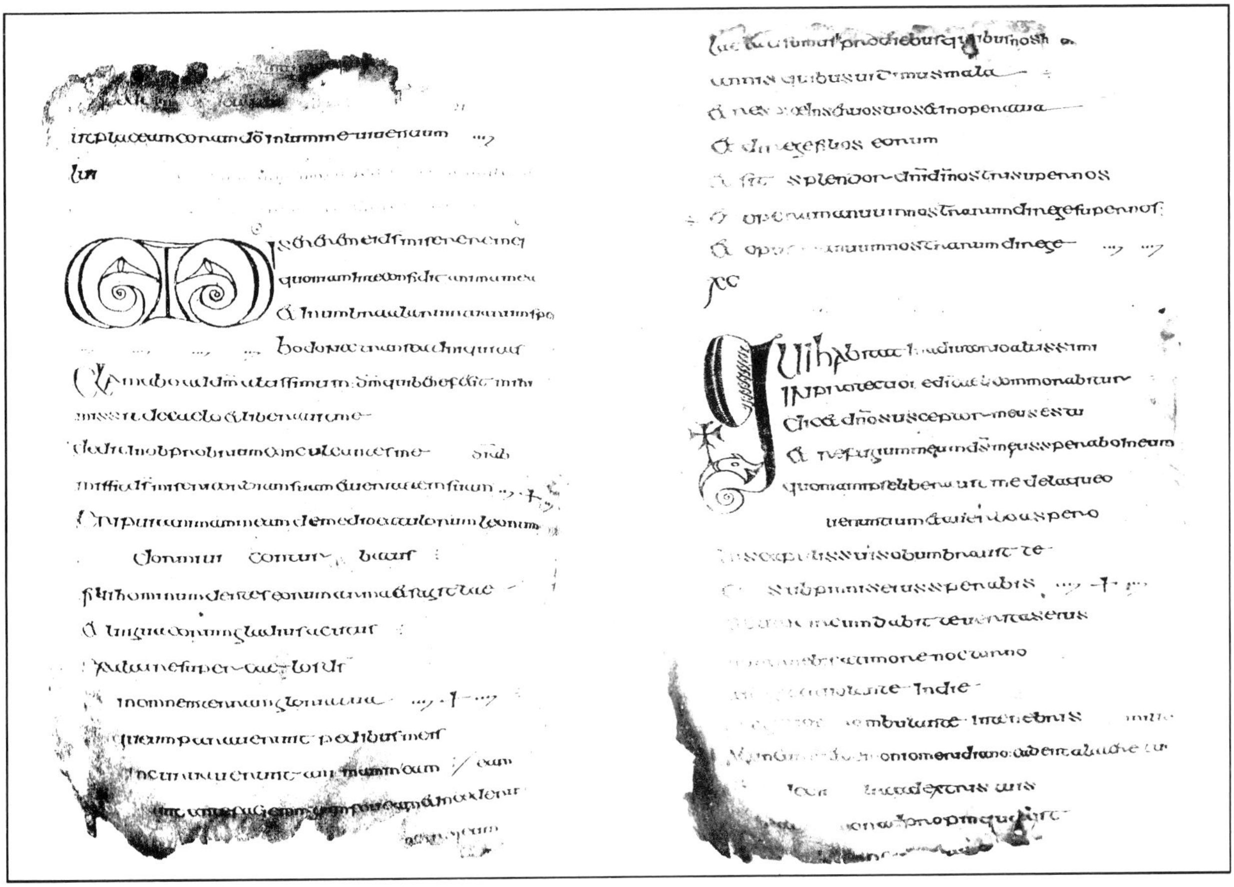

Two pages from the Cathach; Saint Colmcille himself is claimed by some to have been its scribe. (Royal Irish Academy)

found it 'for the most part sown with corn'. The island would have been isolated on its western side by a narrow strip of bog but wooden causeways or *tóchars*, similar to those found elsewhere in Irish bogland, would have crossed it at one or two points, possibly at places marked by streets today. Most of the hills surrounding Derry, on both sides of the river, would still have been tree-covered but some of this land would also have been farmed by the monks and their tenants. Skin boats, or more likely, dugout canoes, similar to those washed up by the River Foyle near Strabane in October 1987, would have been used for crossing the river. On the east bank the traveller would meet the Sligh Midhluachra, the ancient road which wound its way from the ford of Toome in County Antrim towards the royal fort at Aileach.

Besides the mention of Fiachrach, there are no other references to Derry in the annals of the seventh century, although Adomnan's Life of Colmcille does give us some incidental information about the church and its graveyard and how commonplace it was to travel from there to Britain by boat. In 724 the annals record the death of Caech Scuili, the scribe of Derry, whose name implies that he was blind or one-eyed, probably from the excessively detailed work he would have had to do in the primitive conditions of the monastic scriptorium. His main responsibility would have been to copy the gospels and other liturgical works used for worship. These books would have been written on

A monastic scribe from a twelfth-century copy of the *Topography of Ireland* by Giraldus Cambrensis (National Library of Ireland)

'At another time the blessed man was in the midland part of Ireland founding by God's will the monastery which in Irish is called Dairmag [Durrow].'
Extract from an early-eighth-century manuscript of Adomnan's Life of Colmcille, recording the foundation of the monastery of Durrow in County Offaly. The similarity in Irish of the names of Durrow (Dairmag) and Derry (Daire) may have contributed to the later belief that Colmcille was also the founder of the latter monastery. (Stadtbibliothek, Schaffhausen, Switzerland)

vellum and would have been expensive and laborious to produce. The books copied by Caech Scuili may well have been illuminated in the styles that were coming into widespread use in the Celtic monasteries in Britain and Ireland, particularly in the churches associated with the cult of Saint Colmcille. The Cathach, a late-sixth-century copy of the Psalms, is said to have been written by the hand of the saint himself. The Book of Durrow, associated with the midland monastery which Adomnan states was founded by Colmcille, was probably produced during Caech Scuili's lifetime. The Book of Kells was compiled on Colmcille's beloved Iona, within a century of the Derry scribe's death.

In 788 there was a major fire at Derry. No specific cause is recorded and the fire may well have occurred by accident. Most of the buildings would have been made of timber and woven wattles and thus destruction by fire was a constant hazard. Major destructive fires in Derry are recorded on several occasions during the medieval period but fortunately, rebuilding materials were always ready to hand. There are a number of stories in the various Lives of Colmcille about the monks of Derry cutting wood and wattles for the building of the monastery:

> One time Colmcille sent his monks into the wood to cut wattles to make a church for himself in Derry. Where the wattles were cut was in the land of a young man who lived beside the monastery. He was annoyed that the wood should be cut on his land without his permission. When Colmcille heard this he said to his people: 'Take him the value of his wood in barley grain, and let him put it in the ground.' It was then beyond the middle of summer. The grain was taken to the young man . . . and it grew so that it was ripe by the beginning of August.

An angel as depicted in the Book of Kells

Recent archaeological excavations at Carnalbana, near Glenarm in County Antrim, have shown us exactly what some of these wattle houses were like. Two concentric circles of woven hazel rods, roughly seven metres in diameter, formed an inner and outer wall about three metres in height. The gap between the two walls was packed with a primitive insulation of moss, heather and other vegetable matter, which would have kept the wind out and the heat in. The ends of the wattle rods were inserted into stout oak posts which also formed the jambs of the door. The conical roof would have been thatched and a fireplace located at the centre of the room and there was probably no chimney opening for the smoke. Sometimes two of these buildings were attached to one another in a figure of eight or similar shape.

Reconstruction of an Irish early Christian period wattle house at the Ulster History Park, near Omagh, County Tyrone (Omagh District Council)

The monastery of Derry probably contained many of these circular buildings clustered together and it would have been surrounded by an earthen enclosure or possibly a wooden stockade. The monastery would have enjoyed the privilege of sanctuary although this may not always have been respected. Some of the wattle structures would have been the living and sleeping quarters of the monks, others would have had specialised functions and served as kitchens and workshops of various kinds, including the scriptorium where the books were made. The small church or churches inside the enclosure would have been rectangular and initially these too would have been made of timber. Changes in fashion and the desire to erect more permanent structures would have persuaded the monks to build in stone. Nearby would have been the monastic cemetery with the grave of the founder, Fiachrach, in a prominent position. It would have been popularly believed that burial in this graveyard gave added security for the dead when it came to

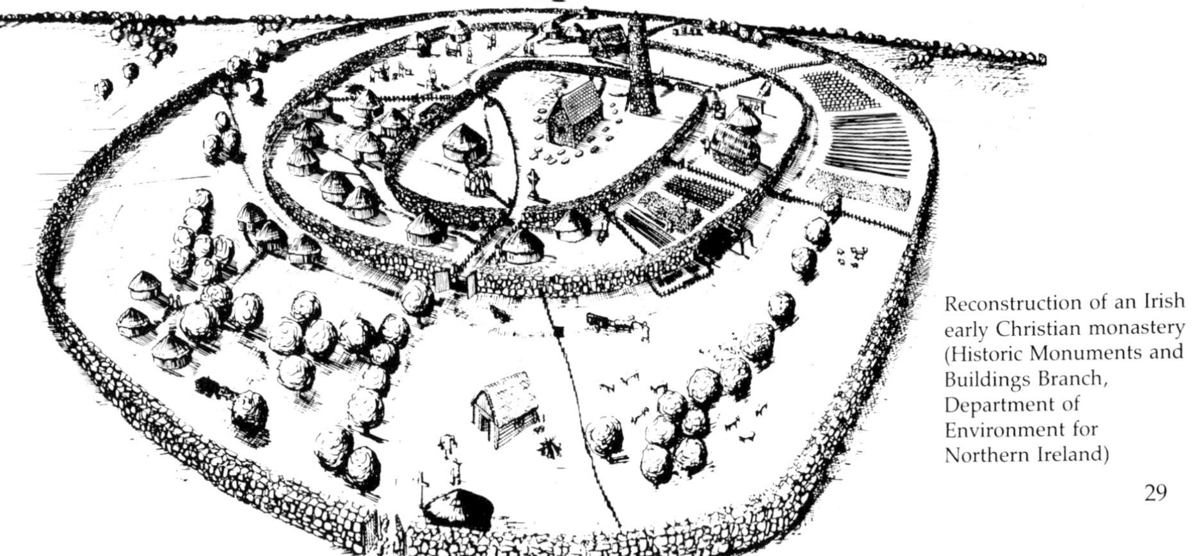

Reconstruction of an Irish early Christian monastery (Historic Monuments and Buildings Branch, Department of Environment for Northern Ireland)

overcoming the hurdles of the next life. Contributions from the wealthy laity of the locality for the privilege of such a burial would have provided a source of income for the monastery.

Apart from some ascetic clergy, the life of the monks was comfortable. They would have eaten well with a varied diet of cereals, dairy produce, pork and beef, vegetables, fruit and eggs. Occasionally, game and wildfowl were available and fish and other forms of seafood seem to have been widely eaten. Water, milk and ale were drunk and honey was used as a sweetener. Clerics were more likely to live longer than their lay relatives and life spans of over seventy years are frequently recorded for the clergy whereas lay people would have been considered old to have reached their forties. There was no specific habit in an ancient Irish monastery – the monks would have worn the long tunic and cloaks which was the dress of their lay contemporaries.

THE VIKINGS

In 795 the Columban monastery on the island of Iona was attacked by a party of seaborne raiders from the Scandinavian countries far to the north. This signalled the first appearance in these islands of the people known as the Vikings. Over the next forty years or so numerous raids were made on the many coastal and riverine monasteries accessible to the Vikings' superb ships. The monasteries in early Christian Ireland, with their collections of church treasures and other valuables, were similar in some ways to towns, and the Vikings, although still pagan, were more interested in stealing the wealth of these institutions than in attacking the monks' Christianity. However, from the second half of the ninth century onwards, Viking communities began to establish themselves in Ireland, founding permanent settlements and becoming involved in highly successful trading activities as well as in the local politics of the country.

Derry did not suffer greatly at the hands of the Vikings, possibly because the monastery was not a particularly wealthy institution. Up to 1100 only two or three incidents are recorded connecting the Vikings with Derry. In 833 the powerful Cenél Eóghain king of Aileach, Nial Càille, was victorious in a battle with the Vikings at Derry. It is not known if the monastery was harmed in any way on this occasion, but in 990 and again possibly in 997 the annals record that Derry was plundered by the 'foreigners'. The Vikings were present in the neighbourhood of Derry, however. One record refers to a group of Vikings as 'the

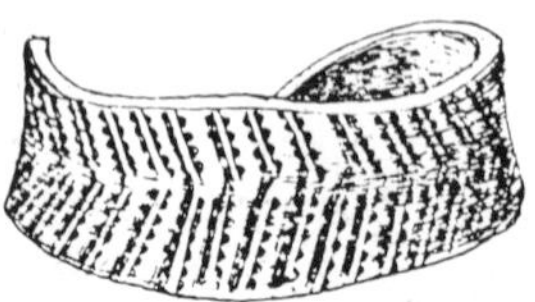

Viking silver bracelets from Glentogher, Inishowen, County Donegal (Royal Irish Academy)

foreigners of Lough Foyle'. The County Tyrone townland of Dunalong, in Irish Dún na Long, meaning 'fort of the ship', upstream from Derry, may have got its name from a Viking encampment. The name is reminiscent of the early Viking camps called by the Irish *longphorts*, meaning 'ship forts', which were formed by drawing several longboats out of the water and arranging them as a makeshift stockade. There have been several finds of Viking material in the hinterland of Derry, including valuable objects such as bracelets made of silver. Nearby Lough Swilly must have seemed very like a Norwegian fjord to the invading Scandinavians and there are strong traditions of their presence there also.

Professor Francis John Byrne, a historian of early Ireland, has noted that the success of the kings of Aileach in wiping out the Viking settlements in the north-west was not to the long-term advantage of the area. Elsewhere in Ireland, wherever the Vikings established successful trading settlements, strong medieval towns were able to develop. This did not happen in Derry. It might have been more beneficial if the local kings had allowed the Vikings to conduct their more usual trading activities. However, the presence of the Mac Lochlainns (meaning 'son of the Viking') as a powerful family in the Derry area during the Middle Ages shows that Scandinavian influences did survive in some fashion. The surname is still one of the most common in the city.

Early Christian period sculpture of an ecclesiastic at White Island, Lough Erne, County Fermanagh (Historic Monuments and Buildings Branch, Department of Environment for Northern Ireland)

THE CLERICS

From the end of the ninth century until the beginning of the twelfth century the annals record the names of many clerics associated with the monastery of Derry. Whenever these can be identified it is clear that they have Cenél Conaill associations. In 882 Muircertach mac Neill, abbot of Derry as well as several other monasteries, died. The deaths of at least nine different officials of the monastery are recorded throughout the tenth century: these include two bishops, four abbots and three erenaghs. In later times the title 'erenagh' signified the steward of the monastic lands and the holder was unlikely to be a cleric, but in the tenth century the erenagh was the abbot. Interestingly, in 967 the death of an anchorite or hermit, Aengus O'Robhartaigh, is recorded. The monastery would have had associated with it at different times varying numbers of monks who led a strict life, somewhat apart from the main concentration of the settlement.

Bishops in the early Irish church did not have the same status as they acquired in later medieval times. In the early monasteries they had no diocesan jurisdiction and were usually subordinate to the abbots, who often held a number of posts. Cinaed mac Domnall, who died in 921, was simultaneously abbot of both Derry and Drumhome in County Donegal. The death notices of many of the clergy of Derry suggest that

Ecclesiastical figures on the twelfth-century Breac Maodhog shrine (National Museum of Ireland)

they were praised for their piety and wisdom and there is no hint of the scandals associated with some of the other Irish monasteries, which had become increasingly secularised.

The annals preserve a continuous, if limited, record of the first five and a half centuries of Derry's history. However, besides the names of some of the chief clerics, very little detailed information has come down to us. Around the end of the eleventh century, members of the Mac Lochlainn family began to involve themselves in the affairs of Derry. From then onwards much more information about the life of the monastery and the settlement that developed around it starts to appear in the contemporary records.

Saint Patrick's Bell shrine, which the Cenél Eóghain king Domnall Mac Lochlainn 'caused to be made' between the years 1094 and 1105 (National Museum of Ireland)

3

DOIRE CHOLMCILLE
THE MONASTIC 'TOWN' IN THE TWELFTH AND THIRTEENTH CENTURIES

The information we have about Derry prior to the twelfth century refers almost exclusively to the affairs of the monastery. While lay people must have been settling around the monastery for some time before 1100, after this date there are more and more references to secular matters, indicating that the settlement at Derry was evolving into a township.

THE TAKEOVER BY THE CENÉL EÓGHAIN

In 1083 the powerful Domnall Mac Lochlainn succeeded as king of the Cenél Eóghain. He soon became a claimant for the high-kingship of all Ireland, in opposition to his chief rival, Muircertach O'Brien, king of Munster. Domnall was no respecter of tradition and as part of his campaign for the high-kingship, he installed his own people whenever and wherever the opportunity arose. It was Domnall who overturned the centuries-old tradition of Derry belonging to the Cenél Conaill. In a poem in the Book of Fenagh he is described as 'the contentious Domnall of Derry'. He died on 9 February 1121 and the Annals of Ulster record his death as follows:

> Domnall, son of Ardgar Mac Lochlainn, high-king of Ireland, the most distinguished of the Gael for form and birth, for good sense and prowess, for happiness and prosperity, for giving treasure and food, died in Derry

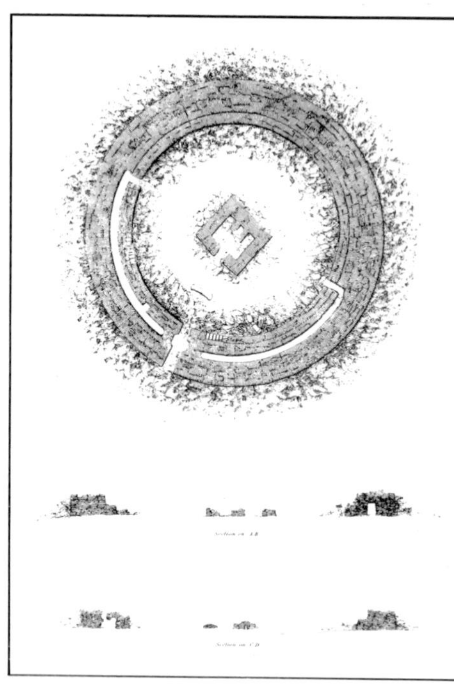

Plan and sections of the dilapidated Grianan of Aileach, as drawn by the Ordnance Survey, *c.* 1830

The restored Grianan of Aileach in the late nineteenth century

> of Colmcille, in the 38th year of his reign and in the 73rd year of his age on the night of Wednesday the 5th of the Ides of February and on the 18th day of the moon and on the feast of St Mochuaroc of the Wisdom.

This is the first occasion when the name Derry of Colmcille (Doire Cholmcille) occurs in these contemporary records. It is used in a literary–cultic manner to achieve an effect similar to 'Joyce's Dublin' or 'Dickensian London'. From this time onwards Doire Cholmcille gradually becomes the usual way of referring to the settlement.

At Derry in 1100, as part of the struggle for the high-kingship, Domnall defeated an expedition of the Dublin fleet that was acting on behalf of Muircertach O'Brien. The following year the ancient headquarters of the Cenél Eóghain, the Grianan of Aileach, was destroyed by another expedition, led by O'Brien himself. On this occasion, according to legend, O'Brien's troops were ordered to carry away the stones of the fortress in their baggage so that it could never be rebuilt. In fact, it was not until the 1870s that a Dr Walter Bernard from Derry and teams of local workmen restored the ruined monument.

The destruction of Aileach in 1101 may indicate that Domnall was already living in Derry. For over a hundred years previously, some of the Gaelic lords in other parts of Ireland had been moving into the Viking towns, or into some of the larger Irish monasteries. Some of these monasteries had grown into sizeable settlements and were beginning to evolve into towns. The O'Briens had settled in Limerick and Dublin, and since at least the end of the tenth century the Cenél Eóghain kings had maintained a house in Armagh. The first hint that Derry had passed into the control of the Cenél Eóghain can be detected

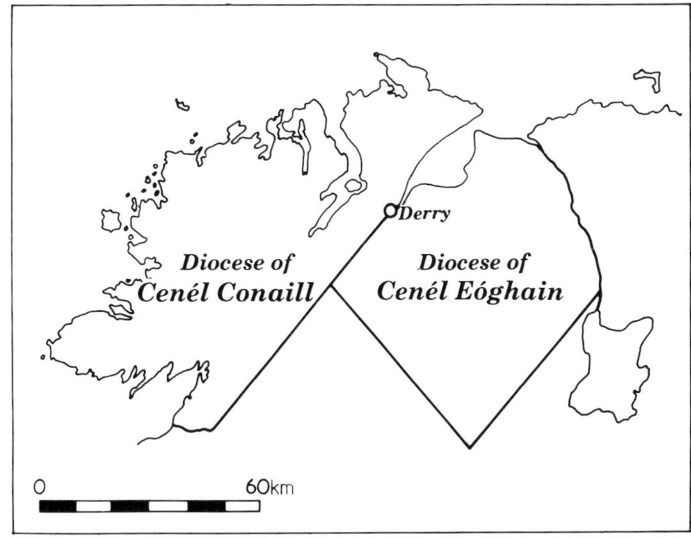

The Cenél Conaill and Cenél Eóghain dioceses, agreed at the Synod of Rath Bresail in 1111

in the records of the Synod of Rath Bresail, County Tipperary, in the year 1111. This met under the presidency of the papal legate, Gilbert, and the patronage of Muircertach O'Brien. It was a council of the leading clergy and some of the leading laity which aimed at setting up a territorial diocesan system for the whole of Ireland, similar to that in use throughout the rest of Christendom. The synod could not decide whether Derry or Raphoe should be the seat of the diocese of the Cenél Conaill. However, Derry was certainly not to be the seat of the diocese of the Cenél Eóghain. The upstart takeover of Derry by Domnall Mac Lochlainn was not going to be given official recognition by a council led by his archrival, Muircertach O'Brien.

However, despite O'Brien's objections, the Cenél Eóghain were now definitely installed in Derry. In 1112 the death occurred, at ninety-four years of age, of Congalach, son of Mac Conchaille, the erenagh of Derry. The Mac Conchaills came from near Lough Neagh and belonged to the Cenél Eóghain. Strictly speaking, they had no business being involved in the affairs of Derry, with its long-standing Cenél Conaill associations. However, they managed to hold on to office there and in 1134 the death in Derry of another member of the family, Bebhinn, is recorded. Bebhinn seems to have been a sister of Congalach and she is the first named woman to appear in the history of Derry. Presumably in the previous six hundred years women had made many contributions to the development of the settlement but these were not recorded. Bebhinn is given the unusual title of female erenagh (*banairchinneach*) of Derry. The precise meaning of the title is unknown but she may have been the founder of a convent of nuns. Some of the 'galliagh' (from the Irish *cailleach* meaning a 'nun') placenames around the city imply such a convent. It is known that there was a 'nuns' church' in Derry at the end of the sixteenth century, sometimes claimed, on very uncertain grounds, to be Cistercian, but there is no evidence to connect Bebhinn with it. The annals record that between the death of Congalach and the death of Bebhinn, two men, Finn Ua Conaingen and Gilla Mac Liag, held the title of erenagh of Derry. This title, although its meaning was to be radically altered in later times, refers to the abbacy of the monastery. Consequently, there must have been a separate religious community for women, although we hear nothing more of it until the end of the Middle Ages.

Coinciding with the Cenél Eóghain takeover of Derry is the elaboration of the claim that Colmcille had been the founder of the monastery there. This may have been originally part of Cenél Conaill propaganda in opposition to the new Cenél Eóghain rulers. By showing that Derry had been founded by the greatest of all their saints, the Cenél Conaill could justifiably claim that the monastery and settlement still belonged by right to them. If this is what happened, it backfired. It was the Cenél Eóghain who were to develop fully the Columban claim and make the most use of it.

In 1137 the great ecclesiastical reformer, Malachy, resigned as head of the church of Armagh. He chose as his successor Gilla Mac Liag, also known by his Latin name Gelasius, who had been erenagh of Derry for the previous sixteen years. The appointment of Gilla Mac Liag to the leading ecclesiastical position in the country gave a new prominence to the monastery in Derry and also brought it into more direct contact with those promoting the reform movement within the Irish church. By 1145 Muircertach Mac Lochlainn was king of the Cenél Eóghain and, like his grandfather Domnall, was making a bid for the high-kingship of Ireland. Also like Domnall, Muircertach took an active interest in the internal affairs of Derry.

FLAITHBERTACH O'BROLCHAIN AND THE CULTIVATION OF A LEGEND

In 1150 there was a major change in Derry: the erenagh, Maelisa Ua Branain, died and was replaced by Flaithbertach O'Brolchain, another Cenél Eóghain ecclesiastic. Unexpectedly, Flaithbertach was not styled

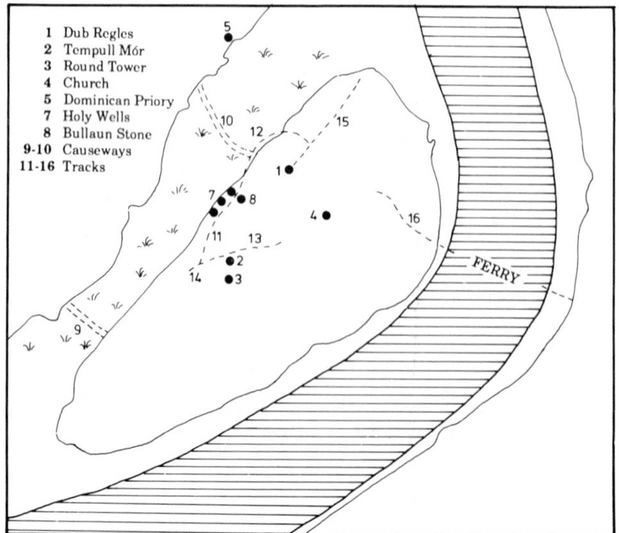

Derry from 1150 to 1250, showing the location of the principal ecclesiastical buildings referred to in the contemporary records

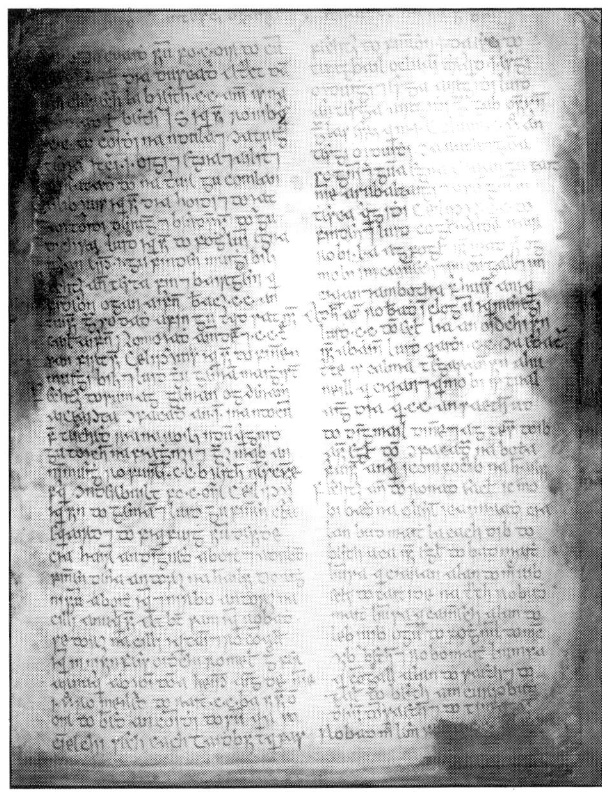

A page from a fifteenth- to sixteenth-century manuscript of the Old Irish Life of Colmcille (National Library of Scotland)

erenagh of Derry on his appointment but instead he was given the more prestigious title of coarb (successor) of Colmcille. For the previous two hundred years this title, and the leadership of the Columban churches in Ireland which went with it, had been reserved for the abbot of Kells in County Meath. By the mid-twelfth century, however, Kells was in decline and the opportunity existed for Derry to make a bid to take over its role. It is unlikely that this decision was taken by the Columban churches acting together. A unilateral move would have been supported by the king, Muircertach Mac Lochlainn, and by Gilla Mac Liag. The O'Brolchain family already had associations with Armagh and Derry. Flaithbertach was probably the son of Mael Coluim O'Brolchain, the Armagh bishop, who died while on pilgrimage to the hermitage in Derry in the year 1122.

As soon as Flaithbertach was appointed, he set about transforming and reorganising Derry, both physically and institutionally. His assumption of the title coarb of Colmcille as abbot of Derry was a break with all tradition, just as the earlier Cenél Eóghain takeover of Derry had been. The 'historians' of Derry set about retrospectively rectifying this situation and sometime between 1150 and 1182 the Old Irish Life of Colmcille was written there. The main thesis of this Life is that Derry was the first monastery founded by the saint and the one most loved by him. If this premise could be established, there could be no objections to Derry assuming the leadership of the confederation of churches which had been founded originally by the saint. The Life clearly sets out the claim that Derry had been founded by Colmcille. It also claims that he

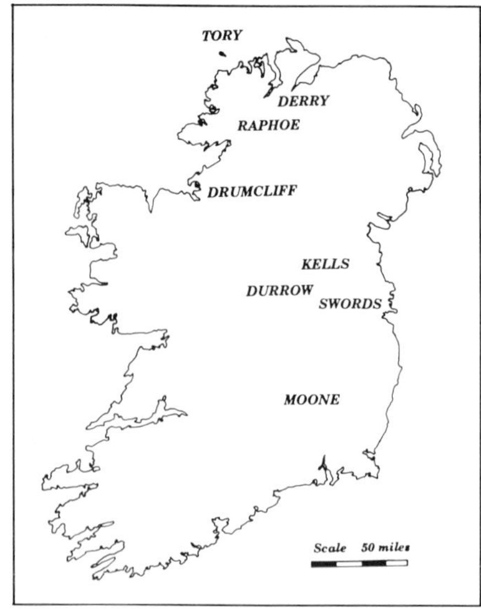

Map showing the principal monastic churches in Ireland of the *Paruchia* (confederation) of Colmcille from the sixth to the twelfth century

founded Kells in County Meath, although there is no doubt that Kells was established in 807, more than two hundred years after the saint's death. The story of the Columban foundation of Derry is no more reliable and its purpose was to bolster the new role for the monastery there.

THE CENÉL EÓGHAIN CAPITAL

With Flaithbertach as abbot and head of the Columban federation, and with Muircertach Mac Lochlainn as a contender for the title of high-king, the importance of the monastery of Derry continued to grow. It was, in effect, the capital of the Cenél Eóghain. It might have been expected that Derry would have been named as the seat of a diocese at the national Synod of Kells in 1152 but this did not happen, probably again as a result of continuing controversy over Derry's connections with the Cenél Conaill. However, in 1158 another synod, held at Bri mac Taidg in County Meath, created a personal episcopal chair for Flaithbertach. This was a formal recognition of his leadership of all the Columban monasteries throughout Ireland.

Saint Colmcille's House, Kells, County Meath; Kells was the principal Columban monastery in Ireland from the ninth to the eleventh century.

Flaithbertach also began his programme of beautifying and reorganising the settlement at Derry. In 1155 the annals record that he built a door for the 'Tempaill'. The reference must be to the construction of a monumental door, possibly in the latest hiberno-romanesque designs. The Tempaill was clearly a different building to the monastic Dub Regles or Black Church. The Annals of Ulster record the following entry for 1162:

> Total separation of the houses from the churches of Derry was made by the Successor of Colmcille (namely Flaithbertach) and by the king of Ireland, that is, by Muircertach [Mac] Lochlainn; where were demolished eighty houses or something more.

A stone wall was built around the churches and a malediction pronounced on anyone who violated the new ecclesiastical enclosure. This

Mellifont Abbey, County Louth. High-king Muircertach Mac Lochlainn, who was instrumental in the building of the Tempull Mór at Derry, was also involved with the construction of the abbey at Mellifont in 1157. (Bord Fáilte)

was a radical attempt to rezone the settlement into separate lay and ecclesiastical precincts. About this time the annals begin to make a distinction between the 'people of Derry' and the 'community of Colmcille'. Obviously an extensive township had developed around the monastery and the demolition of over eighty houses must indicate a settlement of several hundred people at least. In 1163 the annals record the erection of a huge lime-kiln by Flaithbertach which was 'sixty paces in every direction'. This kiln must have been connected with the ambitious construction project undertaken in 1164:

> The great church [Tempull Mór] of Derry was built by the Successor of Colmcille, that is by Flaithbertach, son of the bishop O'Brolchain and by the Community of Colmcille and by Muircertach [Mac] Lochlainn, high king of Ireland. And the [top] stone of that great church, wherein are ninety feet [in length], was completed within the space of forty days.

Muircertach Mac Lochlainn was also involved with the building of the Cistercian abbey at Mellifont in County Louth.

In the thirteenth century the Tempull Mór became a cathedral when a diocesan seat was eventually transferred to Derry. The church also gave its name to a parish of the city, Templemore, which in turn has been used as the name of many of the city's modern institutions.

THE TEMPULL MÓR

The Tempull Mór was allegedly one of the most important buildings in the north of Ireland. The annal references suggest that it had an overall length of between twenty and twenty-seven metres. Unfortunately, the only trace of it which survives is said to be a small inscribed plaque incorporated into the dedication stone of St Columb's Church of Ireland Cathedral, built in the early seventeenth century. However, the lettering on this plaque is clearly of a later date. If the tradition is correct, the plaque presumably was intended to link the new building with its medieval predecessor. The Latin inscription on the plaque reads:

In Templo/Verus Deus/Est Vereque/Colendus.
The true God is in the church and truly he is to be worshipped.

An outline of the plan of the Tempull Mór is shown on Francis Nevill's map which was made about 1690 to illustrate the course of events during the Siege of Derry. Some traces of the building must have survived down to then. The map shows that the location of the Tempull Mór was near the present Long Tower Church. The actual site was probably where the former boys' school building is now situated. The map also shows the building as a cruciform shape with two transepts, which would have been very unusual features in a Gaelic Irish church of the twelfth century, but it is possible that they were added later.

South-west of the Tempull Mór and close to the location of what was until recently the junction of Corporation Street and Barrack Street there was a round tower, which must have been erected about the twelfth century. It is shown on a number of maps of the early seventeenth century but had disappeared by the time of the Siege of Derry in 1689. A windmill tower in the grounds of St Columb's College in Bishop Street is occasionally pointed out, inaccurately, as this round tower. Round towers were principally used as belfries. In the middle of the Bogside area there is a rocky knoll known as Blue Bell Hill. A local tradition explains its name: when the Elizabethan soldiers were coming to take Derry, the monks, fearing that the bell of the monastery would be stolen, took it and buried it somewhere on the hill. It is said to be still there. The round tower also gave its name, in the form 'Long Tower', to the surrounding district of the city.

The round tower of Derry as shown in George Vaughan Sampson's *Survey of the County of Londonderry*, 1814. The attribution is inaccurate; this building, which still survives in the grounds of St Columb's College, Bishop Street, is actually a windmill tower which dates to the seventeenth century.

THE SCHOOL AND SCRIPTORIUM

In 1166 'the greater part of Derry' was burned, including the Dub Regles. Also in that year, Muircertach, the settlement's most important lay patron, died. Shortly before his death Muircertach had fallen into disfavour when he broke a peace treaty with an eastern Ulster king. That treaty had been pledged on the great relics of Armagh and Derry, the Staff of Jesus and the Gospel Book of Saint Martin (Soiscél Martain) respectively, and guaranteed by the coarbs of Armagh and Derry, Gilla Mac Liag and Flaithbertach O'Brolchain. Muircertach's body was taken to Armagh and interred in the burial place of many of his Cenél Eóghain ancestors. The community of Colmcille in Derry, together with their

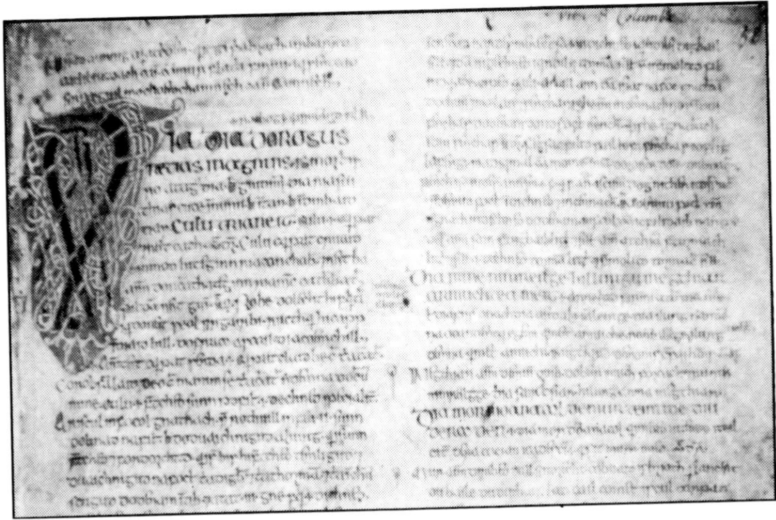

Twelfth-century manuscript of the 'Amra Choluimb Chille' (song of Colmcille), the composition of which is said to have been begun by the poet Dallan Forgail immediately after the Convention of Drumceat in 575, and finished after the saint's death in 597 (Bodleian Library, Oxford)

abbot, Flaithbertach, and the 'leader of the students of Derry', objected strongly to this and they protested in the time-honoured Irish manner by ritual fasting or hunger striking.

From many references like this it is obvious that there was a senior school and scriptorium in Derry during the twelfth and early thirteenth centuries at least. Between 1162 and 1220 the annals refer to four different lectors (*fir leiginn*) and two different senior lectors (*ard fir leiginn*). Members of two of the important ecclesiastical families of the settlement, the O'Murrays and the O'Milligans, held several of these posts as well as many other high ecclesiastical offices in Derry. Only a small proportion of the literary works produced in Derry during the Middle Ages has survived. Both the Old Irish Life of Colmcille and part of the introduction to the 'Amra Choluimb Chille' (song of Colmcille) were most probably written in Derry during this period. There is an abundance of Columban literature, including many verses emphasising the saint's particular love of Derry, which must have been written there around this time:

Derry mine! my small oak grove,
Little cell, my home, my love!
O thou Lord of lasting life,
Woe to him who brings it strife.

and

The reason I love Derry is
For its tranquillity, its purity;
For full of angels white it is,
From one end to the other.

Part of the genealogical material in the medieval Book of Lecan is said by those who compiled it to derive from the so-called Book of Derry. The Book of Derry is lost but presumably it was a compendium of miscellaneous historical and genealogical material such as can be found in many similar surviving compositions from elsewhere in the country. It is known that a set of annals was being compiled in Derry between 1190 and 1220. This, or another copy of it, was later transcribed into the Annals of Ulster. No doubt the entry for the year 546, purporting to record the establishment of the monastery, was inserted into the annals about this time. It has been suggested that two of Ireland's oldest and most treasured illuminated manuscripts, the Cathach and the Book of Durrow (both of which have strong Columban associations) might have been produced in Derry. This is very unlikely, but the Gospel Book of Saint Martin, which was one of the most important treasures of the monastery of Derry, must have been a similarly decorated manuscript. Manus O'Donnell's Life of Colmcille gives an account of how this manuscript came to be in Derry:

> Then Colmcille went on a pilgrimage to Tours of Martin. And he went to the flagstone under which Martin was buried. He lifted the stone from the tomb and he found the book of the Gospels upon the neck of Martin in the tomb. And Martin and that book had been a hundred years in the earth, and God had preserved the book that long for the use of Colmcille, so that it was no better on its first day than the time Colmcille found it. And by the will of God and of Martin, Colmcille took that book with him to Derry, as Martin himself had prophesied at the time of his death.

Saint Martin's Cross, Iona; a cult of Saint Martin was widespread throughout the early Irish church, not least in the monastic settlement at Derry

The same story is told in a simplified manner in the Old Irish Life, implying that the book was actually in Derry at the time the Life was written. It was stolen by a group of Normans in 1182. On this occasion it was probably in use as a talisman by the Irish, in the same way as somewhat later the O'Donnells of Donegal used the Cathach. The Gospel Book of Saint Martin was never recovered. There is an alternative legend as to how it came to be in Derry. According to this version, on his death bed Saint Martin gave the book to Saint Patrick, who brought it with him to Ireland. When Saint Patrick died it was placed in his grave and much later Colmcille exhumed the remains and brought the book back to Derry as a relic.

THE CULT OF SAINT MARTIN

In many similar legends, other Irish saints, anachronistically, were brought into contact with Saint Martin, who was bishop of Tours in southern France from about 371 to about 403. Saint Martin was one of the first people to practise monasticism in western Christianity and it was perfectly natural for the writers of some of the saints' Lives to want to asssociate the founders of the Irish monasteries with him. A cult of Saint Martin was widespread throughout the early Irish church, not least in the monastic settlement of Derry. An entry in the annals in 1204 mentions a graveyard of Saint Martin in Derry and a holy well there was dedicated to him. This was one of three such wells originally located in what later became known as St Columb's Wells Street or Lane. The other wells were dedicated to Saints Columba and Adomnan. The

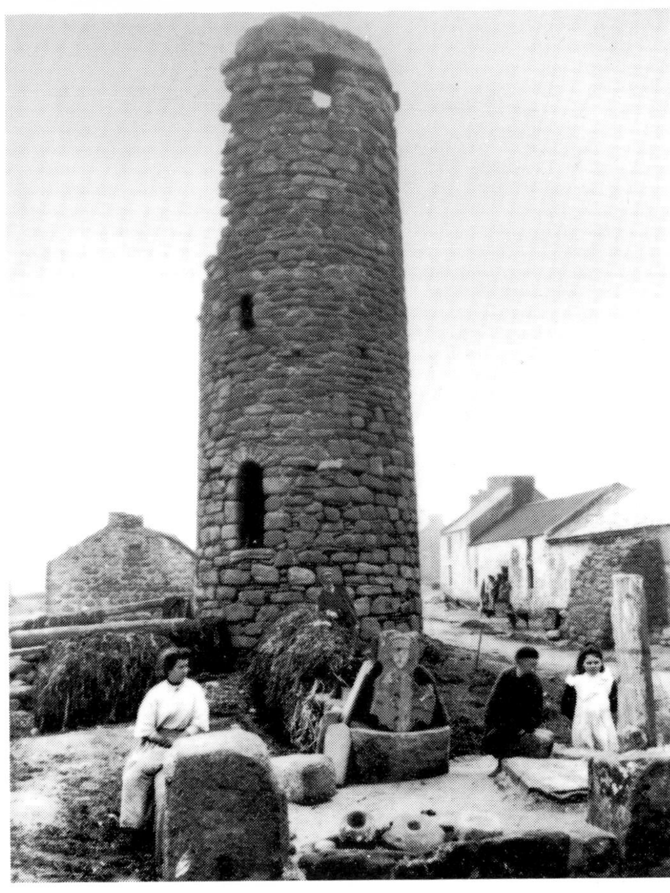

Round tower of the early Columban monastery on Tory Island, County Donegal (Welch Collection, Ulster Museum)

position of St Columba's Well is marked nowadays by the decorative pump erected there in 1897 by Father William Doherty.

An alternative explanation for the unlikely tradition linking Derry and Tours might be found in confused memories of connections with the Columban monastery on Tory Island, off the Donegal coast. The Irish name used for Tours in the legends, Tor Inis, looks suspiciously similar to that of Tory, Inis Torach. The monastery on Tory was run by the local Mac Robartaigh family. Another branch of this family gave its name to Ballymagrorty in south Donegal, where the monastery of Rath Cunga was situated. This branch of the family were the keepers of the great treasure of the O'Donnells of Donegal, the Cathach of Colmcille. A third branch gave their name to Ballymagroarty, on the northern outskirts of Derry. Here, according to the seventeenth-century Inishowen ecclesiastical writer, John Colgan, there was another small monastery. Therefore, it may well be that some of the less likely stories connecting Saint Colmcille and Derry with Tours originally derived from the genuine Columban connections with Tory.

Saint Colmcille's Well and Stone at Pennyburn, as shown on Francis Nevill's 1690 map of the Siege of Derry

THE END OF AN ERA

With the death of Muircertach Mac Lochlainn in 1166, Derry was left without a leading lay patron. In 1167 the new high-king, Rory O'Connor of Connacht, led a huge expedition of nobles to the north

Shrine of the Cathach of Colmcille, originally made about 1090 (National Museum of Ireland)

of Ireland to obtain the submission of the Cenél Eóghain. The expedition brought him to Derry. The Annals of Tigernach described this impressive cavalcade in some detail:

> A hosting by Rory O'Connor, high-king of Ireland, and by the kings of Ireland ie. Dermot McCarthy, king of Desmond, and Muircertach O'Brien, king of Dal Cais, and the kings of Leinster and Osraige with their great muster, and Dermot O'Maelseachlainn, king of Meath, and Tigernan O'Rourke, king of Ui Briuin and Conmaicni, and O'Carroll, king of Oriel, and Ua Eochada, king of the Ulaid, with his mighty gathering; and all these kings were assembled together. Thirteen battalions they were of footsoldiers and seven of cavalry; and they reached Armagh, and remained there for three nights awaiting the Cenél Conaill and the great fleet. They came round Ireland till they reached the harbour of Derry and they went by sea and by land throughout the territory of the Cenél Eóghain . . . And [the Cenél Eóghain] gave eight hostages to the king of Ireland.

The high-kingship of Ireland had clearly passed away from the Cenél Eóghain and from Derry. It never returned.

Within a few years, three of the leading ecclesiastics connected with Derry died. Muiredach O'Coffey, bishop of the Cenél Eóghain, died in 1173. The diocese of the Cenél Eóghain coincided with the territory controlled by the Mac Lochlainns at that time and it later evolved as the diocese of Derry. The official seat of the diocese was the old monastery of Rath Luraigh in Maghera, County Derry, but Muiredach died in the Dub Regles in Derry. He was given a marvellous obituary by the annalists. They called him

> a son of purity, a precious stone, a transparent gem, a brilliant star, a treasury of wisdom and a protector of the canons of the church. After having bestowed food and raiment on the poor and needy – after having ordained priests and deacons and men of every ecclesiastical degree – after having repaired many churches, consecrated many temples and burial places, and performed every ecclesiastical duty – after having

> gained the palm of piety, pilgrimages and penances – he resigned his spirit to heaven in the Dub Regles of Colmcille in Derry on the 10th day of February. A great miracle occurred on the night of his death: from twilight to daybreak the heavens were illuminated, and all the people of the settlement beheld the light; and a great mass of fire arose over the settlement and moved in a south-easterly direction; all arose from their beds imagining it to be day.

Perhaps it was a meteor which caused the extraordinary light on the night of Muiredach's death. In 1174 the death occurred in Armagh of Gilla Mac Liag, who had been a great promoter of Derry and abbot there from 1120 to 1137. His death was followed in 1175 by that of the greatest of all the Derry abbots. According to the Annals of Ulster,

> Flaithbertach O'Brolchain, successor of Colmcille, tower of wisdom and hospitality, a man to whom the clergy of Ireland gave the chair of a bishop for wisdom and for his excellence and to whom was offered the succession of Iona, died piously, after choice tribulation in the Dub Regles of Colmcille.

He was one of the most important men ever to have lived in Derry.

THE TOWNSHIP

From the late twelfth century onwards, the annals record a long series of incidents in Derry, strictly secular in nature. Murders, blood feuds, thieving, an execution, a rape, the deliberate burning of a house over an enemy, and a marriage arrangement are all recorded between 1177 and 1261. In 1222 a terse entry in the annals states that 'Nial O'Neill profaned Derry and the daughter of O'Cahan'. The acts of violence often reflected the continuing rivalry between the Cenél Eóghain and the Cenél Conaill or internal disputes among the ruling families. Also, a number of lay aristocrats died in Derry during this period while on pilgrimage to the Dub Regles of Colmcille. In 1196 the chieftain of the O'Cahans and his wife presented a 'door' to the refectory building of the Dub Regles. This was obviously some kind of special monumental doorway. The mention of a refectory confirms that the Dub Regles was a monastic house with a communal way of life.

With the death of Muircertach Mac Lochlainn, internal disputes had broken out within the Cenél Eóghain. A violent encounter in 1177 is recorded in Derry between Nial O'Gormley, a chieftain of the area around present-day Strabane, and Donchad O'Cairellain, the chief of the Clann Dermot, who by this time ruled the area opposite Derry on the east bank of the River Foyle. The Clann Dermot gave its name, in the form Clondermot, to the parish in the Waterside area. Nial O'Gormley was in a house belonging to one of the clergy of Derry. His attackers set fire to the house, forcing Nial to try to escape by the door, where he was killed. The house and its contents were destroyed and O'Cairellain, who had been accompanied by some of his supporters, was forced to pay compensation. In addition, in order to make 'peace with Colmcille and the people of Derry', O'Cairellain had to promise some kind of unspecified monastic service by himself and his family for posterity. As a guarantee, he donated a valuable drinking horn, 'the best that was in Ireland', as a pledge for sixty cows. This did not stop the feud, as three years later Donchad was killed violently 'through a miracle of Colmcille' by other members of the Cenél Eóghain, probably the O'Gormleys. Another relative, Raghnall, was killed in 'the middle of Derry', again probably as part of this internal Cenél Eóghain dispute. In 1180 a man called Aindiles O'Doherty died in Derry. He was the first person with this surname to be mentioned in association with the settlement. His later namesakes and descendants at various times right down to the present were to make an enormous impact on Derry. Today this surname, in a variety of spellings and pronunciations, is by far the commonest surname in the city amongst both Catholics and Protestants.

The drinking horn which Donchad O'Cairellain had presented in 1177 was known as the 'Mac Riabach'. In 1196 it was stolen, along with three other similar horns (or possibly liturgical chalices) known respectively as the Mac Solus, the Horn of O'Muldory and the Cam Corunn or the O'Doherty Horn, by MacGilla Eidich of the Ciannachta, the tribe based in the valley of the River Roe in County Derry. The horns had all been kept in the Tempull Mór, either as offerings or perhaps just for safe-keeping and were said to be the best of their kind in Ireland. MacGilla Eidich damaged them and removed the jewels but fortunately he was caught after three days and the horns recovered. MacGilla Eidich was hanged on the 'cross of the executions in reparation to Colmcille whose altar he had profaned'. Two of the horns came from the Cenél Conaill families of O'Muldory and O'Doherty and there are other connections between the Cenél Conaill and Derry around this time. Obviously, with the demise of the Cenél Eóghain Mac Lochlainn kings, the Cenél Conaill attempted to re-establish their control over Derry.

There is very little information about the economic basis of this small settlement. Seventeenth-century documents show that by then the monastery owned large amounts of land outside the 'island'. This would have been the case in earlier times as well. For example, in the later Middle Ages, land at Nearabolls, on the Scottish island of Islay, belonged to the Augustinian abbey of Derry. In 1215 Aed mac Maelsechlainn Mac Lochlainn made a foray against the coarb of Colmcille and carried off a herd of cattle. Special sanctions seem to have been available to the distressed abbot as later the same year Aed was killed by the Normans 'through a miracle of Colmcille'. Obviously, natural resources such as the land, the oakgrove after which the place was named, and the local fishing, contributed to the economy. A reference in the annals for the year 1217 seems to imply that there were seagoing fishermen based in Derry at that time. Flaithbertach O'Brolchain had returned from various visitations with large amounts of tribute, and the local aristocrats compensated for their misdemeanours by making contributions to the monastery. No doubt there must have been a secular economy with the produce of different types of craftsmen and other services available. The settlement may even have provided the location for some of the regular markets and fairs which must have been a feature of life at this time but, unfortunately, there are no records of any activity of this sort.

THE NORMANS IN DERRY

In May 1169 a party of Norman warriors from Wales landed on the Wexford coast to help a provincial Irish king, Dermot MacMurrough, regain his kingdom of Leinster, from which he had been forced to flee. The Normans came with the approval of their sovereign lord, Henry II, king of England, at whose request, in 1155, Pope Adrian IV had issued the bull *Laudabiliter*, which granted lordship of Ireland to the king and allowed him to enter the country on the pretext of reforming the church. (A reform under native direction was, in fact, already in progress.) However, Henry, who ruled an extensive empire, had more pressing demands on his energies and was forced to shelve the project until 1171. In that year a combination of difficulties with the papacy, arising from the king's implication in the murder of Archbishop Thomas à Becket, and his recognition that the Norman earl Strongbow might be trying to establish a separate independent kingdom in Ireland, persuaded Henry that he must go there. This was the formal beginning of the Norman conquest of Ireland and of the eight-hundred-year-old connection of the country with the English Crown.

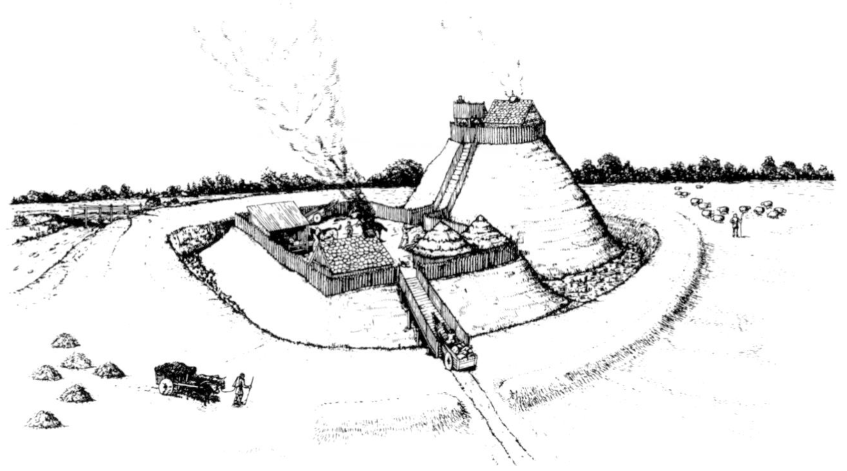

Reconstruction of a Norman motte-and-bailey castle, similar to the type of fortification built by John de Courcy during his conquest of Ulster in the late twelfth century (Historic Monuments and Buildings Branch, Department of Environment for Northern Ireland)

The Normans first came to Derry in 1197. One of two expeditions there was led by Rotsel Piton, who had been installed at the castle of Cill Santain in the Coleraine area, by his lord, John de Courcy. It was de Courcy who had brought the Normans to Ulster and installed himself at Downpatrick in County Down, from where he had established a network of fortifications around the coast to the mouth of Lough Foyle. He was described by his contemporary, the Norman chronicler Giraldus Cambrensis, as 'fair-haired and tall with bony and sinewy limbs. His frame was lanky and he had a very strong physique, immense bodily strength, and an extraordinarily bold temperament.' The Normans seem to have been acting as allies of the Mac Lochlainns, who were trying to regain the power they had lost after the death of their last high-king, Muircertach. Flaithbertach O'Muldory, the Donegal chieftain who, in a dramatic reversal of tradition, was claiming to be lord of the Cenél Eóghain as well as of his own people, the Cenél Conaill, overtook the Normans, along with the son of Ardgar Mac Lochlainn, at the mouth of the Faughanvale river at Lough Foyle. A battle ensued and both the Normans and Mac Lochlainn were slaughtered 'through the miracles of Saints Colmcille, Cainneach and Brecan, whose churches they had plundered'. The churches in question were those at Clooney, Enagh and Gransha, on the east bank of the River Foyle, a few miles downstream from Derry.

Later that year John de Courcy himself came to Derry from his headquarters in County Down, crossing the River Bann by the ford at Toome and travelling onwards via the monastery of Ardstraw. He remained in Derry with his troops for five nights. He returned to impose his authority in Derry in 1199, having already that year plundered the churches of Ardstraw and Raphoe. He remained in Derry for nine days on this occasion, using it as a base to plunder in Inishowen. He only left Derry on hearing that his settlements in eastern Ulster had been attacked by the O'Neills.

In 1212 Thomas Mac Uchtred of the de Galloway family of south-west Scotland, who was in Ireland under the patronage of King John, came on a plundering expedition to Derry with seventy-seven ships. The following year he returned, having received from the king a grant of that part of the settlement of Derry claimed by the O'Neills. At this stage the O'Neills were lords of the Cenél Eóghain and presumably claimed the same rights in Derry as their predecessors, the Mac Lochlainns. On this occasion Mac Uchtred and his men 'plundered Derry completely and took the treasures of the people of Derry, and of the north of Ireland besides, from out of the midst of the church of the monastery'.

Whatever the terms of the grant of Derry to Mac Uchtred were, they were not taken up. The next occasion on which the Normans are mentioned in connection with Derry is almost one hundred years later. In 1306 the bishop of Derry, Geoffrey Mac Lochlainn, sued Henry Mac

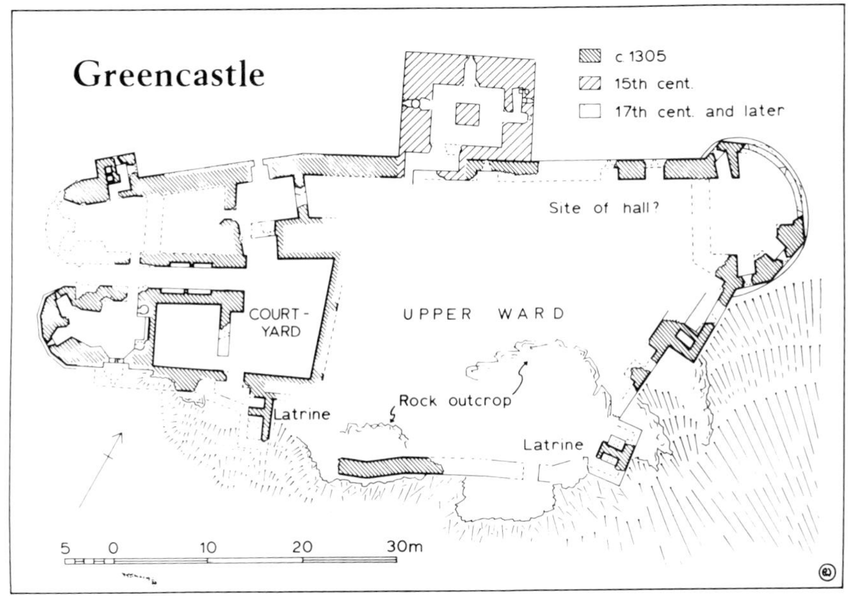

Plan of the de Burgo fortification at Greencastle, County Donegal (Donegal County Council)

an Crossan, bishop of Raphoe, for a large area of land in Derry. In the second half of the thirteenth century the Donegal chieftain, Domnall Óg O'Donnell, had 'unjustly deprived' the then bishop of Derry, Gilla an Choimdedh O'Carolan, of the land and given it to Florence O'Friel, bishop of Raphoe. This must have occurred at a time when the Cenél Conaill had regained some influence in Derry. In 1310 the Earl of Ulster, Richard de Burgo, who in 1305 had built the fortification of Greencastle in Inishowen at the entrance to Lough Foyle, was pardoned by Edward II for accepting, without the royal consent, lands at Derry from both the bishop of Derry and the bishop of Raphoe. In 1311 the king granted Derry to de Burgo but in 1322 de Burgo returned half of the island of Derry to the bishop of Raphoe. This resulted in, or perhaps merely institutionalised, a peculiar partition of the island of Derry between the Cenél Conaill diocese of Raphoe and the Cenél Eóghain diocese of Derry. The arrangement survived to the end of the Middle Ages.

The most logical reason for Richard de Burgo wishing to own land at Derry was in order to develop a colonial town there. However, if this was the case, there is no evidence to suggest that he had any success. The de Burgo earldom itself collapsed by the middle of the fourteenth century and Derry's second opportunity to become a proper medieval town came to nothing. Derry remained almost untouched by Anglo-Norman influences, being situated at the centre of that unexplored territory known as the 'Great Irishry'. Some echo of the Norman connection with Derry may be discerned on the city's coat-of-arms. The lower half is said to be the old arms of Derry prior to the seventeenth-century addition of the London arms for the plantation city of Londonderry. This lower section features a sitting skeleton and although the precise explanation for this device appears to be lost, it is said to represent the death by starvation of Walter de Burgo at Greencastle in 1332.

Coat-of-arms of the City of Londonderry; the skeleton is said to represent Walter de Burgo, who died at Greencastle in 1332. The Latin inscription translates as 'Life, Truth, Victory'.

A DERRY SOLUTION

The partition of the island of Derry between the dioceses of Derry and Raphoe was a harking back to the ancient dispute between the Cenél Conaill and the Cenél Eóghain. The Cenél Conaill tenaciously clung to an involvement in Derry and from before 1180 until 1233 three members of the Cenél Conaill O'Deery family held the office of erenagh. MacCraith O'Deery died in 1180 and was succeeded by Maoliosa, who retained the office for forty years. He in turn was succeeded by Geoffrey, who died in 1233. The O'Deerys continued to hold office until the end of the Middle Ages, although by that stage they had for a long time been joined as co-erenaghs in Derry by the Cenél Eóghain Mac Lochlainn family. With the death of the high-king Muircertach in 1166, the power of the Mac Lochlainns waned. Internal disputes in the Cenél Eóghain, particularly the rise of the O'Neills, and the rise of the O'Muldorys and O'Canannains among the Cenél Conaill, all of whom were becoming involved in the affairs of Derry, affected the role of the Mac Lochlainns. In 1196 another Muircertach Mac Lochlainn died and was 'honourably interred' in Derry. He was the last of his family to be styled king of the Cenél Eóghain. Although the Mac Lochlainns continued to be connected with Derry, their status was that of subordinates.

The Mac Lochlainns, who under their great chieftain Domnall had risen to prominence in the late eleventh century, capturing Derry in the process and claiming the title of high-king of Ireland, had by the start of the thirteenth century lost almost all their power. However, they retained some influence in Derry to the end of the sixteenth century. An 'inquisition', an investigation into the properties of the recently dissolved monastery, was made in Derry in 1609, which throws some light on the fate of the Mac Lochlainns and, ironically, given its more recent history, on the peculiar organisation of the settlement in the later Middle Ages:

> Within the said island of Derry there were two erenaghs belonging to the late abbot of Colmcille, the one called Loughlina [Mac Lochlainn] within the diocese of Derry, and the other called oderry [O'Deery] within the diocese of Raphoe.

This extraordinary partition of the settlement of Derry itself dated back to at least the beginning of the fourteenth century. However, the Mac Lochlainns, who had once been kings in Derry, were now reduced to the status of erenaghs.

THE EPISCOPAL SEAT

During the first half of the twelfth century the diocesan system for the whole of Ireland was being established. Derry was not included among the seats for a bishopric, although in many ways it was an obvious

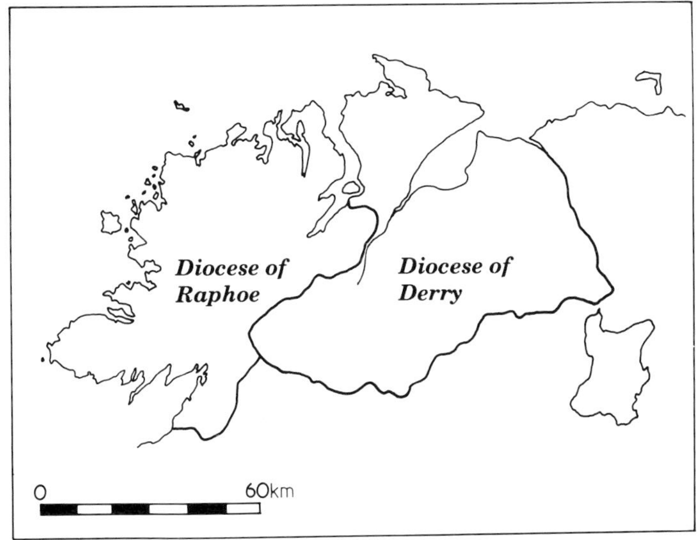

The dioceses of Derry and Raphoe, corresponding to the secular political geography of the late twelfth century

choice. Clearly this was the consequence of secular rather than ecclesiastical political considerations. The recent takeover of Derry by the Cenél Eóghain made it impossible for it to be the centre of the diocese of the Cenél Conaill, with whom it had ancient links. Similarly, fears that its new associations might only be short-lived, together with the influence of the Munster O'Brien kings, who were enemies of the Mac Lochlainns in Derry, ensured that neither was it declared the seat of the diocese of the Cenél Eóghain.

The seat of the Cenél Eóghain diocese was, from 1111, at Ardstraw in County Tyrone, and about the middle of the twelfth century it was transferred to Rath Luraigh in Maghera, County Derry. However, Cenél Eóghain bishops were active in, and possibly living in, Derry from the beginning of the twelfth century. The Armagh bishop Mael Coluim O'Brolchain, though not officially in charge of the Cenél Eóghain diocese, died in Derry in 1122. Flaithbertach O'Brolchain appears to have been his son. Muiredach O'Coffey, bishop of the Cenél Eóghain, died in Derry in 1173. Amhlaibh O'Murray (or O'Coffey), who seems to have been Muiredach O'Coffey's son, died in 1185 at Duncrun near Coleraine and while it is not certain that he operated from Derry, he obviously belonged to the same O'Murray family which provided a number of the lectors and senior lectors to the monastery around this time. The annalists recorded that Amhlaibh's body was brought

Crucifixion scene on the west doorway lintel of St Lurach's Church at Maghera, County Derry. The carving may have been made in the mid-twelfth century, when the building served as the seat of the Cenél Eóghain diocese. (Historic Monuments and Buildings Branch, Department of Environment for Northern Ireland)

'honourably to Derry and there interred at the feet of his father, the Bishop O'Coffey, at the side of the small church'. The annals relate that the Cenél Eóghain bishop, Florence O'Carolan, who died in 1230, was also involved in the affairs of Derry during his term of office.

Florence was succeeded by Gilla an Choimdedh (Gervase) O'Carolan, possibly a close relative, who died in 1279. He was responsible for the official transfer of the seat of the bishopric of the Cenél Eóghain to Derry sometime between 1247 and 1254. In a bull dated 24 June 1247, Pope Innocent IV granted to the chapter of Derry the same rights as had previously been held by the chapter at Rath Luraigh, and this was confirmed on 4 November 1254. The Tempull Mór became the cathedral church. O'Carolan is also alleged to have been responsible for a number of alterations in the territory of his diocese, which was now becoming recognisable as the diocese of Derry. However, it was not until 1293, on the occasion of the death of his successor, another Florence O'Carolan, that the annalists permit themselves to use the title bishop of Derry. Despite the efforts of the twelfth-century church reformers to eradicate the notorious practice of ecclesiastical hereditary succession, the O'Carolan family managed to hold on to the bishopric for over a century from 1185 to 1293.

Conflict between the Cenél Eóghain and the Cenél Conaill, and their leading families, the O'Neills and the O'Donnells respectively, grew to major proportions during the episcopacy of Bishop Gilla an Choimdedh O'Carolan, no doubt some of it arising from the formal moving of the seat of the diocese. However, it is clear that the Cenél Conaill unsuccessfully fought the transfer. In 1261 'sixteen of the most distinguished clerics of the Cenél Conaill . . . were killed by Concubhar O'Neill and the Cenél Eóghain in Doire Cholmcille' but immediately afterwards Concubhar was slain by Domnall O'Breslin, the Cenél Conaill chieftain from the Fanad Peninsula in County Donegal. In 1318 John, son of the chieftain Domnall O'Neill, was killed in Derry by Hugh O'Donnell, who was at that time the chieftain of Donegal.

THE DOMINICAN PRIORY

Gilla an Choimdedh O'Carolan was, apparently, a member of the newly founded order of preaching friars, the Dominicans, who had been introduced to Ireland in 1224. During O'Carolan's episcopacy a Dominican priory was founded at Derry, which was located not on the island of Derry itself but across the bog north-west of the settlement in the area of present-day Abbey Street. According to tradition, the monastery was founded by the O'Donnell chieftains of Donegal but it is also possible that it was brought to Derry by Bishop O'Carolan. In 1281 Domnal Óg O'Donnell, chieftain of Donegal, was killed while fighting the O'Neills in the battle of Desertcreat near Dungannon in County Tyrone. He was brought to Derry and interred in the Monastery of the Friars (Mainistir na mBrathar) and perhaps it was this that gave rise to the O'Donnell–Dominican connection. The surviving parts of the monastery are included on a sketch map of Derry dated 1600. Although no trace of the monastery now survives, 'the foundations of the church' discovered in the Rossville Street/William Street/Abbey Street area at the beginning of the nineteenth century were probably part of that monastery. However, the Dominican connection with Derry proved very resilient: Dominican monks were expelled from the city shortly before the beginning of the siege of 1689.

THE DUB REGLES

By the middle of the thirteenth century Derry had several churches: the Dominican priory; the Tempull Bicc or small church; the Tempull Mór; and the Dub Regles monastic church. Despite all the reforms of the twelfth century, family influence and heredity continued to play a role in ecclesiastical preferment in Derry and it is clear that celibacy was not considered an essential requirement for office.

After 1220 there are no further references to the coarb of Colmcille. The Dub Regles is next mentioned in 1397 when it is referred to as the 'monastery of the Canons Regular, called the Black Abbey of Derry'. At some stage, presumably after 1220, the house, like many other ancient Irish monasteries, adopted the rule of Saint Augustine. It became a monastery of Augustinian canons of Arrouaise, subject to the Abbey of SS Peter and Paul in Armagh, and would survive the rest of the Middle Ages until the English conquest of Ulster in the late sixteenth century.

4

DERRY IN THE LATER MIDDLE AGES

On Monday 8 October 1397 a party of fifteen important ecclesiastics and their attendants set out on horseback from Termonmagurk near Carrickmore in County Tyrone. They travelled over the desolate Sperrin Mountains, passing into the diocese of Derry. There were Gaelic Irish and Anglo-Norman clerics in the group and they were led by John Colton, the archbishop of Armagh. Colton, who was English, was the only person in Irish history to have held the country's two senior positions. For a short time in 1382, before being appointed head of the church, he had been justiciar or head of the king's government in Ireland.

The party's first halt was at Cappagh, near the present town of Omagh. The archbishop summoned the local erenagh and ceremoniously enquired if Cappagh was within the diocese of Derry. Having been assured by the erenagh that it was, the archbishop solemnly explained the purpose of his visit: there was a temporary vacancy at that time in the bishopric of Derry and he had come to exercise spiritual and temporal jurisdiction in the diocese in accordance with ecclesiastical law. The account of his ten-day journey, which was recorded by Richard Kenmore, a priest and notary public 'by apostolic authority', gives us a unique glimpse into the life of the church in Gaelic Ulster.

The strange scene in the Tyrone field on that autumn day was a classic confrontation between a colonial and a native culture. On the one side there was the eminent Englishman, surrounded by his official entourage and the panoply of a prince of the universal church, a man who had been educated and worked at the university in Cambridge, who had occupied the highest offices, both secular and ecclesiastical, who was acquainted with the sophistication of the royal court – a man who was a confidant of the king himself. On the other side there was the erenagh of Cappagh, an unidentified layman, the guardian of a remote church in a remote part of Ulster.

As Cappagh was too poor to lodge the archbishop's party, the erenagh was commanded to bring 'beef for the kitchen' to Ardstraw, where the party stayed overnight. They continued on via Urney and Leckpatrick, reaching the 'city' of Derry on 10 October, where

Dr William Mac Cathmhaoil, Dean of the Cathedral church of Derry, with

Archbishop John Colton's journey through the diocese of Derry from 8 to 17 October 1397 (*Ulster Journal of Archaeology*, 1853)

many others, clerics, members of religious orders, and laymen, reverently came forth to meet the said Father, and conducted him to the monastery of the Canons Regular [Augustinians], called the Black Abbey [Dub Regles] of Derry, and reverently lodged him and his attendants with suitable chambers and accommodation. [The Dean] also procured and caused provisions in abundance to be supplied for the said Lord Primate and his retinue, and for their horses, free and without expense, to the said Archbishop until the following Saturday.

'REFORMATION'

On Thursday 11 October, Colton attended two Masses in the Dub Regles, the first 'solemnly sung, and another without singing'. He took his seat on the 'Tribunal' in the choir, summoned all the canons of the house and asked them 'if they knew of anything relating to the state or government of the said house, which required reformation'. He was informed that after the resignation of their last abbot, Reginald O'Hegarty, the brothers had appointed Hugh Mac Gillibride O'Doherty as guardian of the monastery. He, however, had usurped the common seal of the monastery which previously was kept 'under the custody of three keys', that is, three different people had been jointly responsible for it. Colton enquired of O'Doherty if this was the case and, on discovering that it was, commanded that the seal should be surrendered. A spokesman then rose and complained about the state of discipline in the monastery and the monks, together with the dean and several other clergy, requested the archbishop to draw up a new set of rules for the house. A few days later, while visiting the church at Banagher near Dungiven, the archbishop announced a set of decrees and rules for the monastery. By inference these decrees give us an idea of the daily life of the Augustinian monastery in Derry. References in the decrees to the abbot keeping a concubine should not unduly shock. Although it was undoubtedly illegal by canon law, this sort of practice was not uncommon in the medieval church throughout Europe. John Colton's predecessor as archbishop of Armagh, Milo Sweetman, had to deal with a similar situation in Derry in 1367. During the election of a dean in that year complaints were made that the then bishop of Derry, Simon, a Dominican, had been excommunicated for a variety of offences, the most serious of which were concubinage and adultery. Simon was later rehabilitated but never seems to have returned to the straight and narrow path. Until his death in 1380, he continued to be the subject of similar serious charges.

THE ELECTION OF AN ABBOT

On the morning of Friday 12 October, Archbishop Colton went again to the Dub Regles, where after some debate, he ratified Reginald O'Hegarty's resignation from the abbacy. The canons requested the archbishop to confirm their unanimous choice of Hugh Mac Gillibride O'Doherty as abbot. Colton announced that anyone who had any objections to this appointment should come before him the following day. Next morning the archbishop went to the Tempull Mór. After High

Mass had been solemnly sung the dean announced that he had previously received a mandate from the archbishop directing that

> he the said Dean of Derry should summon or cause to be summoned, peremptorily, on imminent peril of their souls, the Archdeacon and all the members of the Chapter of Derry, likewise all of the clergy of Derry, promoted to dignities or ecclesiastical benefices, or to holy orders, also the erenaghs, and all the officials of the Bishopric of Derry, to appear on the aforesaid 13th October. There to exhibit their charters or letters of dignities, benefices, orders, and dispensations; likewise their charters or letters of erenaghships, lands, possessions, and offices.

Everyone was present, except the archdeacon and the members of the chapter, who failed to appear because they objected to Colton's temporary jurisdiction, particularly the archbishop's claims on the property of the diocese. Twice the crier summoned the recalcitrant archdeacon and chapter and still they did not appear, forcing Colton to excommunicate them.

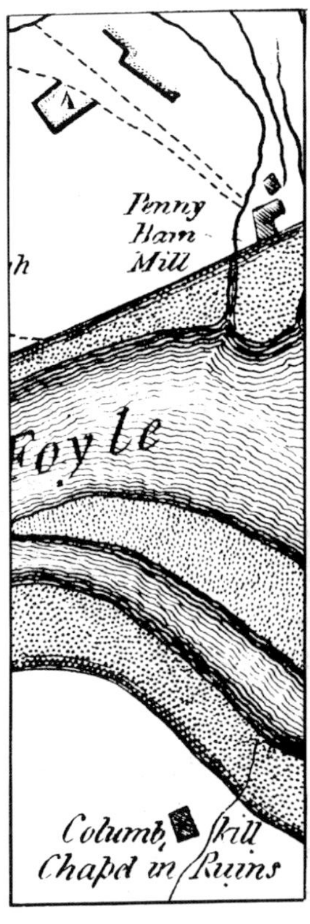

The late medieval church of St Brecan, Clooney, marked Columb kill Chapel on Francis Nevill's 1690 map of the Siege of Derry. This building, or more likely its predecessor on the same site, was where Archbishop John Colton said Mass for 'thousands' of people on Sunday 14 October 1397.

SUNDAY 14 OCTOBER 1397

On Sunday morning the archbishop's party crossed the River Foyle to the parish church of St Brecan in Clooney. Dr Mac Cathmhaoil requested Colton to reconsecrate the church and its cemetery, which had been 'polluted' by the shedding of blood there, a ceremony he had already performed at the church of Ardstraw. Thousands of people had turned up at St Brecan's and a temporary altar for the celebration of Mass had been prepared 'with becoming respect' outside the west door of the church. Before Mass began, the bishop of Raphoe arrived, accompanied by the previously missing archdeacon and chapter of Derry. The bishop requested Colton to absolve the recalcitrants from the sentences of excommunication that he had imposed on them the previous day. Colton relented and instructed the bishop to absolve the members of the chapter according to the rites of the church 'under pain and condition nevertheless of falling a second time under the same sentences, if they did not afterwards obey the mandates and ordinances of the Lord Archbishop'. During Mass the archbishop installed O'Doherty as abbot of the Dub Regles, and when the official business was over, Colton's retinue set out for the 'village' of Dermot O'Cahan, probably at nearby Enagh Lough.

THE LAST DAYS OF THE VISIT

Over the next three days the archbishop went on to visit the church at Banagher and the Augustinian priory near Dungiven. The primate dealt with a number of marriage and divorce issues and with a variety of internal church matters. He also had a meeting with the disobedient archdeacon and chapter of Derry and formally explained the reason and

The interior of the church at Banagher, County Derry, where Archbishop John Colton officiated 15–17 October 1397 (Historic Monuments and Buildings Branch, Department of Environment for Northern Ireland)

legal basis for his visit and then admonished each member of the chapter that they 'should obey himself and his successors . . . solely and exclusively in lieu of the Bishop'. The dean, the archdeacon and the members of the chapter responded unanimously, agreeing that the rights which had been claimed by Colton 'had belonged, now belonged, and ought to belong solely and exclusively to the said Venerable Father'. The dean and the archdeacon each presented a horse to Archbishop Colton in part payment for the rents and other episcopal rights which they had collected during the vacancy of the bishopric and which should have gone to the primate.

The members of the chapter then earnestly requested the archbishop not to grant or farm out any of the possessions of the diocese to the local powerful laymen lest they hold on to them for good. The archbishop gave the dean letters of 'monitions, suspensions, excommunications and interdict' addressed to the chieftains O'Donnell, O'Doherty, O'Cahan, O'Gormley, and Donal and Brian Mór, sons of Henry O'Neill, in respect 'of their usurpation of the episcopal rights of the Church of Derry'. There were few, if any, of the local lords not included in this 'gang of thieves' and yet, surprisingly, as medieval historian Professor John Watt has pointed out, Archbishop Colton had been able to move about the diocese 'in peace and harmony, unharassed by any hostile lay power':

When these affairs were settled . . . the dean, archdeacon, and other

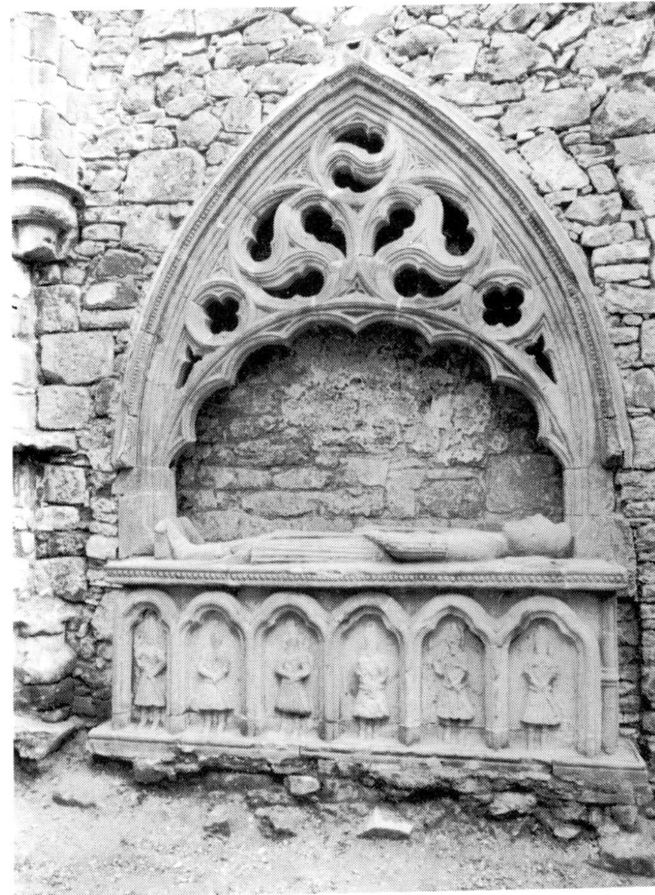

Tomb at Dungiven priory, traditionally said to be the burial place of Cooey-na-Gall O'Cahan, who died in 1395. Two years later, while Archbishop John Colton was on his visit to the district, he excommunicated the O'Cahan chieftain along with several other local lords because 'of their usurpation of the episcopal rights of the Church of Derry'. (Historic Monuments and Buildings Branch, Department of Environment for Northern Ireland)

members of the chapter of Derry accompanying him for about two miles . . . the Venerable Father, proceeding with his retinue through the trackless mountains of Glenelly, came in peace to the church of Desertcreat in the Deanery of Tullyhog, within the Diocese of Armagh.

THE 'FOREIGN BISHOP'

On 25 February 1398 a new bishop, Hugh, was appointed for Derry. Aubrey Gwynn, in *The Medieval Province of Armagh,* states that during the fourteenth and fifteenth centuries the diocese of Derry was 'sorely tried' by a number of 'incompetent and unworthy prelates'. Most of the bishops of that time were of Gaelic origin, with the exception of Nicholas Weston who became bishop of Derry in 1466. Weston probably came from an Old English family but almost certainly spoke Irish. Gwynn states that his career would be unintelligible unless he was accustomed to Irish ways and had a working knowledge of the Irish language. He seems to have fitted reasonably well into the life of Derry and its diocese until his death in 1484. In Manus O'Donnell's Life of Colmcille, written about fifty years later, there is a curious reference to Bishop Weston. The story is told of how Colmcille built a church at Clooney and then prophesied that a 'foreign bishop' would come and tear down the church and use the stones for another building at a place

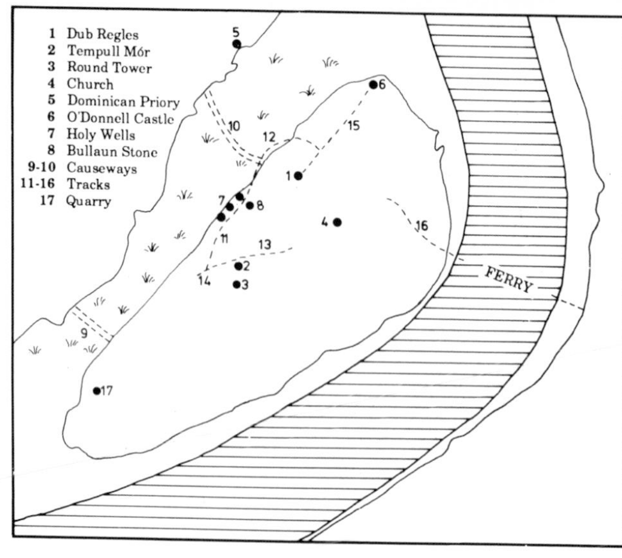

The 'island' of Derry *c.* 1520, showing the position of the principal buildings mentioned in contemporary records

called Bun Sentuinde, probably nearby on the bank of the River Foyle. The saint is said to have composed the following verse:

My sorrow!
Strangers will come to Clooney
And take away my church
To cold Bun Sentuinde.

O'Donnell continues:

> And all this was fulfilled, as is manifest to all today; for there came a foreign bishop called Nicholas Weston, and he destroyed the church to make a palace with it. And that palace was never finished and I am certain that it was by a miracle of Colmcille that they were not able to finish it with the stones of the church.

Unlike his predecessors in the great days of Derry during the twelfth and thirteenth centuries, Bishop Weston seems to have inherited an extremely impoverished diocese. Many of the buildings and institutions of the settlement seem to have fallen on hard times and the township of the earlier period had collapsed. Pope Martin V had granted an indulgence in 1423 to anyone who assisted with the repair of the Dub Regles. In 1469 Bishop Weston, who was probably in Rome at the time, presented a petition to Pope Paul II describing the abysmal state of his cathedral church, the Tempull Mór:

> Owing to many and various misfortunes that for a long time have afflicted these parts, the Cathedral church of Derry, which is quite famous among those of the kingdom of Ireland, is all but roofless, and the bishop has not a house in which he can fittingly dwell; besides, the cathedral, which has but one chalice, and that of tin, is now in need of chalices, books, vestments and other ecclesiastical necessaries, and unless the charitable help of the faithful intervenes, it is much to be feared that the church will quickly fall into ruin.

On 14 December 1469 an indulgence was granted:

> The pope, therefore, desiring that the said church may be roofed, that the said bishop may be able to build himself a becoming house and buy the said ornaments, hereby grants a relaxation in perpetuity of seven years and seven quarantines of enjoined penance to all who, being truly penitent and having confessed, visit the said church on the feasts of St Martin in winter and St Columba and give alms for such rebuilding, restoration and maintenance.

The reference to the lack of suitable accommodation might explain the story in the O'Donnell Life of Nicholas Weston's attempt to build a palace on the opposite side of the river from Derry.

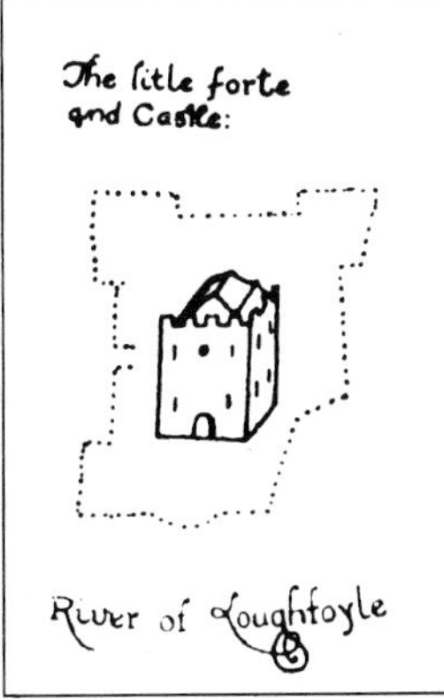

Medieval tower house castle, Derry, built by the O'Dohertys of Inishowen for the O'Donnell chieftain, the site having been purchased from the Mac Lochlainn erenagh for twenty cows. Detail from a map of Derry dated 1611. (Trinity College Dublin)

THE O'DONNELLS IN DERRY

Weston was succeeded in 1485 by Irishman Donal O'Fallon, a friar minor of the observantine Franciscans who were engaged at the time in a major reform of the church in Gaelic Ireland. Their monastery, just outside the present-day town of Donegal, set up by the chieftain Aodh Ruadh O'Donnell in 1474, was a centre of this reform and Donal O'Fallon an important figure of the movement. The Annals of Ulster state that he was 'the preacher that did most service to Irishmen since Patrick was in Ireland'. Aodh Ruadh O'Donnell was probably involved in the appointment of Donal O'Fallon as bishop of Derry. The O'Donnells were regaining control over Derry, a return, in effect, to the ancient Cenél Conaill domination of the settlement. It was probably about this time also that a small castle or tower house was built in Derry by the O'Dohertys of Inishowen on behalf of their overlords, the O'Donnells, in lieu of certain taxes. An 'inquisition' taken in the city in 1609 records that O'Donnell had to buy the land for the castle from the Mac Lochlainn erenagh for twenty cows:

> And further the said jurors doe uppon their oathes finde and point out that the grounde and land whereon the old castle called O'Donell's castle was built, within the lower forte of the citie of Derry, was formerly bought by O'Donell of the erenagh [Mac Lochlainn], as beinge parcell of his herenagh land for twentie cowes, and the said castle was built thereuppon by O'Dogherty for O'Donell's use, in consideracion whereof O'Donell forgave O'Dogherty certen dueties, and that the said castle and grounde thereof is nowe come to [James I's] hands and possession by the attainder of treason of Hugh Roe O'Donell.

We are not certain when this tower house was built but Aodh Ruadh O'Donnell is recorded as having built a castle at Donegal in 1505 and an entry in the annals for the year 1512 records that he set off with an army from Derry on a campaign against Mac William Burke in Connacht. It was located at the north-west corner of the 'island', close to the old river shore line, and the site is now included within the seventeenth-century city walls at Magazine Street. The building, which is shown on several

The O'Doherty Tower, Derry, built in 1986 in the style of a medieval castle (Eason and Son)

seventeenth-century maps, and which survived into the eighteenth century as an ammunition magazine for the plantation city, is depicted as a three-storey structure with crenellations and a hipped, gabled roof. It seems to have been a typical small tower house of the period, with an entrance facing north-east towards the river. The erection of the brand-new O'Doherty Tower on a nearby site in 1986 was an imaginative, if controversial, attempt to re-create the effect of the original castle building.

By 1512 the O'Donnell chieftain was Aodh Dubh, who continued to rule until 1537 when he was succeeded by his son Manus, who compiled the Life of Colmcille. Brendan Bradshaw, in his thought-provoking essay 'Manus the Magnificent', has described this Donegal aristocrat as a Renaissance prince and a humanist, something of a Gaelic-Ulster version of the 'universal man' as idealised by Erasmus and other contemporary Continental writers. For Bradshaw, the composition of the Life, or Betha Colaim Chille, written at the O'Donnell castle near Lifford in 1532, bears 'characteristic marks of the Renaissance spirit'. The book is a huge encyclopedia of everything that was known or believed in Ireland about Colmcille at the beginning of the sixteenth century.

Portrait of Saint Colmcille, from the original manuscript of Manus O'Donnell's Betha Colaim Chille (Life of Colmcille), written in 1532 (Bodleian Library, Oxford)

MANUS O'DONNELL'S LIFE OF COLMCILLE

In compiling the Life, Manus brought together a team who collected and assembled material 'that was scattered throughout the ancient books of Ireland'. The preface states that he 'ordered the part of this Life that was in Latin to be put into Irish, and the part that was in hard Irish to be made easy, so that it might be clear and simple to understand by all'. He dictated the Life 'with his own lips' to a scribe, and he did this 'having conceived the affection and love of a brother for his high-saint, and kinsman by lineage, and his dear patron that he was bound to in steadfast devotion'. Manus was thus well aware that as an O'Donnell he belonged to the ancient line of the Cenél Conaill, the kin-group to which Colmcille had belonged nearly one thousand years earlier. Manus was also very well aware of the ancient association of Derry with the Cenél Conaill despite the interruption of Cenél Eóghain usurpation after 1100. At one point in the Life, having told a story of how Colmcille gave his name to a holy well in Derry, Manus goes on to say that Colmcille left a cleric of the Cenél Conaill in charge of Derry and 'he left the nobility and the honour and the overlordship of that place and of the surrounding district to the Cenél Conaill for ever'. The political implications of this story are plain.

Manus was clearly familiar with Derry. The many stories he relates about the monastery are placed in actual locations. Jesus is said to have appeared at a place referred to as 'the right turn, to the south-west of the Tempull Mór'. The 'Yew of the Saints' is on the left-hand side of the door as you go into the Dub Regles and, in order to protect the trees, that church was aligned north–south rather than east–west, as 'it is manifest to all today'. The saint blessed a well in the hills just to the west of Derry and turned the water there into wine 'so that Maith, that is to say Good, is the name of that Well'.

Another story gives us a glimpse of contemporary economic activity. Once Colmcille was in Derry when a gambler and a poor man came to beg from him. The saint gave a groat (a silver coin worth four pennies) to the gambler and a penny to the poor man. Everyone thought it strange that the holy man seemed to be subsidising the gambler at the expense of the poor man but Colmcille said that the pair should be followed to see what each did with the money: 'And they found the gambler in a tavern drinking the worth of the groat and sharing it with every needy man that came to him.' The poor man was found dead on the roadside with the penny Colmcille had given him sewn into his garments along with the huge sum of five marks. Colmcille said:

> God told me that the poor man had not long to live and even had his life been longer he would have put whatever he had to no use either for himself or for any others, instead he would have hoarded it up as he did with the five marks. And although the gambler was an evil man, yet he did not hoard what he got, but with the worth of the groat he sustained himself and other poor men that were in need. For this I gave him more than I gave to the poor man.

This is the only occasion in the one thousand years of Derry's medieval history that we get any reference to the use of money. Gaelic society practised an essentially self-sufficient, non-monetary economy. More curious is the reference to the tavern either in, or in the vicinity of, Derry. Manus O'Donnell obviously did not think that such an amenity would be considered out of place by his audience. Although the story is fictional, it manifestly hints at a wider but unrecorded practice of commerce.

The insignia of Bishop Rory O'Donnell, who died in 1551. The Latin inscription reads: 'The seal of the Lord Rury, by the grace of God, bishop of Derry.'

Manus tells us in the preface that his reasons for compiling this book were 'God's honour, the raising up of Colmcille's name, the profit of the people who read or listen to it, my own welfare, temporal and spiritual, and the dishonour and destruction of the devil'. It is probable that there was also a more secular reason. Certainly one of the consequences, if not one of the actual intentions of the book, was a bolstering of the O'Donnell hold on Derry in opposition to any claims on the settlement which the latter-day descendants of the Cenél Eóghain, the O'Neills, might make. Manus deliberately has Colmcille say that Derry should belong to the Cenél Conaill for ever. Implicitly, if Derry 'belonged' to Colmcille, it therefore belonged to his descendants, the O'Donnells.

At the time when Manus was compiling his book, Derry must have been something of 'a faded glory'. Its principal buildings were in poor condition and we hear nothing of the tumultuous life of the settlement which had been described in the various sets of annals for the twelfth and thirteenth centuries. Is it possible that the O'Donnells were trying to revive the fortunes of this ancient settlement which was so important in their dynastic history. The erection of a tower house in Derry might have been the first stage in an attempt to establish a new town, and if

Manus was the Renaissance figure which Brendan Bradshaw makes him out to be, then this is not inconceivable. The building of new towns and the revival of old ones was an important element of the European Renaissance. However, Derry was not to be revived on this occasion.

In 1520 Manus's cousin Rory O'Donnell was appointed as the new bishop of Derry, with the support of the O'Donnell chieftain. The O'Donnell hold on Derry was being strengthened. There are very few references to Rory in the ecclesiastical documents of the time, probably because, as Aubrey Gwynn states, 'the normal life of the diocese was continuing without interruption under a bishop who understood his people and was able to win their respect as being one of the ruling dynasty'. Rory and some of the other Derry clergy became politically involved with Manus O'Donnell when he later became chieftain. The diplomatic comings and goings they entered into on behalf of their overlord was part of the history of the Geraldine League and is an element in the wider history of Ireland rather than the more local story of Derry, which was soon to experience major changes of its own.

Map of Ireland by Gerard Mercator, published in Duisburg, Germany, in 1564. The delineation of the coastline of the north-west of Ireland is particularly inaccurate, as are the details for the interior of the region. 'Castell Derrey' is marked near the base of a much-too-narrow 'Log Foyle'. (Reproduced by the National Library of Ireland)

5

THE COMING OF THE ENGLISH

Since the collapse of the Norman colonisation from at least the early fourteenth century, the English Crown had paid little attention to Ireland. When the Tudors came to power in the late fifteenth century, Crown policy was restricted towards ensuring that the country was neither a base for foreign enemies nor a drain on royal resources. Since the 1470s the FitzGerald family, who were earls of Kildare, had virtually monopolised the position of lord deputy, the Crown's chief representative in Ireland. The Geraldine League, formed in the 1530s and comprised of some of the island's most powerful Gaelic and Old English nobles, had been formed in support of the Kildare family, whose position had come under threat from the changed policy of active intervention in Ireland by the new king, Henry VIII. Military opposition to Henry had collapsed by 1540 and was immediately followed by a series of individual treaties, known as 'surrender and regrant', between the Crown and the important Old English and Gaelic leaders. By these agreements the Gaelic chieftains came to hold their lands in a feudal relationship with the Crown rather than in accordance with traditional Irish custom. A parliament held in Dublin in 1536–7 had passed a number of acts extending Henry's Protestant Reformation to Ireland. The consequent distribution of property as a result of the commencement of the dissolution of the monasteries further helped to attach some of these magnates more closely to the king.

Lord Deputy Sir Henry Sidney rides out of Dublin Castle; he was appointed lord deputy in 1565, with a commission to reduce Shane O'Neill to obedience. (from John Derricke, *Image of Irelande*, 1581)

Initially these events left the tiny settlement at Derry unaffected. With the death in 1559 of Conn O'Neill, Earl of Tyrone, supremacy over the chieftains of Ulster passed to Shane 'the Proud' O'Neill, whose authority rested on Gaelic rather than English custom. Elizabeth I and her lord lieutenant for Ireland, the Earl of Sussex, had been extending English local government throughout Munster and Connacht, and they now turned their attention towards Ulster. They sought to break up the vast Gaelic bloc under Shane's control and achieve instead a series of separate treaties with individual local leaders. Sussex's advice to his sovereign was that 'if Shane be overthrown, all is settled. If Shane settle, all is overthrown.'

Despite this, O'Neill's dominance in Ulster continued and William Cecil, Lord Burghley, the Queen's chief adviser in London, thought it better 'to stir no sleeping dogs in Ireland'. However, in 1565, Sir Henry

Sidney was appointed lord deputy with a commission to reduce Shane to obedience. Sidney made a proclamation against O'Neill in August 1566 and the following month marched into Ulster from the south in search of the chieftain. O'Neill eluded the English soldiers, who had to be content with confirming the allegiance of the O'Donnell chieftain, Calbhach. Ancient rivalries between the O'Neills and the O'Donnells, particularly over control of the fertile lands in the Foyle valley, prevented a united front against the advancing English forces. O'Donnell surrendered his chief castle at Donegal to the Crown. Sidney's advance into Ulster was part of a great pincer movement, the other arm of which was the capture and garrisoning of Derry by an English force transported by sea and landed via Lough Foyle.

English soldiers bearing the decapitated heads of native Irish men (from John Derricke, *Image of Irelande*, 1581)

THE FIRST ENGLISH SOLDIERS

On 6 September 1566, about the same time as Sidney was preparing his northward march, a force of one thousand foot soldiers and fifty horse, under the command of Colonel Edward Randolph, set sail from Bristol. Soon afterwards, these arrived in Lough Foyle and landed in Derry, which at this time was part of O'Donnell's territory. Derry was strategically located on O'Neill's borders and on the River Foyle, a water highway into the heartland of Gaelic Ulster. The English made camp at the site of the ancient monastery and expelled whatever few lay and clerical inhabitants were still living there. The soldiers threw up earthen defence works and, according to tradition, used the stone-built Tempull Mór cathedral church as their gunpowder magazine. The seventeenth-century Irish writer, Philip O'Sullivan Beare, in his *History of Catholic Ireland*, described the situation in his characteristically partisan manner:

> The English heretics having landed in this town against the wish and command of O'Donnell expel the priests and monks, invade the holy churches and in one church place for safe-keeping gunpowder, leaden bullets, tow-match, guns, pikes, and other munitions of war. In other churches they performed the heretical rites of Luther, Calvin and others of that class of impious men. They left nothing undefiled by their wickedness. St Columba did not long delay the punishment of this sin.

On 12 October 1566 the Derry garrison was visited by Lord Deputy Sidney, who had so far failed to encounter O'Neill. Before long Randolph's soldiers, not used to the damp conditions of north-western Ireland, began to succumb to a variety of illnesses. The force was quickly reduced to seven hundred men. Shane O'Neill now made an appearance near Derry at the head of a force calculated at about 2,500 to 3,000 men. The Gaelic chieftain did not make a direct attack on the English camp but instead harassed it from a distance. On 15 November Randolph marched out of Derry with a small force of his best men. He was supported by some of the Inishowen O'Dohertys who had come over to the Crown side also. O'Neill's men attacked first but were, nevertheless, put to flight by the better-armed and better-disciplined English soldiers. About four hundred Irish were slain and many others wounded and taken prisoner. There were very few casualties on the English side but Randolph was killed in the fracas. Victorious but crest-fallen, the English returned to Derry to bury their commander. Colonel Edward St Low succeeded his fallen colleague in the command of the English troops.

In a dispatch sent in November from Derry to the authorities in Dublin there was a complaint that their supposed ally, Calbhach O'Donnell, had so far failed to relieve the ailing English garrison. The Donegal chieftain's loyalty was obviously suspect. However, a few months later, another dispatch relates that while Calbhach was on his way to Derry, he died in an accident when his horse stumbled and fell.

Although the garrison in Derry continued to be plagued by illness, St Low was still able to harass O'Neill. In February 1567 the English 'burned [the countryside] to the Bann [and] preyed and spoiled 10,000 cattle'. Some more Gaelic leaders were switching allegiance to the English side. Richard O'Cahan and his wife were 'received to mercy', and other local 'rebels' 'came in' and accepted the authority of the Crown. Reports continued to be sent to Dublin, however, showing 'the death at Derry by cold and infection'. Of the six hundred troops left in Derry, there were only two hundred able-bodied men. In March it was suggested that the isolated garrison should be transferred to the

The submission to the lord deputy, Sir Henry Sidney, of Turlough Luineach O'Neill, who succeeded to the chieftainship of the O'Neills following Shane's death in 1567 (from John Derricke, *Image of Irelande*, 1581)

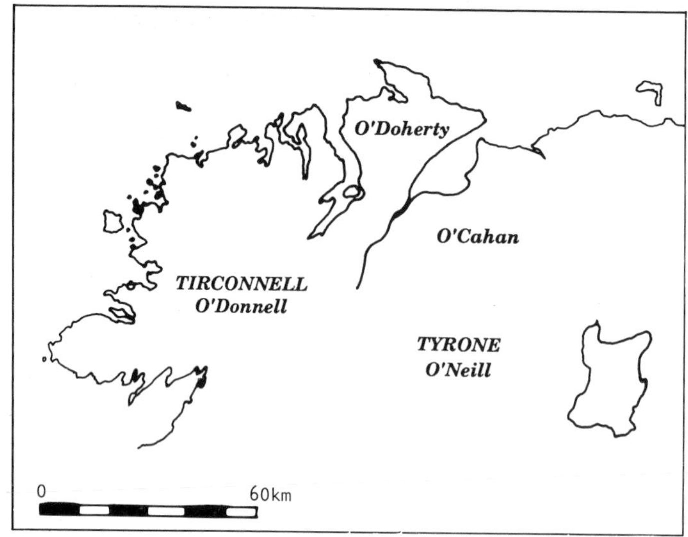

Map showing Gaelic lordships in the north-west of Ireland during the later Middle Ages

Strangford Lough area. Fate, however, intervened. In April a fire broke out in the camp and spread to all the buildings. The flames caught the ammunition store and there was a huge explosion. At least thirty people were killed. The cause of the fire was variously attributed: on the English side an accident in the blacksmith's forge was blamed; O'Sullivan Beare had another explanation:

> The natives confidently assert that a wolf of huge size and with bristling hair, coming boldly out of the nearest wood to the settlement, and entering the iron barriers, emitting from his mouth a great number of sparks, such as fly from a red-hot iron when it is struck, proceeded to the place in which the powder was stored, and spitting out sparks, set fire to powder and church. I will not take upon myself to vouch for the truth of this story; upon fame and long-standing tradition let it rest.

O'Sullivan Beare goes on to describe the destruction and claims that the survivors were well aware of the real author of the tragedy. The English, he says, cried out: 'The Irish god Columba killed us all.'

The damage from the 1567 explosion was devastating. O'Donnell wrote to the lord deputy from his castle at Bundrowes, expressing his 'grief for the ruin of the Derry'. The queen was less upset: Cecil, writing to the Earl of Leicester on 9 May, mentioned that 'Her Majesty perceiving it to come by God's ordinance, beareth it well'. Although there were suggestions that the camp should be rebuilt, the depleted garrison was withdrawn and the first English attempt at a takeover of Derry was at an end. On several other occasions up to the end of the sixteenth century plans for a garrison at Derry were mooted but came to nothing.

'A CATHOLIC DEMONSTRATION'

The physical condition of Derry after the explosion must have been terrible. However, a document collected by the seventeenth-century antiquarian Sir James Ware, and now preserved in the British Library in London, demonstrates that some form of ecclesiastical life continued in

...promouisse et ordinasse presentibus Dominis Deca
no et officiali mac an tsagairt et mauricio o heigceartaigh
Deren diocesis presbiteris cum non nullis aliis clericis
et laicis. Script. in ecclesia cathedrali Deren die
et anno premissis proxime
Remundus Deren Eps.

Derry, at least intermittently, after the English had left. The document is a certificate of the ordination to the priesthood of one Patrick Mac Entagart of the diocese of Clogher, with the consent of his own bishop, Cornelius Mac Ardle, by Redmond O'Gallagher, bishop of Derry. O'Gallagher, who was considered to be 'dangerous' by the Elizabethan government, was the last Catholic occupant of the See of Derry until after the penal period, when Philip McDevitt was appointed in 1766. According to the certificate, the ordination took place on 10 June 1590, Pentecost Sunday, in *'ecclesia cathedrali Derensi'* – the cathedral church of Derry. It is uncertain which building is implied by this designation. According to tradition, it was the Tempull Mór, which had been used as the English ammunition store and which had suffered most damage from the 1567 explosion. There were at least two other churches in Derry at the time and it may well be that one of these functioned as the cathedral for a while.

Certificate of ordination to the priesthood of Patrick Mac Entagart, Pentecost Sunday, 10 June 1590. The ceremony took place in the 'cathedral church of Derry'. (British Library)

It is not clear why this Clogher ordination should have taken place in Derry. One of those present on the occasion was the dean of Derry, William Mac Entagart, who was probably a close relative of the new priest. William, unlike his bishop, who was slain by Crown forces in 1601, later conformed to the Established Church and was reappointed to the Protestant deanery of Derry in 1609. He spoke Latin as well as Irish and served on the jury at the inquisitions into property ownership in Limavady in 1609. The 1590 ordination in Derry showed that some form of ecclesiastical life was possible there around this time despite the destruction of 1567. In this context, historian F.X. Martin has described the Pentecostal ceremony in the Derry cathedral as a 'Catholic demonstration'.

Resentment at the continuing English expansion in Ireland, particularly among the Gaelic aristocracy in Ulster, led the Donegal chieftain Red Hugh O'Donnell to form an alliance against the Government in 1593. The following year a contingent of Scots under Donnell Gorm and MacLeod of Arran came to Derry to meet with Red Hugh and offer assistance against the English. O'Donnell welcomed them and 'they were attended and entertained for three days and three nights with strong drink and every sort of food that was best in the country'. The Scots left behind a force of one thousand men. Towards the end of 1595 Hugh O'Neill took over the leadership of the alliance. The ensuing conflict, which has become known as the Nine Years War, was, in effect, the last-ditch defence of Gaelic Ireland. Its outcome was to transform the future of Derry.

Scripsimus iam Serenissime Princeps, Patri tuo Regi maximo, quam plene per festinan=
tiam licuit quae nobis et Patriae necessaria maxime censuimus. Idem ideo negotio im=
ploramus Celsitudinem ut expectationi quam de generosa indole sua concepimus benigne
respondeat, nosque suorum clientum albo peculiariter adscribat et caussae huic tam piae ac
iustissimae asserendae scilicet Catholicae Libertatis et vindicandae Patriae a tyrannicae
pravitatis iugo clementer suo more suffragetur, sicque Divinae Majestati obsecutus, infi=
nitam animarum multitudinem à tartari faucibus eruens, Christo lucrifaciat, et sathá=
nici furoris ministros ac Reipublicae Xtianae turbones impios aut plane extinguat, aut
ad sanitatem redire compellat. Serenissimae Celsitudini tuae omnia fausta precamur.
In Lesser, May. 16. Anno 1596.

Tuae Celsitudini addictissimi

ONeill

Aodh Odomhnaill

Excellentissimo Serenissimoque Prin=
cipi Hispaniarum Regis Catho=
lici Filio

Madritum.

A letter from Hugh O'Neill and Red Hugh O'Donnell to Don Carolo, son of the king of Spain, seeking assistance in the 'asserting of Catholic liberty and the delivering of our country from the yoke of wicked tyrants'. It was sent from Lifford, County Donegal, on 16 May 1596.

THE ENGLISH RETURN

A plan to dispatch a force of two thousand men and one hundred horse to Derry in 1598 was abandoned when it had to be sent instead to Lecale in County Down. In 1599 the queen wrote to Lord Lieutenant Essex, complaining that Derry, or Loughfoyle as it was often called in the documents of this period, had not yet been garrisoned. The situation was rectified the following year, when, in a manoeuvre reminiscent of the first pincer attack in 1566, an English force under Lord Deputy Mountjoy made an assault on the south-eastern frontier of Ulster while simultaneously Sir Henry Docwra came with a large force by sea to the north-west.

On 14 May 1600, Docwra, with four thousand foot and two hundred horse, entered Lough Foyle. The ships became stuck in the shallow lough and it was not until two days later that they were able to land at Culmore, where there was an old O'Doherty tower house. Culmore, a few miles downstream from Derry, guards the entry from the lough to the river and it has played a leading role in many of the important episodes in the history of the city. At first the English were met with firing from about one hundred Irish on the shore. However, the Irish quickly retired. Docwra spent six days putting his defences in order at Culmore and at Elaghmore, a small castle nearby, he left 150 men.

The ruins of Elaghmore Castle, which was taken by Sir Henry Dowcra on 16 May 1600, prior to his advance on Derry

On 22 May, leaving six hundred men at Culmore, the remainder of the force set out. In Docwra's words, they

> went to the Derry, four miles off upon the river side, a place in manner of an island, comprehending within it 40 acres of ground, wherein were the ruins of a old abbey, of a bishop's house, of two churches, and at one of the ends of it an old castle, the river called Loughfoyle encompassing it all

Contemporary sketch map of the valley of the River Foyle, showing the military fortifications established by Sir Henry Dowcra in 1600, including 'Kilmore', 'the Derry', 'Dounalong' and Elaghmore (bottom left) (National Library of Ireland)

> on one side, and a bog most commonly wet, and not easily passable except in two or three places, dividing it from the main land. This piece of ground we possessed ourselves of without resistance, and judging it a fit place to make our main plantation in, being somewhat high, and therefore dry and healthy to dwell upon, at that end where the old castle stood, being close to the water side, I presently resolved to raise a fort to keep our store of munitions and victuals in, and in the other a little above, where the walls of an old cathedral church were yet standing, to erect another for our future safety and retreat into upon all occasions.

There was no fighting at Derry as Docwra took over. It is probable that few people, if any, were actually living there at the time. The scene which greeted the English commander would have, to some extent at least, resembled that which visitors see today when they approach the great monastic sites at places like Devenish or Clonmacnoise – a collection of ruined early Christian and medieval buildings scattered in a rural setting with a round tower as a focal point. Indeed, when Docwra arrived, most of the 'island' of Derry was sown with corn and he accurately and imaginatively described its geography as it appeared to him: 'It lies in form of a bow bent, whereof the bog is the string and the river the bow.'

Docwra ordered most of the shipping which had carried the troops to Derry to return to base but he sent two ships to scout along the coasts and river banks, and to bring back any timber or other building material which they found. A wood of 'old grown birch' on the east bank of the River Foyle provided for their timber needs, but 'there was not a stick of it brought home but was first well fought for'. They found quarries of stone and slate near to hand and a plentiful supply of cockle shells to make lime:

> Together with the provisions we brought and the stones and rubbidge of the old buildings we found, we set ourselves wholly, and with all the diligence we could . . . to fortifying and framing and setting up of houses such as we might be able to live in, and defend ourselves when winter should come in, and our men be decayed, as it was apparent it would be.

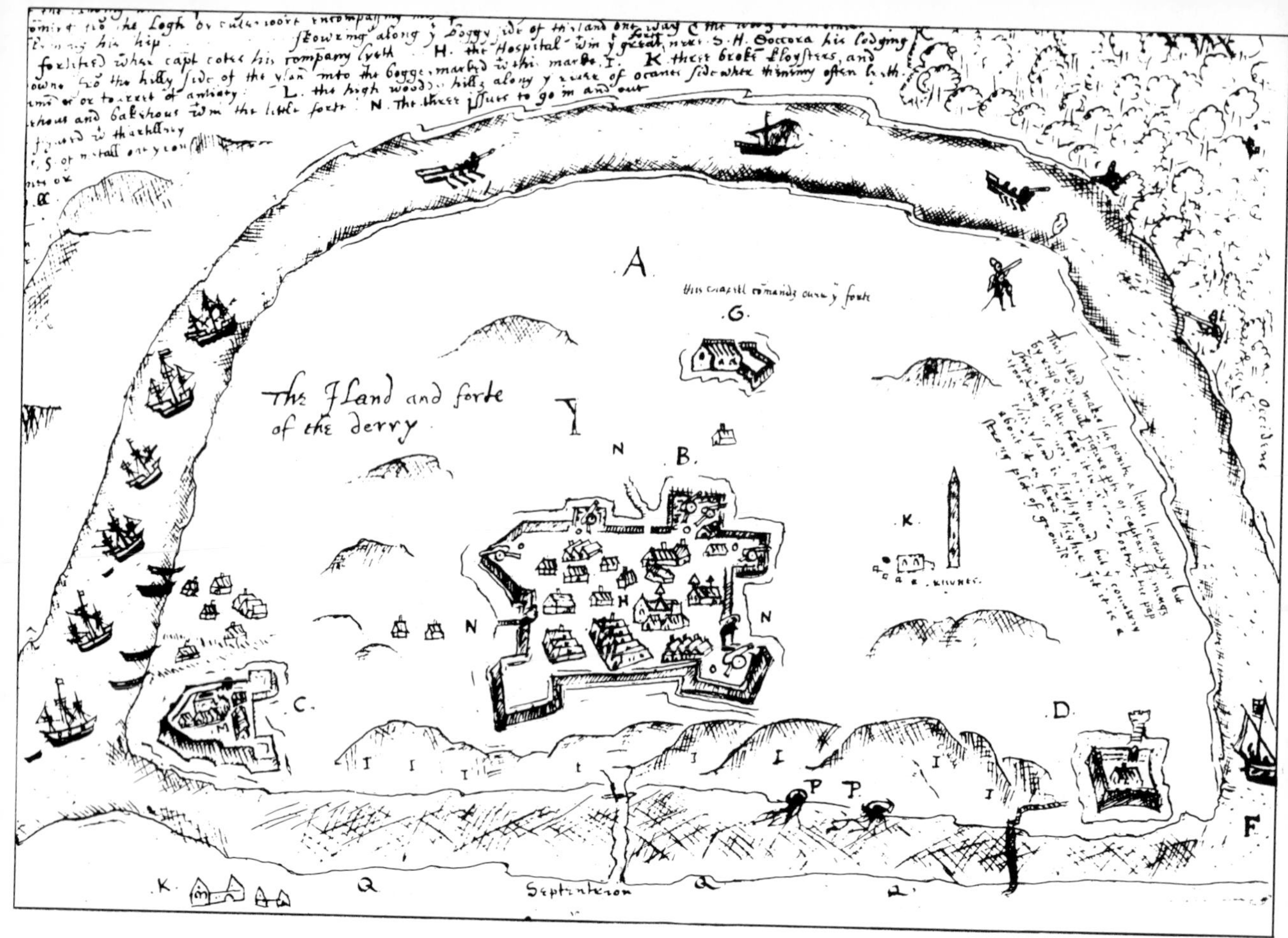

A sketch map dated 1600, the first known map of Derry, gives us a clear impression of what Docwra's camp was like. At each end of the 'island' there was a small fort. The one at the north end was built around the O'Donnell tower house and here was situated both the stores and the bake-house. Around the ruins of the old Augustinian abbey the principal fort was laid out. Inside this, a hospital, lodgings for Docwra, as well as other accommodation were built. On the highest ground on the hill a separate small fort was built around the ruins of another of the medieval churches.

A native Irish description of this camp is preserved in the early-seventeenth-century Life of Red Hugh O'Donnell:

> The English made very large mounds and strong ramparts of earth round the monastery and church first. They made passages and covered ways of earth under the walls and war-towers upon them with windows and loopholes in them for shooting from. They dug deep trenches all round on the outside. They were much stronger and more secure than the dwellings of stone and mortar and the castles, in the making of which much time and great labour were spent. Then they tore down the monastery and the church, and they showed neither honour nor respect to the great Saint [Colmcille], for they destroyed all the ecclesiastical edifices in the place, and made rooms and sleeping apartments of them, and used some of them to eat in.

Sketch plan of Derry, dated 27 December 1600. This is the oldest known map of Derry. Sir Henry Dowcra sent it to London in his dispatches, to illustrate progress in Ulster. The drawing shows a number of English fortifications built since May 1600, including the main fort (centre) based around the medieval Augustinian abbey, and the lower fort at the O'Donnell tower house, close to the river (left). Other medieval and early Christian period buildings can be seen, such as the church-like structure on the summit of the hill (top centre), the round tower, and the ruins of the Dominican monastery (bottom left K). A bog crossed by two causeways isolates 'The Iland and forte of the derry'. (Public Record Office, London)

The O'Doherty castle at Burt, County Donegal, as shown in a drawing made *c.* 1600

At the beginning of July, Docwra established a manned fortification at Dunalong, a few miles upstream from Derry. Later he was able to erect a number of other forts at strategic locations in the hinterland of Derry, including a string of defences along the near-impassable boggy valley that ran between the present-day villages of Carrigans and Newtown-cunningham. Although there were a number of skirmishes and a few half-hearted attacks on Derry, the garrison, for the most part, remained unmolested from the Irish. But, as with Randolph's men on the 1566 expedition, sickness soon began to take its toll. By this stage a number of leading local Irish aristocrats were coming over to the English side. These included Arthur O'Neill, son of Turlough Luineach from Dunalong, and Nial Garbh O'Donnell. With Nial Garbh's support the English were able to capture the strategically important river junction at Lifford.

On 27 January 1601 the Inishowen chieftain Sir Seán Óg O'Doherty died. He had made a series of tentative approaches to Docwra but, for a number of reasons, including the fact that his eldest son Cahir was held hostage by Red Hugh O'Donnell, Seán Óg did not 'come over' and receive the queen's pardon. Red Hugh now set up Seán's brother Phelim Óg as the puppet chieftain of the O'Dohertys. This move infuriated Phelim Reagh and Hugh Buidh McDaid, Cahir's foster guardians, and they instantly made approaches to Sir Henry Docwra. By various double-dealing stratagems, both Red Hugh and Docwra were persuaded to back Cahir. Phelim Óg ceased to be leader and, with the approval of the lord deputy and council in Dublin, the young Cahir became head of the O'Dohertys.

Hugh O'Neill, Earl of Tyrone, who was inaugurated as the O'Neill Mór when Turlough Luineach died in 1595. Hugh's war against the English ended in 1603, when he submitted to Lord Mountjoy at Mellifont in County Louth. (Detail from *La Spada d'Orione Stellata nel Cielo di Marte* by Primo Damaschino, 1680)

Docwra was anxious that Cahir should be instructed in English ways. The governor wrote to the council in September 1601 suggesting that Cahir be sent to England to be educated. However, this did not happen and the teenage leader remained in Docwra's camp at Derry, fully accepted and trusted, absorbing the knowledge and manners which befitted an Elizabethan aristocrat. By all accounts Cahir was allowed to retain his Catholic religion and it is even claimed that Docwra permitted a priest to come to Derry to minister to the youth. When Docwra sallied out from Derry to harass Hugh O'Neill, Cahir usually accompanied him. On one such expedition to the Clogher area, the young man behaved so bravely that Docwra recommended him to the lord deputy for a knighthood. He thus became Sir Cahir O'Doherty.

Coat-of-arms of the city of 'Derrie', which received its charter from James I on 11 July 1604

'A TOWN OF WAR AND A TOWN OF MERCHANDIZE'

The war came to an end in 1603, when Hugh O'Neill surrendered to Mountjoy at Mellifont in County Louth, following which the garrison in Derry was considerably reduced. Docwra remained as governor and obtained permission to begin the civilian and commercial development of the settlement by holding fairs and markets. A small population of merchants involved in provisioning the troops had settled in Derry by this stage. On 11 July 1604, the new king, James VI of Scotland, now

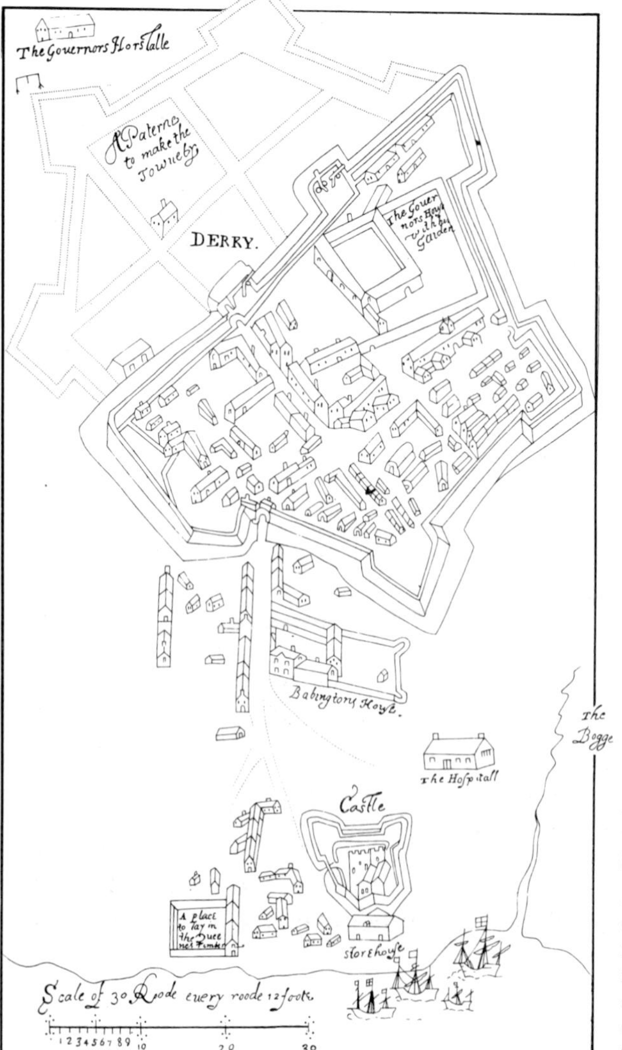

Line drawing of a plan of Derry in 1603, shortly before the settlement was given the status of a city. The O'Donnell 'castle' is shown, as is a proposed extension, 'A Paterne to make the towne by', that is, a layout for additional streets and fortifications. (Original held in Trinity College Dublin)

James I of England, issued a charter creating the city of 'Derrie' with its own corporation and various local powers:

> The town or borough of Derrie is, by reason of the natural seat and situation thereof, a place very convenient and fit to be made both a town of war and a town of merchandize, and so might many ways prove serviceable for the crown and profitable for the subject, if the same were not only walled, entrenched and inhabited, but also incorporated and endowed with convenient liberties, privileges and immunities; and Sir Henry Docwra . . . having . . . repossessed, repaired, and repeopled that town . . . and having begun and laid a good foundation there for the planting of a colony of civil and obedient people in that place, the king . . . did . . . give, grant, and confirm unto him, and the inhabitants of the Derrie . . . for ever a free, entire, and perfect city and county of itself, to be called the city and county of Derrie . . . Sir Henry to be provost for life, as fully as the lord mayor of London.

The little colonial city began to develop but growth was very slow. In September 1605 Lord Deputy Sir Arthur Chichester reported to the council in Dublin on his visit to the city for the assizes. He had 'observed there many good buildings' and as a place of importance he hoped that 'so good a work may not be suffered to decay'. The lord deputy thought that the best way to develop the city was to replenish it 'with merchants, tradesmen, and artificers from England and Scotland which must be commanded by authority to come over and compelled to remain and set up their trades and occupations'. The following year Chichester wrote to Lord Salisbury in London, expressing fears that if the 'infant city' was not supported, it would soon decay, 'being placed among neighbours who long for nothing more than the ruin thereof'. Other similar reports were made to various authorities. A map of the settlement made around 1603, before its city status was granted, indicates plans for its expansion to the south-east of the main fortified area.

In June 1605 the dean of Norwich, George Montgomery, was appointed first Protestant bishop of the united dioceses of Derry, Clogher and Raphoe but he did not take up his new post immediately. In May the following year Sir John Davies, the Irish attorney general, observed that there were no recusants (Old English Catholics) in Derry and that the people of Ulster would be willing to accept the reformed faith 'if the bishop of Derrie . . . would come and be a new St Patrick among them'. In a letter to a relative, dated 10 May 1605, Mrs Montgomery wrote: 'The king has bestowed on [Dr Montgomery] three Irish bishoprics; the names of which I cannot remember they are so strange except one which is Derye; I pray God may make us all merry.' On her arrival she found it better than she had expected. She was living in a small comfortable English-style house and had plenty of English people for company. Dr Montgomery, meanwhile, was engaged on an extensive survey of his dioceses, describing the manner in which the ecclesiastical

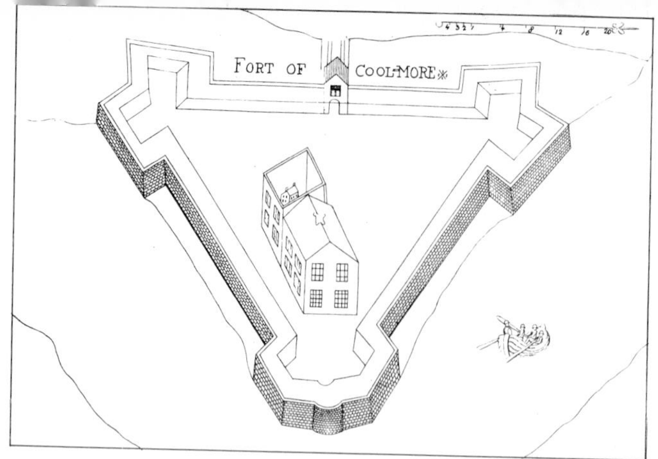

The fort at Culmore was captured by Sir Cahir O'Doherty on 18 April 1608, prior to his attack on the 'infant city' of Derry.

Sir Cahir O'Doherty's sword. O'Doherty's foolhardy rebellion against the English ended when he was killed in a skirmish near Kilmacrennan, County Donegal, on 5 July 1608. (Eason and Son)

system had worked under the Gaelic order. He soon became involved in disputes about property, which for some time to come were the hallmark of the See of Derry.

In 1606, Sir Henry Docwra, apparently frustrated with the lack of development, abandoned the little city which he more than any other had helped to found. Having obtained permission from the Government, he sold his property interests in the city to George Paulett, who took over as commander of the garrison and vice-provost of the town. Paulett was an unfortunate choice, as he quarrelled with everyone, including Bishop Montgomery and, more ominously, with Sir Cahir O'Doherty. Lord Deputy Chichester believed that Paulett was hated by those he commanded and 'neither beloved nor feared by the Irish'.

CAHIR O'DOHERTY'S REBELLION

On 4 September 1607 the defeated Ulster chieftains Hugh O'Neill and Red Hugh O'Donnell left Ireland from Lough Swilly in a celebrated departure which has become known as the 'flight of the earls'. The foreman of the jury which found them guilty of treason after they had left was Sir Cahir O'Doherty. In the aftermath of the 'flight of the earls' Paulett suspected that Sir Cahir was involved in plotting against the Crown also. A number of O'Doherty's close associates had left with the earls. These matters were reported to the lord deputy, who forced O'Doherty to sign an agreement of good behaviour, which exacerbated the already difficult relations with Paulett. O'Doherty was obliged to visit Paulett in Derry early in April 1608; a quarrel broke out between the two men and Paulett assaulted O'Doherty. Some historians suggest that this was the final reason which led the Inishowen chieftain to rebel. However, Brian Bonner, in his book about Sir Cahir, *That Audacious Traitor*, shows that O'Doherty had been planning the uprising from the start of the month and that he had been increasingly anxious for some time about English interference in the affairs of his territory.

In order for Cahir to obtain arms and ammunition for his plan, it was essential to capture Culmore Fort. As a ruse he invited the commander, Captain Henry Hart, and his wife to dinner at Buncrana Castle on the evening of 18 April 1608. O'Doherty and Hart were good friends, as were their wives and they were even godparents to each other's children. The Harts were forced to act as hostages and O'Doherty gained entry to Culmore and was able to obtain the required munitions. The rebels, about one hundred in number, then set out for Derry, arriving at the city at about 2 a.m. on the morning of Tuesday 19 April.

Derry at this time was still a very small and relatively weak place. Six weeks previously the council in Dublin had written to Sir Cahir, who was a burgess of the new city, acknowledging a suggestion that some of the proceeds from the confiscated lands of the departed Gaelic earls should be used to repair the Ulster forts. It particularly recommended assistance for Derry, the plantation of which 'first opened the gap for His Majesty's entry . . . into the bowels of the northern territories'. Two weeks before O'Doherty's rebellion, Lord Deputy Chichester had written to the council about the poor state of Derry:

> The poor infant city daily consumes and wears away, and will be soon resolved unto her first principles again, if she be not forthwith strengthened and restored with some comforts from the King.

O'Doherty split his men into two groups, one of which, under Phelim Reagh McDaid, attacked the main fort near the top of the hill and the other, with Sir Cahir himself as leader, attacked the magazine fort at the old castle, lower down, near the riverside. They completely surprised the sleeping city and by dawn were masters of the two forts. Paulett and a number of his officers were killed, but Lieutenant John Baker was able to hold out for the rest of the day until he obtained an agreement in writing for the safety of himself and his men. About fifteen men were killed on each side, and according to a contemporary report by Sir Josias Bodley, 'the town was wholly spoiled, ransacked, and fired, the most part of the women stripped and led away prisoners'. The bishop's wife and her sister were taken captive and were still being held a fortnight after the other prisoners had been released.

When the dust had settled, only the stone chimneys and some walls were left standing. Thomas Ridgeway, writing to Lord Salisbury in July, pointed out that the old Augustinian abbey inside the main fort, which was being used as the colony's church, and

> whose timber work, either in respect of the height or in devotion to their solemn Collam Kill, the patron of that place, and whose name they use as their word of privity and distinction in all their wicked and treacherous attempts, was not fired.

Sir Arthur Chichester was furious at the treachery of Sir Cahir O'Doherty, 'one so much obliged to the King, so well settled, his country so well inhabited and rich, himself a burgess of the Derrie, and conformable in everything (excepting religion)'. In an outburst that has been echoed down the ages by many of his successors when dealing with Irish affairs, the lord deputy castigated the natives as 'a people that are more dangerous in peace than in war'.

Sir Cahir was eventually killed in a skirmish near Kilmacrennan in County Donegal on 5 July 1608. His foolhardy rebellion had been a complete failure. Derry had been devastated again, and although some houses were rebuilt, the way was now clear for the revolutionary and far-reaching plan which was soon to get under way. In April 1609 Sir John Davies wrote:

> It was the fairest-begun city that ever was made in so short a time, and so well seated upon a goodly river; but now all is wasted saving only the rampiers of the forts; and it is hardly to be brought to its former goodness, unless some great man, who shall be lord of O'Dogherty's country, shall make his principal residence there. In the meantime it is a place of little strength, and lies at the mercy of any that will attempt to seize upon it.

However, the city's rebirth was already being planned.

Lord Deputy Sir Arthur Chichester, who castigated the native Irish as being 'a people that are more dangerous in peace than in war' (from *The Story of the Irish Society*)

Ouer-throw of an

Iriſh rebell, in a late battaile:

Or

The death of Sir *Carey Adougher tie*, who murdred *Sir* George Paulet *in Ireland; and for his re-*bellion hath his head now ſtanding ouer Newgate in Dublin.

Imprinted at London for I. Wright, and are to be ſold at his ſhop neere Chriſt Church gate. 1608.

A contemporary pamphlet giving an account of the 'overthrow' of Sir Cahir O'Doherty in 1608

6

THE ORIGINS OF LONDONDERRY
A TALE OF TWO CITIES

After the defeat of Sir Cahir O'Doherty, the government policy of controlling Ulster by means of anglicising the native population was replaced by a much more revolutionary plan, which involved the systematic colonisation of the province with loyal English and Scottish subjects. In the summer of 1608 a survey was carried out of the six so-called 'escheated' counties in which the land was deemed to be forfeited to the Crown as a consequence of the rebellion and the 'flight of the earls'. The counties involved were Armagh, Cavan, Coleraine (which was subsequently enlarged and renamed County Londonderry), Donegal, Fermanagh and Tyrone. Later that year a London-based committee, which included George Montgomery, the Anglican bishop of Derry, was appointed to draw up detailed arrangements for the plantation. The committee produced two documents, *A collection of such orders and conditions, as are to be observed by the undertakers, upon the distribution and plantation of the escheated lands in Ulster* and *A project for the division and plantation of the escheated lands in . . . Ulster*. For a number of reasons the former county of Coleraine, together with certain adjoining territories in the neighbouring counties of Antrim, Donegal and Tyrone, was excluded from these plans. Instead, a special scheme involving the City of London was suggested for that area.

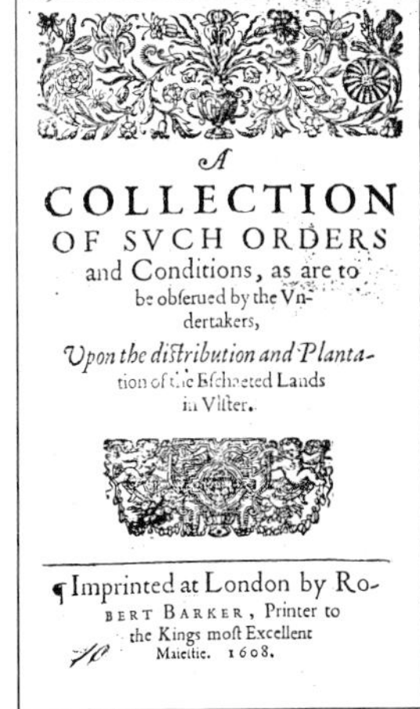

A
COLLECTION
OF SVCH ORDERS
and Conditions, as are to
be obserued by the Vndertakers,
Upon the distribution and Plantation of the Eschaeted Lands in Vlster.

¶ Imprinted at London by Robert Barker, Printer to the Kings most Excellent Maiestie. 1608.

A 1608 pamphlet outlining the regulations to be followed by the 'undertakers' taking part in the plantations in Ulster

Most of this excluded country had been the territory of the O'Cahans. However, the small strip of Donegal which formed part of the London proposal included the strategically important site of Derry, formerly

The county of Coleraine, based on the territory of the O'Cahans, was established in 1603. This land, together with three additional pieces of land (the barony of Loughinsholin, a strip around the town of Coleraine and a strip around the city of Derry), formed the basis of the county of Londonderry when it was established in 1613.

part of the O'Donnells' country. The strip taken in from County Antrim included the equally strategic settlement at Coleraine. The security of these two places was judged to be vital for the success of the entire colony, but the Government was not willing to invest the required resources. The introduction of urban settlements to an area where previously they had not existed on any major scale was considered an essential part of the Ulster colonisation scheme. While some of the smaller Ulster towns set up during the plantation were built under the auspices of certain wealthy individuals, the proposed fortified settlements at Derry and Coleraine were conceived on a larger and more elaborate scale. Investment by a much richer patron was necessary for this undertaking. In May 1609 negotiations began with the wealthy merchants of the City of London.

Robert Cecil, Lord Salisbury, lord high treasurer to James I; Cecil is usually given the credit for initiating the Londoners' involvement in the plantation of Derry. (from *The Story of the Irish Society*)

'THE SUCCESSORS OF . . . LUD WILL THERE REEDIFIE A NEW TROY'

For many centuries the English Crown had been forced occasionally to seek the sometimes unwilling assistance of the financiers of the City of London. An elaborate document drawn up for the privy council, dated 25 May 1609, lists the 'motives and reasons to induce the City of London to undertake the plantation in the North of Ireland'. Among the advantages to be gained were:

> Many thousands would be set at work, to the great service of the King, the strength of his realm, and the advancement of several trades. It might ease [London] of an insupportable burthen of persons, which it might conveniently spare, all parts of the city being so surcharged that one tradesman is scarce able to live by another; and it would also be a means to free and preserve the city from infection, and consequently the whole kingdom, which of necessity must have recourse hither, and being pestered or closed up together can never otherwise, or very badly, avoid infection.

The document also cited the example of how, in the reign of Henry II, Dublin had been successfully given to the 'men of Bristol'.

The credit for initiating the Londoners' involvement in the plantation project is usually given to Robert Cecil, Lord Salisbury and lord high treasurer to the king. However, James I, who had succeeded Elizabeth I in 1603, was actively involved in the development of the London plantation scheme and may have been its original author. As far back as 1600, three years before he became king of England, James, then king of Scotland, had recognised the strategic importance of Derry.

In April 1609, Sir Thomas Phillips, who had been involved in the recent war against the Ulster Gaelic chieftains, for which he had been awarded land in the Coleraine area, visited Lord Salisbury in London. He also had a meeting with James I where the subject of a possible London involvement in a scheme for the colonisation of O'Cahans' country appears to have been discussed. Phillips subsequently sent a

Clemont Edmonds, remembrancer of the City of London in 1609 (Photograph courtesy of Guildhall, London)

lengthy document to Salisbury, outlining the practicalities of the proposal and calculating that it would cost the City about £50,000. The 'motives and reasons' document was based on Phillips's report. Salisbury then wrote to the City of London remembrancer, Clement Edmonds, requesting him to explain the project to the lord mayor, Humphrey Weld. He also requested that Weld meet with Phillips to discuss the proposed scheme. Weld sought the advice of two of the leading aldermen of the City, John Jolles, merchant and draper, and William Cockayne, master of the Skinners' Company and sheriff of London. Both these men had been involved as merchants, supplying provisions to the Crown forces on the Lough Foyle expedition in 1600. The suggested meeting with Phillips took place and on 1 July 1609 the court of aldermen of London, together with 'selected commoners', was convened to discuss the matter. At this meeting the lord mayor issued the following order:

> Whereas, I have lately received from the Lords of his Majesty's most honourable Privy Council a project for a plantation in Ireland . . . with intimation of the King's most gracious favour and love to the city of London, to grant unto us the first offer of so gracious an action, which is likely to prove pleasing to Almighty God, honourable to the City, and profitable to the undertakers. These are, therefore, to will and require you presently to assemble together a competent number of the gravest and most substantial of your Company, to consider advisedly of the said project, and of them to nominate four men of most judgement and

In the early autumn of 1609 four citizen representatives travelled to Ireland to tour the area of the proposed London colony. They spent about a month inspecting land and sampling resources before returning to London to report favourably to the common council. (from *The Story of the Irish Society*)

> experience to join with like number of four of every other of the Companies of this City amongst themselves to consider of and set down in writing such reasons, orders, demands, and other circumstances as are fit to be remembered, required, or performed in the undertaking of so worthy and so honourable an action.

The companies in question were the ancient livery trades guilds, whose origins went back to medieval times. By the seventeenth century they represented all the commercial wealth of the City of London and were intimately associated with its government.

The representatives of the companies submitted their report on 14 July. In the meantime, the city fathers had met again with Phillips to question him about the likely profitability of the proposed plantation. More meetings followed and by 22 July the aldermen seem to have been convinced of the appropriateness of the venture. The individual companies were ordered to draw up lists of the financial contributions promised by their members to the scheme. Ominously, they were also to list those members refusing to invest. By the end of this exercise it was clear that there was little enthusiasm for the scheme and many people were opposed to it. However, at this stage the city fathers were almost inescapably committed to the project. As Thomas Blenerhasset,

Thomas Middleton, one of the first elected members of the Irish Society, which was established in 1613 to oversee the Londonderry plantation (Photograph courtesy of Guildhall, London)

an English settler in Fermanagh, wrote in 1610, curiously referring to the Celtic hero (known in Ireland as Nuadu) who is associated with the ancient mythology of the City of London:

> The successors of the high renouned Lud, will there reedifie a new Troy . . . They have [O'Cahans'] country, and whatever Ireland's Eden can afford . . . will performe this the most honourable action that they ever attempted.

'FOUR WISE, GRAVE AND DISCREET CITIZENS'

It was agreed that 'four wise, grave and discreet citizens' should travel to Ireland in order to inspect the area to be colonised. John Broad, goldsmith, Robert Treswell, painter–stainer, John Rowley, draper, and John Munns, mercer, were selected for the task and given £300 for expenses. The privy council in London wrote to Lord Deputy Chichester, explaining the importance of securing the involvement of the Londoners and of making a good impression on the inspectors. Their guides must

> be able to control whatever discouraging reports may be made to them out of ignorance or malice . . . must take care to lead them by the best ways, and to lodge them . . . where they may, if possible, receive English entertainment in Englishmen's houses . . . that matters of distaste, as fear of the Irish, of the soldiers, of cess, and such like, be not so much as named.

Sir Thomas Phillips was appointed chaperone.

The party landed at Carrickfergus, County Antrim, on 22 August and continued to Coleraine. From there they went to Limavady, where they met Chichester. One of the London party became ill but was restrained from returning home lest this should create the wrong impression. They travelled with Chichester south as far as Lifford and then came back to Derry. They returned to Coleraine by a different route and then turned south again, through the great forests, as far as Toome, where they were shown how local iron ore could be converted into steel. Phillips brought them back to Coleraine down the River Bann by boat, from where they set out for England. The entire journey had taken about a month. Examples of the produce of the country had been procured and samples of rawhides, tallow, salmon, herrings, eels, pipe-staves, beef, yarn, iron ore and other goods were shipped back to London for inspection.

The four travellers reported favourably to the court of aldermen on 28 November and to the common council on 2 December. A committee representing the corporation and the principal companies was then set up, which, on 15 December, presented a set of conditions for the plantation. It was agreed to invest £15,000, later raised to £20,000, and, among many other things, to erect two hundred houses in Derry with room for three hundred more. Serious negotiations now began with the representatives of the king and the first instalment of £5,000 was called in from the individual investors. On 28 January 1610 'articles of agreement' were signed by both the representatives of the privy council and the representatives of the City.

The seal of the Irish Society; the Latin inscription reads: 'The Society of the Governor and Assistants, London, of the New Plantation in Ulster, within the realm of Ireland.'

THE HONOURABLE THE IRISH SOCIETY

The articles of agreement set out the prerogatives and responsibilities of each party to the scheme. As the principal historian of the Londonderry plantation, Professor T. W. Moody has pointed out, the Crown, for its own purposes, 'inveigled' the reluctant City into becoming involved in the colonisation of Ulster. The City made the most of the 'unsought compact'. The original idea was that the City should be a 'foster-mother' rather than a 'beneficial owner' of the two new colonial towns at Coleraine and Derry. However, in their anxiety to secure the City's investment, the representatives of the Crown conceded to all the demands of the Londoners. Under the agreement the City was obliged to build sixty houses in Derry by 1 November 1610 and to complete the remainder, plus the fortifications in Derry and in Coleraine within twelve months.

The agreement was ratified at a meeting of the common council on 30 January and at the same time a special new company was set up to direct and manage the plantation scheme. This company was, to all intents and purposes, a subordinate standing committee of the

The tomb in St Paul's Cathedral, London, of William Cockayne, the first governor of the Irish Society (Photograph courtesy of St Paul's Cathedral)

common council. It consisted of a governor, who was required to be an alderman of the City, a deputy governor, and twenty-four assistants. Five of the assistants were also to be aldermen, while the deputy governor and the other assistants were to be commoners. When the members of the company were elected, William Cockayne was chosen as the first governor.

The new company was officially called 'The Society of the Governor and Assistants, London, of the New Plantation in Ulster, within the Realm of Ireland'. By the second half of the seventeenth century this body was known as The Honourable The Irish Society, or simply the Irish Society. Today the society, which still owns property in Derry, dispenses its resources on philanthropic and charitable projects, with the guidance of a local advisory committee. However, in origin it was set up with the intention of becoming a commercial, profit-making enterprise, like many of the other contemporary joint-stock companies formed for parallel colonising projects in other parts of the world. The Bermuda, Newfoundland and Virginia companies were similar bodies involved in colonisation in the Americas. It was to be a very long time, however, before the Londoners were able to capitalise on their original investment in Ulster.

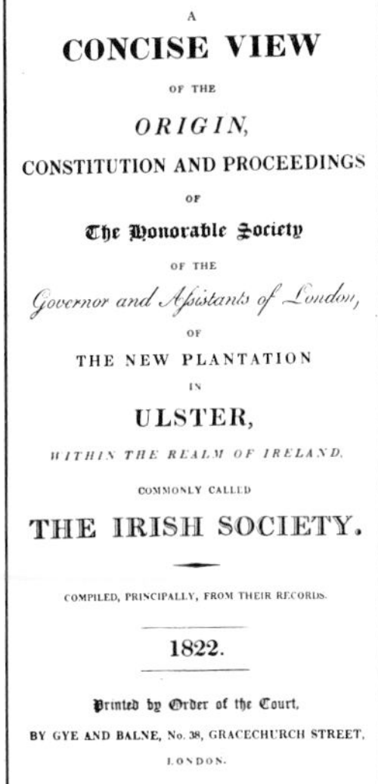

A
CONCISE VIEW
OF THE
ORIGIN,
CONSTITUTION AND PROCEEDINGS
OF
The Honorable Society
OF THE
Governor and Assistants of London,
OF
THE NEW PLANTATION
IN
ULSTER,
WITHIN THE REALM OF IRELAND,
COMMONLY CALLED
THE IRISH SOCIETY.

COMPILED, PRINCIPALLY, FROM THEIR RECORDS.

1822.

Printed by Order of the Court,
BY GYE AND BALNE, No. 38, GRACECHURCH STREET,
LONDON.

Title page of an account of the origins and history of the Irish Society, requested by the members and printed in 1822

BUILDING THE NEW CITY

While discussions continued in London, the task of collecting the promised finance for the scheme was put in hand, which proved a great deal more difficult than expected. So reluctant were the City merchants to become involved that many members of the individual companies

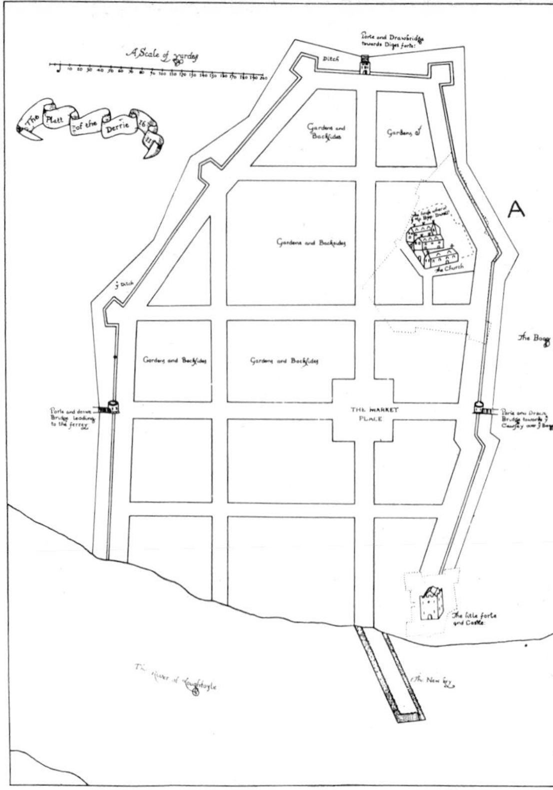

Line drawing of a proposed plan for Londonderry, dated 1611. The outline of the earlier 'city of Derry' can be seen (A). Londonderry, as eventually built, had a similar but slightly different plan. (Original held in Trinity College Dublin)

had to be threatened, and a number actually imprisoned, before the necessary funds were collected. Many in London doubted whether the settlers would be able to 'keep their heads on their shoulders'. In spite of this, operations had begun in Ireland. Early in 1610 about 130 workmen, including masons and carpenters, were sent over to Derry from London. They brought with them tools and some building material. Lord Deputy Chichester was instructed to give every help to the construction project and to ensure that sufficient labourers, presumably drawn from the local native Irish, were available to assist with the work. The former inhabitants of the colonial city of Derry were to be bought out, although many remained, becoming citizens of the new city. Only those houses required as accommodation for the workers were to be left standing, the rest were to be demolished to give a clean sweep for the layout of the new city.

Although no resistance from the native Irish materialised, progress was very slow and by August 1611, when Lord Carew made a survey of the plantation, very little had been achieved:

> Next we came to Derry, where we saw the church well slated and repaired. Two fair houses of stone, two storeys high, slated and finished with cellars to each house. A storehouse covered and walled with deal boards, with a place to work dry in. A thatched house wherein Mr Wray dwelleth. A saw pit covered with deal boards. A fair large smith's forge, with a dwelling-house to the same. Two fair lime kilns. A fair wharf of 300 foot long, and about 14 broad, and 8 or 9 foot high. Two heads of wharfs at

A view of Vitry-le-François, France, in 1634, whose layout bore a remarkable resemblance to that of Derry. The River Marne can be seen at the bottom of the drawing.

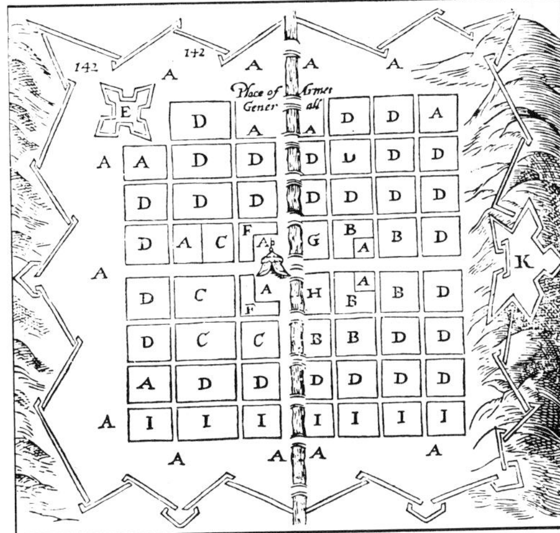

Plan of an ideal military camp, from Robert Barret, *Theorike and Practike of Modern Warres*, published in London in 1598

the ferry-places, on both sides the river. A bark building of 70 or 80 tons, with provisions of plank and other timber for her.

The 'repaired' church was the old Augustinian abbey and one of the stone houses was intended for the Anglican bishop. Carew estimated that approximately 150 workmen and twelve horses were engaged in these operations. There exists a plan, dated 1611, of the proposed walled city, but very little of this was built and the drawing must have been more in the nature of a blueprint. The layout shown on this plan indicated that the proposed city was to be roughly coffin-shaped, surrounded, except on the river side, by a wall and ditch, with the streets arranged in a grid pattern around an off-centre square. The city eventually built, however, had a slightly different plan. The plantation gave its backers an almost unprecedented opportunity to design a new city on what was, in effect, a green-field site. The city built at Derry was the first major piece of urban planning in Ireland.

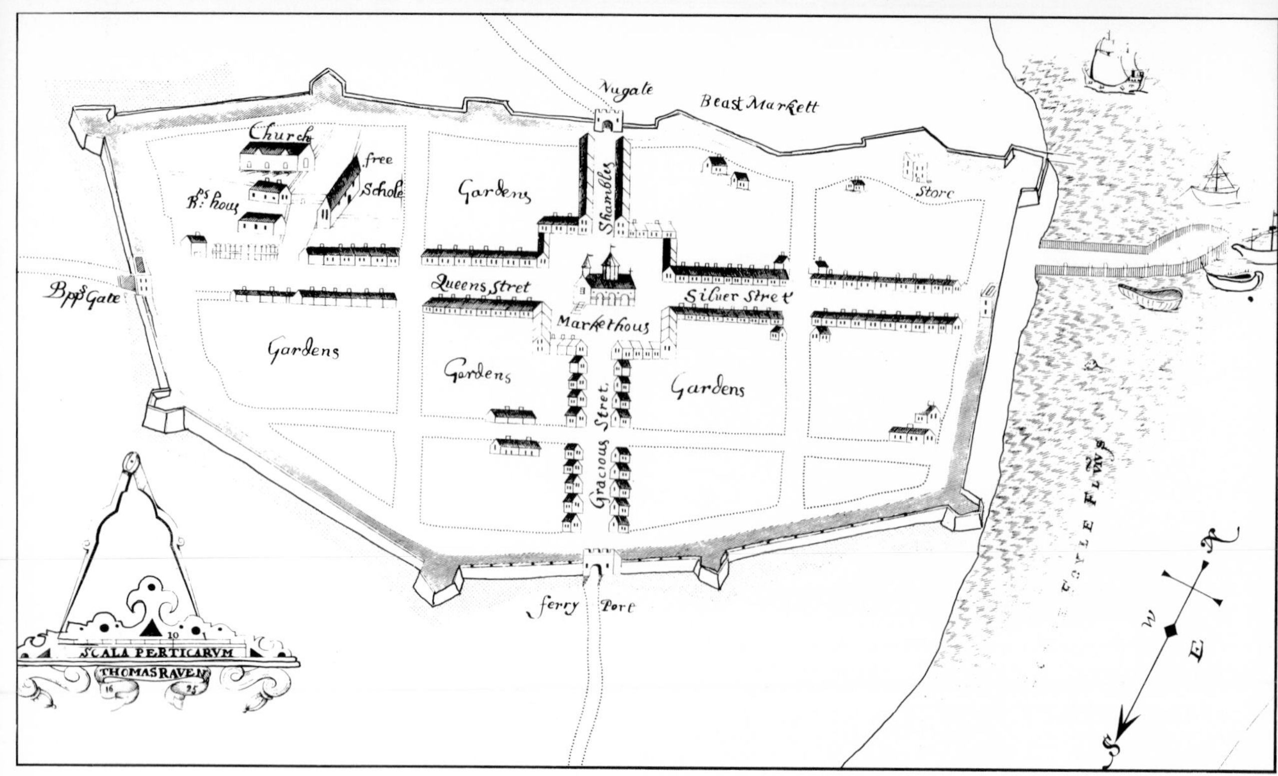

Plan of the city of Londonderry, dated 1625, by Thomas Raven

By this time the design of towns had benefited greatly from the return to classical ideas which had motivated the European Renaissance. The rational, geometric layout of ancient Roman military camps began to influence the design of new towns and cities. One such place was the frontier city of Vitry-le-François, about one hundred miles east of Paris, built by the kings of France and finished about 1560. Vitry-le-François had been designed for Francis I in 1545 by the Italian engineer Hieronimo Marino. In 1598, Robert Barret published *Theorike and Practike of Modern Warres* in London, and included an illustration of an idealised military camp which showed a very close similarity to the layout of Vitry. So among the many 'patterns' for towns circulating at the beginning of the seventeenth century, the one used at Vitry-le-François was undoubtedly known in London.

The layout of the new city at Derry bore a remarkable resemblance to that of the French town. Vitry was also situated on a river, the Marne, but it was bigger than the new city at Derry. However, even the differences between the two cities are instructive, as the truncated Vitry plan adopted at Derry can be explained by local topographical circumstances, particularly by the steep slope to the bog on the western side of the city. The precise manner by which the plan of a new colonial city in Ulster came to resemble that of a French Renaissance town is not clear but it may not be altogether irrelevant to note that the building of Vitry had been finished during the reign of Francis II who was married to Mary Queen of Scots. She was the mother of James I, the king responsible for promoting the London plantation scheme.

It was the American historians of town planning, Anthony Garvan and John Reps, who originally drew attention to the possibility of a Vitry–Derry connection. They were researching the origins of the plans of the early English settlements in what later became the United States. They turned for evidence to the Ulster plantations which had been taking place at the same time as the first English colonies were being set up in America. Reps has suggested that the original plan of Philadelphia shows parallels with the plan of the new city built at Derry. There are, of course, many other similarities between the English colonisations in Ulster and America. Sometimes the same individuals or their close relatives were active in the two enterprises on either side of the Atlantic. In addition, archaeological excavations at post-medieval colonial sites in both Ulster and America have turned up similar domestic material.

The Armes of the Citty of Derry were at first, when the Hon. Sir Henry Docwra, Knight, made the plantation there against the arch traitour Hugh sometyme Earle of Tyrone, the picture of Death (or a skeleton) sitting on a mossie stone, and in the dexter point a castle. And forasmuch as that Citty was since most traiterously sacked and destroyed by Sir Cahire (or Sir Charles) O'Dogharty, and hath since been (as it were) raised from the dead by the worthy undertaking of the Hon. Citty of London, in memory whereof it is from henceforth called and known by the name of London-Derry, I have, at the request of John Rowley, now first Mayor of that citty and the cummunalty of the same, set forth the same with an addition of a chiefe of London, as here appeareth; and for confirmation thereof, I have hereunto set my hand and seale this first of June, M.D.C.XIII.,

Dan. Molineux, *Ulster King of Armes.*

Contemporary explanation of the coat-of-arms granted to the city of Londonderry on 1 June 1613

DERRY BECOMES LONDONDERRY

Although building operations were under way in Ulster, the Irish Society was not pleased with the productivity of the workers. Among the many recommendations which the society issued to its Derry-based agent in November 1612, the following was thought necessary:

> For the more civil and orderly government of our cities, having been credibly informed and in our experience knowing that by the great number of taverns and ale houses much disorder is committed and the poorer sort thereby spend their time and substance, we will have but 2 or 3 taverns at Coleraine and 4 taverns at Derry and not above 10 ale-houses at Coleraine and not above 20 at Derry.

A number of disputes had also arisen between the king and the City about the provisions of the plantation arrangements. Neither side felt that the conditions were being complied with fully by their opposites. However, on 29 March 1613 the royal seal was attached to the document known as the Charter of Londonderry, which changed the name of the city from Derry to Londonderry in recognition of the association with the City of London, and it also set up a municipal corporation. A new associated county, also called Londonderry, based on the former county of Coleraine, was created simultaneously, and its lands were parcelled out among the subscribing companies. The same document formally incorporated the Irish Society and confirmed the various grants and privileges to that body.

The charter gave to the new city the right to make its own bye-laws, to impose fines and punishments for breaches of them, and to hold courts. It had the right to hold markets and fairs and the city was constituted a seaport, the only place for unloading ships in the Lough Swilly or Lough Foyle area. It could collect customs and tolls on imports, and devote the proceeds to the maintenance of the walls and gates of the city. Londonderry was also given the right to send two members to the

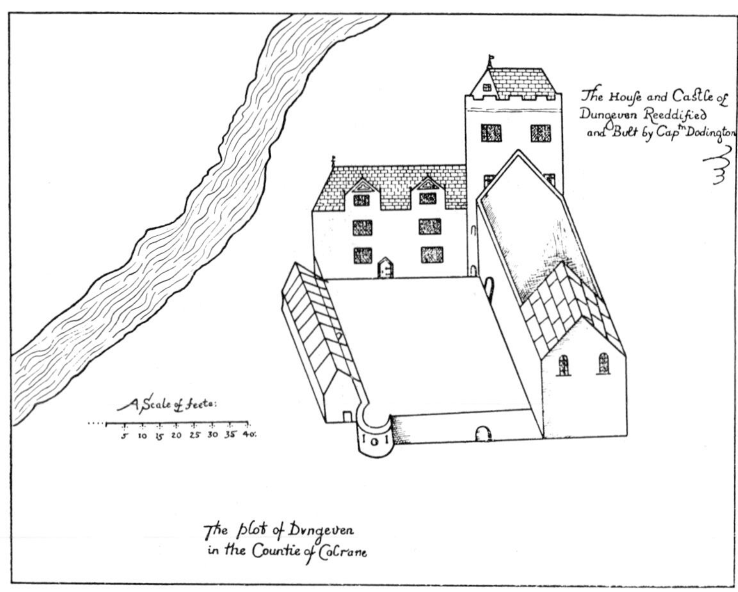

The former Dungiven priory *c.* 1611, 'reeddified' as the house of Sir Edward Doddington, who designed the walls of Derry

Irish parliament. The city did not own the land on which it stood – this belonged to the Irish Society, which thus became an absentee landlord. There were various difficulties for the young city arising from this unusual relationship with the Irish Society, many of which were to surface in the years ahead.

The progress at Londonderry is described in a number of specially commissioned surveys carried out over the next fifteen years. In August and September 1613, Georges Smithes and Matthias Springham, assistants of the Irish Society in London, visited the city and county of Londonderry to inspect developments. They found that the local agents of the society were somewhat corrupt and wasteful and that only thirty-two small houses had been built in the city, although another nine were almost completed. They initiated work on the city's defences:

> We, with the assistance of Captain Panton, and of divers other captains, of special note and good experience being ten in number, have viewed and trod out the ground at the Derry for the fortification there, and have conferred and advised with them concerning the same . . . but [their] advice is, that materials should be first laid in place afore the wall be gone in hand; and we think it fit that the same fortification and the work for the same, be begun and set forward with all convenient speed.

THE CITY WALLS

The layout of the walls of Derry has often been criticised. The highest point on the hill lay outside the walls and, despite the size of the fortifications, the city was exposed to cannon fire from the higher ground on the surrounding hills on both sides of the river. The walls, which originally consisted of a six-foot-thick outer skin of stone backed by a twelve-foot-thick earthen rampart, were built between 1613 and 1618 at a total cost of £10,357. They were designed by Sir Edward Doddington, whose house at the former Augustinian priory in Dungiven was excavated in the mid-1980s. Thomas Raven, official surveyor of the City of London, carried out the detailed survey work. The building of the walls was supervised by Peter Benson, a master bricklayer and tiler from London. He was later the recipient of 1,500 acres of land near Lifford in County Donegal.

The circuit of the walls extended to some 1,700 yards. For almost half their length, on the south and east sides, a large ditch or fosse, ten feet deep and thirty feet wide, ran outside the walls. Small sections of this ditch, which within a century had been filled in, have been excavated recently and produced many thousands of pieces of seventeenth-century ceramics as well as pieces of leather and a variety of wooden objects. It is believed locally that the section of the walls overlooking the Bogside was built from the surviving remains of Docwra's town, and the ruins of the medieval ecclesiastical buildings, of which no traces have ever been found despite systematic examination. Elsewhere the earthen rampart that ran behind the walls, which is now buried inside an inner stone skin, was built with the soil that had been dug out of the ditch.

Londonderry was the last town or city in Ireland to be enclosed by stone walls. It was possibly the last city in Europe to have this distinction, sharing in a tradition which went back several thousand years to the very beginnings of urbanism and civilisation in the Middle East. Derry is the only town or city in Ireland whose full circuit of ancient walls still survive intact. While the walls have been modified in the course of the centuries, particularly by the addition of a number of extra gates, they are essentially the same fortifications that protected the small seventeenth-century colonial city. They are one of the largest single historic monuments in the country and as such belong to the common heritage of Ireland.

PROGRESS CONTINUES

In 1613 Smithes and Springham delivered the Charter of Londonderry to the civic officers and the charter of the former city of Derry was simultaneously surrendered. A communion cup was presented to the church on behalf of the Irish Society. In September 1614, Sir Josias Bodley, overseer of fortifications in Ireland, carried out an inspection of the work in Londonderry on behalf of the Crown. He was critical of the Londoners and found that about £300 had been

> disbursed at the Derry in casting up of earth and breaking of quarries towards the walling thereof, which how it shall be continued either for form or strength, being that . . . no part of the stonework is yet raised, I cannot precisely deliver but only what I gather by the beginnings it is like either to prove more chargeable than it needed or not so strong as were requisite . . . All that [the Londoners] have done of any moment hath been . . . the building of about 130 houses at the Derry after their own distinction of houses of which is a room below with a roof for a house, the

Among the earliest colonists in Derry were orphaned boys sent over as apprentices by the Irish Society from Christ's Hospital in London. (from *The Story of the Irish Society*)

levelling of the uneven ground of the high street for ease of their carriages, the paving of some streets, and the beginning of the work for the wall of the town.

Apart from the workmen, no colonists had yet been sent over from London. In March 1616 the twelve main London companies involved in the plantation were ordered to send over craftsmen and their families. It appears that the companies did not comply with this instruction, although the Irish Society did send ten Christ's Hospital orphaned boys to act as apprentices and servants in Londonderry and two more to Coleraine. It possibly sent other impoverished children as well. In the summer of 1616 the common council of London sent Peter Proby and, for a second time, Matthias Springham to Londonderry:

> For the fortification at Derrie we have exactly viewed the same and find it very commendable and when the same is finished will be very strong and that the walls thereof are wellnigh half done and the houses finished except some 5 or 6 which will be shortly and the whole number of the houses at Derrie are 214 besides the Bishop's house and some thatched English houses and cabins both within and without the Derrie. Also there are two drawbridges finished and one gate was in erecting . . . and whereas it was formerly agreed that on the hill towards the bog the height

The walls of Derry and seventeenth-century cannon, Shipquay Place (Green Collection, Ulster Folk and Transport Museum)

> of the wall should be but 16 foot high which upon view was found to be very low and not defensive we have therefore directed that the wall in that place and in other places where need shall be 19 foot high from the face of the earth and no ditch be made there but the hill to be scarped.

Proby and Springham brought with them two swords for presentation to the mayors of Coleraine and Londonderry. The Derry sword still survives among the city's treasures. Springham also felt moved to donate money for a free school as a gift to the new city and the building of this was begun the following year. That school, which was originally located inside the walls at Society Street, was the ancestor of the present Foyle and Londonderry College.

From December 1618 to March 1619, Captain Nicholas Pynnar, an inspector of fortifications in Ireland, carried out a survey on behalf of the Crown of all the British plantations in Ulster. He described the city of Londonderry as being

> now encompassed about with a very strong wall, excellently made and neatly wrought; being all of good lime and stone; the circuit whereof is 283 perches and ⅔, at 18 feet to the perch; besides the four gates which contain 84 feet; and in every place of the wall it is 24 feet high, and six feet thick. The gates are all battlemented, but to two of them there is no going up, so that they serve no great use; neither have they made any leaves for their gates; but make two drawbridges serve for two of them, and two portcullises for the other two. The bulwarks are all very large and good, being in number nine; besides two half bulwarks; and for four of them there may be four cannons, or other great pieces; the rest are not all out so

> large, but wanteth very little. The rampart within the city is 12 feet thick of earth; all things are very well and substantially done, saving there wanteth a house for the soldiers to watch in, and a sentinel house for the soldiers to stand in, in the night, to defend them from the weather, which is most extreme in these parts. Since the last survey, there is built a school, which is 67 feet in length, and 25 in breadth, with two other small houses. Other building there is not any within the city. The whole number of houses within the city is 92, and in them are 102 families, which are too few a number for the defence of such a circuit, they being scarce able to man one of the bulwarks; neither is there room enough to set up a 100 houses more, unless they will make them as little as the first, and name each room for a house.

The apparent discrepancy in the number of houses built arising from Proby and Springham's 1616 report (214) and Pynnar's in 1619 (92) is explained by the fact that the former report considered each bay to be a house.

Stone houses are shown on the fine map of the city which survives from Pynnar's survey. In 1980 it became possible to excavate the remains of two early-seventeenth-century houses in Linenhall Street, inside the city walls. The frontage of these houses was about thirty feet long by about eighteen feet deep and it appears that they had an upper room but this could not be verified. These houses, like all others in the city, were built of stone with brick detail. Timber-framed houses were not built in the city although they were common in the other settlements of the Londonderry plantation. The ground-floor room in each excavated house had a large stone fireplace with a brick oven set diagonally to one side. The internal walls of the houses were probably plastered. One interesting feature of the arrangements in Londonderry was that each house had assigned to it as a garden about sixty perches of ground in the area of the island outside the walls. In addition, each house had attached to it between six and ten acres of land in the 'Liberties' beyond the island and the bog on the Donegal side.

CONSPIRACY

While building had been going on, a clumsy conspiracy by some of the leading local native Irish was discovered. The perpetrators planned to rise in rebellion and burn the various English colonial settlements, including Londonderry. Between February and June 1615, Lord Deputy Chichester was made aware of the plot and the conspirators were arrested. The attorney general, Sir John Davies, and Dominic Sarsfield, together with the mayor of Londonderry, John Rowley, were appointed to act as judges. There was a fifteen-man jury which, interestingly, included two native Irishmen. The trial was conducted amid the confusion of the half-built city.

Of the seventeen men put on trial, eleven were released and six were found guilty. As Raymond Gillespie relates, the six were sentenced to the mandatory punishment of being 'drawn through the streets of Derry in chains to the gallows where they would be hanged but when only half dead to be cut down, disembowelled, beheaded, the body quartered and then burned'. The heads were to be exhibited on the city gates. One of the six, Brian Crossagh O'Neill, was executed immediately and it seems that the other five were hanged later that year. Gillespie also points out that in a curious reopening of the case at the beginning of the twentieth century the names of these six men were submitted to the Sacred Congregation of Rites at the Vatican as candidates for the title of Martyrs of the Roman Catholic Church. However, the matter was not proceeded with.

'THE DERRY BUSYNES'

Throughout the early years of the plantation there continued to be differences of interpretation about the exact details of the arrangements for the new colony. Property disputes arose between the Anglican bishop of Derry and the municipal authorities in Londonderry, between these authorities and the Irish Society in London, and between the

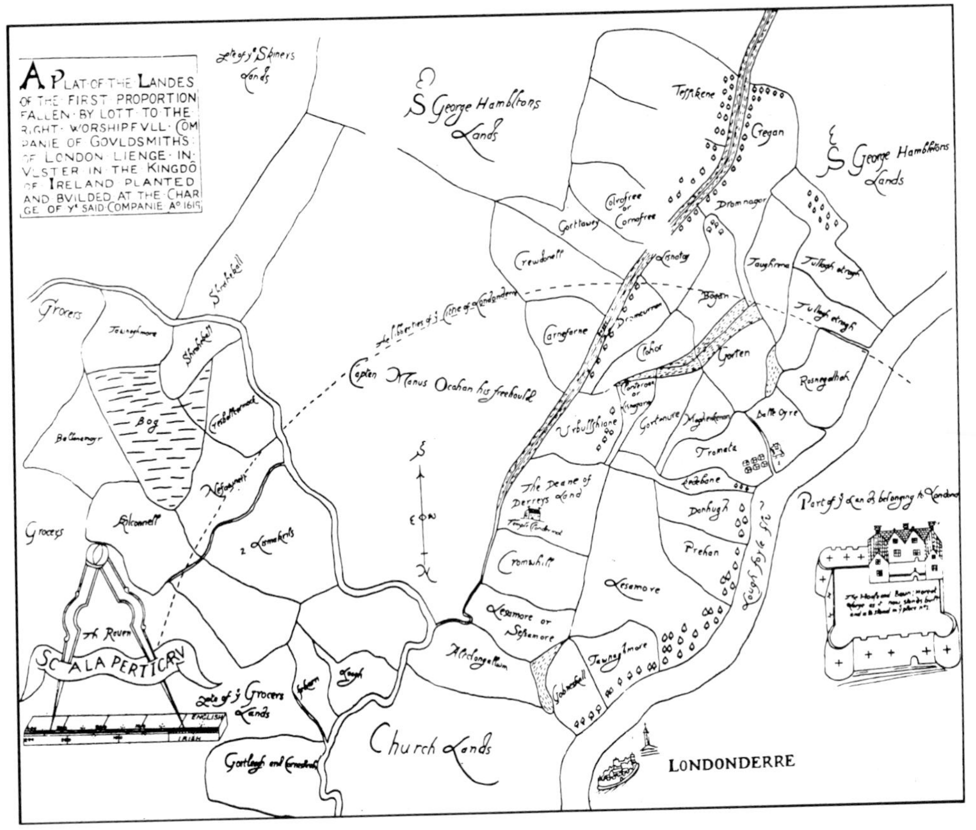

A plan of the lands assigned to the Company of Goldsmiths (including parts of the present Waterside area), drawn by Thomas Raven in 1619. A section of the boundary line of the 'Liberties' (broken line), measured as the area within a three-mile radius of 'the middle of the city', can be seen.

The Court of Star Chamber, which in early 1635 tried the City of London and the Irish Society on charges of mismanaging the Londonderry plantation (Mansell Collection)

society and the municipal authorities of the City of London. Most important of all were the differences between the City and the Crown.

In Ireland Sir Thomas Phillips became an almost obsessive critic of the lack of progress by the Londoners, particularly of their slowness in replacing the native Irish with British colonists. In 1622 he and Richard Hadsor compiled a survey of the state of the Londonderry plantation which was illustrated with a set of beautiful drawings and maps prepared by Thomas Raven. Phillips suggested that the town hall, then in the process of being built in the market place, the present-day Diamond, should be abandoned and a citadel built in its place. He also suggested that a navigable channel should be cut through the bog as an additional defence, thus surrounding the city with water. Raven's plan of Londonderry that accompanied the survey shows the suggested citadel as well as other proposed features that were never built. In 1625 Raven prepared a plan showing the projected channel and other additional defences, but again, these were not constructed.

Phillips's survey of 1622 was submitted as evidence of neglect to the Crown. As a result, the entire property of the Londoners in Ireland was sequestrated on 2 September 1625 by the new king, Charles I. After much debate, the sequestration was removed two years later, but an enquiry was set up to look afresh at the plantation project. The property was sequestrated for a second time on 3 May 1628 but this time the confiscation only lasted three months as the City of London was able to exert pressure on Charles I, whose government was encountering crisis after crisis. Phillips continued his attack on the City and in 1629 submitted another large collection of documents supporting his case. The controversy continued and finally on 28 January 1635 the City of London and the Irish Society were put on trial in the Court of Star Chamber for their alleged mismanagement of the plantation project. On 28 February the defendants were found guilty and sentenced to a fine of £70,000 and the surrender of their Londonderry property. The sentence was appealed and on 16 July 1637 agreement was reached whereby the

City surrendered all its rights in Londonderry and agreed to pay £12,000. Thus was concluded what Phillips referred to in his will as 'the Derry busynes'. However, the society was eventually restored to its property.

'THIS CHURCH AND CITTIE'

Ironically, two years before the Star Chamber trial, the Irish Society had completed work on its principal building in Londonderry, the new church. The place of worship first used by the Protestant colonists was the old Augustinian abbey church which had been repaired. However, there were continuous complaints that this was inadequate for the needs of the growing city, in addition to having to function as the cathedral of a diocese. The Irish Society was not convinced of the need for a new church but in 1628 conceded to the complaints. Work on the building began late in August of that year.

The site chosen for the church was on the highest ground inside the walls, at the south-east corner of the city. On earlier maps, such as Pynnar's in 1618 and Raven's in 1622 and 1625, this area is shown for proposed street and house development. Raven's plan dated 1622, which included a number of buildings which were never, in fact, erected, indicates a large mysterious building on the upper-left-hand side of what was until recently the junction of Richmond Street and Linenhall Street. This building was never constructed but the drawing was possibly a proposed design and location for a new church. The building is shown to have three different sections, each of descending height from south-west to north-east and these probably represented the tower, nave and chancel of a church. The area where the church was

The Irish Chamber, the offices of the Irish Society at Guildhall Yard in the City of London (from *The Story of the Irish Society*)

actually built must have been on or very near to the site of a medieval church referred to by Docwra and shown on maps in 1600 and 1603.

Despite the clean-sweep policy of the Londoners, they did take pains to respect some of the old traditions. They are said to have incorporated a small stone plaque from the Tempull Mór in the dedication stone of the new church. Perhaps more surprisingly, the new church was dedicated from the outset to Saint Columb, the ancient patron of Derry. The erection of the new church on a site already hallowed with ecclesiastical connections would be in keeping with this approach.

The church was built by William Parrott, under the general supervision of Sir John Vaughan, and finished in 1633. It cost the Londoners £3,800 and in 1638 Charles I provided a ring of seven bells costing £500. The architectural historian, James Stevens Curl, has described St Columb's as 'among the finest of Gothic Survival buildings in the British Isles' and as a superb specimen of perpendicular Gothic architecture. Although subsequently it has been altered and added to, the cathedral is one of the most important seventeenth-century buildings in Ireland. St Columb's is both a parish church and the cathedral of the Church of Ireland diocese of Derry. It was the first specifically Protestant cathedral built in these islands after the Reformation and has played an enormous part in the history of the city, particularly during the siege of 1689. Recently, the building has undergone extensive renovations with the support of all sections of the people of the city. Sadly, during this restoration programme, much of the cathedral's historic stained glass and other internal features were damaged by three nearby bomb blasts. Repaired twice already, work on these windows has had to start again.

St Columb's Cathedral, built in 1633, as it looked in the seventeenth century

Near the main entrance to the cathedral is the well-known dedication stone with its famous inscription:

> If stones could speake
> Then Londons prayse
> Should sounde who
> Built this church and
> Cittie from the grounde.

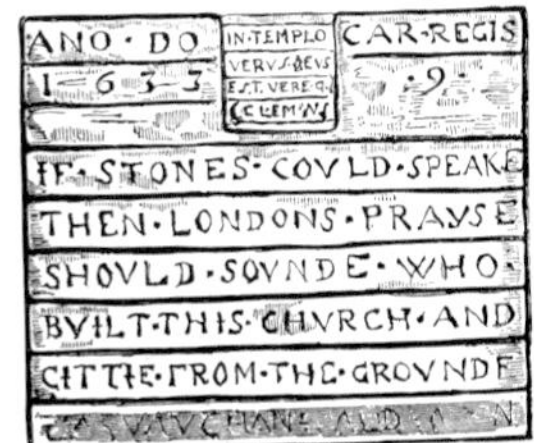

The dedication stone in the porch of St Columb's Cathedral, which is said to incorporate a small plaque taken from the medieval Tempull Mór

THE SEVENTEENTH-CENTURY 'CITY'

Although legally a city, throughout the seventeenth century Londonderry was never larger than a very small town. In 1616, 102 families were living there and by 1620 this had increased to 121, although the size of each family is unknown. The population was smaller than Coleraine at this stage but quickly began to overtake its 'sister' town and by 1628 it was estimated that there were 305 able-bodied men in Londonderry. A rent roll for the city, dated 15 May 1628, interestingly lists a small number of residents with Gaelic Irish names. By 1630 there were about five hundred men living in the city. Small as this appears, it was by far the largest settlement in Ulster.

Initially the population was made up of some of the old Derry settlers, the workmen and officials sent over from London, and young people such as the Christ's Hospital boys. Slowly, with the arrival of new settlers and the birth of children, the population began to rise. Within the walls, houses with back gardens lined the principal streets: Silver Street, leading down to the Ship or Water Gate and the river; Queen Street, leading to the Bishop Gate; Gracious Street, leading to the Ferry Gate and the track to the ferry landing; and the Shambles, leading to the western gate and the bog. Already there were a few houses outside the walls and their numbers gradually increased but were thought to detract from the defences of the city, and in times of crisis were demolished.

The remains of the old medieval tower house had been included within the city walls and it was repaired and served as an ammunition magazine for the city, under the military governorship of Sir John Vaughan. An ornate market house and town hall were constructed in the central square and the cathedral and the former abbey church served the worshipping needs of the Protestant population. The city was a market and service centre for the surrounding district and its quay was busy with ships, importing luxury and manufactured goods and exporting various kinds of raw materials and agricultural produce. Some of the boats trading with the city were locally owned.

THE REBELLION OF 1641

By 1640 opposition in Britain to Charles I had gathered momentum. The struggle between the king, and the English parliament and the Scots, had begun. The City of London sided with parliament and petitioned for redress over the Star Chamber sentence regarding Derry and on 26 August 1641 the House of Commons declared the sentence to have been unlawful and unjust and urged that the confiscated property should be restored to the City. A few months later the king, in a bid to regain some popularity, promised to restore the lands, but events overtook these plans.

Sir Phelim O'Neill, who led the native Irish uprising in 1641 (Reproduced by courtesy of the trustees of the British Museum)

On 23 October 1641 the native Irish, under the leadership of Sir Phelim O'Neill, rose in arms in counties Londonderry and Tyrone, paradoxically claiming to be on the same side as the king. Within a few days most of the centre of Ulster was in the hands of the rebels but no attempt was made to take the city of Londonderry, which became instead a place of refuge for the settlers fleeing before the insurgents. Many set sail from the port for the safety of Scotland. On 10 January 1642 the mayor wrote that 'the terror of the rebellion hath struck such a fear in the British of these parts that their hearts are gone, and, therefore, it is little purpose to stay their bodies'. Temporary houses had to be erected inside the town to accommodate the flood of refugees and there were complaints that the local people were overcharging for these lodgings. Before long, people were dying of starvation. Seven companies were raised for the defence of the city and the surrounding area under the overall governorship of Sir John Vaughan. A 'League of the captains of Londonderry' was drawn up which set out a series of measures to protect the city. It was agreed

> to expell all such Irish out of the city, as we shall conceive to be needful for the safety of this city . . . That after this is done . . . a proclamation be made, that no man or woman so expelled the city shall, upon pain of death, return . . . or make their abode within two miles of the same . . . That we survey the suburbs of this city, and conclude what houses are to be pulled down, and what gardens and orchards to be cut for annoying the enemy's approach . . . All women and children to keep within doors, and hang out lights in their several houses.

Each of the seven captains was assigned a portion of the city walls to repair and then guard. The City of London sent over fifteen 'pieces of ordnance' which together with 'four [it] had before' made up the city's defences. Many of these cannon can still be seen on the walls and in other parts of the city. However, no attack was made on Londonderry. Local regiments were active throughout the western parts of Ulster keeping 'the enemies from our walls' and recapturing strongholds from the Irish. The planned rebellion deteriorated into a series of dreadful spontaneous attacks on the Protestant settler population. Bad as the situation was, even more gruesome, exaggerated accounts began to circulate and spread to Britain, which was itself in considerable political disarray. On 15 April 1642 the Scottish general Robert Monro, with an army of 2,500 men, arrived at Carrickfergus, County Antrim, to help 'their brethren in Ireland' quash the rebellion. From Derry a letter was sent to him aboard a ship 'in his majesty's service', skippered by Captain Strange, who had arrived in the city earlier and lent the forlorn citizens six barrels of gunpowder. The letter, which is dated 27 April and signed by Mayor Robert Thornton, Henry Osborne and Sir John Vaughan, sets out the serious situation in Derry. It explained that while the citizens had made their

> wants and miseries known divers times to Dublin, and to England, and to Scotland, yet no relief ever came to us, but only thirty barrels of powder, brought by Captain Boulton from Dublin . . . want of powder and arms here hath been our ruin . . . It is the great providence and goodness of God, that we are hitherto preserved, having been so ill armed and provided for; all the arms within his majesty's store here were shipped to Dublin last summer, and nothing left here but old decayed calivers . . . for now at this hour, Sir Phelim O'Neill, having gathered from all parts what forces he can make, is with a very great army of horse and foot at Strabane, within ten or twelve miles of this city, intending (by all the intelligence we can get) to set up his rest, and desperately to break in upon us, where all the forces we can make are ready to bid him welcome. Sir Phelim on the one side of the river, and ours on the other, in sight one of the other.

The letter went on to explain how all the food and ammunition had been used up and continues:

> Most earnestly praying that for the love of God, and honour of our king, and the safety of this place and people, ye will dispatch [Captain Strange] back again to us with a good and large proportion of powder, match, and lead, muskets, swords, pikes, some spades and shovels, whereof we have not any . . . for we want all things fit to defend a distressed country and offend a desperate enemy.

While the authorities in Derry were anxious to obtain supplies from the Scots, they did not want Scottish troops garrisoned in the city. The

Englysh Protestantes striped naked & turned into the mountaines in the frost & snowe. whereof many hundreds are perished to death & many lyinge dead in dithes & Sauages upbraided them sayinge. now are ye wilde Iristh as well as wee.
D

A scene from the *Thomason Tracts* (1647) depicting the alleged horrors suffered by Ulster Protestants at the hands of Catholics in 1641. Atrocities did occur but accounts were grossly exaggerated for propaganda purposes.

Scots had requested that the major strongholds of Carrickfergus, Coleraine and Derry should be controlled by them. The English parliament conceded Carrickfergus and Coleraine but, anxious to avoid a conflict with the City of London, refused the Scots access to Derry.

The vast majority of the Ulster settlers sided with the Scots and the English parliament in their struggles against Charles I. Unusually, the mayor of Derry appears to have sided with the king:

> The said Mayor declared to a credible person that he would stand for the King to the uttermost of his power, for the Parliament was too strict with the King and disobedient. He likewise said, it being reported that the parliament were about to send more men to ly in garrison in the city of Londonderry, the Mayor replied, that had they come they should have been kept out.

On 13 June 1643, Sir Robert Stewart, along with some of the Londonderry garrison, defeated Owen Roe O'Neill at the Battle of Clones in County Monaghan. O'Neill, a nephew of the great Hugh O'Neill, had returned from exile on the Continent the previous year. He was now the leader of the Irish Catholic army in Ulster which, ambiguously, was also inclining towards support for the king. Throughout this period overcrowded refuge conditions prevailed in Derry but, despite claims to the contrary by many modern historians, no attack was made on the city by the Irish insurgents during the 1640s.

THE COMING OF PRESBYTERIANISM

In the 1630s John Bramhall, bishop of Derry and an extreme Laudian Anglican, had been vigorous in suppressing any signs of incipient Presbyterianism in Ulster. However, he fled Derry when the rebellion broke out, leaving the way clear for the non-conformists to organise. Although the city had been established by Londoners, the majority of the settlers by this stage appear to have been Scottish. In 1637 the surveyor general of customs estimated that the Scots in Londonderry were 'twenty to one for the English'. Presbyterianism was now formally introduced to the city in the wake of its arrival in Ulster with the Scottish forces under Monro.

In September 1643 the Solemn League and Covenant was concluded between the Scots and the English parliament with the intention of eliminating 'popery, prelacy and profaneness'. Earlier that year the Presbyterians of Londonderry, who appear to have been extremely numerous, applied to the General Assembly of the Church of Scotland to be sent a minister. On 24 April 1644, the Reverend William Adair and the Reverend John Weir, having visited several other Ulster towns, arrived in Derry. They were requested not to enter the city by the now controversial mayor, Robert Thornton, and the governor of the garrison, neither of whom were well disposed towards Presbyterianism.

This seems to have been a minority view, held only by some of the senior authorities in the city, as many of the ordinary people were

> but too much disposed to receive the Covenant. The town was full of factious and seditious persons, who had on former occasions tore the book of Common Prayer, and thrown libels about the streets, threatening everybody who should dare to use it; so that the Mayor, when he went to church, was forced to take a strong guard of English soldiers, of his own company, and plant them about the reader's desk, to secure himself from being insulted, and the book from being tore (as they threatened) before his face.

The ministers ignored the mayor's request but they were not allowed to preach in the cathedral on the following Sunday. They were offered the old Augustinian Abbey church but, because of the large crowds, they chose to preach outdoors in the market place. The ministers asked those who wished

> to enter into Covenant . . . [to lift up] their hands and countenances . . . which was done with many tears by the multitude there; and thereafter, prayer was performed with great solemnity and affection, both in speaker and hearers, wherein they owned God as their God, and gave up themselves to him. This was on the Lord's day [25 April]; and the Mayor and others coming from their sacrament, stood somewhat amazed, yet with reverence did behold what was adoing in the market-place.

On the following day the ministers were allowed access to the cathedral. Although clearly the dignitaries of the city had been opposed to the covenant, they were quickly forced by public opinion to accept it 'to save not the little was left but life itself, such is the violence of the people'. The ministers left Derry to preach in County Donegal but subsequently returned to the city. Eventually, Thornton had the covenant administered to him.

Patrick Adair, the Scottish Presbyterian minister who came to Ulster in 1646, in his *True Narrative of the Rise and Progress of the Presbyterian Church in Ireland,* describes the final events of this first coming of Presbyterianism to the city:

> The ministers, to close the work at Derry, did celebrate the Lord's Supper publicly in [St Columb's Cathedral], where the altar was removed, to give place to the Lord's Table, and God appeared most sensibly and comfortably in that administration, by the power of His Spirit on ministers and people. All things were done with as much order as was possible in such a case. No scandalous or unknown person was admitted and the gravest gentlemen in the town and regiments attended the tables.

The conversion of Mayor Thornton, a Royalist and 'bigoted abettor of prelacy', appears to have been very short-lived. At the General Assembly of the Church of Scotland in January 1645 a complaint was made against him that he had 'in public and official letters, maliciously slandered and otherwise injured' the Reverend John Burne, a Presbyterian minister sent to Derry. The charges against Thornton were considered so serious that the matter was referred to the Scottish and English parliaments. These were not the only complaints against the mayor. At the beginning of 1647 he was in London, explaining the state of his accounts – money allegedly used for the 'relief of poor distressed Protestants in Londonderry' – to parliament. Huge errors were detected and Thornton fled hastily back to Ireland. On 25 January 1647 the House of Commons ordered his arrest to answer for a discrepancy of over £27,500. Thornton, however, died before justice could catch up with him and a year later the House of Commons was still attempting to obtain compensation from his estate.

THE FIRST SIEGE OF DERRY

Throughout the 1640s Ireland, like Britain, was in political turmoil. A plethora of factions emerged in response to Irish events and issues. The situation was further complicated by a layer of differing and changing reactions and allegiances to the contemporary struggles in England and Scotland. So confused was the situation that individuals and groups occasionally appeared to change sides, and temporary alliances were formed almost in contradiction of what had been the case previously.

A seventeenth-century Bellarmine jug, found during the construction of an extension to the Apprentice Boys' Memorial Hall in Derry in the 1930s. These vessels were humorously so called, in Protestant criticism of the allegedly pot-bellied Cardinal Bellarmine, a leading figure in the Catholic counter-Reformation.

The events in Derry in the spring and summer of 1649 were a graphic illustration of these complexities.

The execution of Charles I in January 1649 opened up huge divisions among those who had formerly opposed the king. The Presbyterians of the north of Ireland were disgusted at the extreme radicalism of parliament and 'rose in arms' against the 'republicans', their former allies. At that time Londonderry was garrisoned with troops loyal to the English parliament, under the control of Sir Charles Coote, lord president of Ulster:

> But Sir Charles Coote, notwithstanding he had been seemingly forward before for the Presbytery, and had concurred with them, and was sworn a ruling-elder in Derry, now finding things going in another channel in England, altogether refused to declare against that party in England . . . Upon this, animosities arose between him and those of the army and country there, who had renewed the Covenant and subscribed the same declaration which was subscribed in Down and Antrim by the council of war. And on this occasion the officers there, who had taken the Covenant and declaration, had drawn together some other forces to the fields . . . But Sir Charles sent out a party from Derry and Coleraine, and drew together a considerable number of persons at the rendezvous near Derry. Upon which Sir Alexander Stewart marched towards Derry with his regiment and sat down before it. Others, really affected, joined with him, so that the city was surprised and brought to straits.

Hostilities began at the end of March 1649 as the Presbyterian forces took over the villages and strong points surrounding the city in order to prevent supplies reaching the republican garrison. There were skirmishes throughout April and on 23 April Coote successfully defeated the Presbyterians of the Laggan district in east Donegal at Carrigans, capturing 'a good store of arms' and taking prisoners, some of whom he later exchanged for food. The incident was so important a morale booster that an account of it was soon afterwards published in London with the paradoxical title of *A bloody fight in Ireland, and a great victory obtained by Sir Charles Coote . . . against the British forces of the Lagan.*

At the end of April, Coote ordered the houses outside the walls of the city to be levelled and the trees and other obstructions removed. On 5 May the Laggan forces laid close siege to the city, entrenching themselves within cannon shot. A number of skirmishes took place – one on 13 May at the Gallows Strand, just south of the city, and another on 15 May in the Bogside. On both occasions the besiegers suffered defeat. On 26 May reinforcements arrived for the besiegers but these included 'numbers of the old royalists and prelatical faction, [who] sowed dissension among the besiegers, by discountenancing those who were attached to the Covenant, and [by] endeavouring to monopolise the management of the siege'. On the same day a convoy sent out from the forces in the city to obtain support from their parliamentary allies in

Dublin captured two boats laden with food supplies and shortly after this, another ship arrived from England with two hundred men and supplies of wheat. The besieged garrison was thus well supplied.

Outside the walls the situation was further complicated when more reinforcements arrived, which comprised a party of Catholic Scottish Highlanders and a body of 'confederate' Catholic Irish who had only recently thrown in their lot with the Royalist Marquis of Ormond. The Presbyterians were beginning to find themselves in an uneasy minority among the besiegers and they could see their situation being exploited by the old-style Royalists. On their behalf, Lord Montgomery of the Ards went to see Sir Charles Coote in Derry but no agreement was reached. Montgomery, however, proved to be an ambiguous supporter of the Presbyterians. Apparently his discussions in the city with Coote had been aided by a certain amount of alcoholic refreshment. On Montgomery's return to the besiegers' camp, somewhat loose-tongued he declared, in the presence of some shocked Presbyterians: 'If Coote would engage for monarchical government in the person of the present King [the dethroned Charles II], the devil take him that meddles with religion; let God fight for his own religion himself.'

Charles-Fort, on the west bank of the River Foyle, just north of Derry, built about July 1649 during the first siege of Derry, as shown on Francis Nevill's 1690 map

The uneasy coalition outside the walls survived but with considerable mutual suspicion. The siege continued with occasional sallies by the garrison from inside the walls. Captain Finch, within the city, kept a diary of the events:

> June 8th. The enemy in one night built an incredible piece of work, within almost musket-shot of our town, upon the top of the hill on the way to Ballymackrooty [Ballymagroarty]; the lord-president [Coote] destroyed it next day after a sharp skirmish, and challenged the leaguer [besieging army] to come out and fight him.
> June 13th. A new fort, which we were building at the Windmill, was near finished: but was thrown down by the enemy this night: the wind being high, he was not discovered till done . . .
>
> After three months' siege there is not one sick or feeble body among us, and now in a better condition than the first day of the siege: our greatest want is and will be firing, there being no other firing than old houses, and trees got out of orchards; for we suppose provisions will be plentifully sent us by the parliament.

On 11 July further help came to the besiegers, including twelve pieces of field ordnance. Around this time a gun emplacement, with eleven pieces of artillery, was built, commanding the river channel between Culmore and the city, near to where the boom of the 1689 siege was to be built. It was pointedly named Charles-Fort. Coote ordered a 'parliamentary' frigate which had been operating in Lough Foyle to attack the fort, but the ship had no success. On 26 July, Montgomery, who now held a commission from the dethroned Charles II, returned to the siege with a considerable additional force. He summoned the city to surrender but was refused. Two days later Montgomery attacked the city but suffered greater losses than those inside. On the same day, 28 July, two ships sailed in from the lough to attack Charles-Fort, but the wind subsided, leaving them adrift. By this stage the Presbyterians in the besieging force were convinced that their position was in as much danger from their erstwhile allies, the Royalists under Montgomery, as from the 'enemy' Coote inside the city. On 29 July many Presbyterian soldiers began to abandon the siege. A supporter of Montgomery's wrote:

> Our viscount and general, was hopefull to reduce that important place to his majesty's obedience. The fault was not in his lordship, but in those Lag[g]an men; who no sooner knew of his lordship having accepted a commission from the King without their kirk-pastors' leave, and that he would no longer admit their ministers into his councils, nor walk by their advice, than the whole gang or crew of them deserted the siege and his lordship, they all at once disbanding themselves with one text of Scripture, 'to your tents O Israel'.

The depleted forces continued the siege. A few days later some of Coote's men sallied out of the city and burned several villages in the Laggan area. For some time Owen Roe O'Neill had been trying to organise a mutually beneficial arrangement with the forces in Ireland loyal to parliament. Although Coote's father, one of the original Ulster settlers, had been killed by native Irish Catholics at the beginning of the rebellion, the republican leader now found it expedient to make approaches to the Irish commander to try to obtain assistance for the relief of Derry. The first attempt at an alliance failed but Coote, arguing that God sometimes made 'use of wicked instruments to bring about good design', tried again. Towards the end of July, O'Neill, with three hundred horse and four thousand foot soldiers, marched northwards and successfully drove off the besieging forces, 'who did not expect to see the Roman Catholic party leagued with the republicans in opposing the royalists'. The city was relieved on 8 August and O'Neill entered Derry, where he was entertained by Coote. The siege had lasted twenty weeks. One week later Oliver Cromwell landed in Ireland and eventually the whole country was subdued by the 'republicans'.

Owen Roe O'Neill, who in 1642 returned from exile on the Continent to lead the Irish Catholic army in Ulster. He brought about the end of the first siege of Derry in 1649 by relieving the parliamentary forces being blockaded inside the walls by Presbyterian and Royalist forces. (Armagh County Museum)

RESTORATION

The tiny city of Londonderry gradually returned to normal after the turbulent events of the 1640s. Cromwell issued a new charter to the city on 24 March 1656, but this in turn was replaced by another charter granted by Charles II on 10 April 1662, following his restoration. This document is the only charter to survive in the city's own archives. The census carried out by Sir William Petty in 1659 lists the population inside the city as 586, of which 369 were English and Scottish and the

The decorated initial 'C' of Charles II's Charter of Londonderry, granted on 10 April 1662 (Eason and Son)

remainder were apparently native Irish. Immediately outside the walls there were another 110 English and Scottish and 78 Irish. Among the most interesting residents of the city around this time was George Farquhar, one of the Restoration dramatists. Farquhar is said to have been the son of the rector of Lissan in County Tyrone and it appears that he was born in Londonderry in 1677 because 'his mother had removed [there] for the sake of superior medical assistance, as was then usual with the ladies of the neighbourhood on the approach of their confinement'. Farquhar also received some of his early education at the Free School in the city, before going to Trinity College Dublin.

In 1668 there was a major fire in Londonderry which caused a great deal of damage. From 1673 onwards the minute books of the corporation record many of the minor day-to-day events in the city. Also available from the second half of the century are the registers of St Columb's Cathedral, which detail many of the domestic events in the city such as births, marriages and deaths, at the same time providing information about the variety of tradesmen and shopkeepers who lived and worked there. The city was by no means prosperous but the population did start to grow again and by the end of 1688 it was approximately two thousand. This small colonial city, still wholly contained within its seventy-year-old walls, was about to undergo the greatest challenge since its foundation.

Restoration dramatist George Farquhar, said to be born in Derry in 1677 and educated at the Free School in the city (National Library of Ireland)

Richard Talbot was created Earl of Tyrconnell by James II in June 1685. The king's policies for Ireland were greatly influenced by Talbot, who in June 1686 was made commander of the army in Ireland. (National Portrait Gallery, London)

7

'NO SURRENDER' THE SIEGE OF 1688–9

The crisis known as the Siege of Derry began as a purely local event. However, because of the dramatic circumstances of the time, it acquired a wider significance as part of the War of the Two Kings in Ireland, the Glorious Revolution in Britain and, some would say, the War of the League of Augsburg in continental Europe. Historians have argued about whether or not it was a siege in the strict sense of the word, citing the technicalities of military operations in support of their opinions. Technically, it probably was not a siege. However, what is certain is that for several months the citizens heroically held out against the forces of James II, and won for themselves a reputation which has continued to influence life and politics in the city down to the present day.

When Charles II died in February 1685, he was succeeded by his brother James II, a devout convert to Catholicism. James's policies for Ireland were greatly influenced by Richard Talbot, who was created Earl of Tyrconnell by the king in June 1685. In June 1686 Tyrconnell was made commander of the king's army in Ireland and when he was appointed lord deputy the following year, he quickly set about replacing the overwhelmingly Protestant civil and military establishment, so that by 1688 the army was almost completely Catholic. As part of these reforms, the charters of various cities and towns, including Londonderry, were cancelled and new ones, giving Catholics a greater role in the affairs of the corporations, were issued by James. The all-Protestant corporation in Derry put up a strong resistance to this change. James later commented that he had received little opposition on this matter 'except at Londonderry (a stubborn people as they afterwards appeared) who stood an obstinate suit but were forced at last to undergo the same fate with the rest'.

The Derry charter was changed on 3 August 1687 and a new corporation, with a predominantly Catholic membership, was appointed to run the affairs of the city. It is not certain if the new mayor, Cormack

View of Derry from the north-west, *c.* 1685, by Thomas Phillips, a leading military engineer. One street in the foreground (probably the later Fahan Street) can be seen crossing the Bogside, and to the right the windmill, which was later to play an important role in the siege of 1689, is visible. St Columb's Cathedral (centre), shown without a spire, is probably exaggerated in scale. (British Library, London)

O'Neill, was himself Catholic, although his wife definitely was. There was still a substantial number of Protestants in the corporation, among them several who were to figure in the dramatic events of the coming years. For example, Henry Campsie, later to become a leader of the 'apprentice boys', was a burgess of James's corporation. The council was described by one unsympathetic contemporary as a collection of 'brogue-makers! butchers! raps! and such as these'. No records of its deliberations have survived but it is very unlikely that it was able to influence events in the city. The cancellation of the charter granted to the city by Charles II was not subsequently recognised in Derry, and this document continued to be the basis of its municipal government until the local government reforms of the nineteenth century.

CLOSING THE GATES

At the beginning of the winter of 1688, Derry was defended by a garrison containing some of the few remaining Protestant troops in the Irish army. The regiment was commanded by Lord Mountjoy, William Stewart from Ramelton in County Donegal. Among its officers was Lieutenant Colonel Robert Lundy, a Scottish Protestant married to an Irish woman. The citizens thought of these troops as their principal

William Stewart, Lord Mountjoy, who was in charge of the garrison at Derry in November 1688 (National Trust)

protection against attack by the Catholics of the surrounding districts. Fear of attack was widespread and there were rumours of an impending uprising. Suddenly, Tyrconnell ordered Mountjoy and his men to leave Derry for Dublin. The lord deputy intended that the Protestant garrison, which he was sending to England as support for James, should be replaced by the Catholic troops being assembled by the Earl of Antrim. Antrim's troops were to be ready by 20 November but he had difficulty finding the six-foot-tall men he wanted for his regiment. The new garrison was not prepared when Mountjoy's men left Derry on 23 November. Mayor Cormack O'Neill was absent from the city and so the deputy mayor, John Buchanan (a Protestant), was in charge.

The city was rife with suspicion. There was considerable fear that a re-enactment of the events of 1641 and a massacre of Protestants was imminent. In England the situation was unstable: William of Orange had landed in Devon and was on his way to London. James's throne was far from secure. Several public meetings were held in Derry at which the plight of the city was debated and one of the chief participants was David Cairns, a lawyer, who argued that the citizens should form their own garrison and defend Derry themselves.

Meanwhile, at the beginning of December, at Comber in County Down, an anonymous letter was found addressed to a local Protestant gentlemen:

> I have written to you to let you know, that all our Irish men through Ireland is sworn, that on the ninth day of this month, they are to fall on to kill and murder, man, wife, and child . . . for whosoever of them can kill any of you, they are to have a captain's place . . . give other noblemen warning, and go not out either night or day without a good guard with you, and let no Irish man come near you, whatsoever he be.

Contemporary Dutch print of William of Orange landing in England, 5 November 1688 (Ulster Museum)

Similar letters were found in other places in Ulster but they were all hoaxes, designed to fuel an already tense situation. No evidence of any intention to organise such a massacre has ever come to light but the fear that it was about to happen brought about its own repercussions.

News of the Comber letter spread quickly throughout Ulster, arriving in Derry on 6 December. By that day, Antrim's Redshanks, as the Catholic troops were known, had arrived at Limavady on their way to the city. There were over 1,200 soldiers, accompanied by a large camp following of women and boys. The next morning, Friday 7 December (18 December according to the revised calendar), an advance party arrived on the bank of the River Foyle opposite the city. Two officers were ferried across to negotiate the entry arrangements. The warrant which they had brought with them had not been signed properly, and this gave the city sheriffs the opportunity to delay the admission of the Catholic troops. By this time the streets of Derry were filled with excited, fearful citizens, anxiously discussing what would happen. Many of the more radical, younger people argued that the gates should be shut against the Catholic forces. Although the older citizens counselled caution, many of them secretly agreed with the young townsmen.

About midday, the waiting troops decided to cross the river and began to move up towards the adjacent Ferry Gate, 'but just as the soldiers were approaching the gates, the youthhood by a strange impulse ran in one body and shut the gates, and put themselves in the best posture of defence they could'. Thirteen 'resolute apprentice boys', realising that the moment of decision had arrived, forced the not-too-reluctant guard to hand over the city keys and then rushed to raise

Ferryquay Gate, *c.* 1913. It was a predecessor of this gate which was shut against the Earl of Antrim's soldiers by the 'apprentice boys' on 7 December 1688. (Green Collection, Ulster Folk and Transport Museum)

the drawbridge and close the Ferry Gate in the face of the oncoming soldiers, minutes before they would have entered the city. The apprentice boys closed the other three gates in order to fully secure the city. A shouted threat that a cannon was to be trained on the waiting Catholic soldiers outside the walls sent them running back to the ferry and over to the opposite side of the river.

These events were to have a profound historic significance, sometimes in the least expected of places. In 1989, during the three-hundredth anniversary of the siege, a Sinn Féin spokesman was quoted as describing the action of the original apprentice boys as 'an act of truly revolutionary self-determination which can only be admired'. Indeed, it is difficult not to see, in the impetuous but momentous actions of those Protestant youths, some parallels with the more recent events of 1969, when, as in the late seventeenth century, some of the young people of Derry barricaded their part of the city against the approach of the 'security forces' of their day. Ironically, the 1969 action, this time by Catholic youths, came about during the annual Protestant celebration of the siege of 1689.

'TO STAND UPON OUR GUARD'

In December 1688 there were mixed feelings in Derry about the action of the young men. The two Catholic officers, still inside the walls, and the

Dr Ezekial Hopkins, bishop of Derry in 1688 (from Philip Dwyer, *The Siege of Derry in 1689*)

deputy mayor ordered that the ammunition magazine, located at the old medieval towerhouse at the north-west corner of the city, should be secured. However, they were outmanoeuvred by the apprentice boys, who hurried to take it first. The guard was a Catholic called Linegar and he fired at the group, wounding Henry Campsie in the arm, which further inflamed the atmosphere. The crowd seized Linegar and imprisoned him. Several members of the town's establishment, including the deputy mayor and the two sheriffs, pleaded with the crowd to undo the damage before it was too late. The debate continued for the rest of the day and that evening a meeting was held in the town hall. Again the deputy mayor and other speakers said that the troops should be admitted. Bishop Ezekial Hopkins warned the crowd that James was still their lawful king and that they would bring havoc on themselves if they persisted in this rebellion against his troops. Having failed to influence matters, Dr Hopkins left the city the following day. He never returned.

The shutting of the gates (Stained-glass window, St Columb's Cathedral, Derry)

Other people were also leaving Derry but were being replaced by large numbers of Protestants coming in from the surrounding districts. Some members of the corporation, along with David Cairns, met to plan the defence of the city but it was realised that there was a shortage of arms and at most about five hundred men capable of using them. However, all were called on to play a role. As one participant, Captain Ashe, observed, 'each sex and age joined in the important cause'.

The Earl of Antrim approached Derry on Sunday 9 December and sent George Phillips of Limavady ahead as a messenger. Phillips, unbeknown to the earl, actually sided with the citizens. Initially, to protect his cover, Phillips was taken mock prisoner in Derry, but shortly

David Cairns, one of the leading activists in Derry during the early stages of the siege crisis (Derry City Council)

afterwards the keys of the city were given to him and he was restored to the position of governor of Londonderry, a post he had formerly held under Charles II. A message was sent to Lord Antrim warning him that he dare not try to enter the city. Support continued to arrive in Derry and Cairns formed the men into six companies. Meanwhile, a ship was being prepared to take Cairns, with a letter outlining the situation, to

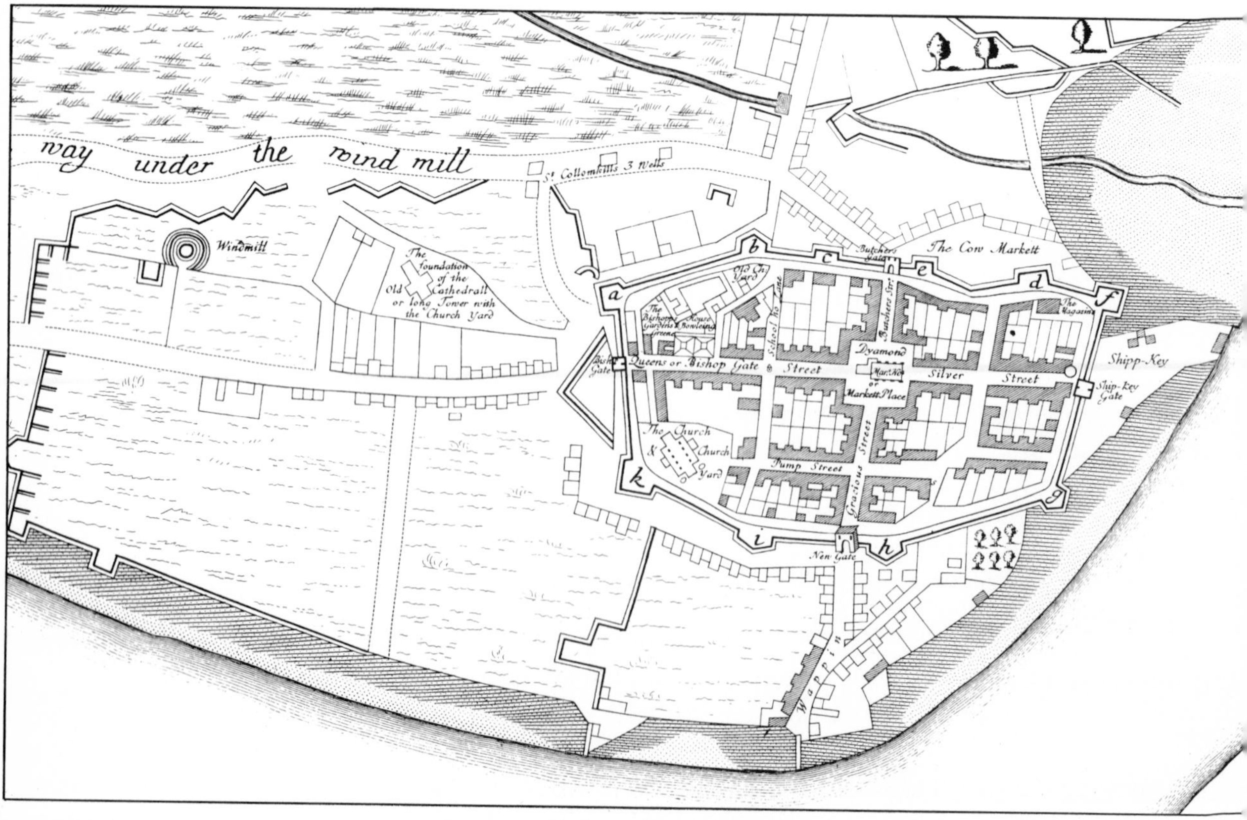

Detail from Francis Nevill's 1690 map of the Siege of Derry. The Ferryquay Gate is labelle 'New Gate'. This map is important as it provides the most complete impression of the remai of the medieval Tempull Mór (to the left of the walled city), here described as 'the Old Cathedrall or long Tower'.

the Irish Society in London. The letter was a model of diplomacy: on the one hand, distancing the local establishment from the actions of the youths, while on the other hand, admitting that they 'blessed God for our present escape, effected by means unforeseen, and against our wills'. A similar letter was sent to Lord Mountjoy in Dublin. The Catholics remaining in the city and a 'convent of Dominican friars' were ordered to leave and a declaration on behalf of the 'Gentlemen of Derry' issued, stating that

> it pleased God, who watches over us, so to order things, that when [the Redshanks] were ready to enter the city, a great number of the younger, and some of the meaner sort of the inhabitants ran happily to the gates and shut them, loudly denying entrance to such guests, and obstinately refusing obedience to us. At first we were amazed at the enterprise, and apprehensive of the many ill circumstances and consequences, that might result from so rash an undertaking; but since that . . . we began to consider it as an especial instance of God's mercy towards us, that we were not delivered over as a prey unto them and that it pleased him to stir up the spirits of the people so unexpectedly to provide for their and our common safety, and preservation: Wherefore we do declare and remonstrate to the world, that as we have resolved to stand upon our guard, and to defend our walls, and not to admit of any Papist whatsoever to quarter amongst us, so we have determined to persevere in our duty and loyalty to our sovereign lord the king.

Paradoxically, in view of what was to happen in the coming months, the declaration goes on to repeat the assertion of loyalty to James, eschewing 'the least breach of mutiny, or seditious opposition to his royal commands'.

NEGOTIATIONS

Lord Mountjoy's regiment had scarcely reached Dublin when news of the events in Derry reached the capital. Tyrconnell immediately ordered Mountjoy to return and within days he was back in Ulster. He presented himself outside the city on 12 December but despite his excellent reputation among the Protestants of Derry and the fact that two of his sons were inside the walls, the regiment was not admitted. Mountjoy insisted that James would protect the citizens but they felt that by now the king was not able to protect even himself. Negotiations were opened and on 21 December an agreement was signed by Mountjoy and representatives of the city, which provided for, among other things, the total withdrawal of Antrim's men and the admission of an all-Protestant garrison. Robert Lundy was given the governorship. Mountjoy returned to Dublin and Tyrconnell deviously sent him to France, where he was imprisoned by the authorities as a traitor to James.

As soon as the gates had been shut the old corporation of Charles II's

The proclamation of William III and Mary II in London on 13 February 1689 (Ulster Museum)

charter began to operate again. It called the first meeting of its common council on 2 January 1689 and confirmed the former mayor, John Campsie, in office. James's Catholic corporation disappeared into oblivion. A committee was set up to collect money for the purchase of arms and an agent dispatched to Scotland to buy them. Other supplies were gathered into the city and letters of appeal were sent to William and Mary, who in February 1689 were proclaimed king and queen in London. Fears of a general Irish uprising lessened in the first few months of 1689 but by then Tyrconnell's forces, led by Lieutenant General Richard Hamilton, were marching on Ulster, determined to reduce the Williamite supporters to submission.

Lundy's position in Derry was very delicate. He was a commissioned officer in Tyrconnell's army, which was still loyal to the deposed king, James, but he was also a Protestant, surrounded in Derry by a populace and citizen garrison which had by this time thrown in its lot with the Glorious Revolution and the succession of William and Mary to the throne. Lundy's need to walk a tightrope between the various conflicting demands on him explains how many of his actions could be interpreted subsequently as treachery by Ulster Protestants.

David Cairns, representing the citizens of Derry, reached London and through the influence of the Irish Society secured an interview with William. The king dispatched the ship *Deliverance* with supplies and instructions for the defence of Derry and a new commission, as governor, for Lundy. The ship, captained by James Hamilton, paradoxically a nephew of Jacobite Richard Hamilton, escorted by the frigate *Jersey*, arrived in Derry on 21 March. Before Lundy was handed the commission he was required to take an oath of allegiance to the new sovereigns. He did this privately but subsequently he refused to repeat the oath in public, giving rise to suspicion about his loyalties. On 22 March there was a ceremony in Derry to publicly proclaim the coronation of William and Mary. Lundy took part in this ceremony; on the surface, at least, he had defected to the Williamite cause.

Cairns returned from London on 10 April, bringing with him additional expressions of support and the promise of help from the new king. Later that night a 'council of war' was held and elaborate preparations decided on for the further defence of Derry on behalf of William and Mary. The following resolution was also adopted:

> We, the officers hereunto subscribing, pursuant to a resolution taken, and agreed upon at a Council of War at Londonderry held this day, do hereby mutually promise and engage, to stand by each other with our forces against the common enemy, and will not leave the kingdom, nor desert the public service, until our affairs are in a settled and secure posture. And if any of us shall do the contrary, the person so leaving the kingdom, or deserting the service without consent of a Council of War, is to be deemed a coward, and disaffected to their Majesties' service, and the Protestant interest. Dated the 10th of April, 1689.

Robert Lundy was among the signatories.

The original local circumstances in which the emergency began had now disappeared. Instead, the defence of Derry had evolved into a national and even international issue. Measures were to be taken to stem the flow of men out of the city. It was subsequently alleged that Lundy, believing that the city could not hold out against an attack by the Jacobite forces, had allowed, and possibly even encouraged, some to leave. To counteract this defeatism, a pair of gallows were to be erected on the double bastion at the south-west corner of the city for the execution of mutineers and traitors. These decisions were popularly received by the citizens when they were published the following day, but the excitement was soon muted by the news that the mayor had died. On 13 April, at the common council, Gervais Squire was appointed as the new mayor. This was the last meeting of this body until after the siege.

THE JACOBITES APPROACH

A small Jacobite force under Richard Hamilton had been successful in bringing the eastern parts of Ulster under its control. While this was happening Derry's importance as a refuge and Protestant rallying point continued to grow. On 13 April, Hamilton's troops appeared for the first time near the city, advancing on the opposite side of the River Foyle on their way from Coleraine to the crossing points further south at Strabane and Clady. A cannon was fired at the city but caused little damage. On the same day the Reverend George Walker, Anglican rector of Donoughmore in County Tyrone, arrived in the city with news

The Reverend George Walker, rector of Donoughmore, County Tyrone, joint governor of Derry during the siege. He was killed at the Battle of the Boyne in July 1690.

that other Jacobite forces were heading in great numbers towards Derry. This was the main Jacobite army from Dublin under the French general, Rosen, which had been accompanied as far as Omagh by James himself.

James had fled to France at the end of 1688, but Tyrconnell begged him to come to Ireland to take charge of the campaign. As one military historian Captain J. A. Read, put it: 'When a man's last card is being played the man himself should be present.' Reluctantly, James sailed for Ireland and landed in Kinsale, County Cork, on 12 March. He was accompanied by a contingent of English, Irish and Scottish supporters. A number of French generals and artillery experts were also part of the expedition and James was attended by a special ambassador of Louis XIV, the Comte d'Avaux. A continuous series of dispatches on the situation in Derry was sent to Louis and his minister of war, the Marquis de Louvois, in Versailles.

THE ROUT AT THE PASSES

On the same day that Hamilton's troops had been sighted near Derry, Lundy, who was being accused of prevaricating, called another council of war. It decided unanimously that

> on Monday next [15 April], by 10 of the clock, all officers and soldiers of horse, dragoons and foot, and all other armed men whatsoever of our forces and friends, inlisted or not inlisted that can and will fight for their

The Marquis de Louvois, chief minister and minister of war to Louis XIV, king of France (Alliance Française)

> country and religion, against popery, shall appear on the fittest ground, near Clady-ford, Lifford, and Long Causey, as shall be near their several and respective quarters; there to draw up in battalions to be ready to fight the enemy, and to preserve our lives and all that is dear to us, from them.

The locations chosen were the strategic 'passes', which if held would keep the Jacobites from advancing on Derry. All men in the surrounding area, from sixteen to sixty years of age, were ordered to assemble for the confrontation and it was estimated that between seven thousand and ten thousand gathered on the Williamite side. Again, there were many accusations that Lundy did not move swiftly enough and Hamilton's force of less than one thousand was able to cross the river. A few miles downstream Rosen's advance troops also managed to cross and the Protestant defenders were forced into a disorderly retreat to Derry.

The impact on the morale of the Protestants was considerable and again most of the blame, rightly or wrongly, was heaped on Lundy. Correspondingly, the Jacobites were jubilant and now believed that the capture of Derry was a foregone conclusion. Lundy was among the first to reach the walled city and once inside, although many troops had yet to return, he ordered that the gates be closed. In defence of this action he later stated that he was anxious to save the limited provisions from the general rabble of refugees that was flooding into Derry. George

Nineteenth-century engraving of Jacobite troops advancing on Derry

Walker claimed that as many as thirty thousand people were crowded inside the walls at the beginning of the siege proper. It is extremely difficult to imagine how so many people could have fitted into so small a space as the fortified area was only about five hundred yards long by, at its greatest, three hundred yards wide. Nevertheless, it is certain that throughout the crisis the city was vastly overcrowded. Many troops returning from the defeat at the passes could not gain admission into the city and, among others, George Walker and his regiment were forced to wait outside overnight.

It was not only the Jacobites who believed that Derry was about to be taken. On the day of the débâcle at Lifford, two regiments sent from England by William arrived in Lough Foyle. The commanders came into Derry on the following day and a council of war was held in the town hall. Complaints were made afterwards that this meeting was attended by career soldiers rather than the leaders of the citizen army, whose zeal to defend Derry to the end was much greater than that of their more cautious professional colleagues. Lundy was the first to speak, painting a depressing picture of a city about to fall to the enemy. His views were echoed, almost unanimously, and finally a statement agreed that

> considering the present circumstance of affairs and the likelihood the enemy will soon possess themselves of this place, it is thought most convenient, that the principal officers shall privately withdraw themselves, as well for their own preservation, as in the hopes that the inhabitants by a timely capitulation, may make terms the better with the enemy.

The two English regiments set sail, taking several of the leading officers of the town with them. When rumours of what was happening reached the citizens, they believed that they had been betrayed and threatened to hang Lundy and his council. George Walker and Henry Baker, out of 'respect for his person', arranged for Lundy to escape from the city in disguise carrying 'a load of match on his back'. Another tradition claims that he fled from the city by climbing down a pear tree which grew beside the city walls. This tree was something of a local monument until it fell in a gale in 1844. He left on the very day that James presented himself in person before the city. Whether or not Lundy was the traitor that Ulster Protestant tradition perceives him to be, using his name as a synonym for treachery, or the pessimist and defeatist that less partisan historians have judged him, will no doubt continue to be debated. Although he escaped the wrath of the defenders of Londonderry in 1689, for the past two centuries at least their descendants have executed his effigy at the annual ceremony in the city marking the anniversary of the closing of the gates. Lundy himself reached Scotland but was arrested and imprisoned in the Tower of London. He was later released and went on to achieve glory against the French at Gibraltar.

Nineteenth-century cartoon of James II outside the walls of Derry, 18 April 1689

'THE KING MUST GO TO LONDONDERRY'

It was essential for James to secure the north of Ireland before he could cross to Britain and attempt to regain his throne. He conceded to the advice of d'Avaux to send a strong army, along with the French commanders, to support the forces of Richard Hamilton, who was already operating successfully in Ulster. Against d'Avaux's advice, however, James decided to accompany the army. He had reached Omagh on 14 April but was then persuaded to turn back towards Dublin, having heard rumours that a large English fleet was bound for Derry. On the morning of 17 April, James, then at Charlemont in County Armagh, received a letter from his illegitimate son, the duke of Berwick, describing the Jacobite successes at Lifford. The duke believed, as did many others, that should the king himself go to Derry, then the city would have no choice but to surrender. D'Avaux did not agree, and writing prophetically to Louis, he promised that he would

> do [his] utmost . . . to hinder the King of England from going to Londonderry, for [he was] persuaded that if [the defenders] are seized by terror, the presence of his Brittanic Majesty will be unnecessary, and if they defend themselves, the King of England will not be in a position to subdue them, and must retire shamefully.

However, others advised that 'the king must go to Londonderry' and so

Henry Baker, appointed joint governor of Derry, along with George Walker, in April 1689. He died three months later on 30 June. (Courtesy of St Columb's Cathedral)

James set off immediately for the city. As J. G. Simms has pointed out, the journey to Derry demonstrated the combination of physical energy and mental lethargy that characterised the fifty-six-year-old king. He rode all day on 17 April and early the next morning arrived at Derry. Negotiations had already started between the Jacobites and the defenders, and it was agreed to give those inside the walls a respite until noon that day so that they could make a decision. In the meantime, no Jacobite troops were to come close to the city.

James, apparently, was not aware of this restriction and advanced 'with flying colours' to the strand at the south end of the island of Derry. The impulsive defenders on the walls immediately began firing and several members of James's own party were killed. Allegedly, the Ulster Protestant cry of 'no surrender' could be heard above the gunfire. James retired a little but spent the rest of the day sitting despondently on his horse, in the rain, awaiting developments. Towards evening, with no sign of a surrender, he moved to quarters in the small plantation castle at Mongavlin, about ten miles south of Derry. Negotiations continued and the council of war even sent an apology to James. However, against the advice of their less radical leaders, the citizens were adamant. They wrote to James:

> The cause we have undertaken, we design for ever to maintain; and question not, but that powerful providence which has hitherto been our guardian, will finish the protection of us, against all your attempts, and give a happy issue to our arms. We must let you know, that King William is as capable of rewarding our loyalty as King James; and an English parliament can be just as bountiful to our courage and suffering as an Irish one: and that in time we question not, but your lands will be forfeited rather than ours, and confiscated into our possession, as a recompense of this signal service to the crown of England.

There would be no surrender. James made four attempts to change the defenders' minds, but without success.

It is one of the most extraordinary paradoxes of the long history of Derry that there can have been few more truly republican acts committed by any of its citizens, past or present, than this defiance of the actual person of James, their sovereign lord according to the doctrine of 'divine right'.

THE SIEGE BEGINS

After Lundy had left the city a new governor had to be appointed. Adam Murray, one of the defenders most determined to prevent a surrender, was initially offered the post. He refused, preferring to play the more active role of a soldier. Eventually Henry Baker and the Reverend George Walker were appointed joint governors, although in the aftermath of the siege there was some debate about the level of authority conferred on Walker. The citizen garrison now set about reorganising the defences, dividing the 7,500 men available into eight regiments, each of which was assigned a section of the city to guard and the council of war issued a set of directions for soldiers and citizens alike. Earlier in the year, a ravelin, or defensive earthwork, had been built by Lundy outside the Bishop Gate and now other similar outworks were constructed. Trees, and even houses, outside the walls were cleared to deny cover for any attempted approach by the enemy. Two guns were mounted on the tower of the cathedral, the highest structure in the city, and some eighteen others were deployed along the city walls. Guns were also trained internally, along the main streets at the four gates, in case the enemy should break in. A new grain mill was constructed inside the walls, as those outside were either in enemy hands or could not be used without danger.

Previous religious and political differences between local Anglicans and Presbyterians were now laid aside and both denominations shared the cathedral for their acts of worship. The senior officers in the city were Anglican, while the junior officers were a mixture of Anglican and

'Roaring Meg' on the city walls, one of the cannon used during the siege, and so named because of its thunderous report when fired. The cannon later acquired the status of an icon for the Protestants of Ulster. (Green Collection, Ulster Folk and Transport Museum)

Presbyterian. However, it has been estimated that less than one in ten, or even one in fifteen, of the ordinary soldiers and people in the town during the siege were Anglican. George Walker, himself an Anglican minister, invited the Reverend John Mackenzie, a Presbyterian, to act as chaplain to the non-conforming members of the governor's own regiment. Differences of opinion about the relative importance of the roles of the two denominations during the crisis would emerge between these two men when the siege was over.

The number of Jacobite troops outside the walls has been disputed by historians. Some estimate that the number of men surrounding the city was less than those inside the walls, others insist that a total of twenty thousand Jacobites besieged the city over the entire period of the siege, although at any one time there were considerably fewer than that number actually engaged in the conflict. The Jacobites were encamped on the hills above the city on both sides of the river. Their lines eventually stretched from the south end of the island of Derry to the old fort at Culmore, four miles downstream, commanding the narrow channel before the river opens out into Lough Foyle.

Placenames that became known internationally in the 1970s and

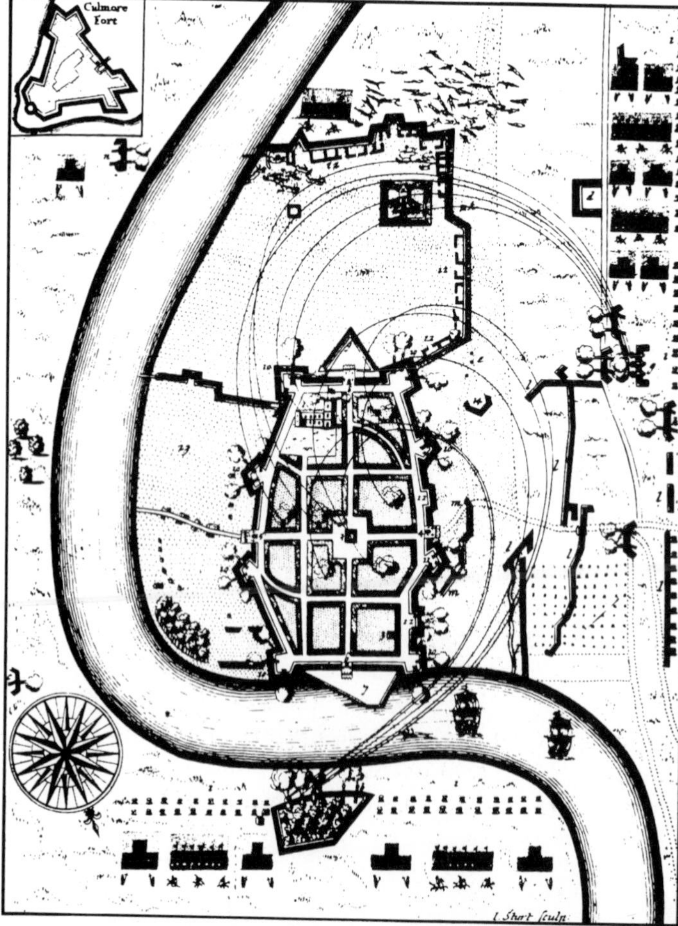

Contemporary stylised map of the Siege of Derry, showing trajectories of mortar bombs and cannon balls fired into the city from the direction of the Waterside and Creggan

Nineteenth-century engraving of Pennyburn Mill, the scene of a major skirmish on 21 April 1689

1980s figure prominently in reports of the siege: Creggan, Bogside, Pennyburn, Waterside and others are frequently mentioned in the contemporary accounts. The defences at these positions were recorded in great detail on a map made by Captain Francis Nevill, who inspected the remains of the Jacobite camps after the siege had ended. Nevill, who had served on the side of the defenders, also described how many of the Jacobite troops built sod huts, sunk four or five feet into the earth for protection, in the absence of proper tents. A number of early Christian ringforts in the locality were also used as fortifications by the besiegers.

No proper siege guns or machinery were available to the Jacobites. They were forced instead to use mortar bombs, fired high into the air, which fell and damaged the upper floors of the houses but left the city walls and defences intact. One estimate suggests that no more than eight cannon were available to the besiegers, the largest of which was a twenty-four pounder, and consequently these guns had to be moved several times throughout the siege period. The defenders reckoned that almost six hundred 'bombs' were fired at the city. The first shots came from Captain Stronge's orchard on the east bank of the river, directly opposite the Ship Quay Gate, but from 24 April until 4 May only about thirty shots were fired. The guns were quiet again until 2 June, but on the following day the firing began in earnest, continuing intermittently until 13 June. The bombardment began again on 21 June, but this time the firing came from the hills to the west of the city, from the direction of Creggan. Sporadic firing continued for a month, but during the last week of the siege, at the end of July, innumerable 'bombs' continuously rained down on the city.

Besides the use of mortars in this way, the besiegers were generally content to blockade the city, hoping to starve and tire the garrison into submission. However, a number of specific clashes did occur. The first encounter took place on Sunday 21 April when the defenders sallied out of the city to take on the Jacobites who had occupied the area around Pennyburn. The besieging troops were badly beaten and Maumont, the

The Number of Bombs thrown into the City of London-Derry, *ſince the beginning of the Siege.*

	Big	Small
April 24.		3
April 25.		3
April 27.		18
From *April* the 27*th* till the 4*th* of *May*, at ſeveral times		6
June 2.	3	1
June 3.	28	
June 4.	37	
June 5.	21	
June 6.	39	
June 7.	6	
June 8.	36	
June 11.		28
June 13.	26	
June 21.		21
June 24.	6	
June 27.	13	
June 28.	22	
June 29.	10	
July 2.		12
July 3.		28
July 4.	14	
July 5.	3	6
July 6.	5	0
July 7.		18
July 8. and tenth		24
July 11.		4
July 14.		18
July 15.		24
July 16.		16
July 17.		14
July 18.		12
July 19.		22
July 21. 28		28
	261	326
Total	587	

Memorandum that one of the great Bombs being brought to the Scale did weigh 272*l.* after 17 *l.* of pouder was emptied out of it.

And that one of the ſmalleſt Bombs being emptied, did weigh 14 *l.*

Till the 22th of *July*.

July

List of 'bombs' fired into the city during the siege from a contemporary edition of George Walker's *A True Account of the Siege of London-Derry*

French commander of the entire Jacobite force at Derry, was killed in the confusion, allegedly by Adam Murray, who had led the attack. Another assault on the Pennyburn detachment was led by Murray on 25 April. On this occasion the French general, Pusignan, was killed. Richard Hamilton was now the besiegers' senior surviving officer but he had insufficient experience for so important a task.

The defenders had turned the area around a windmill, a little outside the walls, into a small fortification. During the night of 5 May the Jacobites made a surprise attack and captured and further fortified this position. The following day a determined effort by the citizen garrison recaptured the area and inflicted major casualties on the Jacobites. On this occasion a pair of yellow banners was seized from the besiegers. Although the cloth has had to be renewed on several occasions since then, the flagstaffs still hang in St Columb's Cathedral, displayed along with many other relics of the siege. George Walker described these encounters:

> Our sallies many times began but with small parties; Capt. Noble, and sometimes other officers, when they saw the enemy make an approach, would run out with about ten or twelve men at their heels, and skirmished a while with them: When the besieged saw them engaged, and in any danger, they issued out in greater numbers to their relief, and always came off with great execution on the enemy, and with very little loss to themselves.

Idealised contemporary impression of the Siege of Derry, published in Germany

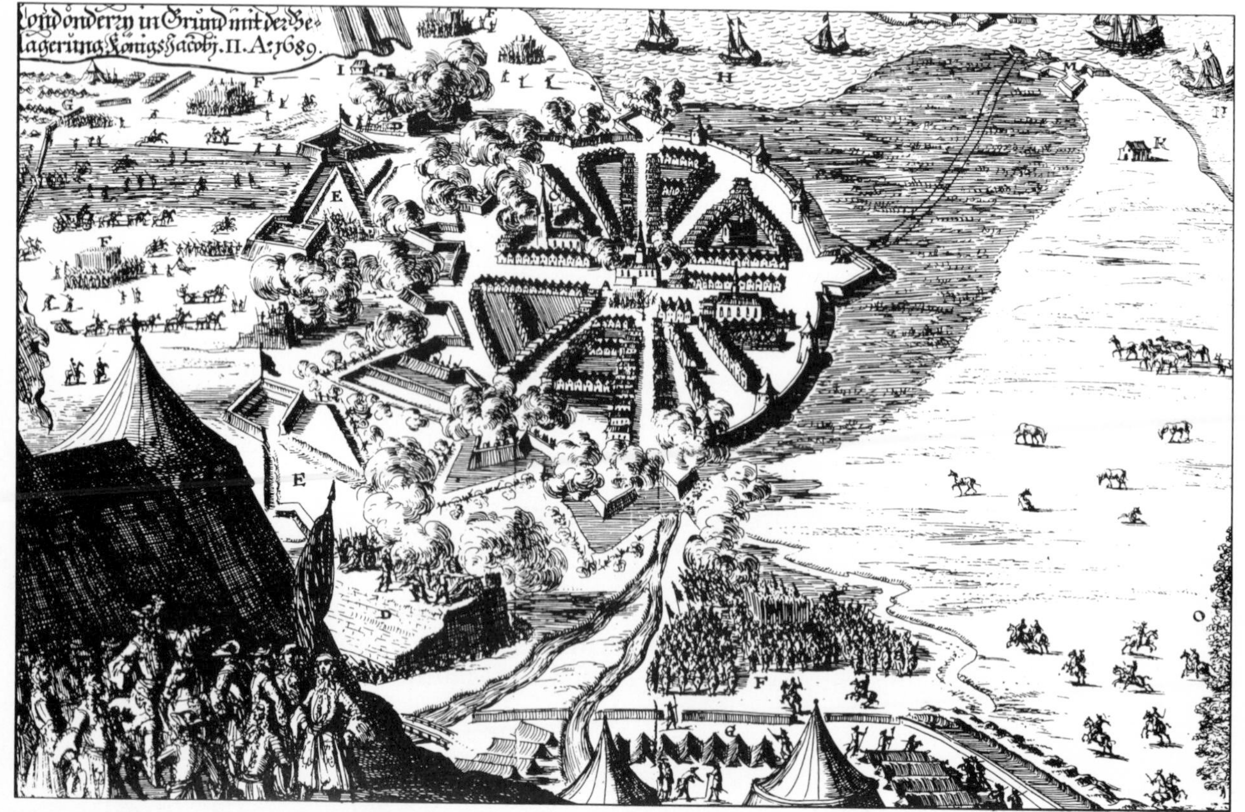

Apart from such minor skirmishes there was no further serious fighting during the rest of May. The Jacobites consolidated their positions, closing in more tightly around the city, but they were still badly armed. One report dated 27 May claimed that 'most of the soldiers in front of Derry have still only pointed sticks without iron tips'. However, another attack was launched against the windmill by the Jacobites on 4 June. As on the first occasion, they were badly defeated, although in some instances some of the younger defenders had nothing more than stones for ammunition. Throwing stones at soldiers is an activity with an ancient pedigree in Derry.

In some ways the Siege of Derry, and the war between William and James of which it was a part, can be seen as a tragic civil war. Former acquaintances and former military comrades and, in certain instances, different members of the same family found themselves on opposite sides. Loyalties throughout were stretched, changed and tested. In reading the various accounts of the siege, one is struck by the willingness of many of the chroniclers to acknowledge the bravery and courage of those on the 'opposite' side. Although the fighting was fierce and some disgraceful incidents occurred, both forces displayed acts of great humanity towards the wounded and other non-combatants on the enemy side. Neither was each side entirely united among themselves and natural suspicions and the stresses of the situation caused several internal disputes and dissensions, both inside and outside the beleaguered city.

HELP ARRIVES

At the beginning of June, Rosen arrived with fresh Jacobite troops to support Richard Hamilton. Throughout the rest of the siege there were difficulties between these two men, particularly on the issue of which of them was in supreme command. Rosen, appointed marshal general by James, was from Lithuania but had fought with the French for most of his life. He had a poor opinion of the Irish troops and the way in which they were being led. He was far harsher in his attitudes than Hamilton and wanted to bring things to a head in Derry. In George Walker's Cromwellian phrase, Rosen

> swore by the Belly of God, He would demolish our Town and bury us in its Ashes putting all to the Sword, without consideration of Age or Sex, and wou'd study the most exquisite Torments to lengthen the misery and pain of all he found obstinate, or active in opposing his Commands and Pleasure.

Hamilton continued to direct the actual blockade of the city while Rosen concentrated on preventing the English relief ships from passing up the river to the besieged city.

A Williamite fleet under the command of Major General Percy Kirke arrived in Lough Foyle during the second week of June. However, it was prevented from reaching the city by a floating barricade or 'boom' which had been built across the river. This had been constructed during the last week of May at a point just a little below the position of the present-day Foyle Bridge. The boom was designed by the French chief of artillery, Pointis, and was located close to Charles-Fort, 'a place of some strength', which had been built during the siege of 1649 on the west bank of the river. Here guns were placed to command the boom. The boom itself was made of timbers about one foot square that had been commandeered from the surrounding houses. These were held together by iron cramps, cables and thick rope. An initial attempt using oakwood was unsuccessful but the fir beams used the second time worked perfectly. The boom was well anchored on each bank and additional firing positions were constructed to cover any possible approach to it by the enemy.

Kirke decided not to try to advance up the river and, tantalisingly from the point of view of those inside the walls, the fleet remained visible but uncontactable from the city. A number of attempts were made by very brave swimmers to carry messages on the river past the Jacobite lines but these were not very successful. Having failed to relieve the city, Kirke sailed around into Lough Swilly and set up camp on Inch Island, from where more attempts were made to communicate with the city. This time the messages were carried, according to Walker's coy words, by

> a little boy that with great ingenuity made two dispatches to us from the Major General at Inch. One letter he brought tied in his garter, another at his second coming within a cloth button. We sent our first answer made up within a piece of a Bladder, in the shape of a Suppositor, and the same way applied to the Boy; our second answer he carried within the folding

Contemporary impression of skirmishing to the north of Derry during the siege. The 'boom' across the River Foyle can be seen in the background.

of his Breeches, and falling among the Enemy, for fear of a discovery he swallowed the Letter.

Luckily the boy made his escape and eventually returned to Inch Island.

DETERIORATING CONDITIONS

On the night of 28 June a small party of Jacobites managed to cross the Bogside and reach the city walls. They were able to approach the Butcher Gate but were overtaken by a garrison force that slipped out through the Bishop Gate coming upon the besiegers from behind and once again the Jacobites were badly defeated. On the last day of June Governor Baker died. He had magnanimously suggested that his replacement should be Colonel John Mitchelburne, which was somewhat surprising as Mitchelburne and Baker had had a serious quarrel at an earlier stage of the siege. Michelburne planted a 'bloody crimson' flag, first on the city walls and later on the cathedral tower, which became a symbol of defiance for the besieged city. The colour crimson has continued to play this role for Derry's Protestants down through the centuries.

Rosen was desperate at the general stalemate and in order to expedite matters he rounded up all the Protestants in the surrounding area, against the express guarantee of their safety by James, and assembled them at the city walls. He hoped that the garrison would feel obliged to admit them, so depleting the already dangerously low stock levels of food inside the city. The garrison retaliated by threatening to hang the Jacobite prisoners held inside the walls. At this point the Jacobite commander, Hamilton, intervened and sent the Protestants home. In fact, the garrison benefited from the affair: about five hundred of the weakest people from the city were smuggled out and replaced by some of the able-bodied men rounded up by Rosen. James, who was in Dublin, was furious when he heard of Rosen's behaviour. Towards the end of June surrender negotiations were initiated and the terms offered by the Jacobites were fairly generous. The defenders seemed anxious to play for time and the discussions went on for several weeks. On one occasion Jacobite conditions for a surrender were shot into the town in a hollow mortar shell, which is still preserved in St Columb's Cathedral:

To the soldiers and inhabitants of Derry

the conditions offered by Lieut. Gen. Hamilton are sincere. The power he hath of the King is real . . . Such of you as choose to serve the King, shall be entertained without distinction in point of religion. If any choose to leave the kingdom, they shall have passes. You shall be restored to your estates and livings, and have free liberty of religion whatsoever it be . . . Be not obstinate against your natural Prince; expose yourselves no longer to the miseries you undergo, which will grow worse and worse if you continue to be opinionate; for it will be too late to accept of the offer now

The hollow mortar shell, now in the porch of St Columb's Cathedral, inside which conditions for a surrender were fired into the city towards the end of the siege

made to you, when your condition is so low that you cannot resist the King's forces longer.

Representatives of the two sides met and parleyed on several occasions, but the defenders' answer was always 'no surrender'. The failure of these talks signalled renewed bombardment.

Conditions inside the city were now atrocious, with food and water becoming increasingly scarce. John Hunter, one of the defenders, wrote:

> I could not get a drink of clean water, and suffered heavily from thirst, and was so distressed by hunger that I could have eaten any vermin but could not get it . . . I myself was so weak from hunger, that I fell under my musket one morning as I was going to the walls . . . my face was blackened with hunger. I was so hard put to it, by reason of the want of food, that I had hardly any heart to speak or walk; and, yet when the enemy was coming, as many a time they did to storm the walls, then I found as if my former strength returned to me.

Many houses were damaged and people had to sleep in the open; the weather was dreadful; there were many wounded people and not enough medical assistance to cope; thousands of the dead had to be buried in backyards or dumped in cellars. Human skeletons, probably from these times, are still found throughout the city. It has been claimed that only about eighty people died in the actual fighting on the defenders' side and that the real killers inside the city were hunger and disease. Fever and other illnesses began to spread as the siege dragged on and food was almost nonexistent. George Walker recorded a price list that gives the cost of portions of horse, dog, cat, rat and mouse meat, and continues:

> We were under so great necessity, that we had nothing left unless we could prey upon one another: A certain fat gentleman conceived himself in the greatest danger, and fancying several of the garrison looked on him with a greedy eye, thought fit to hide himself for three days. Our drink was nothing but water, which we paid very dear for, and could not get without great danger; We mixt in it ginger and anniseed, of which we had great plenty; Our necessity of eating the composition of tallow and starch, did not only nourish and support us, but was an infallible cure of the looseness; and recovered a great many that were strangely reduced by that distemper, and preserved others from it.

On the Jacobite side the situation was not much better. It is generally agreed that they were badly equipped with arms and other necessary supplies. They had endured many losses and casualties and medical support was minimal and primitive. They too suffered from the almost continuous rain, all the more so as they were accommodated in the most basic huts and tents. Their morale and discipline were very poor. Many deserted and those who remained felt humiliated by the resilience and determination of the citizen garrison which they opposed.

(39)

the Enemy in their Trenches. One Regiment draws up againſt them in good Order, but had only three of their Matches lighted; we came upon them over againſt *Butchers-Gate* and kill'd 300 of their Men, beſides Officers. The Execution had been much greater, but many of our Men being much weakned with Hunger were not able to purſue them, ſome falling with their own blows. We return'd without any purchaſe of Cattle, but were adviſ'd to a more eaſie Experiment; having one Cow left we ty'd her to a Stake, and ſet Fire to her. We had hopes given us, that by the Cry and Noiſe ſhe wou'd make, the Enemies Cattle would be diſturbed and come to her relief; and they began to move and ſet up their Tails, ſo that we hoped to have gain'd our point; but the Cow got looſe, and turn'd to no account, only the danger of loſing her.

July 27. The Garriſon is reduced to 4456 Men, and under the greateſt extremity for want of Proviſion, which does appear by this Account taken by a Gentleman in the Garriſon, of the price of our Food.

	l.	s.	d.	
Horſe fleſh ſold for	0	1	8	*per* pound.
A Quarter of a Dog	0	5	6	fatned by eating
A Dogs-Head	0	2	6	the Bodies of the
A Cat	0	4	6	ſlain *Iriſh*.
A Rat	0	1	0	
A Mouſe	0	0	6	

A ſmall Flook taken in the River not to be bought for Mony, or purchaſed under the rate of a quantity of Meal

	l.	s.	d.
A pound of Greaves	0	1	0
A pound of Tallow	0	4	0
A pound of ſalted Hides		1	0
A quart of Horſe blood	0	1	0
A Horſe-pudding	0	0	6
An handful of Sea wreck		0	2
of Chick-weed		0	1
A quart of Meal when found,		1	0

We were under ſo great Neceſſity, that we had nothing [illegible] unleſs we could prey upon one another: A certa[illegible]

The notorious food price-list during the siege, from a contemporary edition of George Walker's *Account*

As time passed there was disquiet that Kirke had not tried to relieve the city. However, towards the end of July he ordered part of the fleet to return to Lough Foyle. He had three victuallers, or supply ships – the *Mountjoy*, the *Phoenix* and the *Jerusalem* – filled with provisions and, with himself on board the *Swallow*, these set sail down the lough for Culmore. The Jacobites had removed their heavy guns from the fort there and brought them up to the city, but once the fleet was seen returning to the lough, they were taken back. Those on board the ships made careful plans: the frigate *Dartmouth* was to engage the enemy at Culmore, while the *Mountjoy* and *Phoenix* passed behind into the river. These were to be accompanied by one of the longboats from the *Swallow*, which was to go ahead and cut through the boom.

The action came just as both sides in the conflict were reaching the end of their resolve. Inside the walls food and ammunition had virtually gone. George Walker records:

> We only reckoned upon two days of life, and had only nine lean horses left, and among us all one pint of meal to each man, hunger and the fatigue of war had so prevailed among us, that of 7500 men regimented, we had now alive but about 4300, whereof at least one fourth part were rendered unserviceable.

Outside the city the Jacobites, who had lost possibly as many as eight thousand or nine thousand men and had many thousands wounded, were contemplating raising the siege. James had more or less authorised such a course. On Sunday 28 July, Walker preached in St Columb's Cathedral in order to spur on his decimated congregation.

The Relief of Derry by William Sadler II (1782–1839) (Ulster Museum)

Early-nineteenth-century impression of the Reverend George Walker

About 7 p.m., an hour after the service had ended, the defenders saw the relief ships moving towards the city. As planned, the *Dartmouth* engaged the Jacobites at Culmore, allowing the *Mountjoy* and the *Swallow* longboat to reach the boom. The men on the longboat attacked the boom with axes and the *Mountjoy* followed, crashing into it. There are several different accounts of what happened next. One version claims that as a result of the collision with the boom the *Mountjoy* recoiled and ran ashore on the east bank of the river. Jacobite soldiers are then said to have rushed to capture the ship. Those on board fired three cannon shots in reply, the main effect of which was to loosen the *Mountjoy* so that she floated on the rising tide. In this version the *Mountjoy* then crashed through the boom as did the *Phoenix*. An alternative view is that the *Mountjoy* ran aground on a sandbank after she had passed the boom.

A TRUE
ACCOUNT
OF THE
SIEGE
OF
London-Derry.

By the Reverend Mr. *George Walker*, Rector of *Donog-moore* in the County of *Tirone*, and late Governou[r] of *Derry* in *Ireland*.

LONDON,
Printed for *Robert Clavel*, and *Ralph Simpson*, in St. *Paul's* Church-yard. MDCLXXXIX.
Also published, A new and exact Map of *London-derry*, and Culmore Fort, draw[n] with great Exactness, by Captain *Macullach*, who was there during the Sieg[e]

Title page of a contemporary edition of George Walker's account of the Siege of Derry, published in London in September 1689

Despite gunfire from the banks, the two ships moved on up to the city, the *Phoenix* arriving first about 10 p.m. that evening. Because of lack of wind, the *Mountjoy* had to be towed by the *Swallow* longboat. This Derry-based ship eventually did reach the city, its triumph lessened by the death of its captain, Michael Browning. Browning was a native of Derry and it appears that Kirke had specially chosen him and the crew of the *Mountjoy* to relieve their fellow citizens and families. At his finest hour, as he urged his men on the last stage of the relief operation, Browning was killed by Jacobite gunfire.

There was jubilation in the city when the ships arrived. The cannon were fired in celebration and the cathedral bells rang out to signal the joyful occasion. Nevertheless, the Jacobites continued to shoot at the city. Three days later, on 1 August (12 August according to the revised calendar), the besiegers conceded defeat and moved away from Derry. As Walker put it:

> Thus after 105 days, being close besieged by near 20,000 men constantly supplied from Dublin, God Almighty was pleased in our greatest extremity to send relief, to the admiration and joy of all good people, and to the great disappointment of so powerful and inveterate an enemy; who were

concerned in point of interest, as well as reputation to have rendered themselves masters of that town.

On Sunday 4 August, Kirke, accompanied by various members of his staff, came up to the city. They were received 'with the greatest Joy and Acclamations'. The keys, sword and mace of the city were offered to Kirke and there followed a civic procession through the streets. Afraid of infection inside the walls, the relief garrison built a camp outside, near the windmill which had played such an important part in the earlier phases of the siege. There was a meeting of the council of war on the following Wednesday and arrangements were made for the initial recovery and government of the city. Much needed to be done to restore even basic conditions. On Thursday 8 August a service of thanksgiving was held in the cathedral and that evening there was a *feu de joie* from the city walls. In the week that followed, arrangements were made by Kirke for demobbing the citizen garrison. This occasioned much disappointment because of the treatment received by many of those who had served during the siege. However, the citizens sent George Walker to London with a loyal address to William and Mary. When the reply from the king arrived in the city, promising restitution for the losses, there was further but, as it turned out, premature celebration.

In the aftermath of the siege and the subsequent war between William and James there were more disappointments for Derry. Although some relief was sent to the city by the London companies, the citizens generally failed to obtain compensation for their service and losses. Also, a serious dispute arose about the interpretation of some of the events of the conflict. One of the principal accounts of the siege, written by George Walker and published in London on 9 September 1689, was challenged by the Reverend John Mackenzie, the Presbyterian minister who had served as a chaplain in Walker's regiment. Mackenzie accused Walker of playing down the role of the Presbyterians in the defence of the city. The controversy was a reflection of the divisions that had existed between these two denominations prior to the siege. It was also a prelude to the discriminatory treatment of Irish Presbyterians, along with Catholics, under the penal laws of the eighteenth century. This division between Anglicans and Presbyterians was to survive as a factor in the political life of Derry for the next two centuries.

Almost as soon as the siege was over, the process by which it acquired a mythic significance began. It became the subject of a library of literary and artistic works, ranging from the unashamedly imaginative and creative to the seriously narrative and historical. This has continued. Sometimes the distinction between the two genres has been more than slightly blurred. More importantly, and particularly since the early nineteenth century, the Siege of Derry has provided a parable and a vocabulary for describing the Ulster Protestant condition.

A VINDICATION OF THE True Account OF THE SIEGE OF DERRY IN IRELAND.

By Mr. GEORGE WALKER, &c.

Publiſhed by Authority.

London: Printed for *Rob. Clavel*, at the Peacock, at the Weſt-End of St. *Pauls*. 1689.

Title page of a contemporary edition of a pamphlet by George Walker, replying to criticisms of his account of the Siege of Derry

AN APOLOGY FOR THE FAILURES Charg'd on the Reverend Mr. George Walker's PRINTED ACCOUNT Of the late Siege of Derry, IN A LETTER to the Undertaker of a more Accurate Narrative of that SIEGE.

Printed in the Year 1689.

Title page of a contemporary pamphlet, published in 1689, which relates to the controversy surrounding the role played by Presbyterians during the siege, in reply to George Walker's partisan account

A view of Derry, *c.* 1800. After the destruction of the siege of 1689, Derry was in a ruined and dilapidated condition. Rebuilding throughout the 1700s resulted in an elegant Georgian city so that by the end of the century Derry could be described as 'the most picturesque of any place'. (from George Vaughan Sampson's *Survey of the County of Londonderry*, 1814)

8

'THE MOST PICTURESQUE OF ANY PLACE' DERRY IN THE EIGHTEENTH CENTURY

The war between the two kings, James II and William III, continued in Ireland for two years after 1689. Some of those who had participated in the Siege of Derry went on to fight at other engagements of the war. The Reverend George Walker, who was fêted and honoured when he arrived in London shortly after the end of the siege, was nominated as bishop of Derry by William following the death in June 1690 of Ezekial Hopkins. However, before Walker had an opportunity to take up his new appointment, he was killed by a stray bullet at the Battle of the Boyne, where, on 12 July 1690, William's army defeated James's.

Romeyn de Hooghe's view of the Battle of the Boyne in 1690. An imaginative depiction of the death of the Reverend George Walker can be seen to the right (10). (Ulster Museum)

In Derry the process of clearing up and returning to normality quickly got under way. Many of those who had sought refuge inside the fortified city dispersed again to their homes and others who had fled from Derry returned. The smell of decaying human corpses was present everywhere in the city. One later account described how in every cellar in the town 'many dead carcases lay piled up one on another in stench and rottenness'. In May 1690 the overseers of the Bishop Street and Church wards were instructed

> to agree with labourers and car men for carrying away the dirt and covering of the graves within your respective wards at the easiest rates. You are to take narrow inspection into all the houses and backsides . . . and cause the several tenants . . . to cleanse the same and send all the rubbish or dry dirt to the churchyards for covering the dead corpses, and all other filth to such other convenient places as will not be nawsoum to the city. You are to cause every inhabitant, before whose door there are any bombshells unfilled . . . to get the same filled up and paved at their proper charge. You are to make strict enquiry for all such persons who of late have buried any dead corpses in any garden or backside within your ward, to give due notice thereof to the Mayor and Governor for preventing the like for the future.

There was also much concern as to how the citizens could afford to repair and, where necessary, rebuild their houses. In addition to everything else, there were many complaints about the soldiers who had come from England to relieve the city. They were still garrisoned in Derry and were making exorbitant demands on the already impoverished citizens with whom they were now quartered.

George Walker had appealed in London to the Irish Society and the House of Commons for financial aid for the ruined city, but despite the fact that parliament voted a sum of £10,000 for assistance, the money was never paid out. In 1705 it was calculated that, apart from other considerations, a total of £134,958 3s. 3d. was owed in wages to the men who had served in the various citizen regiments that had defended the city. Only a tiny fraction of that sum was ever secured. One appeal after another was sent to London and although a number of parliamentary committees expressed support for these claims, the money itself was not forthcoming. Neither did the city receive anything from the proceeds of the extensive confiscations that took place in Ireland after the Williamite victory in the war.

Several individuals who were virtually bankrupt went to London in order to press their own claims or those of the city to the authorities and a number of them actually ended up in the debtors' prison. One of the jailed claimants, William Hamill, calculated in 1721 that the accumulated unpaid wages and other expenses owed to the citizen garrison had by then reached a total of almost £350,000. Hamill lambasted the

Bee it knowne unto all men by these presents that wee Collonell John Michelburne of the City of Londonderry Alderman and Captain Stephan Heard of [illegible] Gent doe confess and acknowledge our selves to bee oweing and stand justly and truly indebted unto James Strong of Gobnascale within the liberties of Londonderry Gent the [illegible] and full summ of One Thousand pounds Sterling Currant and lawfull mony of and in England, to bee paid to the said James Strong his heirs Executors Administrators or assignes, To the which payment well and truly to bee made and done, Wee the abovenamed Collonell John Michelburne and Captn Stephen Heard doe binde our selves, our Heirs Executors And Administrators and every of us Jointly and severally in the whole and every part thereof firmly by these presents sealled with our seales dated the Twentieth day of September In the yeare of our Lord One Thousand six hundred Nyntie And Two

The Condition of the above Obligation is such that if the above bounden Collonell John Michelburne his heirs, Executors, or Administrators, and every of them, doe and shall from tyme to tyme, and at all tymes hereafter well and truly observe, performe, fulfill, pay, and keep, all and every the Covennants Grants, Articles, payments, and agreements, which on his and their parts & behalfs are and ought to bee observed, performed, fulfilled, paid and kept, specified and comprized in a certain pair of Indentures of Lease, bearing date with the date of these presents, made between the above bounden Collonell John Michelburne Susanna Michelburne his wife, and [illegible] Jackson her daughter on the one part And the abovenamed James Strong on the other part, And that in all things accor-ding to the true intent and meaning of the said Indentures, That then the above obligation to bee voyd, or els to remaine in full force and vertue.

Signed Sealled and Delivered in presence of

John [illegible]

John Buchanan

[illegible]

[illegible] Notr Publ.

[illegible]

Stephen Heard

A bond signed in 1692 by Colonel John Mitchelburne and others for £1,000 loaned during the siege by Captain Stronge (from C.D. Milligan, *The Siege of Londonderry 1689*)

Government in a passionately argued pamphlet entitled *A View of the Danger and Folly of being Public Spirited and Sincerely Loving One's Country.* He protested that despite the extraordinary sacrifices which the defenders of Derry had made, they had 'nothing for it these thirty years but royal promises, commissions without pay, recommendations from the throne to Parliaments and reports and addresses back to the throne again'.

William was anxious that Derry's citizens should be treated justly, but parliament had other more pressing demands. Apart from a few minor settlements, the city was never properly recompensed. One of those who was owed money was Captain Stronge, from whose orchard, on the east bank of the river directly opposite the city, Jacobite bombardment had commenced on 24 April 1689. Two IOUs signed by Colonel John Mitchelburne, for a sum of £1,000 lent to the city's defenders, survived in the Stronge family home at Tynan Abbey, County Armagh, until 1981. In that year, the Irish Republican Army (IRA) broke into the house, shot dead Sir Norman Stronge and his son James, and burned the building. It was estimated that together with the unpaid interest the accumulated value of the loans was in the region of £60 million.

Dramatis Perſonæ.

London-Derry beſieged by the *Iriſh Army*

Conrade d' Roſin, Mareſchal and General of the *Iriſh* Army.
Hamilton, Lieutenant-General.
Ramſey, Brigadier-General.
Sheldon, a Brigadier-General.
Dorington, Colonel of the Foot-Guards, and Brigadier.
Waubop and *Bochan*, two Brigadiers.
Clancarty and Sir *Neil*, two Colonels.
Sir *Bryan* the *Iriſh* Judge.
Teague, the Executioner to hang and quarter the *Britiſh* Rebels taken Priſoners.
Rapparees and Attendants.
Trumpets, Drums and Hautboys.

Defended by the *Derry* Men, and *Engliſh* Forces.
Landvill, Firſt Governor of *Derry*.
Baker, call'd *Antony*, Second Governor.
Mitchelburne, called *Granade*, Third Governor.
Walker, call'd *Evangeliſt*, Commiſſary of the Stores.
Camill and *Monrath*, two Colonels.
Forgus, the Town-Major.
Buff, and *Step-ſtately*, two Aldermen of the City.
Amazon, *Betitia*, *Gertrude*, *Felicia*, and *Deborah*, Female Warriors.
Black Jack, the Executioner, to hang and quarter the *Iriſh* Rebels taken Priſoners.

Cartel agreed upon. *No exchange of Priſoners, but hang and quarter on both ſides.*

Ireland Preſerv'd;

OR, THE

SIEGE of LONDON-DERRY.

A TRAGI-COMEDY.

ACT the FIRST.

SCENE I. *Repreſenting the Suburbs of the City as on Fire.*

Enter GRANADE, *knocking at a Perſon of Note's Door.*

GRANADE.

OH! how we are betray'd, ruin'd, and undone! what will become of theſe thouſands that muſt now periſh by the treachery and wicked deſigns of ſome men? It almoſt diſtracts me to think what miſery and deſtruction attends this diſmal place: Let patience guide me; nor let my thoughts and ſpirits ſink under the intolerable burden: Oh, *England, England!* think of this diſtreſſed city, and ſend us timely ſuccour. Oh, thou divine power, let our arms be ſtrong to fight; judge if we fight for any more than our own, or our country's liberty and freedom, and to defend ourſelves from thoſe that would deſtroy us.

Servant opens the Door.

Is the governor ſtirring yet?

Serv. My maſter was late up laſt night with ſome friends; but he will be ſtirring in a ſhort time.

Gran. Pray tell him my name is *Granade*: and that I have brought up the rear of our flying army.

[*Exit Serv.*

Oh, with what eaſe and quiet do ſome men ſleep, when ſafe and ſecure and in no danger of an enemy's approach; they are certainly friends to them and not

A 2 to

PROTESTANT 'HERO' AND CATHOLIC 'SAINT'

Colonel John Mitchelburne was another of the defenders of Derry who later found themselves in the debtors' prison. He was jailed in London in 1709 while attempting to obtain what he believed was owed to him for his service. Mitchelburne, the former military governor of the city, had gone on to serve William at the Battle of the Boyne and elsewhere during the remainder of the war with James. The governor had lost his wife and children during the siege but had, nevertheless, successfully commanded the garrison and maintained its morale. However, in 1690 he was unsuccessful in his bid to be elected mayor of Derry and he also failed to obtain from the Irish Society the governorship of Culmore. Eventually, he did receive some compensation from the Government for his military services, but this still fell far short of what he believed his entitlement to be.

Ireland Preſerv'd;

OR, THE

SIEGE

OF

LONDON-DERRY.

Being the ſecond part

OF THE BATTLE OF AUGHRIM.

Written by a GENTLEMAN who was in the Town during the whole SIEGE.

DUBLIN:

Printed for THOMAS WILKINSON, Bookſeller and Stationer, No. 40, Winetavern-ſtreet, the Corner of Cook-ſtreet; where may be had all Kinds of Novels, School books, Plays, and Merchants Account-books, with every article in the Stationary Way.

Colonel John Mitchelburne, governor of Derry during the siege, and most probably the author of two plays that use the Siege of Derry for their plots. He died on 1 October 1721. (from C.D. Milligan, *The Siege of Londonderry 1689*)

It is almost certain that Mitchelburne was the author of two plays that use the Siege of Derry for their plots. *Ireland Preserved, or the Siege of Londonderry. A Tragi-Comedy written by a Gentleman who was in the town during the whole siege* and *Ireland Preserved, or the Troubles of the North; being a preparatory to the Siege of Derry; a Tragi-Comedy* were both published in London in 1705. The suggestion has been made that Mitchelburne may have been assisted in his literary task by dramatist George Farquhar and certainly, in literary terms, the plays go well beyond mere propaganda. Farquhar would have been about eleven or twelve years of age at the time of the siege and whether or not he was in the city at the time, he must have been greatly influenced by the extraordinary events of the period. Mitchelburne's plays, or versions of them, were very popular throughout the eighteenth century and were regularly published and performed.

John Mitchelburne died on 1 October 1721 at the age of seventy-six. He wished to be buried at Enagh Lough but was, in fact, interred in Glendermot graveyard beside his former comrade at the Siege of Derry, the fearless Adam Murray. In his will, which, appropriately, he signed on 12 July, a few months prior to his death, Mitchelburne left a sum of £50 'for maintaining the Flag on the steeple of Derry'. The flag in question was the 'Bloody Crimson' banner that he had placed on the tower of St Columb's Cathedral during the siege as a symbol of defiance. He also left various sums of money for the education and support of the poor of the district and his charitable and philanthropic image survived for a long time after his death. An interesting story about him, reflecting this reputation, was collected for the Ordnance Survey *Memoir* (Clondermot parish) about one hundred years later. During his later life, Mitchelburne, who had married again, retired to a house on the east bank of the River Foyle, in the Gobnascale area of the Waterside district. Somewhere close to this house, probably near where the present Craigavon Bridge reaches the Waterside, there was a spring well. About 1714 the elderly and, clearly, contemplative old soldier had a small shed erected beside this well. Inside the shed he placed his coffin. For the remainder of his life he 'used to take a walk every morning from his house to this well along the side of the River Foyle in order to pray'. He employed a number of young boys from the neighbourhood to keep the grass around the well tidy.

By the 1830s, when the Ordnance Survey was under way, the practice of the local 'superstitious people [was to] tie rags on the bushes and throw pins into the well, and say [that] as Col. Mitchelburne was so pious a character there must be some healing virtue in the water'. The memoir continues: 'Stations [local religious practices] are performed at this well by superstitious Roman Catholics.' Although the writer is not explicit, it is clear that the spring had become a holy well for the local Catholics (elsewhere referred to in the memoir as 'ab origines') and

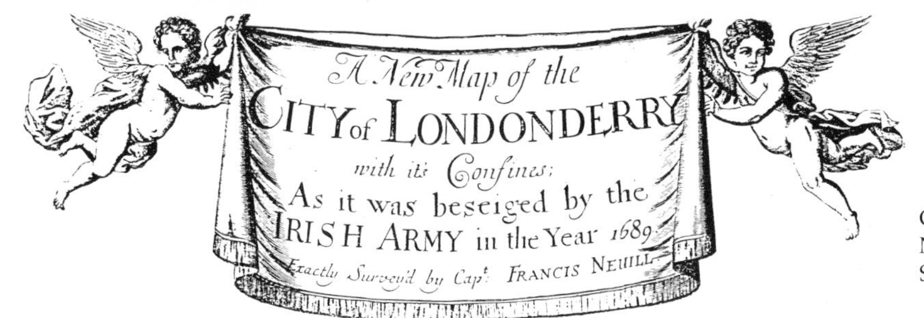

Cartouche from Francis Nevill's 1690 map of the Siege of Derry

more extraordinarily, by extension, Mitchelburne had acquired the status of its presiding 'saint'. In 1836 the Irish Society erected a marble tomb over his grave so that 'the burial place of so brave a soldier, and so great a benefactor to the poor . . . ought not to be unknown to posterity'. Mitchelburne was not forgotten and his name appears on the banners and drums of many modern-day loyalist groups. But the story of his holy well is perhaps the most paradoxical legacy of the Siege of Derry.

SUCCESSES AND DISAPPOINTMENTS

Immediately following the end of the siege, the Irish Society in London collected £100 apiece from each of the twelve principal companies of the City for the relief of conditions in Derry and it also made other contributions, mainly by abating rents. By the summer of 1690 the corporation in Derry was concerned about the state of the town house, which had been badly damaged 'by the enemies bombs':

> Upon application made to their majesties King William and Queen Mary by the corporation of Londonderry, they were graciously pleased as a mark of their favour, to give a largess of £1500 towards the building an Exchange, the repairs of the church, gates, and walls of the city; appointing the mayor, aldermen, and burgesses to dispose of the money to that use, which trust they most faithfully discharged to the best advantage; and to promote this great and good undertaking the gentry of the grand jury for the city and county were pleased to grant an applottment of £300 towards finishing the Exchange, with the court of judicature, guard house, guard chambers, common councillroom, grand and petty jury rooms.

Building work on the new town house or 'Exchange', designed by Captain Francis Nevill, began in April 1692.

Dr William King, Anglican bishop of Derry from 1691 to 1703, when he was appointed archbishop of Dublin (Trinity College Dublin)

The new town house ('Exchange') was designed by Captain Francis Nevill, a member of the corporation. In 1690 Nevill presented the Irish Society with 'a survey, taken by himself, of the damages done to the city of Londonderry, and a map of the city, during the late siege'. This survey was the basis of a printed map of the siege, published shortly afterwards. A report dated 6 May 1691 records that sixty tons of timber from the Irish Society's forests in County Londonderry were made available 'towards rebuilding the market-house, repairing the gates, and other public buildings in Derry' and on 4 December 'one hundred and twenty tons of timber, and forty thousand laths, were allowed for building the town-house of Derry'. The foundation stone was laid in the market place on 15 April 1692 by the mayor, Alderman Lecky, and the new Anglican bishop, Dr William King.

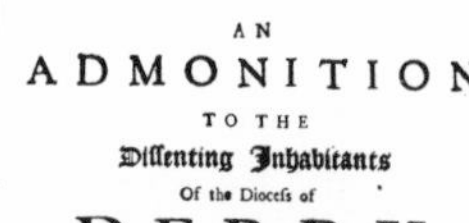

AN
ADMONITION
TO THE
Diſſenting Inhabitants
Of the Dioceſs of
DERRY,
Concerning a Book lately Publiſhed by Mr. J. Boyſe;
Entituled,
Remarks on a late Diſcourſe of WILLIAM
Lord Biſhop of DERRY:
CONCERNING
The Inventions of Men in the Worſhip of God.

My Friends and Brethren,

I Have told you in this Diſcourſe (when firſt Printed, *p.* 170.) *That no Man ought to take it ill that another propoſes Reaſons againſt his Opinion; but to ſcoff at, or revile any Practice, or Opinion that another believes to be Founded on the Word of God, is*
A 2 *not*

Title page of a book by Dr William King, published in 1694

King was very much involved in resolving some of the apparently interminable property disputes that had arisen between his predecessors in the See of Derry and the Irish Society. These disputes, relating to the ownership of several valuable fishing rights on the Bann and Foyle river systems and to the disputed former monastic lands of Termonderry, close to the city on its western side, had persisted for most of the seventeenth century. Dr King brought the issue of the Termonderry lands to the Irish House of Lords, where he won his case in 1697. However, the Irish Society appealed to the English House of Lords and a major constitutional conflict between the two kingdoms was narrowly averted. The Irish Society won on this occasion but the bishop continued to ignore the ruling. The king ordered that the bishop should be taken into custody and brought to London to answer for his contempt, but Dr King pleaded illness and the matter was quietly dropped. Another controversy over fishing rights soon broke out, but finally, in April 1703, agreement was reached on all issues and a compromise incorporated in a private act of the English parliament.

The silver mace presented to the city of Derry by William III as a gift for the rôle that the city had played during the siege (Eason and Son)

Besides the donation for the new town house and other restoration projects, William and Mary made a number of other gifts to Derry as a mark of respect for the role that the city had played on their behalf during the siege. Copies of the official coronation portraits by Sir Godfrey Kneller, a new gold mayor's medallion and a silver mace were bestowed on the city, all of which still survive among the city's treasures. However, despite his graciousness, the king was unsuccessful in persuading parliament to pay the arrears of wages to the citizen soldiers.

Another major disappointment for the citizens was the manner in which Irish Presbyterians were treated in the aftermath of the siege and the Glorious Revolution. Under the influence of the Anglicans, not the least vocal of whom on this issue was Dr King, Presbyterians were subjected to a series of discriminatory measures. Although these never reached the level of the penal laws against Catholics, they had an enormous impact on the morale of the Presbyterians who, justifiably, felt that they had played a significant role in the success of the Williamite revolution. These attitudes had already manifested themselves in the post-siege controversy between George Walker and John Mackenzie. Dr King published several tracts attacking the Presbyterian mode of worship. His *Discourse Concerning the Inventions of Men in the Worship of God*, published in 1693, had been replied to by, among others, the *Answer* of Mr Robert Craighead, the Presbyterian minister in Derry. The bishop responded with *An Admonition to the Dissenting Inhabitants of the Diocese of Derry*, which forced Mr Craighead into print again in 1697 with a second *Answer*.

In 1689 'An Act for Exempting Their Majesties Protestant Subjects Dissenting from the Church of England, from the Penalties of Certain Laws', commonly known as the toleration act, was passed in England but was not extended to Ireland. In 1704 'An Act to prevent the further growth of popery', commonly known as the test act, required that all holders of public offices in Ireland, both civil and military, had to qualify by taking the sacrament of communion in their local Anglican parish church. As a direct consequence of this act, twenty-four Presbyterian members of the thirty-eight-man corporation in Derry had to resign, having refused from principle to qualify in the manner prescribed:

AN
ACT
To Prevent the
Further Growth
OF
POPERY.

DUBLIN:
Printed by *Andrew Crook*, Printer to the Queen's most Excellent Majesty, on the *Blind-Key*, MDCCIII.

> Robert Rochford, recorder of the city, advised the mayor, etc. to elect other members in their place. The mayor, therefore, to leave the dissenting members without excuse, caused the sergeants to summon them

The river front at Derry, *c.* 1780. Derry was probably the premier port for the American emigration trade throughout the eighteenth century. (Engraving from an original sketch by John Nixon in the possession of Ronnie Adams)

> twice; none, however, attended, consequently he proceeded to a new election on the 12th August, and filled the vacancies.

Those who had been obliged to resign had been influential in the civic life of Derry. Of the ten aldermen involved, six had previously held the office of mayor, while the remaining four had served as sheriffs and two of the fourteen resigning burgesses had also served as sheriffs. Of the twenty-four who resigned, fifteen were elders of their congregation.

THE BEGINNINGS OF EMIGRATION

Many Ulster Presbyterians were so shocked by the impact of the penal laws on their community that they resolved to leave the country altogether. The freedom of the American colonies proved very inviting to many, including some of those who believed that they had been defending just those freedoms during the Jacobite–Williamite war. One of the first transatlantic emigrants was the Reverend James McGregor of Aghadowey in County Derry, who had fought at the Siege of Derry. He took most of his congregation with him to North America. In a sermon on the eve of their embarkation, Mr McGregor compared their departure from Ireland with the story of Moses leading the chosen tribes to the promised land. The party arrived in Boston on 4 August 1718 and the towns of Derry and Londonderry in the state of New Hampshire were among the settlements which developed from this particular migration.

In the same summer, another Presbyterian minister, the Reverend James Woodside, led a party of over one hundred emigrants to America. They sailed from Derry on the seventy-ton ship *McCallom* and arrived in Boston in September. The forty-five-ton *Mary and Elizabeth* also carried a hundred or so passengers from Derry to Boston that year.

Modern writers on eighteenth-century emigration from Ulster have stressed the importance of economic rather than religious factors on those who decided to leave. It has also been shown that not only Presbyterians but also Catholics and Anglicans made the hopeful journey. Many of these emigrants left from Derry, which was probably the premier port for the American emigration trade throughout this period. Most of the ships used belonged to local businessmen and the emigrant trade became a major element in the economy of the city. In July 1729 a local merchant in Derry reported that as many as twenty-five ships had left the port already that summer, destined for America and that each ship had 140 passengers on board. Another report, for 1759, described how more than three thousand people had recently left from the ports of Derry and Coleraine. It was reported to the Irish Customs Commissioners that in the years 1772 and 1773 about six thousand emigrants had left from Derry. This scale of emigration was confirmed by an article in the *Maryland Journal* of 16 October 1773, which claimed that 3,500 people had left from Derry in the previous twelve months. Throughout the century emigrant ships left from many Ulster ports, but especially from Derry, destined for South Carolina, Nova Scotia and particularly Philadelphia, as well as other places. R.J. Dickson, in his classic study, *Ulster Emigration to Colonial America*, quotes an advertisement in the *Belfast News-Letter* of 3 June 1766, for the 250-ton ship *Hopewell*, which was about to leave from Derry for Nova Scotia:

> It would swell the advertisement to too great a length to enumerate all the blessings those people enjoy who have already removed from this country to said province, it may suffice to say, that from tenants they are become landlords, from working for others they now work for themselves, and enjoy the fruits of their own industry.

Similar advertisements appeared in the city's first newspaper, founded in 1772, the *Londonderry Journal and Donegal and Tyrone Advertiser*. (Today, as the *Derry Journal*, it is Ireland's second-oldest newspaper.)

However, many of those who went to America financed their passage by signing on as indentured servants, in effect mortgaging their future labour. In July 1770 the cost of a passage from Derry to Philadelphia was 3 guineas. The Ulster-Scots, as these migrants came to be known, played a major part in the establishment and subsequent history of the American republic, and provided the new nation with many of its leaders and heroes, such as President Andrew Jackson, lawyer and banker Thomas Mellon, Charles Thompson, who was first secretary of the US Congress, and Francis Mackemie, founder of the Presbyterian Church in the United States.

'THE HEARTS . . . AS MELTING WAX'

In 1706 the population of Derry was estimated at 2,848. When the scientific writer Dr Thomas Molyneux visited the city two years later he remarked on the many new and restored buildings, but thought that the trade and commerce of the city had not recovered since the siege. He also discovered that a library was being established adjacent to the renovated schoolhouse. This was the diocesan library founded by Bishop William King before he left the city in 1703 to become archbishop of Dublin. He had augmented his own book stock, which he bequeathed to the city, by buying the collection belonging to his predecessor, Bishop Ezekial Hopkins. The library still survives and is now housed in the Church of Ireland diocesan premises in London Street.

In 1724, philosopher George Berkeley was appointed to the prestigious and lucrative office of Anglican dean of Derry. He held the post until 1732, although apart from one visit in the early summer of 1724, he never lived in the city. Instead, he let the tithe lands associated with the deanery for a sum of £1,250 per annum and devoted himself to establishing a college in Bermuda for the education of the American colonists and the training of native Americans as missionaries to their own people. However, Berkeley was favourably impressed by Derry, as revealed in letters he wrote during his visit:

8 May 1724

My house is a fashionable thing, not five years old, and cost eleven hundred pounds. The Corporation are all good churchmen, a civil people, and throughout English, being a colony from London. I have hardly seen a more agreeable situation, the town standing on a peninsula in the midst of a fine spreading lake, environed with green hills, and at a

A view of Londonderry, *c.* 1729, by William van der Hagen, one of the first major landscape painters to work in Ireland. The painting, which is now missing, may have been used for the design of the huge tapestry *The Siege of Derry*, one of a pair along with *The Battle of the Boyne*, which were commissioned for the chamber of the Irish House of Lords and hung there in 1733. (The former parliament building in Dublin, including the House of Lords, where the tapestries still hang, is now owned by the Bank of Ireland.) (Photograph, Magee College)

George Berkeley, philosopher, and Anglican dean of Derry from 1724 to 1732 (John Smibert, National Gallery of Ireland)

A view by John Nixon, *c.* 1780, from the quayside area, looking through the city's main gate and up Shipquay Street to the town house in the market place or Diamond (from George Vaughan Sampson's *Survey of the County of Londonderry*, 1814)

distance the noble ridge of Ennishawen [Inishowen] mountains and the mighty rocks of Magilligan form a most august scene.

8 June 1724

The city of Londonderry is the most compact, regular, well built town, that I have seen in the King's Dominions, the town house (no mean structure) stands in the midst of a square piazza from which there are four

A view of the city of Derry from the Waterside, showing the first wooden bridge, which opened to pedestrians in 1790 and to horse-drawn traffic the following year (Bartlett engraving, Ulster Folk and Transport Museum)

principal streets leading to as many gates. It is a walled town, and has walks all round on the walls planted with trees, as in Padua.

In spite of the disapproval of the authorities, from early in the eighteenth century houses for poorer people began to be built again outside the walls. By the end of the century there was a small network of suburban lanes and streets, although paintings and maps made around this time still show a compact city surrounded by a rural landscape.

There were several years of famine in the eighteenth century and the Derry area experienced appalling poverty. In 1721 the bishop of Derry, Dr William Nicholson, wrote:

> One of my coach-horses, by accident, was killed in a field within view of my house. Before the skin could be taken off, my servants were surrounded with 50 or 60 of the neighbouring cottagers, who brought axes and cleavers, and immediately divided the carcase: Every man carrying home his proper dividend for food to their respective families.

By this stage Catholics had begun to move back to the city and its suburbs, some of them as servants to the wealthier Protestant citizens. In 1709 there were complaints that many Catholics had come to Derry to work as car men but had no grazing land for their horses, which were trespassing on private property. There were more car men than the city could support, 'whereby the city comes to be overburdened with poor, and such strangers' children are often left as a charge upon the parish'. A number of tradesmen in the city were prevented from working when it was discovered that they were, or had become, 'papists'. In the mid-1700s measures were introduced to prohibit Catholics from living in the city, but despite this, they continued to come back in.

Many of these Catholics settled just outside the city walls in the area now known as the Long Tower district. In the more relaxed period of tolerance at the end of the penal era they were served by their parish priest, Father John Lynch, who, along with his bishop, Dr Philip McDevitt, took the oath of allegiance in 1782. According to tradition, Father Lynch said Mass under a well-known hawthorn tree on the side of the hill overlooking the Bogside. Here, in 1784, this much-loved priest began building a small church with the support of Dr Frederick Hervey, the Anglican bishop of Derry, who was known for his advocacy of Catholic emancipation. Dr Hervey, an inveterate traveller, greatly admired the baroque splendour of Continental Catholic churches and he donated four Corinthian columns, said to have been brought specially from Naples, to the new church in Derry. These now frame the high altar of the Long Tower Church. Dr Hervey also donated £200 to the building fund and, at his behest, the all-Protestant corporation gave another £50. The spirit of 'enlightenment' had come to Derry. Unfortunately it would not survive for long.

Dr Philip McDevitt, Catholic bishop of Derry from 1766 to 1797 (from *The Story of the Long Tower Church 546–1946*)

Father Lynch's building was the first Catholic church to be erected in Derry since the plantation. It was constructed near the site of the Tempull Mór, which, in the popular mind, was believed to have been the site of the ancient monastery of Saint Colmcille. As the church was extended over the years with the growth of the numbers of Catholics

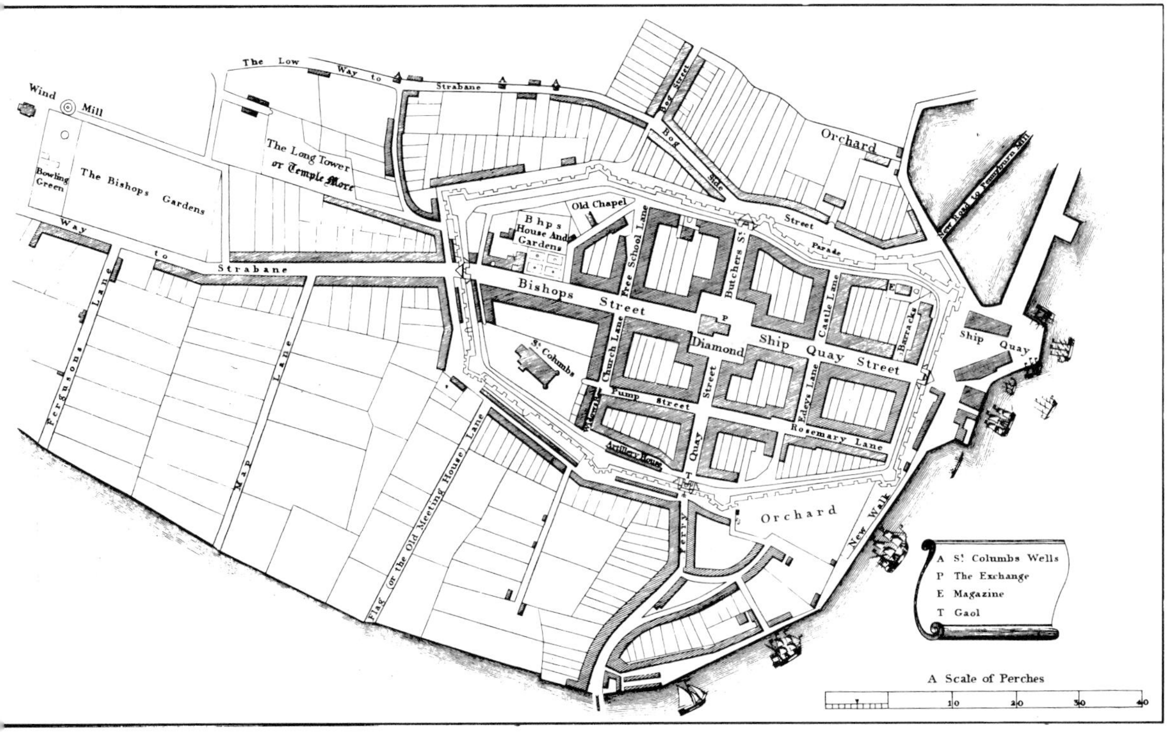

Map of Derry as it looked in 1788, the centenary year of the shutting of the gates

living in its vicinity, this tradition about its location grew and was enshrined in its iconography. Despite the building of St Eugene's Cathedral in the city in the middle of the nineteenth century, St Columba's (Long Tower Church) continues to occupy a central place in the affections and traditions of the Catholics of Derry.

John Wesley, the English founder of Methodism, made his first visit to Derry on 11 May 1765 to minister to the fledgling Methodist congregation. On that day he preached 'to the largest congregation [he had] seen in the north of Ireland' and on the following day to 'near all the inhabitants of the city'. Wesley recorded that he was amazed at the 'honesty' of the citizens: 'None scruples to leave his house open all day and the door only on the latch at night. Such a thing as theft is scarce heard of at Derry, no one has the least suspicion of it.' He made a total of ten visits to Derry and came for the last time in 1789, the eighty-sixth year of his life, when he was pleased to find 'a neat convenient preaching house just finished; a [Methodist] society increasing and well united together; and the whole city prejudiced in favour of it. The hearts of the people seemed to be as melting wax.'

THE SIEGE CENTENARY

The year 1789, the one-hundredth anniversary of the siege, was one of unity and harmony in the city. On 15 October 1788 the mayor, John Conyngham, issued a notice stating that the

> Corporation of Londonderry, zealous to revive in the breasts of the Protestant generation, and transmit to posterity such principles as actuated their heroic ancestors, had resolved on a secular commemoration of the return of that memorable day, the seventh of December, 1688, when the gates of their city were closed against a bigoted tyrant, a day so honourably interwoven with that aera of our Constitution, the Glorious Revolution, which to our happy experience, has been terminated by extensive and elaborate provisions for the general liberty.

A committee was set up to plan the centenary events. On 4 November, the eve of the anniversary of the 'gunpowder plot' (when it was alleged that there was a conspiracy of Catholic gentlemen who intended to blow up the houses of parliament when the king was actually present) and the anniversary of the landing of William of Orange in England, a 'day of public commemoration' was declared and special religious services were held. There was a public meeting in the town hall which endorsed the corporation's suggestion for a ceremony to mark the 'shutting of the gates'. It also recommended that a public monument should be erected. The Irish Society contributed £50 to the celebration fund.

In 1829 the Reverend John Graham, rector of Tamlaghtard in the diocese of Derry, published a detailed, if somewhat slanted, account of these celebrations:

Burning the Effigy of Lundy in Derry, c. 1830 (artist unknown, Ulster Museum)

> On Thursday, the seventh of December, (old style date) 1788, the dawn was announced by the beating of drums, the ringing of bells, and a discharge of the cannon which had been used during the siege; and a red flag, the emblem of a virgin city, was displayed on the cathedral. If a magistrate or military officer had interfered to prevent the hoisting of this flag or the ringing of these bells on this occasion, he would have been sent to a lunatic asylum, and the mob of all denominations would have pelted him with stones on the way. The city was almost immediately in motion, each person seemed eager to bear his part in the rejoicings of the day, and the glow of honest enthusiasm was apparent in every countenance.

The procession, which started at 10.30 a.m. from the ship quay and proceeded to the cathedral, was comprised of representatives from a variety of organisations in the city and of all its leading citizens. Although every inch of the route was occupied, hundreds of people had to be turned away and 'the city never before witnessed so throng an assembly'. Following a service in the cathedral, and a sermon delivered by the dean, John Hume, sections of Handel's oratorio *Judas Maccabaeus* were performed. The procession then went to the Presbyterian meeting house, where the Reverend Robert Black gave an oration.

HMS *Porcupine*, commanded by Captain Brabazon, sailed into the harbour, elaborately decorated for the occasion, and was saluted by a discharge of twenty-one guns from the city walls and returned an equal number. It was claimed that such a large war ship had never before been

Design for the triumphal arch, by Henry Aaron Baker, for the Bishop Gate, whose first stone was laid on 12 August 1789 by Mayor Thomas Bateson, during the celebrations marking the centenary of the relief of Derry. When the arch was actually built, the equestrian sculpture was not added.

seen in the harbour of Derry. The naval cutter *Sea-flower* also arrived. John Graham's account continues:

> The first procession had scarcely terminated when another of a different kind commenced. Some of the lower-class of citizens had provided an effigy representing the well-known Lundy, executed in a very humourous style, with a bundle of matches on its back; with this they perambulated the streets, and having repeatedly exposed it to the insults of the zealous populace, they burned it in the market-place with every circumstance of ignominy. This piece of pageantry afforded no small entertainment to innumerable spectators, nor was it barren of instruction to an attentive mind, as it marked out in striking characters, the unavoidable destiny of Traitors, who having sacrificed to their own base interests the dearest rights of honour and conscience, are deservedly consigned over to perpetual infamy, and become everlasting objects of detestation even to the meanest of people.

At 2 p.m. the 46th Regiment and the Volunteer corps paraded through the town. The Apprentice Boys Company of the Volunteers, supported by other Volunteer sections, and regular soldiers enacted the ceremony of the shutting of the gates. All then returned to the market place, now called the Diamond, where a *feu de joie* was fired, in concert with gunfire from the batteries on the walls and the ships in the harbour. At 4 p.m. the dignatories of the town, including the Catholic clergy, attended 'a plain but plentiful dinner' in the town hall:

> The toasts were constitutional, and well suited to the occasion; no man was idiot enough to object to drink to the Glorious Memory of that great Prince who saved the religion of the Protestant and the liberty of all other professors of Christianity. The assembly was necessarly mixed . . . the

John Hume, Anglican dean of Derry from 1783 to 1818 (Courtesy of St Columb's Cathedral)

> guests amounting nearly to a thousand persons, and yet regularity, decorum, and complacency pervaded the whole company. Religious dissensions, in particular, seemed to be buried in oblivion, and Roman Catholics vied with Protestants in expressing, by every possible mark, their sense of the blessings secured to them by the event which they were commemorating, and the part which they took in the celebration of this joyful day was really cordial.

Among the guests at the dinner was a man who had been present at the siege. Born a short time before it began, he had been nursed in a cellar during the conflict. This venerable old man, who 'had breathed the same atmosphere with the immortal Walker, Mitchelburne, and Murray' created such an impression that a collection was taken up for his support.

Many other events were organised for the day. The windows of the town hall were ornamented by illuminated paintings, depicting a variety of scenes, including 'the genius of Londonderry fixing the imperial crown upon the head of KING WILLIAM, and trampling on a figure representing despotism' and 'a medallion, in which the genius of the Maiden City appeared in contest with a tiger'. The day ended with a display of fire-works from the Shipquay Gate. About noon on the following day, the carcase of an ox, decorated with orange ribbons, was drawn through the streets to the Diamond, where it was cut into pieces, and distributed with bread and beer to the poor of the city. The two days of festivities ended with a ball and supper.

THE 'RELIEF' CELEBRATIONS

In August 1789 further celebrations were held to commemorate the centenary of the breaking of the boom and the relief of the city. The festivities were held on 1 August, according to the old-style calendar. A great procession made its way to the cathedral, led by the Anglican bishop, Dr Hervey, and accompanied by Dean Hume and the clergy of

Frederick Augustus Hervey, 4th Earl of Bristol, and Anglican bishop of Derry from 1768 to 1803, from a painting by Pompeo Batoni. St Columb's Cathedral can be seen in the background. (from Brian Fothergill, *The Mitred Earl*)

The Earl Bishop's palace, built in 1780, at Downhill near Coleraine (from Brian Fothergill, *The Mitred Earl*)

the Established Church. Among others in the procession were the Catholic bishop, Dr Philip McDevitt, and his clergy, the Presbyterian clergy and elders, the mayor, Thomas Bateson, members of the corporation and civic officers, and a corps of the Londonderry Independent Volunteers. At the cathedral a sermon was given by the Reverend George Vaughan Sampson, which was subsequently published to general acclaim. He told his listeners:

> If ye would draw from the example of your fathers a lesson, suited to this solemn hour, you must not only be pious in your courage but also humane in your opinions, – you must not only say in your hearts – 'Glory be to God in the highest'; but also – 'and on earth Peace, good-will towards men!'

The procession proceeded to the Bishop Gate, where the foundation stone of a new triumphal arch was laid by the mayor. It was originally intended that there should be an equestrian figure on top of the arch but this was never added. The relief celebrations continued with several *feux de joie*, fire-works and a dinner, and by another ball on the following evening.

The centenary of the relief of Derry had been celebrated in a manner that gave pleasure to many and offence to few. As historian Desmond Murphy has observed, the small Catholic community, 'keenly aware of the vulnerability of their position . . . even tried to legitimize the siege celebrations by their participation in them'. However, historian Roy Foster has pointed out the unfortunate irony that 'the invention of this tradition coincided, not only with the high point of Protestant Ireland's colonial nationalism, but also with a revival of sectarian tension, which would have a far longer life'.

Engraving of St Columb's Cathedral, from a painting by P. Sandby, published on 1 May 1780. In 1776 Bishop Hervey provided £1,000 to build a new stone spire (228 feet tall), but the heavy structure proved to be dangerous and had to be taken down in 1802.

THE EARL BISHOP

The relief procession had been led by Dr Frederick Augustus Hervey, Anglican bishop of Derry and 4th Earl of Bristol, who originally came from Ickworth in Surrey. Through the favour of his brother George, who was lord lieutenant of Ireland, Hervey had been appointed in 1768 to the See of Derry, the richest episcopal prize in the country. While the bishop's behaviour was often eccentric and at times bizarre, he proved to be an extremely popular pastor as he set about governing his diocese with great enlightenment. His principal dwelling was at Downhill but his town house was at the palace in Bishop Street (now the Masonic Hall) and he also built a summer house in a garden owned by the diocese outside the city walls, a site now occupied by St Columb's College. Although Hervey spent much of his time abroad – a string of Bristol hotels on the Continent commemorates his love of travel – his frequent and prolonged visits to his diocese proved very valuable. In this, he compares more favourably than the other great eighteenth-century cleric associated with the city, George Berkeley.

The 'Earl Bishop' quickly began to involve himself with the affairs of his diocese, both in the spiritual and secular spheres. He became involved in an exploration for coal in Magilligan and Aghanloo in County Derry. As well as improving the accommodation for his clergy and congregation (he added, as it proved, a dangerously tall spire to St Columb's Cathedral, which had to be taken down in 1802) he was even involved in the building of roads. But perhaps the bishop's greatest contribution to his adopted city was his unstinting support for the building of a bridge across the River Foyle, no doubt in the belief that he

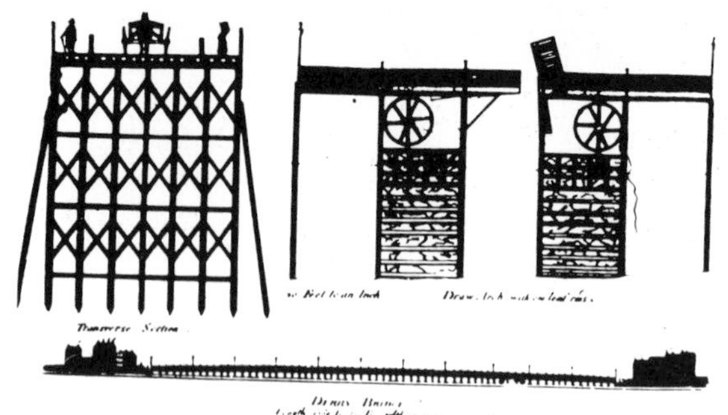

Contemporary drawings of Derry's first bridge across the River Foyle, built between 1789 and 1791. The sections show the wooden support structure and the opening which allowed boats to proceed upstream. (Magee College)

would be one of its most frequent users. Since ancient times the only method of crossing the one-thousand-foot-wide river had been by ferry. In 1759 one visitor to the city, Judge Edward Willes, found that three large boats were engaged, one carrying 120 passengers, and the other two around 80 passengers each. There were endless complaints about the inconvenience and delays of this system but little, if anything, was done about the matter until the arrival of Dr Hervey.

Throughout 1769 there were frequent communications on the subject of the bridge between the corporation in Derry and the Irish Society in London. The bishop wrote to a friend in France to enquire if anyone could provide a plan and elevation of the bridge at Schaffhausen in Switzerland, which he thought might serve as a model for Derry. A 'Sardinian' architect, Davis Duckart, or Daviso de Arcort, who was working in Ireland at the time, wrote to Hervey on 13 February, describing the progress made on the designs for a stone bridge and

The late-eighteenth-century wooden bridge in 1863, shortly before its demolition. The toll house at the 'city' end of the bridge can be seen. (Magee College)

LONDONDERRY, OLD WOODEN BRIDGE, 1863.

guaranteeing that the cost would not exceed £32,000. He offered to come to Derry 'before the next assizes' so that his plans could be 'perused and examined by people of taste and knowledge'. The bishop contributed £1,000 to the 'bridge' fund. However, these plans were not proceeded with.

It was not until 1789 that work on the bridge commenced. The contract was given to the Boston firm of Lemuel Cox and Jonathan Thompson, who had a lot of experience in New England constructing bridges over rivers as wide, deep and rapid as the Foyle. The bridge became usable by pedestrians in 1790 and the following year was opened to horse-drawn traffic. It cost £16,294 6s., was 1068 feet long, 40 feet wide, with a footpath and gas lamps along each side. The supporting piers were sixteen and a half feet apart and near the city or western end there was an opening device to allow boat traffic to pass upstream. This was necessitated because the citizens of Strabane, with the support of Lord Abercorn, had opposed the building of the bridge on the grounds that it would interfere with their trade. Water and gas pipes were later laid across the bridge, involving a complicated process

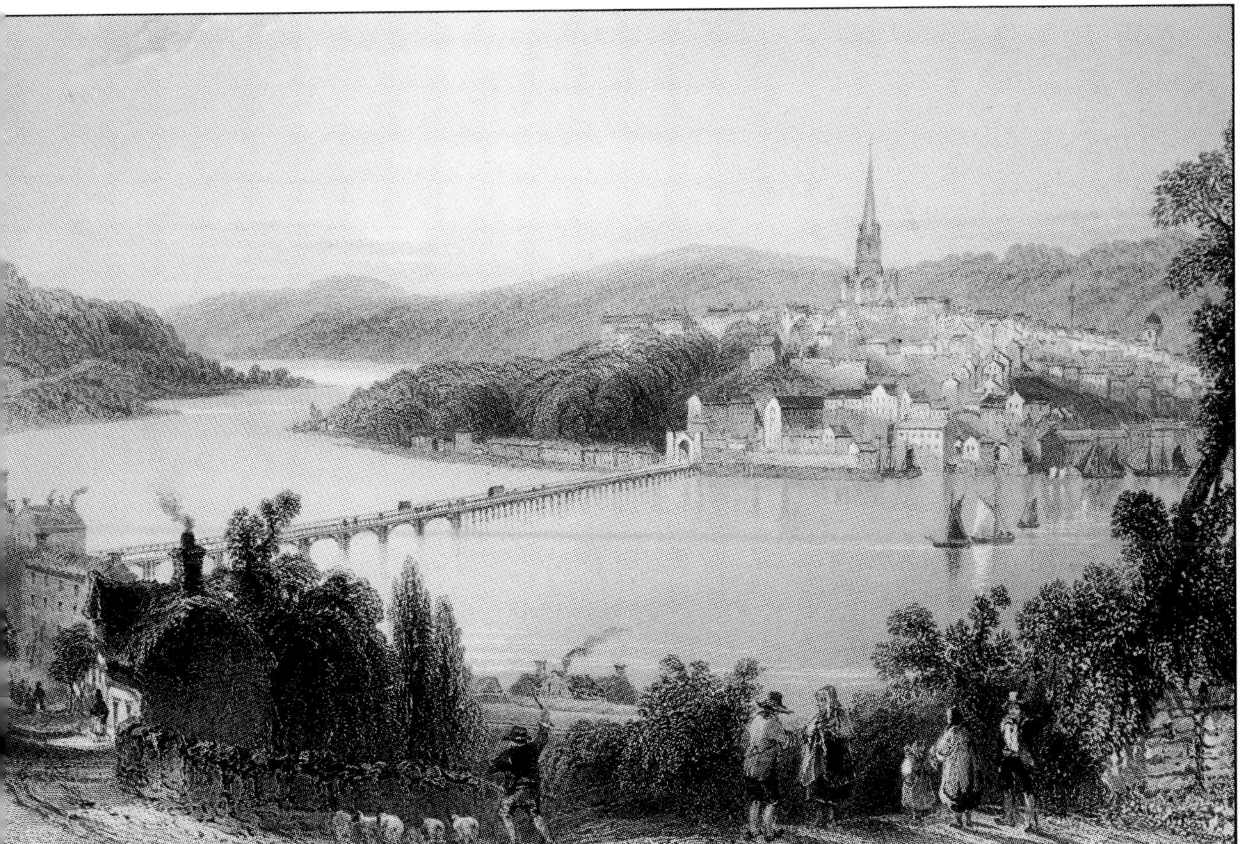

A romanticised view of Derry, *c.* 1800 (Ulster Folk and Transport Museum)

of disconnection whenever shipping wished to move upstream. A toll-house was built at the city end of the bridge, which occasioned the tongue-in-cheek complaint that the inhabitants of the Waterside had the 'free' pleasure of being able to perambulate the length of the bridge without having to pay the fee. Consciousness of discrimination has always been highly developed in Derry.

THE VOLUNTEERS

After the relief centenary celebrations in 1789, Dr Hervey set out again on his travels. He returned to the city a year later, on 30 November, and his entry was a triumph. At about 3 p.m. he was met on the nearly completed bridge by the corporation and a company of the Derry Volunteers. He was accompanied to his palace by a civic procession, where several speeches were made and volleys of shots fired in his honour. That night a great banquet was held and the bishop's contributions to the city, most notably his campaign for the bridge, were praised repeatedly. Among the groups prominent in this welcome and in the previous siege centenary celebrations, were companies of 'Volunteers'. The Volunteers, a paramilitary organisation, had come into existence in 1778 to defend Ireland against French invasion, at a time when most of the regular troops were either in America or garrisoning Britain. The Volunteers, who were influenced by the success of the American rebels in shaking off restrictions imposed by Britain, quickly took a radical direction and soon they began to influence Irish politics. They forced a number of concessions from the British government, including the abolition of Poyning's Law, which had subordinated the parliament of Ireland to that of Britain since the later Middle Ages.

Volunteer medal, 1782

A number of Volunteer companies had been formed in Derry and the surrounding areas – the Londonderry Fusiliers, the Londonderry Independent Company, the Blue Volunteers, and the Apprentice Boys. Dr Hervey showed little interest in the movement for the first few years of its existence but many of its radical demands coincided with his own views about how society and government should be reformed in Ireland, including radical improvements in the treatment of Catholics. In the summer of 1782 there was a cordial meeting between the city's Volunteer companies and Father John Lynch, and in the same year, Dr Hervey wrote to the Derry Volunteers offering his support and assistance. An apocryphal story claims that the bishop later presented a number of cannon to the Volunteers, with an inscription written on the barrels which read: 'O Lord open thou our lips and our mouths shall show forth thy praise.'

Early in 1783, Dr Hervey joined the Volunteer movement, quickly becoming colonel of the Londonderry corps, a position that gave him a powerful role in the political affairs of the country. But his real ambition was to become national leader of the Volunteer movement throughout the whole of Ireland. His rival was the existing commander in chief, James Caulfield, Earl of Charlemont. The showdown between the two men came at the Grand General Convention of the Volunteers, held in Dublin in November 1783. Dr Hervey's journey from Derry to the capital was another triumphant procession, which took three days to complete; he was attended by officers and men of the Derry Volunteers and he was given civic receptions at a number of towns along the route. His entry into Dublin rivalled that of royalty, going so far as to interrupt, with a fanfare of trumpets, the proceedings of the House of Lords and of Commons. This elaborate pageantry had been staged as part of the war of nerves with Charlemont, who, however, secured victory at the convention. One contemporary, referring to Hervey, wrote: 'The Volunteer of Derry is of no consequence.'

The Volunteer movement was now fully in the hands of conservative forces and its influence began to wane. Among the casualties was a commitment to the enfranchisement of Catholics. Hervey left his Derry diocese in 1791 and although he did not die until 1803, he never returned to Ireland. The city, which under his episcopal direction had had a brief flirtation with enlightenment values, soon reverted to more traditional attitudes. In 1792 the corporation declared itself opposed to any measures which would weaken the Protestant ascendancy.

Derry escaped any major entanglement in the events surrounding the 1798 rebellion. To help control the area during the growing political crisis in the country, the Londonderry Militia had been brought into existence in 1793. Later, the Londonderry Yeomanry Cavalry was formed by local gentlemen. There was fear for the strategic location of the city in the event of a French invasion through Lough Swilly. However, the authorities were successful in preventing the spread of the rebellion to the western parts of Ulster, and Derry remained quiet throughout the course of the uprising.

SOCIETY AND ECONOMY

By the end of the eighteenth century the population of the city had reached eleven thousand, nearly four times its size at the beginning of the century. Clearly there had been a great deal of growth, although there had been very little physical expansion beyond the original walled area. Arthur Young, who visited the city in the 1770s during his tour of Ireland, described Derry as 'the most picturesque of any place I have seen'. Another report by an English visitor, Charles Abbot, in 1792, describes a 'neat' city, most of whose houses were built of brick. Several of these elegant eighteenth-century houses still survive in Shipquay Street. Abbot recorded that there were about fifty to sixty ships belonging to the port and although there was much poverty in the city it nevertheless had a lively social life.

Coteries or society gatherings were held fortnightly throughout the winter and there was for a brief period at the end of the century a theatre in London Street. Dramatic and musical performances were also given regularly at other venues throughout the 1700s by travelling companies. Horse racing, which used to take place in the seventeenth century on the strand or foreshore just to the north of the city (now reclaimed and built over as the Strand Road), moved in the early eighteenth century to the Shantallow–Ballyarnett area. In 1777 a proper race-course was built there and this was in use by 1780. Racing continued at that location until the 1920s, although its days of glory had ceased around 1880.

The economy of the city did not develop to any great extent in the earlier part of the eighteenth century. However, by the mid-1700s the situation was beginning to improve, the linen industry and emigrant trade to America making the largest contributions. The original ship quay was improved and expanded and new quays built out into the river. However, the American War of Independence and the later war with France interrupted this development. A linen hall was built in 1759. In 1802 Robert Slade, the agent for the Irish Society, described the linen market in the city:

> The linen market of Londonderry forms an object of great curiosity; it is held twice in every week, and lasts for two hours only, within which short period of time I was assured linens were purchased in single webs of the manufacturers, to the amount of £5,000 and upwards in ready money. These manufacturers do not reside in the city, but are dispersed in cabins round its neighbourhood, where they have each of them a few acres of land for the sake of keeping a cow and raising some potatoes and flax, and for which, by means of their looms, they are enabled to pay a heavy rent.

A small sugar factory was established in the city about 1755 and continued in operation until 1809. Tobacco and snuff were manufactured but these industries seem to have declined towards the end of the century. Suspicions that some people in the city were involved in a notorious tobacco-smuggling trade in Inishowen led to Derry being dropped from the list of ports licensed to handle tobacco in 1788–9. Brewing and distilling were also carried on although on a domestic scale. In 1780 there were twenty-eight distillers in the city and another twelve in the Waterside. Most of the other businesses in the city were concerned with servicing the local economy.

A TRAGIC LOVE STORY

One of the best-known stories connected with Derry in the eighteenth century is the tragic tale of young Mary Anne Knox of Prehen House, and her would-be lover, 'Half-hanged' John McNaghten. Mary Anne was the daughter of Andrew Knox, a member for Donegal in the Irish parliament. She was just fifteen years old when she first met the much-older McNaghten. A contemporary described her as

> of a middling stature, very elegantly formed, her hair was light with an agreeable tendency to the golden hue, serving only to enliven her complexion, which nothing could exceed.

McNaghten, although he had been a sheriff of County Antrim, was a notorious gambler and many believed that his first wife had died through worrying about his behaviour. Andrew Knox invited McNaghten to visit Prehen as a house-guest, where he laid eyes on the beautiful Mary Anne. Whether it was love or, as some allege, an attempt to secure her inheritance, McNaghten determined to marry the young woman against the wishes of her father.

McNaghten cajoled Mary Anne into reading through the marriage service with him at the house of Joshua Seetenham in Derry and on the basis of this 'ceremony', he claimed her as his wife. Andrew Knox was livid and forbade any contact between the two, but the wily McNaghten is said to have flouted the injunction, going to Prehen regularly in disguise. Whatever the facts, McNaghten won the support of the common people of the time, including some of the servants at Prehen. He made plans to abduct Mary Anne and nearly succeeded when she was taking the waters at Swanlinbar in County Cavan.

On the morning of 10 November 1761, the Knox family set out from Prehen for Dublin. Andrew was on his way to parliament and decided to take his family with him in order to safeguard Mary Anne. A few miles down the road at Cloughcor Wood, McNaghten had gathered with a few accomplices. In the débâcle which ensued after they had stopped the coaches, McNaghten, possibly in a tragic error, shot Mary Anne and she died four hours later. A conspiracy of silence enveloped McNaghten but after six weeks on the run, he was captured at Portrush in County Antrim, just as he was about to escape to Scotland. He was taken, wounded, to Lifford Jail and was later tried and found guilty of murder.

McNaghten's popularity among the common people had continued and at first no one could be found to build the gallows or remove his fetters so that he could be hanged. Finally, with great remorse for his crime, McNaghten threw himself off the gallows. Unbelievably, the rope broke. The spectators quickly opened up a gangway for McNaghten to escape but he declined, saying that he did not wish to be known as the 'half-hanged man'. He returned to the gallows and on the second attempt the rope held. Throughout Ireland and even further afield the story became one of the great romances of the century.

At the end of the eighteenth century Derry was an elegant, picturesque Georgian city. With the exception of its walls and cathedral, both of which had been altered also, virtually the entire city had been rebuilt since the end of the siege of 1689. Most of the city's overwhelmingly Protestant population still lived inside the walls but a commercial and industrial quarter had developed along the river front. In the rural

A contemporary cameo of Mary Anne Knox (Courtesy of Mrs C. Peck), and the Knox family home, Prehen House, on the hill, built *c.* 1745, near Derry (from George Vaughan Sampson's *Survey of the County of Londonderry*, 1814)

hinterlands, particularly in County Donegal, a growing mass of desperately poor people struggled for survival. In the midst of appalling conditions of poverty, added to which were the penal restrictions on their Catholic religion, many of them began to look to the prosperous city of Derry in the hope of a better life. The arrival of these people and their descendants in Derry during the nineteenth century would profoundly alter the character of the city and once more change the direction of its historical development.

9

THE GROWTH OF THE CATHOLIC COMMUNITY 1800–50

The late-eighteenth-century flirtation with liberalism in Derry was very short-lived. Political influence in the city at the time was totally in the hands of a few wealthy Tory and Anglican families. There was virtually no opposition to this oligarchy from the Presbyterian merchants and artisans, and Catholics were a tiny, poor, disenfranchised minority. There was strong support in the city for the union of Ireland with Britain when the proposal emerged in 1799–1800.

The plantation city of Londonderry had been colonised with British Protestants in the seventeenth century but in the nineteenth century there began an influx of Irish Catholics. The tensions resulting from this unforeseen change dominated affairs throughout the 1800s but, as the century began, the city was quiet and stable. Fears of an imagined Catholic uprising, the basis of the infamous 'siege mentality', had dwindled to the point where deliberate expansion beyond the walls could be contemplated. By 1844 the local prejudice that 'it was not respectable to live outside the walls' was disappearing. Nevertheless, in 1815 strong opposition had been expressed at the decision to build the new military barracks at Ebrington in the Waterside, which, although directly opposite the city, was still considered to be on the 'wrong' side of the river.

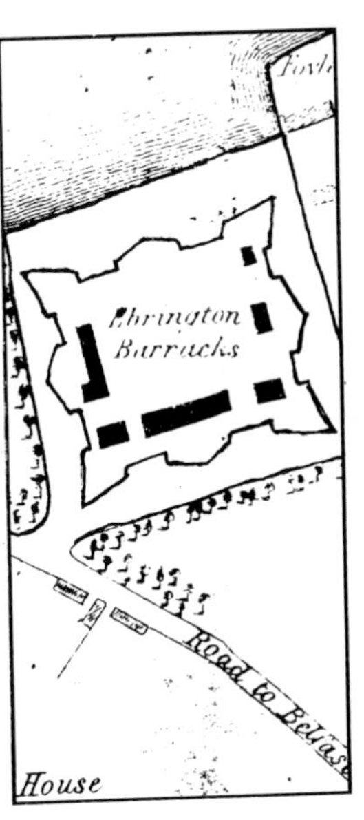

Ebrington Barracks in the Waterside, built in 1839 on lands purchased for the purpose many years before. As early as 1815, opposition had been expressed at the decision to site the new barracks across the river from the city.

TOWARDS A CATHOLIC MAJORITY

In the early nineteenth century some of the city's middle classes were moving to the Waterside, and to the new suburbs being opened up in the Great James Street–Queen Street area to the north of the walled town. Meanwhile, the city's growing working-class communities were being concentrated in the Bogside and Fountain areas, both of which huddled close up beneath, but outside, the city walls. From this time these districts acquired the strongly denominational character that they have retained to the present day – the Fountain area became predominantly Protestant while the Bogside was predominantly Catholic. As was the case with similar working-class areas in other cities, poverty, disease and high mortality were the common lot of the people who lived there. On 29 November 1836, a letter to the editor of a local newspaper called

The Bogside overlooked by the city walls and the Walker Pillar, which was erected between 1826 and and 1828. Since at least the middle of the eighteenth century the Bogside area had developed as the Catholic ghetto of the city. A township of appalling hovels developed there, housing impoverished immigrants, most of whom came into the city from County Donegal. (Bartlett engraving, Ulster Folk and Transport Museum)

the attention of the public to the fact, that there are more deaths at present in this city and suburbs, from typhus fever, than were at the time the cholera raged here in its greatest fierceness. I state this fact, for the purpose of shewing the necessity of taking proper measures to prevent the spread of this frightful contagion.

In the 1830s the compilers of the Ordnance Survey *Memoir* for the city also observed very bad conditions:

> Among the labourers of Derry great poverty prevails, from the want of steady employment, and their consequent exposure to dissipation, together with the total absence of employment for their children. The better class inhabit huts, which let for about £3 a year; but the poorer frequently lodge in garrets, or out-houses, chiefly in the Bogside, at a rent of about 1s. 3d. a week, – and yet even in these hovels they contrive to let shares of their rooms at 6d. a week.
>
> A great number of the labourers are from the mountains of Donegal. The majority are employed in serving masons etc., from May to November, – the rest in provision yards, etc., and in casual works during the export season, from November to May. Their only resources, when unemployed, are the pawnbrokers, and, in some instances, small potato-patches. When enfeebled by age or disease their condition is such as it would be painful to describe, but which is only an epitome of the wretchedness that prevails among the lower orders throughout Ireland.

Daniel O'Connell (1775–1847), the leader of the campaign for Catholic emancipation (George Mulvany, National Gallery of Ireland)

Contemporary drawing of Sir George Hill, who was MP for the city of Londonderry from 1801 to 1830 (from *The Protestant or True Blue Loyal Songs*, c. 1820)

The Catholic working class in Derry was increased after 1820 by a huge influx from Inishowen, when the extensive and illegal local poteen-making industry collapsed there under the onslaught of the Government's newly recruited excise men. In 1814 the Irish Society was informed that the population of the city and surrounding district had grown to 14,000. Twenty years later, Richard Griffith and the Grand Jury Valuation found that the population was just under 19,000, of whom 9,864 were Catholics. By the 1851 census Catholics were a clear majority in the city. However, it would take 120 years before that majority would be translated into municipal power.

The increase of Catholics in the city in the late eighteenth century had not been a source of tension. Under their astute bishop, Dr McDevitt, the Catholic population had quietly accepted the political status quo. At first the small community received some support from the city's Protestant establishment but, as its numbers began to grow and in the more reactionary atmosphere following the 1798 rebellion, tensions rose. Sectarian trouble began to focus on the siege anniversary parades which were now being held annually. There was tension from 1809 to 1811, which contemporaries blamed on the influence of Daniel O'Connell's national campaign for Catholic emancipation. A large rally attended by almost every Catholic in the city, with the exception of the local clergy, was held in support of O'Connell in 1811. Attempts to defuse the agitation were made by Bishop Charles O'Donnell, who had succeeded Dr McDevitt in 1798, and who was anxious to pursue the conciliatory policies of his predecessor. Dr O'Donnell's co-operation with the corporation and the city's Member of Parliament, Sir George Hill, brought him into conflict with the local Catholic Committee and

Derry Jail, Bishop Street, *c.* 1830 (Derry City Council)

earned him the soubriquet 'Orange Charlie', and the committee, of which he was a 'nominal' member, denounced him.

Among the leading agitators in the city at the time was Father Cornelius O'Mullan, a powerful orator who was a strong supporter of O'Connell and an associate of the local agrarian secret society, the Ribbonmen. In January 1813 attempts at a compromise between the two factions of the Catholic community in the city failed. The bishop retaliated by accusing Father O'Mullan of planning his assassination, reported the cleric to the local civil authorities and prohibited him from officiating as a parish priest. On 28 November of that year, Dr O'Donnell organised a meeting in the Long Tower Church to try to capture control of the Catholic Committee. During the meeting Father O'Mullan, supported by an angry mob which included several Ribbonmen, arrived in the church and physically and verbally threatened the bishop, who was forced to flee to the courthouse for protection. A number of people were hurt in the ensuing fracas. O'Mullan was immediately ex-communicated by the bishop and arrested by the civil

The courthouse in Bishop Street, built between 1813 and 1817 (Derry City Council)

authorities. Although O'Connell sent Nicholas Purcell O'Gorman to Derry to defend O'Mullan, he was found guilty and sentenced to six months' imprisonment. There was a huge and vociferous demonstration by the Catholics of the city against the decision of the court but trouble quickly subsided. During 1814 the Protestant Apprentice Boys of Derry Club was founded, the precursor of the present organisation. However, sectarian tensions in the city faded temporarily.

CATHOLIC EMANCIPATION

An increase in political disturbances throughout Ireland in 1822 led to an attack on the annual Protestant parade in August and tension continued in the city for a few weeks afterwards. The new Catholic bishop, Dr Peter McLaughlin, tried quietly to tackle the concerns of his people. Apart from the frustration of being excluded from local political influence, the problems had been heightened by the national campaign for Catholic emancipation. A Catholic Association was formed in the city in 1823, but under Dr McLaughlin's guidance this organisation concerned itself more with spiritual than political matters. In 1837 the compilers of the Ordnance Survey *Memoir* described the bishop as

> being very generally esteemed by the various classes, for his zealous and unremitting exertions to promote concorde and good feeling among all sects within his diocese, – interfering in political matters only so far as to endeavour to prevent the people of his own persuasion from indulging in party violence.

Medal to commemorate the foundation of the Apprentice Boys of Derry Club in 1814

However, the bishop's calming effect was jeopardised in 1826 by the arrival, in the middle of a national controversy about the conversion of Catholics, of a group of proselytising Protestant itinerant street preachers, which resulted in a sectarian riot. That same year, the foundation stone of the elegant Walker Pillar was laid on a site overlooking the Bogside. For 147 years the monument was a well-known symbol of the city and an icon for the Protestant siege celebrations. It was blown up in 1973 in the course of the current Troubles.

In 1828 two members of the missionary Reformation Society visited Derry to help establish a branch of the organisation in the city. A meeting held in the courthouse on 11 March was attended by a number of Catholics, including several priests, determined to prevent the society from engaging in any proselytising activities among their people. The meeting ended in uproar and the organisers had to adjourn it until the next day, when admission was by ticket only. However, the second occasion proved just as tumultuous as the first:

> It was in the course of this very unpleasant conflict of opinion, that a charge having been thrown out by one of the deputation, and repeated by one of the Protestant clergy present, as that the Roman Catholic clergy in their opposition to the Society only wished to avoid discussion, a distinct

The Walker Pillar, made of Portland stone, was eighty-one feet tall and was surmounted by a nine-foot plinth and statue of the Reverend George Walker (joint governor of Derry during the siege), by the Dublin sculptor John Smyth. An internal spiral staircase of 110 steps ascended to a viewing platform. Until its destruction in a bomb blast in 1973, the pillar figured prominently in various siege anniversary commemorations organised by the Apprentice Boys. (Bartlett engraving, Ulster Folk and Transport Museum)

> declaration was made on their part, that their objection was to the formation of such Societies as that contemplated; but if the question of the establishment of the Society were once disposed of, and the Protestant clergy were still anxious for discussion, the Roman Catholic clergy were ready to enter on it immediately. This was met on the part of the Protestant clergy, by a frank and ready avowal, that, as their only interest in the Society arose from the hope it offered of promoting such a discussion, they would willingly accede to any arrangement of the kind. A motion to the above effect having been made by Dean Blakely, and put by the chairman to the meeting, and the general feeling seeming to be in favour of the proposal, it was finally arranged that the meeting of the Reformation Society be now adjourned sine die, and that a discussion on the respective merits of the two Churches should immediately commence between six of the clergy of the Church of Rome, and six of the clergy of the Established Church of Ireland.

The result of this motion was the so-called 'Derry Discussion', a series of unprecedented public debates which began on 12 March 1828 and lasted for a fortnight. Each day up to seven speakers addressed a wide range of contentious religious issues, such as transubstantiation, purgatory, the papacy, Martin Luther, and the Scriptures. Each side was made up of six speakers – six Protestant ministers and six Catholic priests – and individual contributions lasted about forty-five minutes. The transcripts of these unparalleled debates were published in Dublin in a book of nearly eight hundred pages later that year, because

> those circumstances will surely not be thought unworthy of record, which have suddenly drawn forth, from the quiet walk of professional duty, so many Ministers of the long severed Churches of Rome and of Ireland, which have led persons, hitherto of retired habits, to stand forward in the public eye and ear, to contend on those great elements of faith and hope, on which they differ.

The Protestant community in the city was variously affected by the

The Londonderry Sentinel.

campaign for Catholic emancipation. The MP for County Londonderry in 1828 was G. R. Dawson, who was related by marriage to the leading English politician, Sir Robert Peel. That year Peel announced his conversion to the Catholic emancipation cause and Dawson, who up until then had professed strong Protestant opinions, felt it necessary to follow the lead of his eminent relative. However, he chose an unusual platform to announce his Damascus-like conversion. Speaking at a siege commemorative dinner held in Derry on 12 August, Dawson described his change of heart to his, no doubt, astonished audience, and was immediately subjected to public scorn. As a result, the Protestant community in the city was split into two separate and mutually critical factions.

The emancipation crisis in the city also precipitated a radical alteration in policy of the local newspaper, the *Londonderry Journal*. From its establishment in 1772 by Scotsman George Douglas, who ran a stationery business in the Diamond, the paper had had a solidly Protestant and conservative editorial policy. In 1829 its new owners decided to support the demand for Catholic emancipation. The editor, William Wallen, vehemently disagreed and left the *Londonderry Journal* to found his own newspaper with a number of similarly minded friends. The *Londonderry Sentinel and North-West Advertiser* was first published on 19 September 1829, six months after the Catholic relief act became law, removing all the important remaining restrictions on Catholics. Its first editorial proclaimed the philosophy for which it stood:

> The state of Ireland is pregnant with alarm. Ill-timed and timid concession has borne its natural fruits – discontent has ripened into disloyalty – turbulence into open sedition – and the men who promised the most unreserved submission to gain their favourite end, now loudly complain, that Emancipation has been but an empty boon, and that they have got only ashes for bread.
>
> We judge of men by their actions, and unstudied declarations; and taking these as our guide, we do not hesitate to say, that there is a large party in Ireland, who in return for the sacrifice of the Constitution to their views, are determined to separate this country from England. Agitation, disturbance, and intimidation are kept up as a means of serving their object, and they already fancy the Protestants of Ireland at the tender mercies of a Popish Parliament sitting in Dublin . . .
>
> The Protestants have been deceived, not by the open enemy, for then we could have borne it, nor by the adversary that did magnify himself against us, but by friends and guides in whom we trusted. We will learn wisdom from the past; and as WE have formed no bargain with, or sought no protection from, public men, and have moreover little confidence in

The Diamond, *c.* 1913, the former location of the statue of Sir Robert Ferguson, 'The Black Man' (left), who was elected MP for Derry in 1830 and held the seat for thirty years. The statue is now located in Brooke Park. (Green Collection, Ulster Folk and Transport Museum)

> them, we will fearlessly exact from them the penalty of their station, and bring them, no matter who they may be, to the bar of public opinion, whenever we deem their conduct worthy of reproof. – If the Schoolmaster is abroad the PROTESTANT SENTINEL is at his post.

Sales returns indicate that the proprietors of the *Londonderry Sentinel* were in closer touch with the attitudes of the reading public in Derry than the owners of the *Londonderry Journal*, for within five years it was selling more than twice as many copies as its rival. From January to September 1829 another newspaper, the *Londonderry Chronicle*, had been published in the city and there were other similarly transient publications in the early nineteenth century, such as the *Londonderry Recorder* and the *Londonderry Reporter*. The *Londonderry Sentinel* has continued to be closely identified with the Protestant community in the city and at least some of the views expressed in its inaugural editorial could still be found in its pages today.

The Catholic community of Derry reacted to the passing of the emancipation act with a demonstration on St Patrick's Day 1830 and a renewed demand for further national and local political reforms. These issues were taken up with the mayor, Sir Robert Ferguson, one of the candidates in a parliamentary bye-election for the city of Londonderry in August of that year. The Catholics had little hope of success. Sir Robert was returned and, supported by a united Protestant community, he retained the seat for thirty years.

ECONOMIC AND SOCIAL LIFE IN THE EARLY NINETEENTH CENTURY

In the 1820s and 1830s the population of Derry was growing, with large numbers of migrants coming into the city from its Donegal hinterland.

Londonderry Shipping List,

AND GENERAL PRICE CURRENT.

No. II. THURSDAY, SEPTEMBER 19, 1833. PRICE 3D.

Published (by Government Authority,) every Thursday, by JOHN EVANS, *of the Custom-House.*
Price to Subscribers Half-a-Guinea per annum—to be paid in advance.

A great number found work quickly in the thriving port and in the construction boom which had arisen as the city expanded beyond its original walled enclosure. Many of the city's major public buildings, such as the courthouse, the asylum, Foyle College and the Great James Street (the 'Scotch') Presbyterian Church were built about this time. But the economy of the city was anything but healthy: it had failed to develop any major industries and those which had been established, such as glass-making and sugar-refining, had either already collapsed or were about to.

Around this time a local man, William Scott, set up a small weaving business. Fashions in men's shirts were changing from the older flannel kind to a lighter cotton garment which had a stiff linen front and collar.

GLASGOW AND LONDONDERRY
STEAMERS.

ST. COLUMB, - *Captain Wyse, and*
FOYLE, - - - *Captain Coulter,*

SAIL regularly between the above Ports, calling at GREENOCK and CAMPBELTOWN, and weather permitting, at PORT RUSH, near the GIANTS' CAUSEWAY; leaving Glasgow for Londonderry every Tuesday and Friday, and leaving Londonderry for Glasgow on the same days.

INTENDED HOURS OF SAILING.

FROM GLASGOW.

St. Columb,	Tuesday, 2d Sept.		10	Morning.
Foyle,	Friday, 5th —		12	Noon.
St. Columb,	Tuesday, 9th —		3	Afternoon.
Foyle,	Friday, 12th —		7	Morning.
St. Columb,	Tuesday, 16th —		10	——
Foyle,	Friday, 19th —		12	Noon.
St. Columb,	Tuesday, 23d —		2	Afternoon.
Foyle,	Friday, 26th —		6	Morning.
St. Columb,	Tuesday, 30th —		9	——
Foyle,	Friday, 3d Oct.		12	Noon.
St. Columb,	Tuesday, 7th —		2	Afternoon.
Foyle,	Friday, 10th —	½ past	6	Morning.
St. Columb,	Tuesday, 14th —		9	——
Foyle,	Friday, 17th —		11	Forenoon.
St. Columb,	Tuesday, 21st —		1	Afternoon.
Foyle,	Friday, 24th —		3	——
St. Columb,	Tuesday, 28th —		8	Morning.
Foyle,	Friday, 31st —		10	——
St. Columb,	Tuesday, 4th Nov.		1	Afternoon.
Foyle,	Friday, 7th —	½ past	3	——
St. Columb,	Tuesday, 11th —		8	Morning.
Foyle,	Friday, 14th —		10	——
St. Columb,	Tuesday, 18th —		12	Noon.
Foyle,	Friday, 21st —		2	Afternoon
St. Columb,	Tuesday, 25th —		7	Morning.
Foyle,	Friday, 28th —		9	——

FROM LONDONDERRY.

Foyle,	Tuesday, 2d Sept.		10	Morning.
St. Columb,	Friday, 5th —		11	——
Foyle,	Tuesday, 9th —		6	——
St. Columb,	Friday, 12th —		7	——
Foyle,	Tuesday, 16th —		9	——
St. Columb,	Friday, 19th —		10	——
Foyle,	Tuesday, 23d —		1	Afternoon.
St. Columb,	Friday, 26th —		6	Morning.
Foyle,	Tuesday, 30th —		8	——
St. Columb,	Friday, 3d Oct.		10	——
Foyle,	Tuesday, 7th —		12	Noon.
St. Columb,	Friday, 10th —		6	Morning.
Foyle,	Tuesday, 14th —		8	——
St. Columb,	Friday, 17th —		10	——
Foyle,	Tuesday, 21st —		12	Noon.
St. Columb,	Friday, 24th —		6	Morning.
Foyle,	Tuesday, 28th —		7	——
St. Columb,	Friday, 31st —		9	——
Foyle,	Tuesday, 4th Nov.		12	Noon.
St. Columb,	Friday, 7th —		6	Morning.
Foyle,	Tuesday, 11th —		8	——
St. Columb,	Friday, 14th —		9	——
Foyle,	Tuesday, 18th —		11	Forenoon.
St. Columb,	Friday, 21st —		1	Afternoon.
Foyle,	Tuesday, 25th —	½ past	6	Morning.
St. Columb,	Friday, 28th —		9	Morning.

THE TIME OF SAILING FROM GREENOCK IS TWO HOURS AND A HALF LATER THAN FROM GLASGOW.

Goods require to be alongside One Hour before the time of Sailing.

AGENTS.

T. CAMERON & CO. GLASGOW.
N. KHULL, - - GREENOCK.
G. LYON, - - LONDONDERRY.

25th AUGUST, 1834. *Muir, Gowans, & Co. Printers.*

William Scott, the 'founder' of Derry's shirt industry (Magee College)

A view of the Butcher Gate area and the River Foyle, *c.* 1840 (St Columb's Cathedral)

The Scott family business, in which the men did the weaving and the women made up the garments, was one of the first to supply this new demand. In 1831 Scott travelled to Glasgow, taking some of his samples with him, where they were an immediate success. Orders soon followed from London, and from as far away as Australia. The female members of the family could not keep up with the demand, and the business was forced to expand through a system of outstations. Country women, who had inherited the local skill of sprigging (white embroidery on a white background), were trained and assigned a 'station' at their homes. A large warehouse was set up in Derry, where the material was cut for the outworkers and the results inspected when they were returned. An article published in the *Derry Standard* in 1928 describes how the original outstation system survived:

> Trained girls were placed in charge of the stations. They instructed local girls in the trade. They gave out materials, collected the finished garments, examined them and paid the workers. These stations covered an area from Strabane and Claudy; Inishowen and East Donegal. Wages for the girls employed in making the shirts ranged from 3/6 per dozen upwards. The actual making of the shirts was carried out in the homes of the workers.
>
> The constant comings and goings of carts from the stations to Scott's weaving shop made it necessary for the family to open larger premises in the Old Military Hospital in Bennet Street. In the new site, there was space for weavers, cutters and sewers, who prepared the materials for the outworkers; and for the examiners and for the packers who organised the finished goods for despatch . . .

A general view of the city of Derry, *c.* 1840, featuring the Ship Quay area (St Columb's Cathedral)

> Such was the eagerness of the people to make shirts, that they came distances of 10 and 12 miles and upwards – from Claudy, Carndonagh, Redcastle, Strabane, etc. They used to remain in front of Mr Scott's doors all night, patiently waiting to get in, in the mornings, and such were the crowds of workers, that it was necessary to make an arrangement by which each individual got a ticket, with a number on it, which after the doors were closed in the evening, they dropped into a letter-box, as they came forward, and when the place was opened on the following morning, the contents of the letter-box were turned upside down, so that workers who had waited longest, and whose tickets would be at the bottom, were called forward and attended to first. Some of the workers, however, more knowing than the rest, devised a plan by which they for some time got themselves attended to before others, who had waited much longer. This was by means of putting a crooked wire into the letter-box, lifting up the tickets that had been put in before theirs, and slipping their own underneath. This trick, however, was soon discovered, and willing sentries afterwards kept watch at the letter-box.

In spite of its humble beginnings, an industry was to grow that would be the mainstay of the city's economy for almost a century.

Growing puritanical influences in the city were leading to the disappearance of lucrative local festivities and social occasions. By the time of the Ordnance Survey *Memoir* in 1837 the theatre had been

> converted into a coach-house . . . the concerts have been discontinued; the coteries presided over by a King and Queen of the night, have died

Shipquay Street in the middle of the nineteenth century

away; and even the horse-races are probably less attractive than the meetings of the farming societies, and seem marked with all the symptoms of decay.

The same report suggests the kind of atmosphere prevailing in the city at the time:

> That gravity of character is indeed the most striking feature of the inhabitants of Derry is evident to the most careless observer. It is manifested by the appearance of the city at night, when the streets, at a comparatively early hour, are nearly deserted, and the repose of the inhabitants rarely disturbed by the noise of a drunken brawler. It is exhibited still more remarkably on Sundays, when every thing indicates strict order, decorum, and scrupulous observance of the Sabbath. It is apparent also in the prevailing indifference to public amusements, to polite literature, and to the fine arts.

The result of this sensible, if dull, way of life was that many of the upper-class residents of the surrounding counties, who previously had patronised the social facilities and retail outlets of the city, now deserted it. The 1837 description continues: 'The removal of many of the more wealthy inhabitants from the town to the country has left its occupation chiefly to those who have yet their fortunes to gain.' This could not have

Bishop Street in the middle of the nineteenth century

happened at a worse time, as within a few years, the growth of the railway network emanating from Belfast brought the retail outlets of that city within the grasp of many of Derry's former customers.

On 30 November 1836 the city acquired another newspaper, the *Londonderry Standard*, which later changed the description of its place of publication to the more commonly used Derry. It was established by two local men of liberal opinions, J. Walker and T. McCarter, and became the principal public organ of Derry's Presbyterian community. It outlined the principles for which it stood in its first editorial:

> The Londonderry Standard is indebted for its existence neither to partizans of faction nor to the hirelings of patronage – it is the offspring of a sense, in its conductors, of the great good and manifest blessings to a community attendant on a principled and devoted employment of all their energies to the elucidation of truth . . . with us, power is nothing, place is nothing, but Truth is everything . . . The Standard will be the guardian of those civil and religious institutions for which our forefathers fought and conquered, it will advocate the principles of the Revolution, and the religion of the Reformation . . . And where should such an appeal be successful . . . if not here, where the very air is eloquent with the echoes of former triumph – here, where the memory of our ancestors' patient endurance has become a very romance and poetry of chivalrous

> loyalty – here, where the very stones are letters of an historic page, luminous with unequalled glory – here, in this citadel and stronghold of a pure faith – in this armory of constitutional feeling? here we plant our STANDARD.

The newspaper was to become a powerful voice in Derry and it was said of many of its supporters that 'the Bible and the *Standard* were the only literature they read'. (In 1932 the *Derry Standard* made the news itself, when its employees took over its ownership and ran it as a workers' co-operative, the first of its kind in Ireland. It eventually closed in 1964, an omen, perhaps, of the coming reduction of Protestant influence in the city.)

THE ORDNANCE SURVEY

A great deal is known about Derry in the 1830s, largely because of the publication in 1837 of the Ordnance Survey *Memoir of the City and North Western Liberties of Londonderry Parish of Templemore.* This extraordinary 350-page volume gives, in minute detail, a description of the city and the surrounding district at this important stage in its development. Surprisingly, although the memoir also outlines the general history of the city, it virtually ignores what many of its citizens would have seen as the most important event in that history – the siege of 1689. It was published at a time when there was much controversy about siege commemorative events and its authors were forthright in their opinions:

> As long as the citizens were exclusively Protestant, or as the community generally participated in [the siege commemorations], they might be

Foyle College, built in 1814. In 1968 the school moved to new premises at Springtown but 'Old Foyle' has been restored as an arts centre (Magee College)

considered as harmless and unobjectionable. But as these circumstances had greatly changed, and the perpetuation of such customs had become a subject of contention, it was well that the legislature interfered to smooth down a cause of useless dissension.

Colonel Thomas Colby (1784–1853) was director of the first Ordnance Survey of Ireland in the 1820s and 1830s. He married a Derry woman, Elizabeth Boyd, and for a while lived in Shipquay Street. (from Colonel Sir Charles Close, *The Early Years of the Ordnance Survey*)

The Ordnance Survey originally planned to publish memoirs for every parish in Ireland as a companion to the detailed six-inch-to-the-mile maps being compiled at the same time. The memoirs were to be the 'biographies' of the country, to complement the 'portraits' shown on the maps. In the preface to the Templemore volume, the authors convey the economic and developmental role which they envisaged for the memoir scheme:

> It is scarcely necessary to remark, that a map is in its nature but a part of a Survey, and that much of the information connected with it, can only be advantageously embodied in a memoir, to which the map then serves as a graphical index . . . The direction in which a rail road or canal should be made might be indicated by the maps, but the necessity for making it must be sought in the objects to be attained by it when made. This required a knowledge of the social and industrial state of the people, of the effects which had been produced by similar improvements under similar circumstances; and, in order that the present condition of the country might be exhibited in every useful light, it was necessary to divest History of fable and error, and to hold up the past as a beacon and a guide to the future.

However, the Government decided to abandon what appeared to some contemporaries to be an enormously expensive, and possibly even dangerous, luxury. The Templemore volume was the only memoir to be published contemporaneously.

Derry has several other associations with the first Ordnance Survey. The original base-line from which the whole of Ireland was subsequently mapped was laid out on the level terrain of Magilligan sands,

Contemporary drawing of the first Ordnance Survey of Ireland in operation *c.* 1825 (from W. Yolland, *An Account of the Measurement of the Lough Foyle Base*, 1847)

about eighteen miles north of the city. The English director of the survey, Colonel Thomas Colby, married a local woman, Elizabeth Boyd, and for a while during the course of the operations they lived in a house in Shipquay Street. In 1980 the Derry-based Field Day Theatre Company premiered the much acclaimed and controversial play *Translations*, by Brian Friel, which takes the work of the first Ordnance Survey as its principal theme and dramatic locale.

LABOUR RELATIONS

The 1830s also saw a series of trade-union and industrial disputes in Derry. In 1834 George Kerr, a Belfast cabinet-maker, came to public attention when he acted as chairman of a meeting called in that city to protest at the treatment of the Tolpuddle Martyrs. (These were six farm workers from Tolpuddle in Dorset who in 1834 had been sentenced to seven years' transportation for forming a trade union.) He was invited to Derry to help the local cabinet-makers form a union and fight a decision by the employers to cut wages by up to one-third. A meeting was held and a Derry branch of the union set up. Shortly afterwards the mayor, Joshua Gillespie, who naturally supported the employers, had some of the union leaders arrested on false charges of administering illegal oaths. Kerr, by this time back in Belfast, was also arrested and brought back to Derry, but he and the others were later released and the charges dropped. It was the mayor who had been guilty of illegality. Kerr wrote an account of the incident in a pamphlet entitled *Exposition of Legislative Tyranny and Defence of the Trade Unions*:

> While in [Londonderry], I made it my business to have a meeting with some of the Cabinet-makers, in order to learn the state of their trade; and also to acquaint them of the state of the Cabinet-makers' trade in Belfast, to which last mentioned body I belonged. After mutual explanation on both sides, it was at length agreed, that as there had been a great falling off, and frequent reduction of the Cabinet-maker's wages, to the extent of thirty, forty, and in some instances even sixty per cent, we came to the determination of joining the Trades' Union, or Friendly Society, which had for its object the unity of all Cabinet-makers in the three kingdoms; that they might the more effectually be enabled to support their sick, and bury their dead; and that they might be enabled to support their idle brothers who could not get employment, and also to support the travelling operative, who wandered from town to town in quest of employment, and in short to endeavour by every means in our power to check the evils of society, by recommending and providing to our members the means of moral and intellectual improvement . . .
>
> Every one who reads this cannot but see the most determined spirit evinced by the Mayor of Londonderry to punish and harass the Trades Unionists, merely because they were poor; for as I have already remarked, he observed, with a malicious sneer, that the Trades Unionists could not find in all their mighty society, two men to qualify for forty

Shipquay Street in 1844

> pounds each, thus at once showing that their poverty was as much a crime in his eyes as anything else . . . Nevertheless, although the Trades Unionists individually are not wealthy; still will they be able to produce from among their ranks, men as talented – men as virtuous – men as humane – men as honest – and perhaps, men as rich, as the Worshipful Joshua Gillespie, Esquire, Mayor of Londonderry. Alas! alas! what a pity it is, that poverty should be looked upon as a crime!

Kerr's pamphlet has been pointed to by labour historians as being an extremely valuable document in the early history of trade unionism in Ireland.

There were struggles in other trades and industries in the city around this time. Workers retaliated against the tactics of their employers with intimidation and even attempts to assassinate some of the blacklegs who had been brought in. In 1837 the printers managed to achieve some modest successes, but the following year the local newspapers were unusually unanimous in their celebration of the defeat of the same workers. The economic situation in the city at the time was not conducive to the improvement of workers' conditions and by 1840 trade unionism in Derry had been effectively defeated.

Dr Edward Maginn, Catholic bishop of Derry from 1845 to 1849 (from *The Story of the Long Towe Church 546–1946*)

THE CATHOLIC GHETTO

During the early 1830s there were frequent disputes in Derry over the rights to hold 'traditional' marches. Catholics had responded to the two existing Protestant marches, on 12 August and 18 December, by holding their own march on 17 March, St Patrick's Day. An act making these commemorations illegal became law in 1832 but 'modified' demonstrations continued. Finally, in 1836, the authorities in Dublin Castle prohibited all such marches in the city. The easing of tension as a result of this ban caused a withdrawal from political activity by Derry's Catholics and most of their energies were devoted instead to the development of church infrastructure. In 1838 building work began on a second Catholic church, St Columb's in the Waterside.

The two communities in Derry remained relatively tranquil under the control of their respective leaders: the bishop in the case of the Catholics, and Sir Robert Ferguson MP in the case of the Protestants. The passing in 1840 of the Municipal Corporations (Ireland) Act provided for the first public elections to local authorities. Prior to this, the corporation of Londonderry had been a self-selecting body. The act gave a vote to a restricted number of citizens, based on a minimum £10 valuation of their residences. But because wealth in Derry was largely confined to Protestants, the reform did not result in adequate representation for the Catholics of the city.

In 1845 Dr Edward Maginn took over as Catholic bishop of Derry. He was a strong supporter of Daniel O'Connell and the repeal movement, which sought to break the union with Britain, and was much more of a political activist than his Catholic episcopal predecessors. On the outbreak of the Great Famine in 1845 he became involved in a public dispute about responsibility for the disaster. The Famine did not begin to affect Derry to any extent until the end of 1846. By that time many of the stricken country people from the surrounding districts were pouring into the city, looking for relief. However, the municipal authorities reacted quickly to the threat of the 'potatoe crop' disease and as early as November 1845 the corporation passed the following comparatively radical motion:

> The Council having ascertained that the potatoe crop in this district has

LONDONDERRY POOR-SHOP ACCOUNT,

FOR THE YEAR ENDING 31ST DECEMBER. 1834.

Dr.

1834.		£	s.	d.
Jan. 1.—To balance on hands this day, per account published,		535	14	1
DONATIONS.				
Hon. Lord Decies,	£5 0 0			
Irish Society, for half-year ending March, 1834,	12 10 0			
Ditto, for half-year ending September, 1834,	7 10 0—	25	0	0
Listing sold,		0	2	1
Dec. 31.—Interest to this date,		8	19	3
		£569	15	5

Cr.

1834.		£	s.	d.
By expenses of Management,	£5 13 11½			
— Printing and Stationary,	6 3 6			
— Loss by defaulters,	0 18 2			
— Rent and Taxes,	12 17 7½—	25	13	3
Dec. 31.				
By Stock on hand, viz. :—				
— Due by instalments,	£162 5 9			
— Goods on hand,	22 16 0			
— Bank Receipts,	350 0 0			
— Cash in Treasurer's hands,	9 0 5—	544	2	2
		£569	15	5

ARTICLES SOLD DURING THE PAST YEAR.

301 Pairs Shoes—65 Coats, Waistcoats, and Trowsers—127 Flannel Drawers and Waistcoats—21 Boys' and Babies' Suits—283½ Pairs Blankets—48 Counterpanes—56 Linen and Flannel Shirts—28 Shawls, Bonnets, and Bedsteads—226 Flannel Petticoats—54 Cloaks—132 Bedticks—178 Gowns and Curtains, (containing 1484½ yards Scotch Drugget)—239 Sheets—60 Linen and Calico Shifts. Total, 1,819 arricles.

AUDITED, { THOS. HARVEY. P. GILMOUR.

2D JANUARY, 1835.

The Poor-shop was established in 1821 by Lady Hill, wife of Sir George Hill MP, 'to provide the indigent with clothes and bedding at prime cost'.

been attacked by the Mysterious disease now general over the Kingdom, feels imperatively called on, to express to the Government its unanimous opinion, that as a matter of precaution immediate measures should be taken, to guard against the melancholy consequences, of the scarcity of food, which must be experienced, if the progress of the disease shall not be arrested:– Resolved that the Mayor be requested to convey this resolution to the Government and to request that an Order in Council may be issued admitting the immediate importation of Corn at a minimal duty and prohibiting the exportation of provisions to foreign parts, until the pleasure of Parliament shall be taken on the subject.

Sentinel house and city walls in dilapidated condition, *c.* 1830

The corporation then left responsibility for relief measures to the clergy of the city. A committee was set up which, to some degree, was able to deal with the crisis, but the authorities made it clear that refugees were not welcome. As historian Desmond Murphy says of Derry: 'The hostile atmosphere . . . must have deterred all but the most destitute from seeking relief there.'

Extreme poverty in Derry was not confined to the Famine victims. The city itself was suffering from economic decline which exacerbated the plight of many of its citizens and turned their attention to agitation and protest. Dr Maginn was quick to seize on this opportunity and he began a campaign against the Protestant parades which, although officially banned, had started up again in the 1840s. In March 1848 the St Patrick's Day Catholic celebration was banned and a threatened attempt to ignore the ban became the subject of a satirical 'lay'. The poem was dedicated 'To the Officers and Men of the different Services whose patriotic gallantry on the ever-memorable 17th March 1848, sheds additional lustre on the "Union Jack" ':

From Bogside round to Bennet's Lane,
The Rebels one and all,
Have sworn that they this night will sup
Within the City wall!
Ha! not so fast, ye caitiffs;
Little ye know the men,
Who guard the ancient Citadel
From such rebellious den! . . .

St Patrick's eve the Mayor felt
His Civic Crown at stake!
St Patrick's eve, the men who wore
The Magisterial Gown
Took council for the safety
Of the good old Maiden Town.
Oh! 'twas a goodly sight to see
These wise and loyal men
Guarding the ancient City
From such rebellious den! . . .

Joy, joy the Maiden City
Remains a maiden still;
No rebel footstep taints thy sod,
Time honoured Blue-Bell-Hill!
No rebel arms have clasped the maids
Fast verging to decay
But all is dull and quiet
As the mud in Ross's Bay.

In August 1848 Dr Maginn unsuccessfully appealed to the corporation to have the relief parade stopped. Following the peaceful 18 December parade, the bishop organised a counter-march by Catholics through the walled city, which led to further demonstrations. On St Patrick's Day 1849 rioting broke out after Protestant groups tried to prevent a Catholic march. The authorities panicked and mobilised troops in expectation of further trouble.

Dr Maginn died in 1849, and the appointment as new Catholic bishop of Dr Francis Kelly, a man with a very different outlook than his predecessor, helped to restore order to the city. He focused the attention of his congregation on ecclesiastical matters. He introduced the Irish Christian Brothers, the Sisters of Mercy, and the Society of St Vincent de Paul to the city to develop educational and welfare services for the community. He also initiated building work on the new Catholic cathedral on its impressive and appropriate site overlooking the Bogside district. The cathedral was dedicated to Saint Eugene, the founder of the ancient church of Ardstraw in County Tyrone, the first seat of the bishopric which subsequently evolved into the diocese of Derry. The sheer size of the cathedral, dwarfing its Church of Ireland neighbour, Christchurch, was an architectural symbol of the arrival of a confident Catholicism in the city. However, the inability of the Catholic community to influence municipal politics, and the absence of a strong Catholic middle class, ensured the predominant influence of the clergy and the inevitable formation of a Catholic ghetto. More than a century would pass before attempts would be made to breach the walls of that ghetto.

The *Great Northern*, from the *Illustrated London News*, 14 January 1843 (Hulton-Deutsch Collection)

10

THE INDUSTRIAL CITY

Up to 1850 industrial development in Derry had been minimal. In the second half of the nineteenth century, however, that situation was to change, giving the city a very different character.

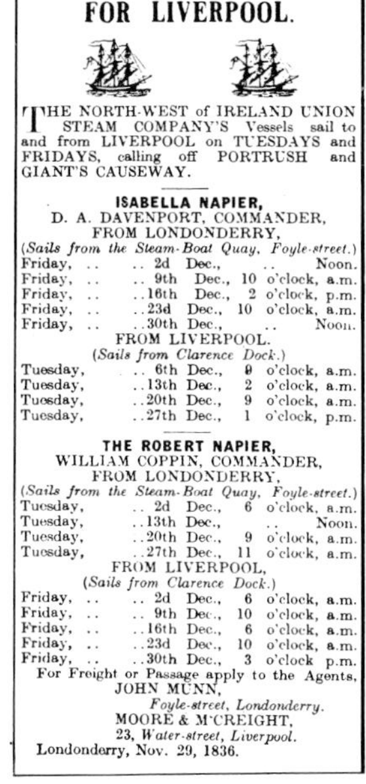

FOR LIVERPOOL.

THE NORTH-WEST of IRELAND UNION STEAM COMPANY'S Vessels sail to and from LIVERPOOL on TUESDAYS and FRIDAYS, calling off PORTRUSH and GIANT'S CAUSEWAY.

ISABELLA NAPIER,
D. A. DAVENPORT, COMMANDER,
FROM LONDONDERRY,
(*Sails from the Steam-Boat Quay, Foyle-street.*)
Friday, ... 2d Dec., .. Noon.
Friday, ... 9th Dec., 10 o'clock, a.m.
Friday, ...16th Dec., 2 o'clock, p.m.
Friday, ...23d Dec., 10 o'clock, a.m.
Friday, ...30th Dec., .. Noon.
FROM LIVERPOOL.
(*Sails from Clarence Dock.*)
Tuesday, .. 6th Dec., 9 o'clock, a.m.
Tuesday, ..13th Dec., 2 o'clock, a.m.
Tuesday, ..20th Dec., 9 o'clock, a.m.
Tuesday, ..27th Dec., 1 o'clock, p.m.

THE ROBERT NAPIER,
WILLIAM COPPIN, COMMANDER,
FROM LONDONDERRY,
(*Sails from the Steam-Boat Quay, Foyle-street.*)
Tuesday, .. 2d Dec., 6 o'clock, a.m.
Tuesday, ..13th Dec., .. Noon.
Tuesday, ..20th Dec., 9 o'clock, a.m.
Tuesday, ..27th Dec., 11 o'clock, a.m.
FROM LIVERPOOL,
(*Sails from Clarence Dock.*)
Friday, ... 2d Dec., 6 o'clock, a.m.
Friday, ... 9th Dec., 10 o'clock, a.m.
Friday, ...16th Dec., 6 o'clock, a.m.
Friday, ...23d Dec., 10 o'clock, a.m.
Friday, ...30th Dec., 3 o'clock p.m.
For Freight or Passage apply to the Agents,
JOHN MUNN,
Foyle-street, Londonderry.
MOORE & M'CREIGHT,
23, *Water-street, Liverpool.*
Londonderry, Nov. 29, 1836.

SHIPBUILDING

Some shipbuilding had been carried on in Derry since the late eighteenth century but there were no adequate slipways or dry docks. In 1830 Pitt Skipton had built a slip dock where a small shipbuilding and repair business was operated. This yard was taken over in 1835 by Captain William Coppin, who successfully began building sailing vessels for the Atlantic crossing and steamers for the cross-channel business. His clients were mainly local businessmen. In 1843 a public holiday was declared in the city when Coppin launched the *Great Northern*, the largest screw-propulsion vessel of its kind yet built anywhere in the world. Allegedly over twenty thousand people turned up to see the launch. Coppin, however, failed to sell the vessel to the Government as he had intended, so he took the ship to London himself where the *Illustrated London News* of 14 January 1843 described her:

> The *Great Northern*, this extraordinary steamer in the East Indian Dock, is the object of general astonishment. Her great length, breadth, and depth exceeds we believe the dimensions of any steamer ever in existence. She was built in Londonderry by Captain Coppin and is a remarkable monument of marine architecture. She is propelled by Archimedian Screws which work on each side of the rudder. The engine is 560 horse power, no paddles are required, and but for the funnel which is seen amidships she might pass for a square rigged ship of the larger class. She

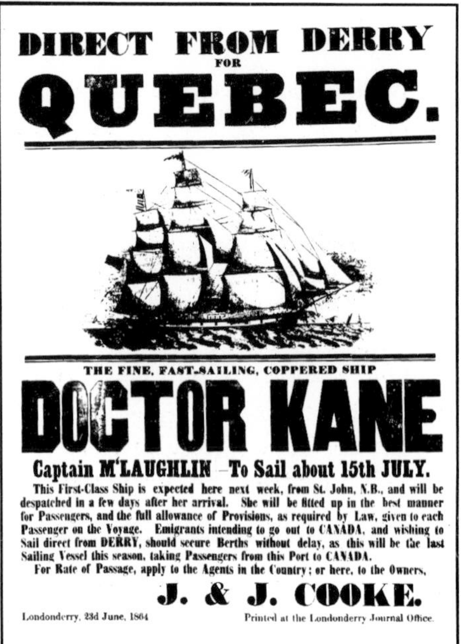

has three masts with lower and upper yards and is rigged in respect of a frigate or sloop of war. During the week many persons visited the dockyard to gaze at this really wonderful object. Her dimensions are as follows. Length 274 feet, beam 37 feet, depth 26 feet, and her speed averaged 13½ knots.

Despite this eulogy, Coppin found it difficult to find a buyer for the *Great Northern* and eventually he was forced to accept a considerable loss on the transaction. He returned to Derry and immediately set about building a similar ship, which was completed in 1846. Just as the vessel was about to be launched, it was completely destroyed by fire. This second disaster forced Coppin out of the shipbuilding industry altogether, although he continued a ship-salvaging business and an engineering and foundry works in the city until the 1870s. Thus the first opportunity to develop a thriving shipbuilding industry in Derry was lost.

It was not until 1882 that another attempt was made when W. F. Biggar opened his Foyle Shipyard at Pennyburn and the business continued there until 1892. In its ten years of operations the Foyle Shipyard built 'some of the loveliest little barques and ships that were ever seen in the days of sail'. A total of twenty-six sailing vessels and six steamships were built before the company closed. In 1899 the Londonderry Shipbuilding and Engineering Company was set up at the former Biggar yard and survived for five years, building a total of nine steamships. In 1912 the yard was taken over by the Tyneside company of Swan and Hunter under the title of the North of Ireland Shipbuilding and Engineering Company. The yard had a brief boom during the years

EMIGRATION OFFICE,
LONDONDERRY.

FREE PASSAGE TO LIVERPOOL.

FITZHUGH & C. GRIMSHAW,
of Liverpool,

DESIROUS of affording every facility in their power to Emigrants proceeding through Londonderry to embark in their Vessels at Liverpool for the UNITED STATES of AMERICA, have appointed

MR. FRANCIS M'MULLAN,
Ship-Quay, Londonderry,

Their Agent for the Counties of Londonderry, Tyrone, Donegal, and Fermanagh, and the Town of Coleraine, and its neighbourhood, who will furnish, on application to him, every information respecting their vessels and their time of sailing from Liverpool to New York.

FITZHUGH & C. GRIMSHAW
Have a Regular Line of Superior First Class
AMERICAN SHIPS,

Which sail from Liverpool for New York, at intervals of every eight days throughout the year, fitted up comfortably for the accommodation of Cabin, Second Cabin, and Steerage Passengers.

The superiority of their Vessels, their kind treatment to Passengers, and punctuality of sailing their Ships at the dates advertised, are already sufficiently established to render unnecessary all further reference to them.

For passage, apply to
FRANCIS M'MULLAN, General Agent,
Ship-Quay, Londonderry.
Londonderry, 18th Nov. 1836.

N.B.—Fitzhugh & C. Grimshaw's American Orders for Cash Payments in the above counties punctually attended to by F. M'Mullan.

of the First World War but the depression dealt a final blow to shipbuilding in Derry. The company was wound up and the yard closed in 1924.

DERRY 'KAY' – EMIGRATION IN THE NINETEENTH CENTURY

The shipping trade was closely tied to the business of emigration. Derry's position as one of Europe's most westerly ports meant that it was an ideal location for embarkation to the New World. Emigration to North America had started from the city at the beginning of the eighteenth century. Most, but by no means all, of those who left at that time were Presbyterians – the so-called Ulster-Scots – but Catholic emigration began to increase in the nineteenth century and the flow was considerably quickened by the tragedy of the Famine. In the summer of 1847 the Catholic bishop of Derry, Dr Edward Maginn, had written: 'In the diocese of Derry we have a Catholic population of 230,000 souls; of these at the present time there are at least 50,000 in actual starvation.' On 5 May of the same year the *Londonderry Journal* reported that about 5,000 emigrants had left from the port since January, directly for North America, while another 3,500 had gone from Derry via Liverpool: 'And from the crowds who daily throng our streets enquiring for vessels to carry them from famine-stricken Ireland it is calculated that close on 8,000 more will have left before the month of September next.'

In the early years of the nineteenth century most emigrants were carried on American-owned ships which each spring arrived from New York into the port of Derry with consignments of flax seed for the Ulster linen industry. The ships were then refitted for passenger transport for the return journey and if conditions were favourable some ships could manage a second round trip during one summer season. By 1815 some of the Derry merchants were beginning to take an interest in this lucrative trade. They bought Canadian-built sailing vessels and carried emigrants on the outward journey to places like Saint John, New Brunswick, and then returned with a cargo of timber. During the winter some of these ships would be sent under ballast to the southern American ports of Charleston, Savannah, and, more importantly, New Orleans, where they would load up with a cargo of cotton destined for Liverpool. Having crossed the Atlantic in the hazardous winter conditions, the ships would be back in Derry in time for the spring passenger sailings. Most of the ships used on these journeys were relatively small, up to three hundred tons, and traffic was at its greatest during the 1820s and 1830s.

Not all emigration from Derry was to the North America. A letter dated 18 October 1838 from James Dempsey, who was emigrating to Sydney, Australia, was posted before the ship left Lough Foyle:

> The ship moved down from Derry the south of Culmore on Saturday evening and the weather being unfavourable, stopped there till Thursday

John Cooke, who died in 1895, was one of the founders of the Derry shipping company of J. and J.L. Cooke (from Sholto Cooke, *The Maiden City and the Western Ocean*)

> morning and she is now down the length of Moville and intends going off the first opportunity this evening: it is serious to behold in all corners of the ship there are sick and women fainting but thank God we are all in good health as yet: the first and second day that we went on board there was a great deal of complaints with the emigrants of their rations being too small and many of them wishing to go ashore and return home but I endeavoured to peacify all that I had any influence with knowing it was impossible that two hundred and sixty four passengers to be all righted according to their wishes at once.

By 1840 the smaller vessels had disappeared and been replaced by a locally owned fleet of larger ships, which sailed to various ports, including New York, Saint John and Quebec, but principally to Philadelphia, where more Derry passengers were landed than any other port in the United States. In the spring of 1847 alone, one company, J. and J.L. Cooke, sent eight vessels to Philadelphia with 1,197 passengers on board. The ships were so full that many intending emigrants could not get passages.

The need for greater investment in larger ships meant that fewer merchants were able to take part in the transatlantic trade. Gradually, the business passed into the hands of a small number of Derry families and after the Famine only two firms, Cookes and William McCorkell and Company, were still involved. The quality of the ships had been steadily improving and they were now much faster. Although the outbreak of civil war in the United States in the 1860s threatened at first to depress the transatlantic trade, in fact the Derry merchants did quite well, carrying war supplies and emigrant replacements for the American workers who had become involved in the war. A local tradition,

Bartholomew McCorkell, who died in 1887, a member of the well-known Derry shipping family (from Sholto Cooke, *The Maiden City and the Western Ocean*)

also claimed in other parts of Ireland, says that the city's clothing manufacturers supplied uniforms to both sides in the American war.

At the end of the war the Derry shipping and emigration trade was at its peak, but although 'the number and quality of Derry-owned ships had never been higher', the boom was coming to an end. During the war, steamships had entered the transatlantic business, and although the Derry sailing vessels had kept pace with all the latest improvements, they were no match for the new kind of vessel. Sholto Cooke, in *The Maiden City and the Western Ocean*, has pointed out:

> The harvest of increased emigration to the States would be reaped by steamship lines calling in the Foyle, and not by the traditional Derry sailing ship. In spite of all the efforts which the owners could make, the [1860s] saw the flower and decay of the passenger trade in Derry-owned sailing vessels.

Cooke was a descendant of the Derry family that had played such an important role in the shipping trade. After the boom of the American war years, harder times set in for the Cooke line. It was engaged in the Canadian timber-importing business but suffered enormously from increased competition in the 1870s, to the point where it almost went out of business. The firm was given a short reprieve, however, from the transportation to Britain of the newly available pitch-pine which came from the clearing of virgin forests in the southern American states of Georgia and Florida.

The McCorkell line diversified into grain importation, using its sizeable fleet, which was expanded in the 1870s to transport large quantities of wheat and Indian meal from Baltimore in Maryland. It was not until the following decade that McCorkells began to suffer the effects of competition from the steamers. Again, it diversified into carrying coal and other cargos from Britain to the less-developed ports of the east and west coasts of South America. McCorkell ships could even occasionally be seen as far north as San Francisco. But these extraordinarily long voyages were an indication of the marginalisation of the Derry shipping trade, not of its vitality. Gradually the industry collapsed in the face of competition from steamships. In 1896 the McCorkell shipping business was wound up with the sale of its remaining vessels, which included the celebrated *Minnehaha*. When this beautiful ship joined McCorkell's fleet in 1860, she set a standard by which all future vessels would be judged. She was named after the heroine of Longfellow's poem *The Song of Hiawatha*, and six other McCorkell vessels took their names from characters in the poem. The last of the Cooke ships, the *Twilight*, came to an ignominious end when she was washed up on the treacherous sands of Trawbreaga Bay in north Donegal on 25 November 1889.

By comparison with the ports of London, Liverpool, Glasgow and so on, the Derry portion of the transatlantic trade had been insignificant, and yet, for the size of the city, it was enormous. A comparatively large service industry developed in the city to cater for the needs of the ships

The *Minnehaha*, probably the best-known ship of the McCorkell line (Derry City Council)

A view of Derry in 1854 (from J.B. Doyle, *Tours in Ulster*)

and their passengers. There were even businesses which advertised themselves as 'emigrants' outfitters'. Besides the economic impact that the trade made on Derry, its quays throughout this period were the scene of a thousand individual human dramas. Derry 'Kay' entered the imagination of the century and was commemorated, if not actually celebrated, in many ballads and stories:

From Derry Kay, we sailed away
On the 23rd of May.
We were boarded by a pleasant crew,
Bound for Amerikay.
Fresh water there, we did take on,
Ten thousand gallons or more,
In case we'd run short, going to New York,
From Paddy's green shamrock shore.

SHIRTS AND TRAINS

The invention of the small portable sewing machine in America in 1845 helped to revolutionise the existing cottage industry that had been built up in the Derry area. The original Scott family business, which relied on hand-sewing, continued to prosper, but when the founder, William, died in 1858, competition from better-organised rivals was already established in the city. In the 1850s the Glasgow shirt and collar manufacturer, William Tillie, introduced the first sewing machine to Derry. He and his partner, John Henderson, had come to the city in 1851

Marshall Tillie of the Derry shirt-manufacturing company of Tillie and Henderson (Magee College)

Tillie and Henderson's shirt factory in Foyle Road

and in January 1857 they opened their massive factory at Foyle Road. After a private dinner to celebrate the opening, the partners and their friends

> adjourned to the new factory, where the workers and their friends, to the number of four or five hundred, had already assembled . . . The middle floor of the factory . . . had been tastefully decorated with drapery, flowers, and evergreens, and brilliantly lighted with gas . . . The female portion of those present were very tastefully dressed, and the utmost decorum and good nature were everywhere prevalent. A temporary orchestra had been erected at the end of the room, and here were placed the band of the Derry Militia, who performed at intervals throughout the evening . . . After tea, the company removed to the ground floor, where dancing was commenced, and continued with great spirit for some time. Returning to the upper room, several songs were sung in good style, and the party separated at three o'clock in the morning.

In 1864 a new shirt factory in Queen Street was opened for the firm of McIntyre Hogg and Company and in 1876 the London firm of Welch Margetson opened a huge factory on Carlisle Road. This street was beginning to develop in response to the construction of the new bridge which had been opened in 1863, a short distance upstream from its wooden predecessor. Unusually, like the present Craigavon Bridge, Carlisle Bridge had two levels, the lower deck to accommodate transfer between the two railway termini which had been established by this time on opposite sides of the river.

The Londonderry and Enniskillen Railway was set up in 1845 on the same day as the Londonderry and Coleraine Railway. The former company, after many vicissitudes and mergers, became part of the Great Northern Railway with connections to, among many other places, Belfast and Dublin. The route via Coleraine was eventually connected to Belfast and is the only railway line into Derry that now survives. The first train out of the city ran on 19 April 1847 on the Enniskillen route, but the line only extended to Strabane and did not

Derry, *c.* 1863. Carlisle Bridge (left) has been built but the old wooden bridge (centre) has not yet been removed. The terminus of the Londonderry and Enniskillen Railway can be seen on the far side of the river between the two bridges.

reach Enniskillen until August 1854. As reported in the *Londonderry Journal*, the official inauguration from the inconvenient terminus at the Letterkenny Road was something of an anti-climax:

> Captain Coddington having, after his late inspection of the completed portion of this Railway, reported his entire approval of the works, and the necessary authority from the Board of Works having been received by the local directors, the Londonderry and Enniskillen Railway between Londonderry and Strabane was opened for general traffic on Monday last under most favourable circumstances. About 600 passengers availed themselves of its advantages during the first day, few of whom could have been actuated by curiosity, as the directors had previously given repeated trips to the citizens as far as Strabane . . . Omnibuses and cars are at the terminus on the arrival of each train, and convey passengers to and from Foyle Street and Shipquay Gate for 3d. each.

On the opposite side of the river, the line to Coleraine was opened in July 1853. In 1863 the first of Derry's two narrow-gauge railways, later to be known as the Londonderry and Lough Swilly Railway, or simply the 'Swilly', opened a line to Farland Point and the Rathmullan ferry. By

City Shirt Factory in Queen Street in the early twentieth century (Magee College)

> and we rejoice at the erection of all such factories in our city, because they are a pledge that a branch of employment which has been found so useful will not be of a fluctuating character, but will become a permanency amongst us; and its advantages will be all the more felt, as, by the fact that Messrs. Tillie and Henderson employ all the workers directly, the latter are preserved from those annoyances inseparable from the 'middleman' system which formerly prevailed.

Working conditions, however, were severe and wages much lower than for equivalent work in other cities. One factory owner, giving evidence in 1875 to a commission set up to investigate the shirt industry, under the Factories and Workshops Act, stated:

> The hours of labour which have prevailed in the trade during the past 25 years have been 61 hours a week, 8 to 8 with an hour for dinner [11 hours Monday to Friday and 6 hours on Saturday] . . . Regarding the working hours on Saturday, we have never felt any inconvenience or seen any bad results to the hands from working 6 hours at a stretch and the hands themselves unanimously prefer the present hours to any other which would require them to come in without breakfast.

Most of the women earned between 5 and 12 shillings per week, while the 'hands' and 'forewomen' earned between 10 and 20 shillings. The employees were fined a penny or halfpenny if they were five to ten minutes late for work. There was no holiday pay during the annual shut-down for two weeks in August and, if a machine broke, the operative had to suffer the loss in earnings until a mechanic could repair it.

James McKnight, a political campaigner who argued for a distinct Presbyterian identity, became editor of the *Londonderry Standard* in 1848 (Magee College)

LIBERAL PRESBYTERIANISM – ITS RISE AND FALL

The growth of the shirt industry during the 1850s, with consequent modernisation and population increase, set in train a series of social developments, not least among the city's Protestant community. Derry was still governed by an élite that was Tory in its politics and Anglican in its religion. Many well-to-do Presbyterians often 'changed over' or married into the Church of Ireland in pursuit of greater social respectability. At the other end of the scale, working-class Presbyterians found in the Apprentice Boys organisation an outlet for much of their energy and need for social cohesion.

However, the 1850s saw a new breed of Presbyterianism emerge in the city. Initially this took the form of an evangelical revival, led by a number of laymen prominent in the business life of the city, including William Tillie, the shirt factory owner, and William Biggar, a local merchant. These men became involved in various religious activities such as the Londonderry Presbyterian City Mission, the Sunday School movement and in collecting for Presbyterian church funds. They also reversed the trend of wealthy Presbyterians conforming to Anglicanism. Another voice arguing for a separate Presbyterian opinion in Derry was James McKnight, who had become editor of the *Londonderry Standard* in 1848, having previously served in that position with the *Belfast News-Letter*. McKnight was a leading figure in the tenant right agitation during the 1850s and an ally of the Young Ireland movement leader, Charles Gavan Duffy. He was also a strong opponent of the power that the Catholic clergy exerted over their congregation, of Tory landlords and of the official position of the Church of Ireland: 'I have no language sufficiently strong to convey my contempt for policies which, under the hypocrisy of religion, degrade Christianity to an engine of state intrigue.' He was the very personification of Presbyterian liberalism or radicalism, whose ethos has been described by historian Peter Brooke as

> an orthodox Presbyterian sectarianism opposed to the Unitarian, Catholic and Church of Ireland interests, but prepared to ally with Unitarians, Catholics and Anglicans in pursuit of particular social and economic demands such as tenant right and the abolition of tithes, it being clearly understood that they would stand in a solid Protestant bloc with the Church of Ireland if and when the great issue of the Union was at stake.

McKnight campaigned for a distinct Presbyterian political identity in Derry. An opportunity to put these ideas into practice arose when long-serving MP Sir Robert Ferguson died in 1860, bringing to an end the focus of unity around which the city's various Protestant strands had gathered previously. The subsequent bye-election saw the struggle between the various sections of the community brought out into the open. The main contest was between William McCormick, a railway developer and landowner who had the support of the Church of Ireland voters, and Samuel McCurdy Greer, who represented the liberal Presbyterian position. The two hundred Catholic votes, which had been promised originally to the Liberal candidate, were split when McCormick applied pressure through his Catholic employees. McCormick won the seat.

A closer alliance between the Presbyterians and Catholics at the 1865 election still lost out to the Tory candidate, Lord Claud Hamilton. One of his first moves was to gain control of the Apprentice Boys, changing that organisation's previous party political neutrality to a position of firm support for Tory policies, including the defence of the Church of Ireland as the Established Church. In the opinion of liberal Presbyterians, this transformed the nature of the anniversary parades and raised the question of their continuation. Derry Catholics had continued to press unsuccessfully for the total suppression of these demonstrations, and saw their failure as proof of the bias of the authorities. Growing political tension nationally had been paralleled by mounting

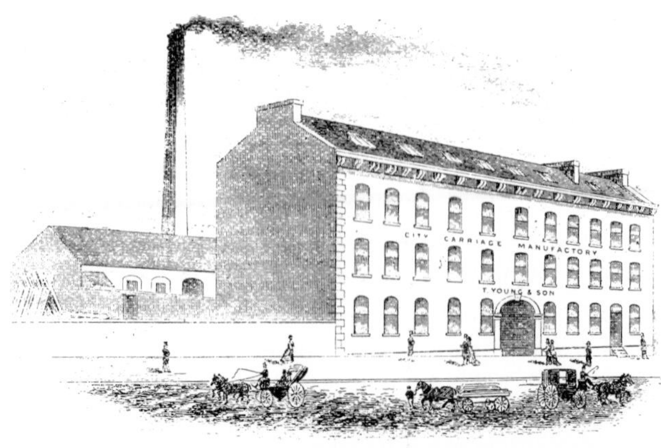

T. Young and Son's carriage factory in Clarendon Street in the late nineteenth century

Commercial Buildings in Foyle Street in the middle of the nineteenth century

militancy within the Apprentice Boys. The movement and its parades were also growing in strength, as the expansion of the railway network allowed large numbers of supporters from other parts of the province to travel to the city on the various anniversary days.

In an atmosphere of increasing disquiet and street violence, an alliance of liberal Presbyterians and Catholics managed to win the parliamentary seat from Hamilton at the 1868 election and Richard Dowse was returned as MP for the city. Blunders of local Tories ensured that this coalition held together for a few years, despite the real likelihood of a break along denominational lines. The Tory administration in the city exacerbated the situation by banning the Liberal victory parade.

On 28 April 1869 three people died when police opened fire on rival demonstrators. The occasion was a visit to the city by Prince Arthur, a son of Queen Victoria's. Excitement and tension had grown throughout the day, although the prince himself was not affected by any of the disturbances. Around 8 p.m. a group of Apprentice Boys on one side and people from the Bogside on the other clashed, in the Butcher Street, Society Street and Diamond area in the centre of the city, shouting and throwing stones at each other. As the situation grew more heated, two Bogsiders were arrested. 'Shots were exchanged between the parties' and the police, who were in the middle attempting to keep the two crowds apart, fixed bayonets and returned fire, although at this stage no one was injured. The report of the public inquiry into the events of the day, and subsequent associated events, makes ominous reading in the light of what happened in Derry almost exactly one hundred years later:

> It was now near 10 o'clock, and there was a crowd of people at the lower end of Bishop-street, and in the Diamond, apparently 'a mixture of both parties'. Butcher-street was quite clear, but a number of persons had collected on the adjoining wall. When Mr. Thompson and the constabulary officer left the Mayor, they resolved to do what they could to keep the

A mid-nineteenth-century view of the rear of the old Corporation Hall in the Diamond (Derry City Council)

> peace, and the officer marched his men back to the Diamond, halting them there, and leaving them in charge of the head-constable. Both gentlemen then went over to the crowd to persuade the Bogside party to go home. Some of them, addressing the officer, said, 'Mr. Stafford, we will go home, if you will get the other parties off the wall; for if we go down there we will be murdered.' There were from eighty to a hundred of this party in the Diamond, and their direct way to the Bog-side lay through Butcher's Gate, which those on the wall, who were flinging stones, and it was said firing pistols also, from it, had the command of. Those on the wall were of the Apprentice Boy party. At Mr. Thompson's suggestion, Mr. Stafford and he went to get these men away, and saw on the wall over the gateway a few of the city police, trying apparently to drive them up towards the Walker testimonial. Mr. Ferguson [Apprentice Boys leader] came up then, and also endeavoured to get his party away. After a little they succeeded, and as Mr. Stafford thought got all the men into Society-street, and into the gun-room there, at which point he was separated from the others. Believing all was made secure, he returned down the wall, but on his way heard the report of a pistol, and the glass of an adjoining window broken. He turned into Butcher-street quickly, which was now full of people, on whom he called to run away, or they would be shot; but they pelted him with stones, and he had to fly. He hurried back up Meetinghouse-row, and by Society-street into Bishop-street; and when near the Meeting House he heard the report of fire-arms. When he got into Bishop-street there was hardly anyone in view; but on getting within twenty or thirty yards of the Corporation Hall, he heard that men had been shot. He then saw a man lying on the flags perfectly still, and another 'writhing backwards and forwards'. Some of the city police were by him.

By the time order was restored three people were dead.

With rising sectarian feelings in the city, the leaders of the local Liberal Party called for a ban on all parades. This was not conceded. In August 1869 a Catholic Workingmen Defence Association was established in Derry, led by John O'Donnell, a publican from William Street. On 18 December 1869 two rival parades were held in the city but they passed off reasonably peacefully. The local Liberal leaders were privately critical of the actions of the Catholic activists, but publicly they supported them. Intermittent street violence continued throughout the first half of 1870. The Government banned a proposed Catholic counter-demonstration to the 12 August Apprentice Boys march and serious rioting ensued. O'Donnell was determined to force a showdown on 18 December.

By this stage the report of the inquiry into the killings of the previous year was available and it seemed to indicate that the primary cause of these disturbances had been the toleration of various Orange demonstrations. The upper-class sections of the Apprentice Boys now distanced themselves from the more militant working-class members. The Government responded to the report by banning the December demonstration, and although there was an attempted breach, the prohibition was generally successful and was maintained the following year. Toryism in the city seemed to be in total disarray.

In 1870 a fairly moderate and conservative Home Rule movement was founded by Isaac Butt, a leading Protestant barrister who had formerly been a Tory. Its objective was to have an Irish parliament that would have control over domestic issues. From 1879 onwards the movement became more radical in its tactics under the leadership of Charles Stewart Parnell and succeeded in converting the Liberal leader, William Ewart Gladstone, to its cause. Attempts by Gladstone, as prime minister, to enact Home Rule legislation were defeated in 1886 in the House of Commons and in 1893 in the House of Lords. In 1890 the revelation of Parnell's adulterous relationship with Kitty O'Shea led to a major split in the Home Rule movement itself.

Charles Lewis, who was elected MP for the city of Londonderry in a parliamentary bye-election in 1872. The election was the first in Ireland to be conducted using the new secret ballot arrangements (Derry City council)

The 1872 parliamentary bye-election in Derry suggested that the local coalition of liberal Presbyterians and Catholics was doomed to a short life. The election came about when the Liberal MP for the city, Richard Dowse, was elevated to the House of Lords. Despite the fact that the Presbyterian J. G. Biggar was standing as a Home Rule candidate, the Catholic bishop, Dr Francis Kelly, and his clergy endorsed the Liberal (and Catholic) candidate, Christopher Palles. A London Presbyterian, Charles Lewis, stood as the Conservative candidate. In the election – the first in Ireland to be held under the new secret ballot arrangements – Lewis beat Palles as a result of former liberal Presbyterians deserting to the Conservative side. Biggar came a very poor third but from now on Catholic political energies began to be focused on the issue of Home Rule.

From 1877 onwards the determination of Catholics to have the same rights as Protestants to march inside the walled city was increasingly asserted. The early 1880s were marked by many confrontations over marches and there was increased sectarian tension. Reforms introduced in 1884 meant that almost equal numbers of Catholics and Protestants were entitled to vote in parliamentary elections, although the ward arrangements for municipal contests ensured Protestant dominance in the city itself.

The Apprentice Boys' Memorial Hall in Society Street, which was built in 1873 (Magee College)

The general election of 1885 brought the Tories and Presbyterian Liberals in the city together against a journalist, Justin McCarthy, who was standing for the Irish Parliamentary Party, with Catholic support. McCarthy lost but captured the seat in a historic bye-election the following year. This was the first time that Catholics had triumphed in a parliamentary constituency contest in Derry. The anti-McCarthy electoral coalition had cemented the two strands of the Protestant community together again. In 1889, during the fairly muted celebrations for the second centenary of the Siege of Derry, Protestant unity, in the face of growing Catholic influence, was the dominant theme. An editorial in the, by now, totally nationalist *Derry Journal* (it had changed its name in 1880) could not resist the temptation to poke fun at this coming together of the two Protestant traditions that had been at odds with one another in times past. Referring to the Anglican bishop's speech at the siege bicentenary dinner, it commented:

> Painfully hampered as was his position – Dissenters to the right of him; Dissenters to the left of him – his first move was careful and shrewd. 'You

Justin McCarthy, who was elected MP for the city of Londonderry in 1886. A member of the Irish Parliamentary Party, his victory gave the Catholics of Derry their first parliamentary electoral success. (Harold Waite, National Gallery of Ireland)

Magee Presbyterian College, opened in 1865 (Magee College)

> must excuse me,' said this full-hearted Churchman, 'if I speak of the present and the immediate future rather than the past.' At a banquet commemorative of the events of two centuries ago and thereafter, 'the past' might be supposed to come into the speech with some warrant. But his lordship knew a method worth two of that. 'The past' is a hot subject for Prelacy and Dissent . . . No doubt it made the Presbyterians feel very proud in being permitted to grace the Orange-Tory 'triumph' of the banquet hall. It is not every day – or rather it was not – that Episcopal dignity deigns to pat on the heads mere Dissenting Presbyterians.

But despite this effort to push a wedge between Anglicans and Presbyterians in the city, Protestant unity was now a reality. By the mid-1880s the Catholic and Protestant communities in Derry were politically polarised.

COLLEGIUM MAGEENSE APVD DERRY
FAC ET SPERA
A D MDCCCLXV

MAGEE COLLEGE

The mid-1860s saw the resolution of an age-old conflict between the corporation of Londonderry and the Irish Society in London. The corporation claimed that the society's refusal to grant perpetual leases restricted the economic growth of the city. It persistently sought to have the situation altered and even petitioned parliament to abolish the society on the grounds of its neglect of its offspring city. As a result of this dramatic move the society changed its position and concord was achieved between the two parties.

The support of the Irish Society was useful in the campaign to bring the proposed Presbyterian theological college to Derry. In 1865 Magee

Presbyterian College was opened after a long-drawn-out controversy within the Presbyterian Church. It was named after the bequest of Martha Magee, the wife of a Presbyterian minister who had lived in Dublin and had left a sum of £20,000 for the project. In 1845 the city had lobbied Prime Minister Sir Robert Peel, requesting that Derry should be considered as the site of the new Queen's College about to be established in the north of Ireland. On that occasion, however, the decision had gone in favour of Belfast.

There had been much discussion about the establishment of a Presbyterian college in Derry. As early as 1850 strong civic interest was being shown in the project but one of its critics dismissed the city as 'the back of God speed'. The Reverend Richard Dill, a trustee of the Magee bequest, wrote – ironically in view of developments one hundred years later – 'The choice seems to be between Derry and Coleraine and the Trustees will fix on the place which will offer the largest amount of support and best prospect of success of the proposed seminary.' Eventually Derry was chosen and work began on the college buildings. Although established primarily to prepare men for the Presbyterian ministry, the college was also intended to have a broader role. At the foundation ceremony on 18 August 1856, one of the trustees, Dr John Brown from Aghadowey, promised that

> no surly janitor shall stand at the gate to say to men of any denomination, 'Here is a fountain of science and piety at which you may not drink.' On

Martha Magee, the wife of a Presbyterian minister who had lived in Dublin, whose bequest of £20,000 helped establish Magee College (from R.F.G. Holmes, *Magee 1865–1965*)

The interior of the Grianan of Aileach, which was restored between 1874 and 1878 by Dr Walter Bernard of Derry (Welch Collection, Ulster Folk and Transport Museum)

St Columb's College, which was opened in 1879 at Casino (Magee College)

> the contrary, men of every creed and no creed, if they conform to the laws of order and decency, may attend its lectures and share its literary distinctions.

The foundation of Magee College brought with it a major addition to the intellectual life of Derry. Many of the city's doctors and other professionals joined organisations such as the Natural History and Philosophical Society of Derry, which held its inaugural meeting and first 'Conversazione' on the evening of Friday 19 November 1869. The opening address

> was delivered before a very large and enlightened audience representing the intellect, respectability, and, we add, the beauty of the city and its environs. The address met with general approval from the critical assemblage for its terseness, breadth of thought, and the general acquaintance with scientific subjects displayed. The objects of the Society – the necessity for the study of science at the present day – its extent and wonderful researches – the revelations of the spectroscope – the study of botany and zoology, especially with reference to the development of the local flora and fauna – meteorology, and the necessity for records of local variations in temperature and humidity – the microscope and its minute wonders – the ends which the members of the Society ought to propose individually for himself and his work; all these subjects were passed in review.

Professor John Robinson Leebody, one of the first professors at Magee College (from R.F.G. Holmes, *Magee 1865–1965*)

Among the founding members were Professor John Robinson Leebody from Magee (who lectured to the society on no less a topic than 'The Sun'), and Dr Walter Bernard of Queen Street, who from 1874 to 1878 directed the restoration of the ancient Grianan of Aileach.

The reorganisation of university education in Ireland in 1908 proved unfavourable to Magee; according to Professor Leebody, it was to be 'the one College out of the five associated Colleges of the Royal University to be treated with special disfavour'. However, Magee went on to develop an association with Trinity College Dublin, an arrangement which endured down to the 1960s.

ST COLUMB'S COLLEGE

The Catholic clergy in the city had been concerned for many years with the need for a college for the young men of the diocese. In 1879 'St Columkille's Church and Derry Diocesan Seminary at Casino, Londonderry' was opened. The college advertised that it would take 'day

The mayor of Derry's garden party at Boom Hall on 9 August 1898 (Derry City Council)

scholars' and boarders, it would prepare students for Maynooth and other ecclesiastical colleges, and for civil service examinations, and would provide special teaching 'for those intended for Mercantile pursuits'. Since its inception, St Columb's College has exerted a powerful influence on the life of Derry Catholics. The school motto, '*Quaerite primum regnum Dei*' (seek ye first the kingdom of God), is almost a summary of the political advice of the majority of the city's Catholic clergy to their congregations throughout the past two centuries. Journalist Eamonn McCann has written of his alma mater:

> Catholic Derry is steeped in the influence of St Columb's. Almost every Catholic teacher, Catholic doctor, Catholic solicitor, Catholic architect, accountant and businessman in the city was schooled there . . . Before the introduction of state scholarships St Columb's was the preserve of the Catholic middle class and, until the school got used to it, Bogsiders who arrived were made aware that they were intruding.

Since the 1947 education reforms, St Columb's has provided the early education of a galaxy of talented students, many of whom went on to make their mark on the wider international stage. The names of Seamus Heaney, Seamus Deane, Brian Friel, John Hume and Phil Coulter, and many other distinguished Derrymen figure among the lists of its former pupils.

A garden fête at Nazareth House Convent in Derry, 27–30 June 1905 (Courtesy of the McCloskey family)

For a variety of reasons both Catholics and Protestants saw the Derry parliamentary seat as the most critical in Ulster. The 1886 election had shown how close, in electoral terms, the city's two communities were to one another. Each was forced into developing a political machine that would deliver every vote and the work of the registration agent played a vital role as each side battled to maximise its own vote and diminish that of its opponents. Politically the two communities were controlled by their traditional leaders – in the case of the Protestants the aristocratic Hamilton family provided the dominant influence, while the local priests had a similar function within the Catholic community. The Parnell crisis actually helped the Catholic clergy to strengthen that dominance in Derry.

In 1892 the parliamentary seat was lost to the Unionists but it was

Late-nineteenth-century Derry football team. Until the late 1880s Protestants, by and large, had a monopoly with regard to soccer in Derry. From then onwards, for the Catholic men of the city, under the encouragement of their priests who were anxious to move them away from the extreme nationalist influences of the GAA, soccer became a dominant element in their social life. (Magee College)

recaptured by nationalists three years later. In that same year, 1895, the corporation, fearing that parliament might intervene to reform the undemocratic form of local government in the city which had not been revised since 1841, produced its own plan for reorganisation. As a consequence of internal nationalist squabbling at Westminster, the Unionist-backed Londonderry Improvement Bill was passed, which resulted in an electoral and ward system that gave a greater advantage to the Unionist voter than to the nationalists – the so-called gerrymander. Although the census of 1891 showed that there were 4,500 more Catholics than Protestants in the city, the nationalists secured only sixteen of the forty seats at the local election held the following year. The expectation by Derry nationalists that some reform was inevitable was dashed. In 1900 the nationalist seat at Westminster was lost to a Unionist, the Marquis of Hamilton.

Despite these circumstances, the city was generally quiet during this period, with little of the sectarian violence that had been prevalent in earlier years. One development which occurred at this time, pointed out by historian Desmond Murphy, continues to affect the city. Up to the late 1880s the Catholic clergy had urged their congregations to take an interest in Gaelic games, while at the same time, the Protestant working class were involved in soccer. The support for Parnell in the Gaelic Athletic Association (GAA) after the Kitty O'Shea divorce scandal, and the emergence of a strongly republican element in that organisation at a national level, pushed the Catholic clergy in Derry to alter their sporting allegiance. Priests began to encourage their working-class male parishioners to play soccer, and within a short time a professional team, Derry Celtic, was formed. The Catholic clergy deliberately exploited football as a means of influencing and controlling the men of their congregations. Since that time Derry has been 'a soccer city'.

An opportunity to demonstrate Catholic confidence and organisational ability came about in June 1897, the thirteen-hundredth anniversary of the death of Saint Colmcille. Under the leadership of Father William Doherty of the Long Tower Church, an impressive programme of devotional and public events was planned. Catholic Derry had begun to use the associations and legends of Colmcille in much the same mythic way that Protestants exploited the legacy of the siege.

A trades council was established in Derry in 1887 and from 1890 onwards there were a number of small victories for employees in an atmosphere of revived trade-union activity. The workers were defeated, however, in a bitter dispute with the Londonderry and Lough Swilly Railway Company during the winter of 1903–4:

May the rose of England always glow,
And the thistle of Scotland always blow,
And the harp of Ireland always play,
Till the 'Swilly' porters get more pay.

An inspection party in August 1881, including the mayor of Derry, Sir Edward Reid, on far left, at Cabry in County Donegal, checking available sources for increased water supplies to the city (Derry City Council)

Laying the foundation stone for the Guildhall in 1887 (Derry City Council)

The Guildhall, the home of the corporation, which was opened in 1890, was almost completely destroyed by fire on 19 April 1908 (Derry City Council)

This defeat encouraged other local businessmen to take on the unions. In the midst of an economic depression, one indicator being that the population of the city fell between 1901 and 1911, the employers began to cut wages, resulting in the increased unionisation of unskilled workers and a series of strikes. The workers made no political claims – they simply wished to improve their economic situation and to obtain parity with conditions and wages in Belfast. Despite the appearance of trade unionists in the local elections in 1896 and 1904, there was still no political party to represent the working class in Derry. Instead, workers were split by the sectarian division within the city, although individuals who bitterly opposed each other on religious grounds could, nevertheless, co-operate on labour issues. The Catholic clergy made no attempt to frustrate the rise of trade unionism. Both in secular and spiritual areas they dominated their people to a level undreamed of by their Protestant colleagues. Occasionally, priests co-operated with factory owners on matters of mutual benefit, and hence were able to set up a variety of sodalities and clubs inside the workplaces.

By 1900 the population of Derry was 40,000 and this increased to 45,000 by the outbreak of the First World War in August 1914. The city had continued to expand, with new suburbs being built for both working- and middle-class people in areas like Rosemount. The city's entrepreneurs, cautious of protecting their capital, preferred to invest in housing rather than the manufacturing industries. In the early 1900s,

Rebuilding the Guildhall, *c.* 1909 (Derry City Council)

Joseph Cordner of Derry, one of the first aviators in Ireland (Ulster Folk and Transport Museum)

despite some appallingly overcrowded conditions, particularly in Catholic areas, the city had a glut of accommodation and many empty houses. Sanitation and public-health arrangements in working-class areas were abysmal. The indifference and complacency of the corporation to these issues dramatically backfired in 1908, when on 19 April, Easter Sunday, the lack of an adequate water supply and fire brigade contributed to the virtual destruction by fire of the very home of the corporation – the new town hall. The Guildhall had been opened in 1890, outside the walls on a site reclaimed from the slob-land of the river. Following the fire, it had to be almost totally reconstructed.

The city had experienced an economic boom since the 1860s but at the beginning of the twentieth century decline was setting in. Business at the port, and for those services which were dependent on it, dropped off sharply as the transatlantic trade declined and as the strong influence of the railway cartels diverted business to other places. The Great Northern Railway Company was particularly active in this, promoting the port of Greenore in County Louth, which it owned, at the expense of Derry's harbour. The railways also affected the city's retail business by distributing Belfast goods in areas where previously Derry had enjoyed a monopoly. This commercial crisis was exacerbated by internal factors: cuts in wages imposed by employers struggling with increased international competition further reduced the availability of disposable income within the city. Some achievements were possible, however: in 1908 a bicycle-shop owner from John Street, Joseph Cordner, became one of the first persons in Ireland to fly a plane. He is said to have invented wing flaps, a device copied by the de Havilland company when Cordner's patent ran out in 1919.

BALDRICK & CO.

With the construction of the Guildhall, the old Corporation Hall in the Diamond was converted for use as a school of art. That building, along with others in the city, was elaborately decorated and transformed in medieval style for the visit of King Edward VII and Queen Alexandra on 28 July 1903. (Derry City Council)

HOME RULE OR EXCLUSION

Derry nationalists were disorganised and had been damaged by a series of internal conflicts following the Parnell débâcle. In 1898 a Dublin printer, Arthur Griffith, founded the *United Irishman*, a weekly paper in which he preached the doctrine later to be espoused by Sinn Féin – a movement advocating the cultural, economic and political independence of Ireland. In the election of 1900 the Unionists recaptured the parliamentary seat and consolidated their electoral majority. Although attempts were made to establish Sinn Féin in the city, primarily with a cultural rather than a political agenda, these were not successful. Efforts by Sinn Féin supporters to reintroduce Gaelic games and develop an appreciation of Irish culture, as was happening elsewhere in Ireland, had to contend with the enormous influence of the Catholic clergy and the importance of soccer in the city.

In 1906 Father Doherty called a meeting of the various Catholic

Opposite
The proclamation of Edward VII by the mayor of Derry, Sir Henry Miller, and the high sheriff, Sir John Johnston, in the Diamond on 29 January 1901. The guard of honour was provided by the Royal Irish Rifles. (Derry City Council)

An anti-Home Rule rally at Shipquay Street on 20 September 1912. Sir Edward Carson and the Duke of Abercorn are seated in a carriage, and F.E. Smith, a leading English Tory supporter of the Ulster Unionists, is standing. (*The Graphic*)

groupings in the city with a view to restoring unity, which resulted in a vastly improved nationalist political machine. A bye-election in 1913 turned out to be of great importance as this seat would secure a seventeen to sixteen majority of Ulster parliamentary seats in Westminster. The Catholic clergy, whose authority on the choice of nationalist candidate was total, surprisingly selected David Hogg, an elderly shirt manufacturer and a Protestant, and although he gave no commitment to back Home Rule, the nationalist vote held solid and Hogg was elected by a narrow majority.

By late 1913 rumours were beginning to circulate that Ulster would be excluded from any Home Rule settlement for Ireland. Agitation against this proposal began immediately in Derry, led by the Catholic bishop, Dr Charles McHugh. John Redmond, the leader of the nationalists at Westminster, intervened, and promised Dr McHugh that Derry would be protected against any 'exclusion' propositions that might be forwarded. Historian A. T. Q. Stewart has pointed out that in 1833, in reply to Daniel O'Connell's repeal demands Lord Macaulay, speaking in the

David Hogg, who with Catholic support was victorious in a controversial parliamentary bye-election in 1913 (Magee College)

House of Commons, had first suggested a partition solution. Ironically, he suggested that any arguments for Irish independence 'would in a tenfold degree apply in favour of one domestic legislature in Dublin, and another in Derry, or some other large town in the north of Ireland'.

In February 1914 the Irish Volunteers began to organise in Derry and quickly gained recruits among the Catholic working class. The Volunteers were a nationalist paramilitary movement set up in Dublin in November 1913 in response to the formation in January 1913 of the loyalist Ulster Volunteer Force (UVF). The UVF was already organising among the Protestant working class in Derry.

As the national and international political situation deteriorated, in June 1914 the Government indicated that as a compromise it would provide for the six Ulster counties (which would later form the state of Northern Ireland) to opt out of the Home Rule settlement. However, events abroad now began to take precedence over local issues. By early August Britain was at war with Germany. Derry men from every walk of life, and from both communities, joined the forces. Local conflicts were put aside, but they were not forgotten.

11

THE GATHERING STORM
1914–68

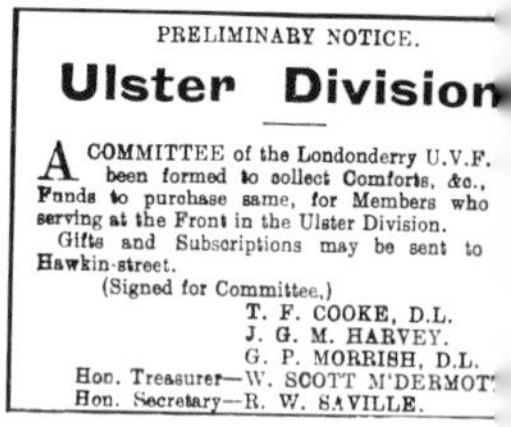

PRELIMINARY NOTICE.

Ulster Division

A COMMITTEE of the Londonderry U.V.F. been formed to collect Comforts, &c., Funds to purchase same, for Members who serving at the Front in the Ulster Division.

Gifts and Subscriptions may be sent to Hawkin-street.

(Signed for Committee.)

T. F. COOKE, D.L.
J. G. M. HARVEY.
G. P. MORRISH, D.L.

Hon. Treasurer—W. SCOTT M'DERMOT
Hon. Secretary—R. W. SAVILLE.

At the outbreak of the First World War the virtual unity of opinion in favour of Britain's opposition to Germany brought about a decrease in tension among Catholics in Derry despite the fact that the Government now saw partition as a serious option. Most nationalists, few of whom had ever taken the Unionist position seriously, were content to wait until the end of what they expected to be a short war to resolve the Home Rule issue. The Catholic bishop of Derry, Dr McHugh, and his clergy encouraged support for the war effort and the war introduced a temporary boom to the city's industries. The shipyard reopened and there were plenty of jobs and relatively high wages. The population began to grow again and political agitation virtually ceased, Sinn Féin

Men of the 36th (Ulster) Division before the Battle of Cambrai, November 1917 (Imperial War Museum)

and the Irish Volunteers becoming all but extinct. On 7 August 1914 the *Derry Journal* reported the departure of some of the reservists. The occasion did not pass without controversy:

> Though the orders for General Mobilisation of the reserves were only posted late on Tuesday there was a very prompt response to the call, nearly a thousand men leaving Derry alone by various trains . . . [Many] members of the National Volunteer Force also left, some to join the Royal Inniskilling Fusiliers reserve, others the Dublin Fusiliers, and also some to join the Connaught Rangers. The men were quite cheerful, though they took a serious view of the object of their journey. At the railway stations there was a certain amount of demonstration of a partisan political nature in connection with the departure of certain Protestant reservists, some of whom were members of the Ulster Volunteer Force . . . [When the trains departed] the demonstrators returned home seemingly quite content with the valuable contribution of ignorant lip service which they provided for the defence of the Empire.

Somewhat hypocritically, in view of what it had just said, the *Derry Journal* went on to criticise the reporting of this event by its principal rival:

> In the demonstrative description of the departure of the Army reservists from this city which appeared in the Derry Sentinel of yesterday the allegations of party dissension said to have shown itself on the part of the reservists is serviceable only for German purposes and is likely to be communicated to Germany, so as to give that country the impression that there is still a divided Ireland, where it is so essential in the face of the present crisis to have a united front.

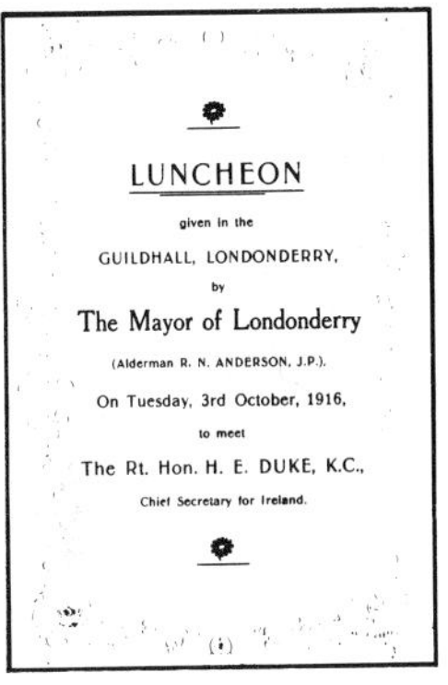
LUNCHEON

given in the

GUILDHALL, LONDONDERRY,

by

The Mayor of Londonderry

(Alderman R. N. ANDERSON, J.P.).

On Tuesday, 3rd October, 1916,

to meet

The Rt. Hon. H. E. DUKE, K.C.,

Chief Secretary for Ireland.

Even at war, although ostensibly fighting on the same side, the ancient divisions between the two communities continued to be reflected. Separated from their Catholic fellow citizens who went into regiments of the 16th (Irish) Division, the former UVF members were absorbed into the 36th (Ulster) Division. In July 1916 the men of the Ulster Division were to suffer appallingly at the Battle of the Somme. Three months prior to the Somme there had been little or no noticeable sympathy in Derry when the Easter Rising broke out in Dublin on 24 April. Four days later, the *Derry Journal*, noting that the city had reacted calmly to the rising, reported that 'the conduct of all classes of the citizens, and of the north-west generally, has been admirably cool and sensible'. Echoing the conservative approach of the bulk of its Catholic readers, the newspaper continued: 'The urging of people like the Dublin dockers with little political sagacity and less discriminative capacity to senseless and positively suicidal action is deplorable beyond powers of expression.' On 3 May the newspaper, with an obvious degree of relief, informed its readers that 'the authorities have succeeded in suppressing disturbance and restoring order. This is highly satisfactory.'

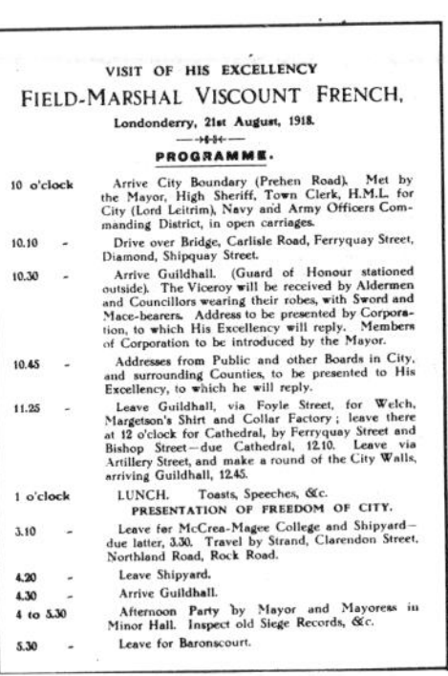
VISIT OF HIS EXCELLENCY

FIELD-MARSHAL VISCOUNT FRENCH,

Londonderry, 21st August, 1918.

PROGRAMME.

10 o'clock	Arrive City Boundary (Prehen Road). Met by the Mayor, High Sheriff, Town Clerk, H.M.L. for City (Lord Leitrim), Navy and Army Officers Commanding District, in open carriages.
10.10 -	Drive over Bridge, Carlisle Road, Ferryquay Street, Diamond, Shipquay Street.
10.30 -	Arrive Guildhall. (Guard of Honour stationed outside). The Viceroy will be received by Aldermen and Councillors wearing their robes, with Sword and Mace-bearers. Address to be presented by Corporation, to which His Excellency will reply. Members of Corporation to be introduced by the Mayor.
10.45 -	Addresses from Public and other Boards in City, and surrounding Counties, to be presented to His Excellency, to which he will reply.
11.25 -	Leave Guildhall, via Foyle Street, for Welch, Margetson's Shirt and Collar Factory; leave there at 12 o'clock for Cathedral, by Ferryquay Street and Bishop Street—due Cathedral, 12.10. Leave via Artillery Street, and make a round of the City Walls, arriving Guildhall, 12.45.
1 o'clock	LUNCH. Toasts, Speeches, &c. PRESENTATION OF FREEDOM OF CITY.
3.10 -	Leave for McCrea-Magee College and Shipyard—due latter, 3.30. Travel by Strand, Clarendon Street, Northland Road, Rock Road.
4.20 -	Leave Shipyard.
4.30 -	Arrive Guildhall.
4 to 5.30	Afternoon Party by Mayor and Mayoress in Minor Hall. Inspect old Siege Records, &c.
5.30 -	Leave for Baronscourt.

The leading Home Rule politician John Redmond (1856–1918). In 1916, on behalf of Herbert Asquith's government, Redmond tried to persuade Ulster Catholics to accept partition as a 'temporary' arrangement. (Henry Jones Thaddeus, National Gallery of Ireland

Dr Charles McHugh, Catholic bishop of Derry from 1907 to 1926, and a leading campaigner against partition (from *The Story of the Long Towe 546–1946*)

ANTI-PARTITION

In the aftermath of the rising, Prime Minister Herbert Asquith proposed the immediate introduction of Home Rule for Ireland with the exclusion of six Ulster counties, including Londonderry. The nationalists at Westminster, now called the United Irish League and led by John Redmond, tried to persuade Ulster Catholics to accept this 'temporary' arrangement. Dr McHugh was furious and announced that he would not go along with any concensus on the issue and the proposal was abandoned after a few weeks. But, forewarned about the real likelihood of partition, at a meeting held in Derry on 20 July, Dr McHugh formed his own political party – the Anti-partition League (later the Irish Nation League). The league attempted to make the subject of partition an issue in Irish national politics but, despite some limited success in Derry itself, the new party was a failure. Even in Derry its main effect was to weaken the position of the United Irish League, thus further preparing the way for the rise of the much more radical Sinn Féin.

Caricature of Eoin MacNeill, former president of the Irish Volunteers. He was elected Sinn Féin representative for Derry in 1918 and went on to take his seat at the breakaway Dáil Éireann. He was later appointed Minister of Education in the Irish Free State government and acted as its representative on the ill-fated Boundary Commission. (Magee College)

The first meeting of the Pearse Sinn Féin Club was held in Derry in August 1917. The following month the club organised a rally to which the well-known nationalist figure Eoin MacNeill was invited. MacNeill, originally from the Glens of Antrim, was a leading activist in both the Gaelic League and the Irish Volunteer movement and was also a noted scholar of early Irish history. Desmond Murphy has commented that the Pearse Sinn Féin Club

> was probably the first [Catholic] movement in Derry since the 1860s where the clergy were not the directing influence. Rather, leadership of Sinn Fein was provided by the petty bourgeoisie with occupations such as

The Butcher Gate, leading to the Catholic Long Tower and Bogside districts of Derry, *c.* 1912. Second-hand-clothes shops can be seen outside the city walls and a member of the RIC surveys the scene. (Green Collection, Ulster Folk and Transport Museum)

clerk, butcher and small shopkeeper being dominant on the organising committee.

In the changed political circumstances the club had little difficulty in establishing itself.

However, the nationalists and the anti-partitionists were still stronger in Derry than Sinn Féin. Following the end of the war, a crucial general election was called in December 1918. To avoid splitting the anti-Unionist vote, a single unity candidate was required and disagreement arose between the two parties. Similar disputes were taking place elsewhere in Ireland. The archbishop of Armagh, Cardinal Michael Logue, was invited to apportion the Ulster constituencies and Derry was awarded to Sinn Féin. Ironically, as Eamonn McCann has pointed out, the campaign in Derry on behalf of the Sinn Féin candidate was largely run by the stronger local nationalist party. Without nationalist opposition, the Sinn Féin candidate, Eoin MacNeill, easily defeated the Unionist, Alderman Robert Anderson. In total, seventy-three seats

Local solicitor Hugh C. O'Doherty, nationalist mayor of Derry from 1920 to 1923 (Harry Bryson)

were won by Sinn Féin, and MacNeill, along with the other Sinn Féin candidates, took his seat at the breakaway Dáil Éireann (unofficial independent Irish parliament) in the Mansion House in Dublin rather than in the House of Commons in London.

The end of the war brought an end to the period of temporary economic improvement in Derry. Almost immediately men began to lose their jobs and the wages of the women in the shirt factories began to fall. Ex-servicemen returned to the city, many of them with prospects of nothing but unemployment. Poor housing and social conditions provided a seedbed for the spread of republicanism among the Catholic population. And yet there was one brief moment when unity among the city's working-class people might have proved possible. There was a revival of trade-union activity in the city in early 1919, connected with the outbreak of the general strike in Belfast. However, the Derry trades council failed to give decisive leadership and sectarianism was free to prevent cross-community working-class collaboration. A Unionist Labour Association was established in the city, with Alderman Robert Anderson at its head, which stressed the importance of Unionist solidarity for the protection of jobs for the Protestant people and successfully argued that trade-union activism was synonymous with republican subversion. The authorities banned the May Day rally later that year, claiming that it would be nothing more than a republican demonstration.

Following Sinn Féin's national victory at the 1918 general election, the Government moved to frustrate any further similar successes. Proportional representation (PR) was introduced for local authority elections in Ireland. In Derry this had the effect of further exposing the tenuous Unionist control of the corporation. Although Catholics now outnumbered Protestants in the city by about five thousand, Protestants still held power in the municipal government. The Unionists tried to overcome the dangers for them in the new PR system by manipulating the ward boundaries. However, their attempt failed, and a Catholic or nationalist majority of twenty-one to twenty councillors was returned at the local election held in January 1920. With the support of an alliance of nationalist and Sinn Féin councillors, Hugh C. O'Doherty, a local solicitor, became the city's first Catholic mayor (with the possible

The Guildhall, seat of the municipal government of Derry, *c.* 1913. It was rebuilt after a disastrous fire in 1908. (Green Collection, Ulster Folk and Transport Museum)

exception of Cormack O'Neill for a short time in 1688–9). In his inaugural speech O'Doherty stated:

> Today a long and painful chapter in the history of Derry is closed, and a new one opened. I trust that when it comes to be written it will show a spirit of tolerance and forbearance amongst all creeds and classes. So far as in our power lies, my Nationalist colleagues and I mean to conduct the business of this Corporation without giving offence.

The *Derry Journal* was euphoric and proclaimed somewhat exaggeratedly: ' "No Surrender" Citadel Conquered After Centuries of Oppression. Overthrow of Ascendancy.'

CIVIL WAR

The unexpected change in power at the Guildhall was signalled by a series of alterations, largely symbolic in character. The Union Jack was no longer flown and the corporation ceased to be represented officially at government functions. There were a number of other similar superficial reforms, but when it came to more substantial matters, the new corporation was not as decisive. Its members vacillated about their relations with the Dáil and continued to have links with the official British local government board in Dublin.

Although political excitement continued to mount in Derry, the city remained comparatively peaceful in the first few months following the election. Trouble began in mid-April, when a group of republican prisoners were brought to the city jail. Rival Catholic and Protestant

The Apprentice Boys' Memorial Hall in Society Street, constructed originally in 1873 and extended in 1937. Sectarian hostility between Derry's two communities was underpinned by a range of mutually exclusive institutions and myths. For the Protestant community the siege and the Apprentice Boys' organisation provided a cohesive force. (Derry City Council)

groups who had gathered to watch the event clashed and a riot ensued. The *Derry Journal* reported:

> The most violent conflict took place at the junction of Long Tower Street and Fountain Street, outside Bishop's Gate, a great storm centre in party fights in the city . . .
>
> The Sinn Fein crowd sang Republican songs and waved the tri-colour. On the opposite side a crowd of Unionists were equally demonstrative, singing 'Rule Britannia' and 'Dolly's Brae'.
>
> Soon the rival parties became more aggressive and blows were exchanged, the Unionist crowd being rushed up Albert Street by the opposing crowd. Stones were thrown freely, and the crash of glass was heard continuously . . . For fully an hour a desperate conflict raged.

On 18 April shots were fired into the Bogside and on the same day police, with bayonets fixed, charged a group of Catholics near the centre of the city. Similar incidents occurred in other parts of Derry during the following weeks. Rioting and disorder flared again on the weekend of 14–16 May. On 15 May a fierce gun battle between the police and the IRA lasted for four hours and the head of the Royal Irish Constabulary (RIC) Special Branch was shot dead – the first policeman to be killed in the six counties. The police were also engaged with nationalist rioters in and around Bridge Street. Meanwhile, units of the re-formed UVF repeatedly took over nearby Carlisle Road and the bridge without interference from the police or army. The *Derry Journal* reported some of these incidents:

> A mob of masked and armed Orange rowdies took possession of Carlisle

St Columb's Hall, Newmarket Street, built in 1888. By the late nineteenth century the city's two communities were polarised, both socially and politically. The Catholic community developed a range of institutions and organisations exploiting the legacy of Saint Colmcille, in much the same mythic way that Protestants used the siege. (Derry City Council)

Bridge and held it for almost two hours. Every pedestrian crossing the Bridge during that period was stopped, challenged, and had to declare his religion, and if it were found he was a Catholic he was maltreated . . . Gangs of masked Unionist outlaws, emerging from Fountain Street, Wapping Lane, and other haunts, again created for a couple of hours a reign of terror. Some of these ruffians had their faces blackened, others wore black masks, and a few had handkerchiefs on their faces with holes for the eyes. Armed with revolvers they took possession of Carlisle Road and indulged in indiscriminate revolver firing.

Ironically, a young Catholic ex-soldier, recently returned from the war where he had been gassed and wounded, was killed on this occasion. As a result of growing fears among working-class Protestants, and without 'official' approval by the local Unionist establishment, the UVF had been reorganised in the city. The number of volunteers had been increased by the availability of many war veterans, who were no strangers to fighting.

More trouble occurred in mid-June, when a group of Catholics was attacked at Prehen, on the east bank of the River Foyle. During the following week there were several incidents, including a major riot in the Waterside, where, on 18 June, Catholic houses were attacked. The following day the UVF launched a fierce gun attack on the Bogside, having already taken over the Diamond and Guildhall Square areas of the centre of the city. Four Catholics and one Protestant were killed. Neither the police nor the army intervened. The following Monday's *Derry Journal* reported:

Derry was on Saturday night the scene of appalling bloodshed and brutality, following a wild outburst by Unionists, who, armed with rifles and revolvers, turned some streets of the city into a veritable shambles. Many lives were lost. The Long Tower, an exclusively Catholic district, was kept for hours under a deadly fire from the City Walls and Unionist strongholds of Fountain Street and Albert Street. At least three men were shot dead and many persons including a baby in arms were wounded. In the Diamond and at Butcher Street men were also killed and at other parts of the city many received serious injuries.

The IRA responded immediately by entering the walled city, where several battles broke out. The better-equipped UVF drove the republicans out beyond the walls again, but the premises of Unionist supporters in the Bogside were destroyed in retaliation. The city descended into anarchy. People from both sides of the community had to flee their homes and some individuals who were caught in the 'wrong' area were killed. One of the Protestants killed in reprisal was Howard McKay, a son of the leader of the Apprentice Boys. On 21 June members of the UVF attempted to take control of the grounds of St Columb's College, the scene of their ancestors' famous victory at the Battle of Windmill Hill during the siege of 1689. The IRA quickly dislodged the Protestants on

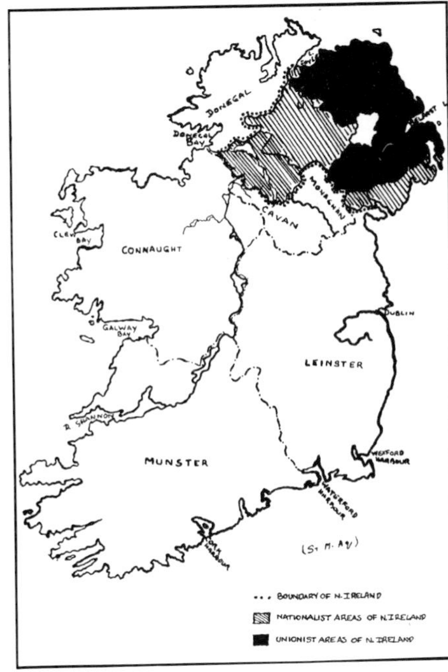

Map showing the Irish border and the nationalist and Unionist areas of Northern Ireland, in a 1945 anti-partition pamphlet published by the *Derry Journal* (from Cahir Healy, *The Mutilation of a Nation*)

this occasion and they retired to the nearby corner of Abercorn Road, from where the battle continued. An IRA spokesman later told the press:

> As far as the attack on St Columb's College was concerned, [the IRA was] asked by the President of the College to furnish him with as many men as would protect the institution. The [IRA] went there and took over control, but they merely confined their efforts to locating snipers. A number of men who had been sniping at the College were now casualties.

By 23 June eight Catholics and four Protestants were dead. At this point the British Army intervened with 1,500 men, and a curfew was imposed. The troops mounted heavy machine guns on armoured cars and aimed them at republican and nationalist areas of the city: six Catholics were shot dead. The troops immediately began weapon searches in the city's Catholic districts. A number of Catholics in the RIC resigned, alleging collusion between the army and some of their police colleagues with the UVF. Members of the UVF, who were not disarmed, were allowed to carry out patrols openly, using a password prearranged between themselves and the army. Over the following months, a close liaison developed between the UVF and the troops stationed in the city.

A total of forty people were killed in this 'civil war'. The IRA, aware of its inferiority locally to the UVF, virtually ceased to operate in Derry for the time being. Meanwhile, the establishment of an auxiliary police force, the B Specials, in November 1920 gave the Protestant paramilitaries official sanction. The Government of Ireland Act was passed at Westminster in December, providing for the setting up of two local parliaments, one in the north and the other in the south. By Christmas 1920 Ireland was effectively partitioned. Derry was part of Northern Ireland.

The Catholic bishop of Derry, Dr McHugh, now returned to political activity. He helped to organise a campaign of protest against the elections for the new parliament of Northern Ireland, held in May 1921. The bishop was pragmatic, however. In December 1921 he frustrated an attempt by republican councillors to have the corporation pass a motion of allegiance to Dáil Éireann. With the signing of the Anglo-Irish treaty in December 1921 and the formal acceptance of partition by the southern state, Catholics in Derry began to look forward to the recommendations of the Boundary Commission, which was to be set up to finalise the detailed line of the new frontier.

In September 1922 the government of Northern Ireland abolished PR for local authority elections. It also approved a rearrangement of the electoral areas in Derry which restored the former Unionist advantage in the city. The population of the city at this time was 23,000 Catholics and 18,000 Protestants. At a public meeting in the city in November it was recommended that the Catholic community should not take part in the forthcoming election but should look to the Boundary Commission instead for a resolution of its problems. The meeting concluded:

> In Derry City alone, where Catholics are an overwhelming majority of the population, they are, owing to a system of gerrymandering and other mean devices, being disenfranchised, permanently excluded in future from all share in the management of the city and placed at the mercy of a privileged, intolerant minority.

In the municipal elections which followed in 1923, Unionists again took control of the corporation. The nationalists withdrew from the chamber in protest against the 'gerrymandered victory'. They did not return to take part in corporation business for another ten years.

A delay in setting up the Boundary Commission gave the government of Northern Ireland time to consolidate its territorial position. This infant government refused to appoint an official delegate to sit on the commission when it was eventually established. Instead, in 1924, the British government was forced to appoint the prominent Ulster Unionist, J.R. Fisher, as the northern representative. The southern government had appointed Eoin MacNeill, the former Sinn Féin representative for Derry. The 'neutral' chairman was Richard Feetham, a South African Supreme Court judge. The commission began meeting in secret at the beginning of November 1924. A number of visits were made to Derry, including a celebrated occasion when the mayor organised a Sunday-afternoon excursion to the Grianan of Aileach. The incident gave rise to subsequent slanderous and totally false allegations against Eoin MacNeill, that this eminent Gaelic professor was more interested in archaeology than in the fate of the nationalists of Derry.

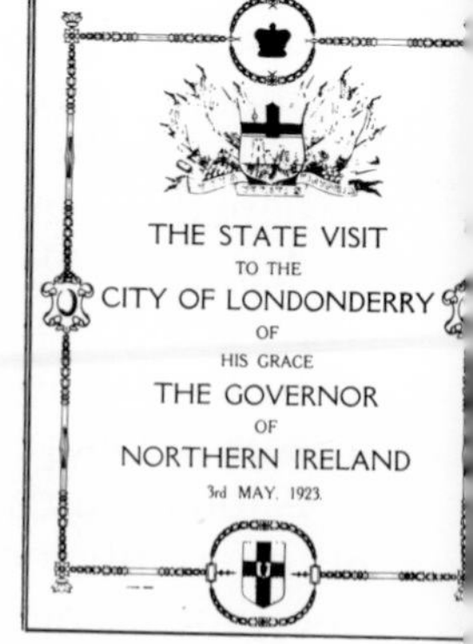

THE STATE VISIT
TO THE
CITY OF LONDONDERRY
OF
HIS GRACE
THE GOVERNOR
OF
NORTHERN IRELAND
3rd MAY. 1923.

Full hearings before the commission, in relation to Derry and its hinterland, took place in the city from 14 May to 5 June 1925. Detailed evidence was presented on both sides of the argument but the historian of the commission, Geoffrey Hand, believes that the case for the nationalists was 'mismanaged':

> The Committee of Nationalist inhabitants of the city claimed, firstly, that the desire of the majority of the inhabitants was the unity of all Ireland; secondly, that failing the unity of Ireland the majority of the inhabitants wished that the city should be included in the Irish Free State. The Committee based its claim on the fact that the majority of the inhabitants as Catholics had always desired to be associated with an autonomous Government in Dublin, and on the contention that the economic life of the city was largely dependent on its connection with Tirconaill [Donegal]. In the course of the hearing of evidence certain witnesses put forward an alternative scheme in favour of a boundary following the line of the Foyle, and dividing the city so as to include the Waterside Ward in Northern Ireland and the remainder in the Irish Free State . . .
>
> The claims put forward for the transfer of the city were opposed –
>
> (a) on legal grounds –
> 1 that the city is mentioned in the Government of Ireland Act 1920 as a constituent part of Northern Ireland;
> 2 that no part of the city actually touches the present boundary;
>
> (b) on economic grounds –
> 1 that the transfer would endanger the prospects of the city's industries;
> 2 that the greater part of the trade of the city and its port is with Northern Ireland;
> 3 that the city is closely linked economically with the Protestant districts to the East . . .
>
> The Londonderry members of the Shirt and Collar Manufacturers' Federation contended that this industry imported its material from and exported the bulk of its products to Great Britain, that many of its factories were allied with British undertakings, and that its continued prosperity depended on costs being kept at a level which would enable the Derry factories to hold their own against English factories.

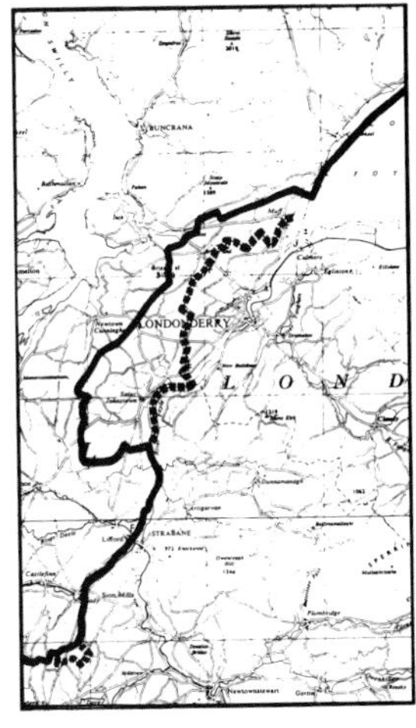

The hinterland of Derry, from a map illustrating the report of the Boundary Commission (1925), showing existing frontier (broken line), and proposed extension of Northern Ireland into County Donegal (solid line). The report was abandoned and its proposals were not implemented.

Judge Feetham announced to his commission colleagues that he considered that 'economic and geographic factors' should take precedence over the 'wishes of the inhabitants' and that specific places with a nationalist majority, such as Derry, should remain in Northern Ireland. This view was leaked to the press on 7 November 1925, most likely by Fisher. Extremely embarrassed by these disclosures, MacNeill resigned from the commission on 20 November, followed shortly afterwards by his resignation as minister for education in the southern government. The following year an agreement was signed between the three governments involved, abandoning the Boundary Commission. Its report was not finally published until 1969 and a number of minor readjustments to the border were never implemented. Derry remained part of Northern Ireland and of the United Kingdom.

THE BOUNDARY PROBLEM.

MR. FIGGIS'S FORECAST.

Great Resentment Shown by Derry Nationalists.

MYTHICAL TEN MILE RADIUS.

Derry Nationalists are very angry over Mr. Darrell Figgis's article on the boundary question, in which he foreshadowed not only the inclusion of a considerable portion of East Donegal, but the peninsula of Inishowen in the Northern area, and the "Derry Journal" yesterday stated that strong exception is taken in the city and district to such forecasts.

It says the forecast of Mr. Figgis is based on the assumption that by bringing part of Donegal into the Six Counties Derry city can

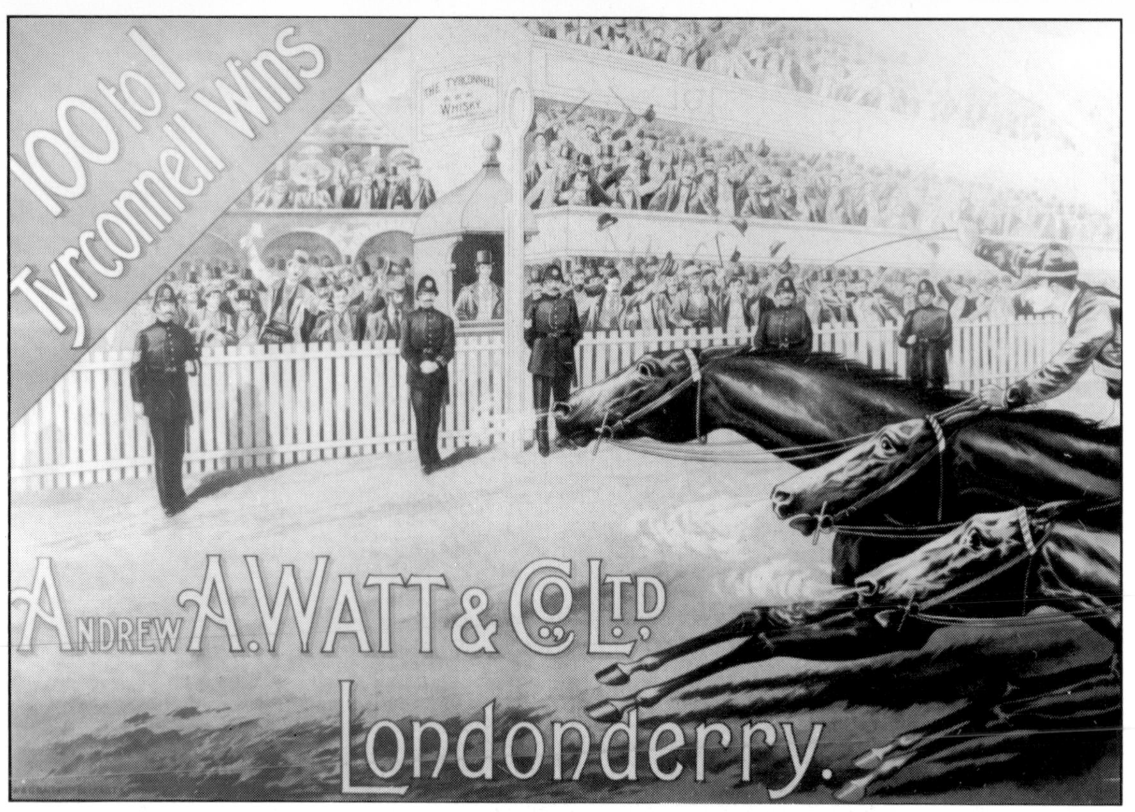

Watt's distillery, Derry, makers of the famous Tyrconnell whiskey, closed down in 1920 (Derry City Council)

The arrival of partition coincided with the intensification of the postwar economic depression in Derry. Watt's distillery, makers of the famous Tyrconnell whiskey, closed in 1920 and the shipyard shut down in 1924. The new border separated the city from its Donegal hinterland and some businesses transferred into the Irish Free State in pursuit of their traditional customers. The border created unprecedented barriers to trade and communication: one of the four railway networks out of the city crossed the new frontier seventeen times. Several other major businesses closed in the city in the 1920s, and by 1926, the official unemployment figure was 28 per cent. However, it is difficult to gauge the precise impact that partition made in a period of general economic decline. Certainly, the depression and unemployment affected the Catholic population disproportionately and many people reacted by availing of the only opportunity open to them – between 1926 and 1936 about three thousand men from Derry 'took the boat' and emigrated.

BRANDY AND THE BORDER

DONEGAL CUSTOMS PROSECUTIO

COAT BOUGHT IN DERRY.

FARMER'S £16 PENALTY

An aged man who alighted at St. Jo
ston Railway Station from the De
train wearing two overcoats was the
fendant in a prosecution at Raphoe D
trict Court yesterday. He was Jose
Gamble, whose age was given as seven
of Bready, Carrigans, who was char
with attempting to evade payment of
Customs duty on an overcoat and kn
on 27th March, and also with obstruct
the officer in the execution of his duty.
Mr. Hugh C. O'Doherty, for the
fence, raised three preliminary point
first, was a Guard a duly authorised p
son to serve the summons in this instan
secondly, had the sanction of the Reve

THE 1930S

Despite its many problems, and unlike troubled Belfast, Derry remained a peaceful, even sleepy, town throughout the 1930s. In 1932 the city's name was brought to world attention when the first woman to fly solo across the Atlantic, the indomitable Amelia Earhart, landed accidentally and somewhat ignominiously in a field at Ballyarnett on the northern outskirts of the city. She had intended to arrive in Paris in imitation of the epic flight of Charles Lindbergh. The following year the city was the scene of more international aviation attention when it

Amelia Earhart, the first woman to fly solo across the Atlantic, with members of the McLoughlin family and Dan McCallion at Shantallow, Derry, on 22 May 1932 (Derry City Council)

became the refuelling depot for a transatlantic Italian flying-boat armada led by General Italo Balbo. The expedition was essentially a propaganda exercise for the Fascist government of Benito Mussolini. It was given an enthusiastic welcome by the citizens of Derry, especially by the small community of Italian immigrants, and a civic reception was organised by the mayor, Sir Dudley McCorkell.

An archaic feature of life in the city which had survived to the 1930s were the Rabble Days, or annual hiring fairs. These were held on each of the three Wednesdays which succeeded 12 May and 12 December, when local farmers could inspect and hire agricultural labourers and domestic servants. Huge crowds gathered in the Diamond and nearby streets, which were lined with street entertainers' booths and various sideshows. Gradually, improved conditions for workers put an end to what must have been a humiliating way of obtaining employment.

In October 1932 the city's unemployed organised a peaceful march to the Guildhall, where a deputation submitted to the corporation a series of proposals for job creation, which included:

> The erection of houses, the removal of petrol tanks to safer positions, the

From 2 to 5 July 1933, Derry played host to the Italian air minister, General Italo Balbo, and one hundred airmen who were taking part in a trans-atlantic flying-boat propaganda armada on behalf of the Facist government of Benito Mussolini. The Italian party is seen here with the mayor, Sir Dudley McCorkell, returning to the Guildhall after a wreath-laying ceremony at the War Memorial in the Diamond.
(T. McDonald and D. Biggar)

> erection of proper lavatories in all the wards of the city and the removal of the present unhealthy urinals, a new sewerage scheme, the provision of municipal playgrounds, baths, and washhouses, and concreting of all footpaths, the provision of fire stations with sleeping quarters, a new slaughter-house, the removal of the Infirmary wall and of dangerous corners at William Street and Creggan Road, the substitution of zinc water barrels for wooden barrels and ashbins instead of ashpits, and the erection of libraries in each ward.

In view of the seriousness of the situation, the corporation decided on unprecedented action and 'ordered that with a view to alleviating unemployment during the winter months we forthwith advertise for tenders for annual clothing supplies which are not usually taken until March'. What effect the corporation felt this measure would have on the numbers of those out of work is not recorded.

In the Stormont election of the following year, the sitting Nationalist member for the Foyle constituency in the city, J. J. McCarroll, was opposed by a Sinn Féin candidate, Sean McCool. McCool's supporters, referring to the well-known politicians of the day, sang:

Craig and Devlin save your face,
Now, McCarroll, leave your place,
Here's a man that's no disgrace,
McCool is on the border.

Londonderry Corporation with guests, seated outside the Guildhall in the late 1920s (Magee College)

However, McCool's Nationalist opponents labelled him a Communist. In the year following the religious fervour of the 1932 International Eucharistic Congress, held in Dublin, McCarroll, with the support of the Catholic clergy and the *Derry Journal*, which he owned, easily held the seat. The year 1933 also saw the opening of the Craigavon Bridge, named after Lord Craigavon (previously Sir James Craig, the first prime minister of Northern Ireland). The new bridge, like its predecessor, had the unusual distinction of having two decks, the lower of which was intended for rail traffic.

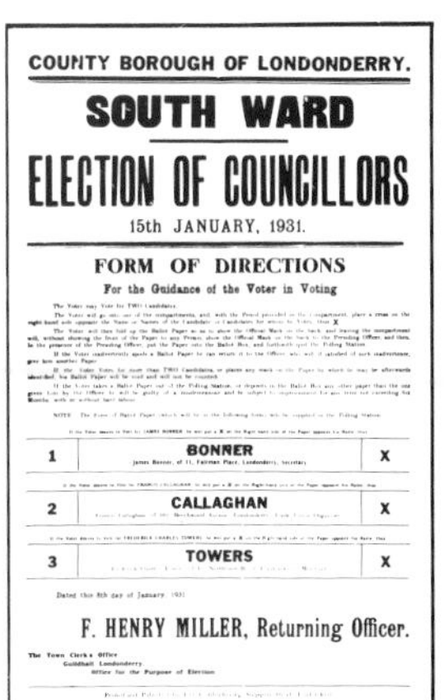

COUNTY BOROUGH OF LONDONDERRY.

SOUTH WARD

ELECTION OF COUNCILLORS

15th JANUARY, 1931.

FORM OF DIRECTIONS

For the Guidance of the Voter in Voting

1	BONNER James Bonner, of 11, Fairman Place, Londonderry, Secretary	X
2	CALLAGHAN	X
3	TOWERS	X

Dated this 8th day of January, 1931.

F. HENRY MILLER, Returning Officer.

The Town Clerk's Office
Guildhall, Londonderry.
Office for the Purpose of Election.

GERRYMANDER

By 1936 the continuing increase in the city's population was threatening to upset the carefully worked out ward arrangements which gave the Unionists control of the corporation. To protect their majority in the council, the Unionists drew up a radical plan which proposed to reduce the number of councillors from forty to twenty-four and the number of wards from five to three. Nationalists opposed the scheme and called for a public inquiry, which was held before an inspector of the Ministry

A hiring fair in the Diamond, Derry, in the 1930s (Magee College)

of Home Affairs from 7 to 9 October 1936. Most of the Unionist witnesses argued that the rearrangements were necessary for the better administration of the city but the frank evidence of Archie Halliday caused a sensation. Halliday, who was English, was the principal of a commercial college in the city and a member of the North Ward Unionist Association. During cross-examination he was asked what he thought the purposes of the proposals were:

> Halliday – 'I think I should not say anything too strong if I say it really is due to the fact that there is a fear that the Unionist majority in the North Ward will, in the course of a year or two, be wiped out.'
> Cyril Nicholson [barrister for the Nationalists] – 'And it is your suggestion that this is the purpose of the scheme?'
> Halliday – 'Oh yes! I think so.'

Another Unionist witness was Councillor James Welch, a director of a local shirt factory. Nicholson put it to Welch that the scheme, whereby nine thousand nationalists would elect eight councillors and seven thousand Unionist voters sixteen, would be 'extraordinary':

> Welch – 'Put that way it looks . . .'
> Nicholson – 'A bit funny?'

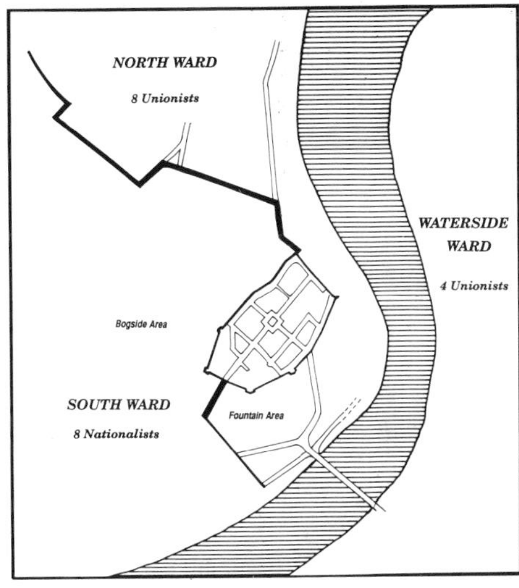

The 1936 gerrymander arrangements, which persisted until 1968 and resulted in a twelve to eight permanent Unionist majority on Londonderry Corporation

Welch – When you put it that way it looks a bit . . .'
Nicholson – 'A bit unjust? You are a businessman and a fair-minded man, what does it look to you?'
Welch – 'It looks a bit slightly out of proportion.'

At the end of October 1936 the Ministry of Home Affairs wrote to the corporation outlining its decision on the proposed scheme:

> Very considerable opposition was offered to the scheme at the Inquiry, while the evidence put forward in support of it was of a most unsatisfactory character. The new line proposed as a boundary line between the two wards not separated by the river, followed in some parts, a course very difficult to define and no evidence was given in justification of this complication and none of the witnesses examined on behalf of the scheme had ascertained or were aware how this boundary would actually run.

The Unionist scheme was rejected. Nevertheless, two months later, in December 1936, the Northern Ireland government made an order effectively implementing the proposed arrangements. One modification was made: the number of councillors was reduced to twenty, allowing a Unionist majority of four rather than eight as suggested in the original scheme. These changes had been carried out by the time the 1938 municipal elections were held. The South ward had been drawn so as to include almost the entire Catholic population of the city and it returned a full complement of eight Nationalist councillors. Similarly, the North and Waterside wards returned their full complement of twelve Unionist councillors. The paradox was that in the city as a whole there were only 7,444 Protestant electors while the Catholics had 9,691 votes, a majority of more than 2,000. At the first meeting of the new corporation the leader of the Nationalists, Paddy Maxwell MP, claimed that 'by a shameless gerrymander scheme, we have been deprived of our rights. The city has been carved up to give an ever decreasing minority control over an ever increasing majority. But numbers will tell in the end.'

Councillor James Welch, a local shirt-factory director, who gave evidence to the public inquiry into proposed electoral changes – the gerrymander – in 1936 (Derry City Council)

THE SECOND WORLD WAR

When the American 'civilian technicians' arrived in Derry in 1941 one of the first things they did was to take groups of local children to the pictures, giving each child a bag of sweets (T. McDonald and D. Biggar)

As in 1914, the outbreak of the Second World War in 1939 occasioned a truce in local political conflicts. The war brought much activity to the city: once again the shipyard reopened and a massive amount of wartime construction created plenty of jobs. One Derry woman, Mary Lynch, recalled:

> I was working in a shirt factory during the war years in Derry . . . However, when the war broke out we started making trousers as well as shirts for the troops in the Middle East . . . At that particular time I was a buttoner in the factory. The girls used to slip notes into the orders, hoping to receive a reply from the troops [and] one time we did. The soldiers thanked us for writing to them and added that they would love to get their hands on the girl who put the buttons on their shirts because every time they put the shirts on, the buttons flew off.

A secret agreement with the Americans, signed in 1941, even before they had entered the war, provided for the establishment of a US naval base in Derry. The first group of 362 'civilian technicians' arrived on 30 June 1941, and over the next five months the numbers more than

The US Naval Operating Base, Londonderry, officially came into operation on 5 February 1942. (Imperial War Museum)

doubled. In December 1941, when the United States did enter the war, a vast array of facilities, including a radio station, a ship repair base, ammunition and storage depots, personnel camps, an administrative headquarters and one thousand feet of new quayside at Lisahally, had been provided. Later, additional facilities were constructed. The Americans quickly won friends in the city. One local man, Jim Girr, remembered

> when they took over the picture houses. Every child of school age was marched over to the pictures. You got a big bag of sweets going up to the picture show which lasted three or four hours. It was a great treat as sweets were scarce. The American 'technicians' paid for everything.

On 5 February 1942 the 'US Naval Operating Base, Londonderry' was officially commissioned. Derry replaced Reykjavik in Iceland as the terminal for US convoys bound for Britain. Some of the puritanical traditions of the city shocked the American sailors, but it was a definite improvement: 'Londonderry, a stronghold of strict Irish Presbyterians, offered bluejackets slight recreation on the Sabbath, but seemed like Coney Island after Reykjavik.' The American base continued in operation in Derry until July 1944. With the Normandy landings, the installations were handed over to the British and by the beginning of September, only a US radio station was left in the city. (The Naval Communications Base in the Waterside was finally closed in September 1977.) According to an official American source, 'Until the creation of Exeter, Londonderry was the main supply depot for our naval activities

A wartime dance at the Guildhall (Derry City Council)

in the British Isles, and throughout the war, it was the major United States naval radio station in the European theatre.'

Derry was also of great importance from the British point of view. Professor J. W. Blake, the official Northern Ireland war historian, has written:

> Londonderry held the key to victory in the Atlantic . . . [It] became our most westerly base for the repair, the working up, and the refuelling of destroyers, corvettes and frigates . . . By that critical Spring [1943] when the battle for the security of our Atlantic lifelines finally turned our way, Londonderry was the most important escort base in the North-Western approaches. Everybody at Londonderry co-operated in this supreme effort, and all was controlled from Combined Naval and Air Headquarters, housed in Magee College.

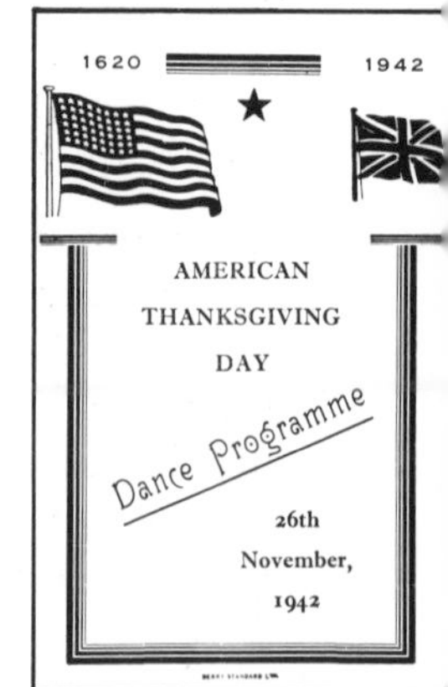
1620 1942

AMERICAN
THANKSGIVING
DAY

Dance Programme

26th
November,
1942

In April 1943, 149 ocean-going escorts were based at Derry, twice the number at Liverpool and Greenock combined. In addition, four military airfields were built close to the city, on the level terrain along the eastern shore of Lough Foyle.

There were nearly as many Canadians as Americans at the base and other contingents from the 'free' forces of France, Belgium and Holland increased the cosmopolitan atmosphere in the city. Some refugees from

Gibraltar were also sent to Derry. Paradoxically, the war brought a lot of 'life', and a touch of glamour which is still fondly recalled. Leading entertainers visited the city to perform for the troops and many Derry women married 'Yanks'. Charlie Gallagher, a local air raid precautions warden, recollected that the local men were not always too happy about the excitement caused by the foreigners, especially the Americans: 'We were getting our eyes wiped left, right and centre . . . The British used to say of the Americans that they were "over-fed, over-paid, over-sexed and over here". The American reply was that the British were "under-paid, under-fed, under-sexed and under Eisenhower".' Derry women who went out with the Americans were sometimes the butt of caustic jibes:

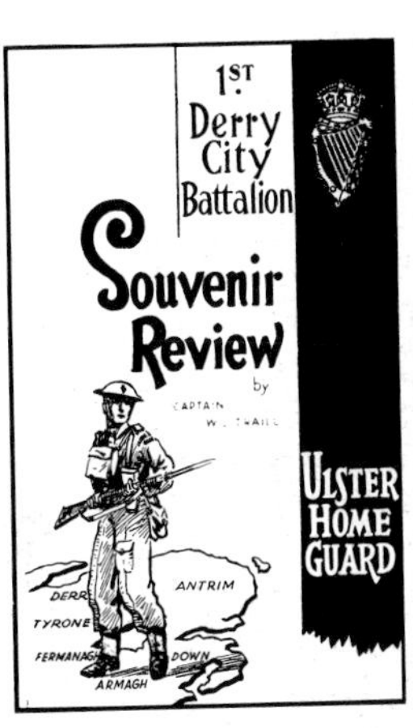

> Coming in with a yank on a jeep,
> All the girls in Derry think its cheap,
> With their clothes up to their bums
> And their chewing yankee gum,
> Coming in with a yank on a jeep.

The city's location beside the border with Éire was no security risk. The Irish policy of benevolent neutrality was repeatedly exploited and wartime smuggling became part of the local economy as well as of the folklore. A well-known Derry character, Patrick 'Barman' Duffy, tells the story of a Derry lad who worked in a knackers' yard in the city who was sent 'across the border' to collect an ailing horse. By mistake, a good horse was put down rather than the intended victim:

> Now this boy and his mate were in a quandary for they had to pay the old farmer for the horse they had destroyed by mistake. So they had an idea; they went into a bar and bought so many bottles of whiskey for smuggling. Then they split open the belly of the horse and put the bottles inside; they then brought the horse up to Derry. There was no danger of a Customs Man searching inside the guts of a dead horse – even if he thought there was anything in there.

Apart from the Derry men killed overseas, casualties in the city were limited to one occasion. On 15 April 1941, Easter Tuesday, a single German bomber dropped two parachute mines over the River Foyle – they were probably intended for the busy ship-repair base. One of the bombs fell on Messines Park, a small ex-servicemen's housing estate about half a mile from the dockyard. The bomb exploded, killing fifteen people and injuring as many more. The second bomb fell into a sandpit at Pennyburn, damaging a nearby Catholic church. One, no doubt, 'shell-shocked' observer claimed that he saw a statue of Saint Patrick on the church actually push the bomb away from the building. On the same night, two hundred German bombers caused devastation in Belfast. Over two hundred tonnes of bombs fell on the city, more than nine hundred people died and twice as many again were injured. Over

3,500 houses were destroyed or severely damaged. Glasgow was also bombed on the same night.

The Germans did not come into contact again with Derry until 1945, at the conclusion of the war. Following the end of hostilities, German U-boats at sea were instructed to surface and make their way to indicated ports and a number of U-boats of all types were escorted into Lisahally. The surrender of the first group of eight submarines was formally taken on 14 May 1945 by Admiral Sir Maxwell Horton, Commander in Chief of the Western Approaches, watched by the prime minister of Northern Ireland, Sir Basil Brooke. Twenty-eight submarines were towed out into the Atlantic and sunk during the following winter.

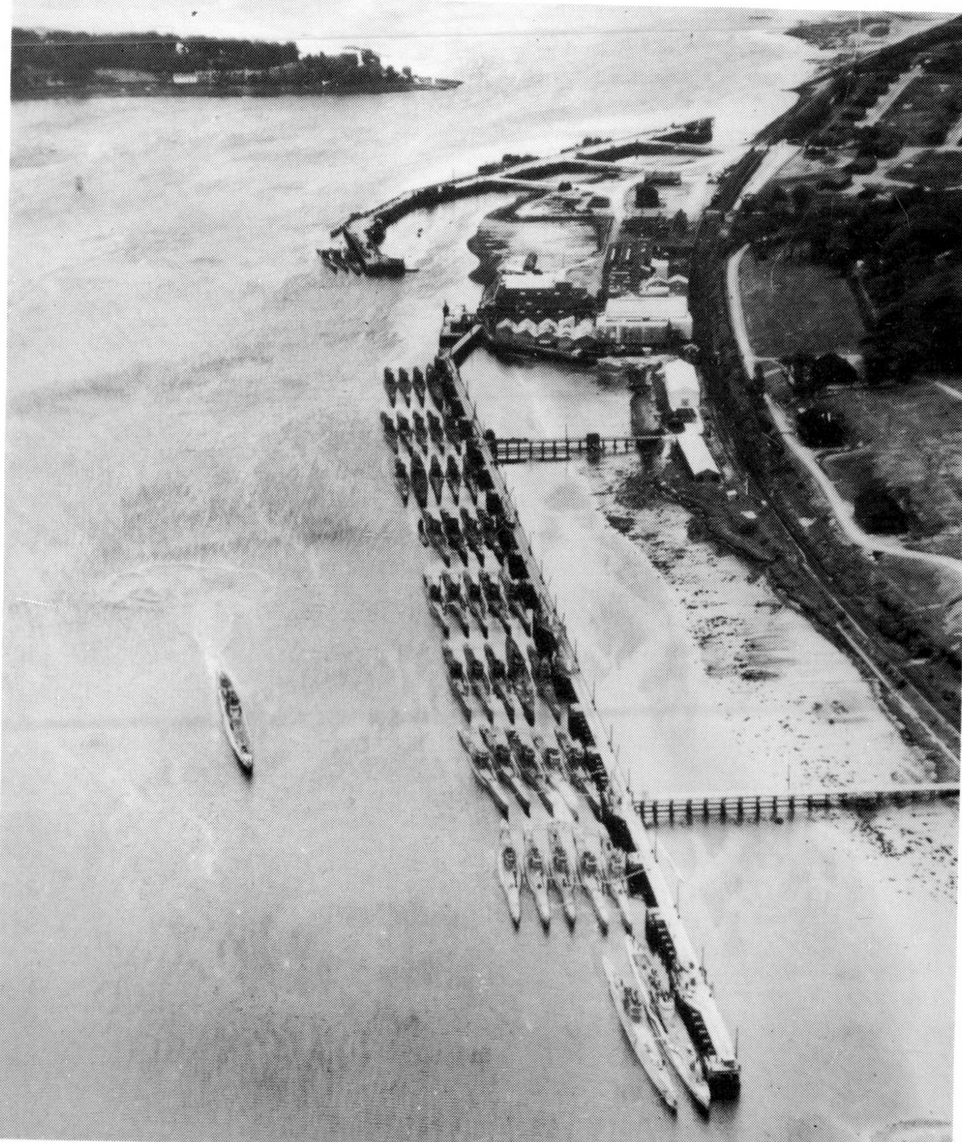

Surrendered German U-boats at Lisahally, near Derry, 1945 (Imperial War Museum)

Eamonn de Valera in Derry in 1951 to open a festival of Gaelic cultural and sporting events (Frank McFadden)

As in the First World War, Derry men from both communities had joined the British Army and fought overseas. The war meant that local differences and conflicts were subsumed by the great world cataclysm. But despite the temporary wartime prosperity and excitement, the city's deeper problems remained intact, ready to surface again when peace was declared everywhere else.

THE POSTWAR PERIOD

The end of the war brought the city's underlying economic, social and political difficulties into the open again. Although the IRA made a brief appearance in the city in 1951, raiding Ebrington Barracks and escaping with a quantity of arms, Derry continued to be free from serious violence. Nationalists were divided as to whether or not they should organise street demonstrations to highlight their grievances. When a march down Shipquay Street with an illegal Irish tricolour was organised on St Patrick's Day 1951, it was baton-charged by the Royal Ulster Constabulary (RUC). Traditionally, this area was restricted to Protestant marches. A similar incident occurred the following year. One nationalist 'victory' was achieved on the night of 24 April 1951, Easter Saturday, when a local republican, Manus Canning, boldly climbed the Walker Pillar and attached the banned tricolour to the top. The pillar, which overlooked the Bogside, was the most important siege monument in the city and its flagpole was usually bedecked by emblems with more loyalist associations. The *Derry Journal* reported the incredible incident:

> Our reporter says that by the time the sky had cleared and in the light of the full moon the Tricolour could be quite clearly seen. It had been

Destruction at the Great Northern Railway terminus in Derry during the IRA border campaign of the late 1950s, when a goods train was hijacked and sent driverless, at full speed, into the station (Magee College)

perfectly raised to the top of the vertical flag-pole and fanned by a slight breeze from the south-west it floated fully spread out and presented an impressive sight. It was right over the head of the Orangemen's hero, Rev George Walker.

Another symbolic victory for the nationalists of Derry occurred in the same year, when Eamonn de Valera, then temporarily out of government office in the Irish Republic, visited the city. He came, without a civic invitation, to open a festival of Gaelic cultural and sporting events. Eamonn McCann, in his book *War and an Irish Town*, captures the ephemeral excitement of the occasion:

> The kerbstones were painted green, white and orange, and flags and bunting hung everywhere. When he came up Rossville Street in an open car the crowds surged forward and almost swamped him, waving their arms, delirious, cheering, laughing, and jumping up on one another's shoulders to be sure to see him. Women craned precariously out of upstairs windows waving handkerchiefs, frenetic, screaming 'Dev, Dev, Dev!' He who had fought in 1916, the last living leader of the single most glorious episode in all our history, was come here among us, and for a day at least all care was quite forgotten. Everybody said afterwards that it was the greatest day there had ever been in Derry. That was the measure of our Bogside innocence, that the old Fagin of political pickpockets could, by his mere presence, excite such uncensorious fervour.

In 1953 Eddie McAteer stood as the Nationalist candidate in the safe Derry constituency of Foyle and comfortably won the seat. In the words of journalist Frank Curran, McAteer became 'the image of Northern nationalism for the next sixteen years'.

During the IRA border campaign in the late 1950s, there were a number of incidents in Derry. Several electricity transformers and other installations were damaged in explosions and a goods train on the Great

Overcrowded and bad housing in the Bogside, dominated by St Eugene's Cathedral (Harry Bryson)

Northern line was hijacked and sent, at full speed, without a driver, into the city, where it badly damaged the Foyle Road station. Many local men were interned without trial, but once again the city remained comparatively calm.

HOUSING, JOBS AND VOTES

The housing situation in Derry during the postwar years was so bad that many of its homeless squatted in abandoned, temporary wartime structures. A local joke explained the enigmatic skeleton on the city's coat-of-arms as symbolic of a Derry Catholic waiting for a house. The local government franchise was restricted to householders, so providing someone with a house meant giving them a vote also. Inevitably, for the Unionists to give a house to a Catholic was tantamount to political suicide, unless the house in question was located in the safe South ward. This area was already extremely overcrowded, but in 1947 the first new local authority houses in the Creggan Estate were ready for occupation. Creggan, situated on a hillside overlooking the Bogside and the walled city, was within the South ward, and so allocation to Catholics of houses here or in the Rossville Street 'high flats', built in 1966, did not upset the political balance. But this was not the case with other new estates being built elsewhere in the city.

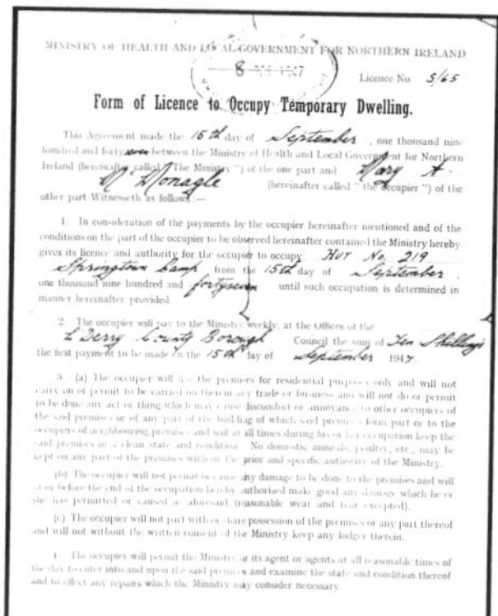

MINISTRY OF HEALTH AND LOCAL GOVERNMENT FOR NORTHERN IRELAND

8 ... 1947

Licence No. 5/65

Form of Licence to Occupy Temporary Dwelling.

This Agreement made the 15th day of September, one thousand nine hundred and fortyseven between the Ministry of Health and Local Government for Northern Ireland (hereinafter called "The Ministry") of the one part and Mary A. McMonagle (hereinafter called "the occupier") of the other part Witnesseth as follows:—

1. In consideration of the payments by the occupier hereinafter mentioned and of the conditions on the part of the occupier to be observed hereinafter contained the Ministry hereby gives its licence and authority for the occupier to occupy Hut No. 219 Springtown Camp from the 15th day of September, one thousand nine hundred and fortyseven until such occupation is determined in manner hereinafter provided.

2. The occupier will pay to the Ministry weekly, at the Offices of the L'Derry County Borough Council the sum of Ten Shillings the first payment to be made on the 15th day of September 1947.

3. (a) The occupier will use the premises for residential purposes only and will not carry on or permit to be carried on therein any trade or business and will not do or permit to be done any act or thing which may cause discomfort or annoyance to other occupiers of the said premises or of any part of the building of which said premises form part or to the occupiers of neighbouring premises and will at all times during his or her occupation keep the said premises in a clean state and condition. No domestic animals, poultry, etc., may be kept on any part of the premises without the prior and specific authority of the Ministry.

(b) The occupier will not permit or cause any damage to be done to the premises and will at or before the end of the occupation hereby authorised make good any damage which he or she has permitted or caused as aforesaid (reasonable wear and tear excepted).

(c) The occupier will not part with or share possession of the premises or any part thereof and will not without the written consent of the Ministry keep any lodger therein.

4. The occupier will permit the Ministry or its agent or agents at all reasonable times of the day to enter into and upon the said premises and examine the state and condition thereof and to effect any repairs which the Ministry may consider necessary.

A licence to squatters allowing them to occupy temporary dwellings at the former military base at Springtown

Recently, the loyalist writer Paul Kingsley has defended Londonderry Corporation's practice in housing matters, arguing that a points system was always in use. He further argues that most of the housing reforms implemented after 1969 by the Londonderry Development Commission and the Northern Ireland Housing Executive had been 'drawn up and endorsed' by the corporation before it was abolished in 1968. However, it is difficult to see how an objective system could have resulted in a situation that was repeatedly comdemned. The crisis was undoubtedly exacerbated by the continuing expansion of the population. The 1961 census demonstrated that at an increase of 21.2 per

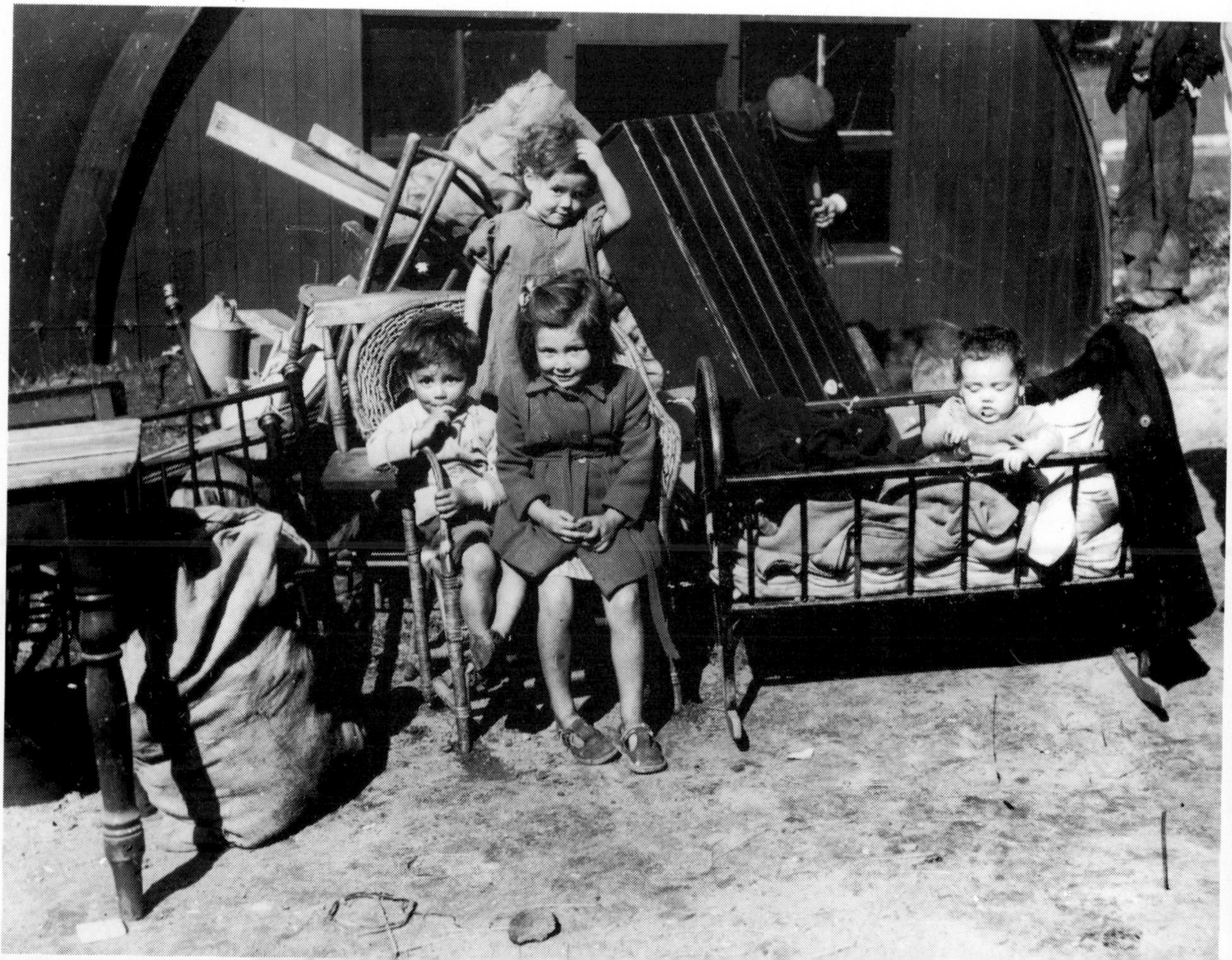

Moving into an abandoned military camp near Derry (*Derry Journal*)

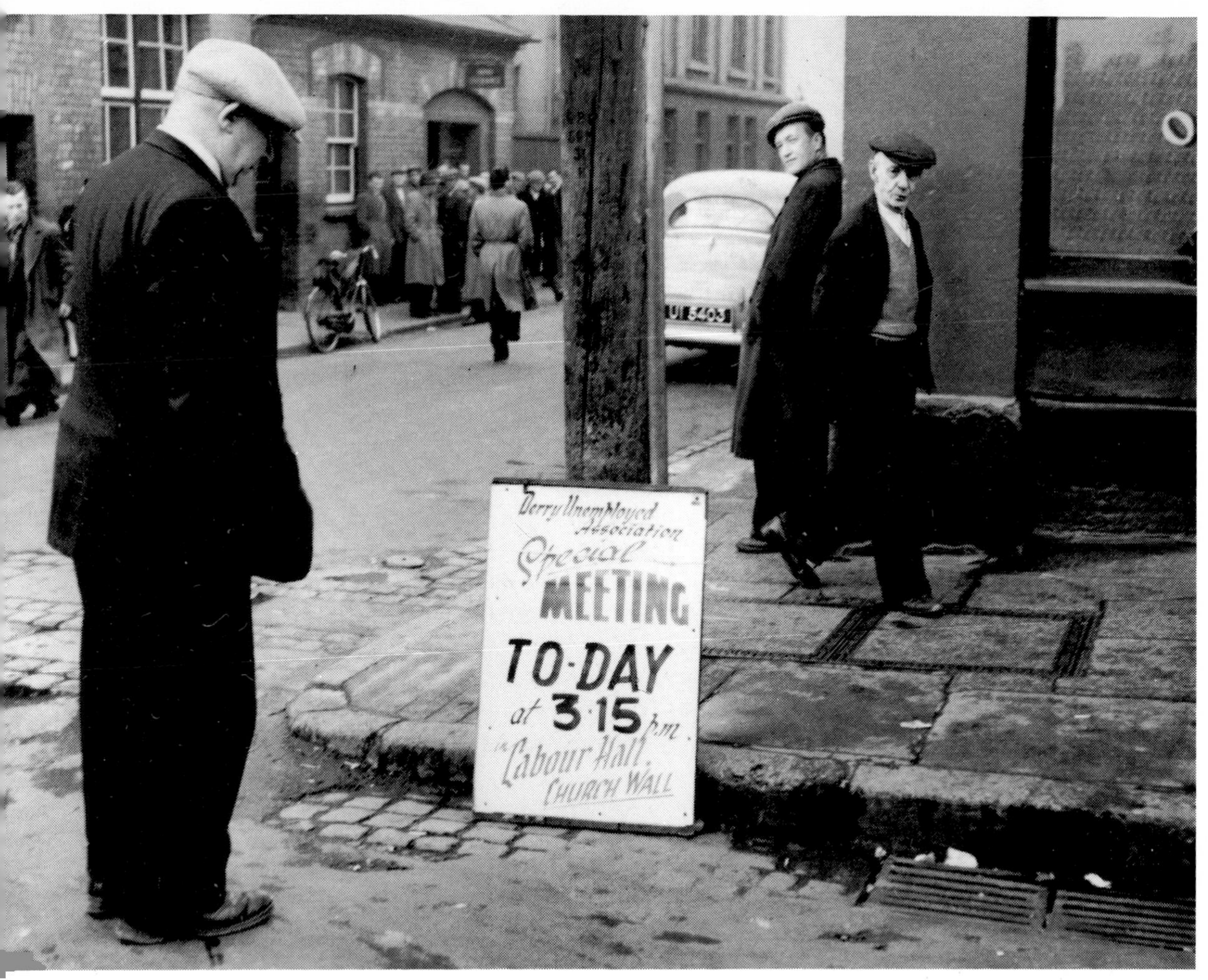

Living with unemployment in Derry in the 1950s and 1960s (Bert Hardy, Hulton-Deutsch Collection)

1,000, the growth in Derry was almost twice that of Northern Ireland as a whole, and nearly four times that of England and Wales. Most of this increase was among the poorer Catholic section of the community: 80 per cent of births in Derry were to Catholic mothers. Yet this growth had taken place simultaneously with a huge increase in emigration, as jobs disappeared after the war. In the decade after 1951 the official estimate was that 12.6 per cent of the population of the city had emigrated.

The unemployment figure for Derry during the postwar period averaged 20 per cent, although by 1966 it had fallen to 10 per cent. In 1951 Birmingham Sound Reproducers (BSR) took over a large government-built factory in the city. This was the first of sixty-eight such overseas businesses already attracted to Northern Ireland by the Government to be located in Derry. Du Pont began operating in 1960 at an industrial estate opened up on an abandoned wartime airfield at Maydown. By the mid-1960s seven such industries had been set up in the city, although local critics were quick to point out that more had been provided in other Northern Ireland towns with much smaller unemployment figures. While Derry's geographic position was no doubt partly to blame for this state of affairs, many believed that there was a deliberate policy of discrimination against the city by the Stormont government. However, Paul Kingsley has argued the opposite case, citing a reduction through government policy of the unemployment figures by over two thousand between February 1967 and October 1968, the eve of the civil rights confrontations. Kingsley also quotes Brian Faulkner, who subsequently became prime minister of Northern Ireland, as saying that in 1966 the Government was looking forward to 'full employment in the city of Londonderry within a few years through industries already established or in the pipeline'.

In 1960, Altnagelvin Hospital was opened, just outside the city. This was the first general hospital to be built in the United Kingdom in the postwar period. A new psychiatric hospital was also built nearby at Gransha. However, from inside the city, conditions seemed bleak. By 1966 only one of the original four railway lines into the city remained open, and this had narrowly escaped closure because of a campaign of protest from Derry and other towns along its route.

The 1966 electoral revision showed that there were 20,102 Catholic voters and 10,274 Protestant voters in Derry, but in the local government elections held the following year the usual number of eight Nationalists and twelve Unionists were returned to power. This result was achieved by means of a careful manipulation of the wards and a property-based, multiple-vote system. In order to maintain this advantage, it was necessary for the Unionists to keep accurate documentary records, monitoring every minute alteration which could affect the electoral outcome. However, no system of records could camouflage or halt the tide of resentment.

Eddie McAteer, 'the image of northern nationalism', was MP for the Derry constituency of Foyle from 1953 until 1969 (Courtesy of the McAteer family)

In 1964 the Dublin-based Radharc television team filmed a documentary examining the gerrymander and housing situation in the city. Because of the possible danger to improved north–south relations expected from the historic meeting in January 1965 between the Taoiseach Sean Lemass and the northern premier, Terence O'Neill, Radio Telefis Eireann (RTE), the national television network in the south, decided not to show the programme. It was not broadcast until September 1989, twenty-five years after it was made.

THE UNIVERSITY FOR DERRY CAMPAIGN

As early as March 1960, Eddie McAteer, supported by the Unionist MP for the city of Derry, Edward Jones, recommended in a speech at Stormont that Derry would be an obvious location for a second university for Northern Ireland. At this time Magee College was a small, but lively, academic institution. Despite partition, its non-theological students went on to complete their degree courses at Trinity College Dublin. As the debate on the issue gathered momentum, there appeared to be widespread support for McAteer's idea in Derry. The Unionist-dominated corporation published a submission to the

Government, fully backing the proposal, and promising a contribution from the rates if the institution was set up in the city. However, in 1965 the Stormont-appointed Lockwood Committee recommended that the new university should be located at Coleraine, and the Government agreed with its conclusions.

A cross-community University for Derry Action Committee was set up under the leadership of John Hume, a young teacher at St Columb's College who had come to prominence in the credit union movement and other local self-help initiatives. At a packed public meeting in the Guildhall on 8 February 1965, the local population demonstrated unusual unanimity, applauding both the Unionist mayor, Albert Anderson, and the Nationalist leader, Eddie McAteer, who claimed that, 'when the people of Derry and Londonderry get together as one, surely [Stormont] will have to listen'. To highlight the unity of opinion, a massive motorcade to parliament buildings at Stormont, in Belfast, was organised on 18 February. Twenty-five thousand people, almost half the population of Derry, are estimated to have taken part in the demonstration. It was a veritable crusade. There was almost total agreement in Derry on the issue: some employers not only gave their workers time off but also gave them expenses so that they could make the journey. The two political leaders from opposite sides of the ancient community divide travelled together in the mayor's official car. The *Derry Journal* reported:

> Virtually every business house in the city had at least one representative in the cavalcade – and there must have been few households which did not have a representative taking part. All creeds and classes and all shades of political opinion were included . . . Clergy of all denominations joined with business and professional men, factory workers, dockers, school teachers and students in a motorcade which varied from the stately limousines to furniture vans, coal lorries and bread vans . . . milk vans, petrol lorries, break-down vans and cars of every make and size.
>
> On the way through the city girls wearing 'University for Derry' streamers as head-coverings and waving red and white coloured scarves, greeted the cavalcade.
>
> The city itself had a holiday atmosphere, with shops, schools and public houses closed. A two-minute silence was observed in the city. Most traffic stopped and pedestrians stood bare-headed as the Guildhall struck three. 500 workers in the Monarch Electric factory stopped work. Many others were away in the motorcade, while some could not stop assembly lines at that particular moment. The motorcade was an impressive sight as it moved through the western counties. It was joined by official delegations at Strabane, Omagh and Dungannon. But despite its size there were few, if any, hold-ups, mainly due to the smooth arrangements made for its passage by the RUC.

In the parliamentary debate which followed at Stormont there was notable criticism of the Government's attitude, even from within the ranks of its own party. A former Unionist attorney general, Edmund Warnock, warned that the decision was 'political madness and the penalty will have to be paid by the people of Northern Ireland'. When the issue came to a vote, the Government applied the party whip and the measure, ratifying the Lockwood recommendation, was passed. Some Unionists defied the whip and abstained or voted against the Government, including the Derry-born MP for Shankill, Desmond Boal. The attorney-general, Edward Jones, who had originally supported Eddie McAteer in 1960, followed the party line. In the aftermath of the defeat it was alleged that there had been a number of local Unionists, the so-called 'faceless men', who while publicly supporting the case for Derry had all the time been plotting with the Stormont government against the city.

Magee was made a part of the New University of Ulster (NUU) when it was established with its main campus at Coleraine. In 1972 the limited undergraduate programme available in Derry was withdrawn and Magee was assigned to adult education. With its courses in foundation studies for mature students, the college successfully pioneered in Ireland a new development in 'second chance' learning for adults who had been disadvantaged by the existing educational system. In 1984, in an attempt to bolster the university at Coleraine, which, unsurprisingly, had not lived up to its expectations, the University of Ulster was created by the merger of NUU with the Ulster Polytechnic at Jordanstown and its Art and Design Centre at York Street in Belfast. Within this four-campus institution, Magee College was promised a new and developing role in university education. Since that time a limited range of undergraduate courses have commenced at Magee, additional staff have been appointed and new buildings have been constructed. A critical city, barely able to restrain a communal 'I told you so', now waits for further progress.

Many people believe that the university for Derry campaign of the mid-1960s was a form of dramatic, political, street education for the people of the city, the bitter results of which were to emerge in the tumultuous years ahead.

FRONTLINE UNIONISTS

The disappointment over the university issue in 1965 was soon followed by another calamity for the city. In January 1967 the three Monarch Electric factories closed down completely. Monarch Electric started operations in 1961, having been re-formed from the former BSR company, which had folded in 1960 – a stratagem that took advantage of tax concessions. At one stage the factories employed some 1,800 people. By March 1967, with other industrial closures, the official unemployment figure for the city, at 20.1 per cent, was double what it had been twelve months previously. This made it nearly three times the

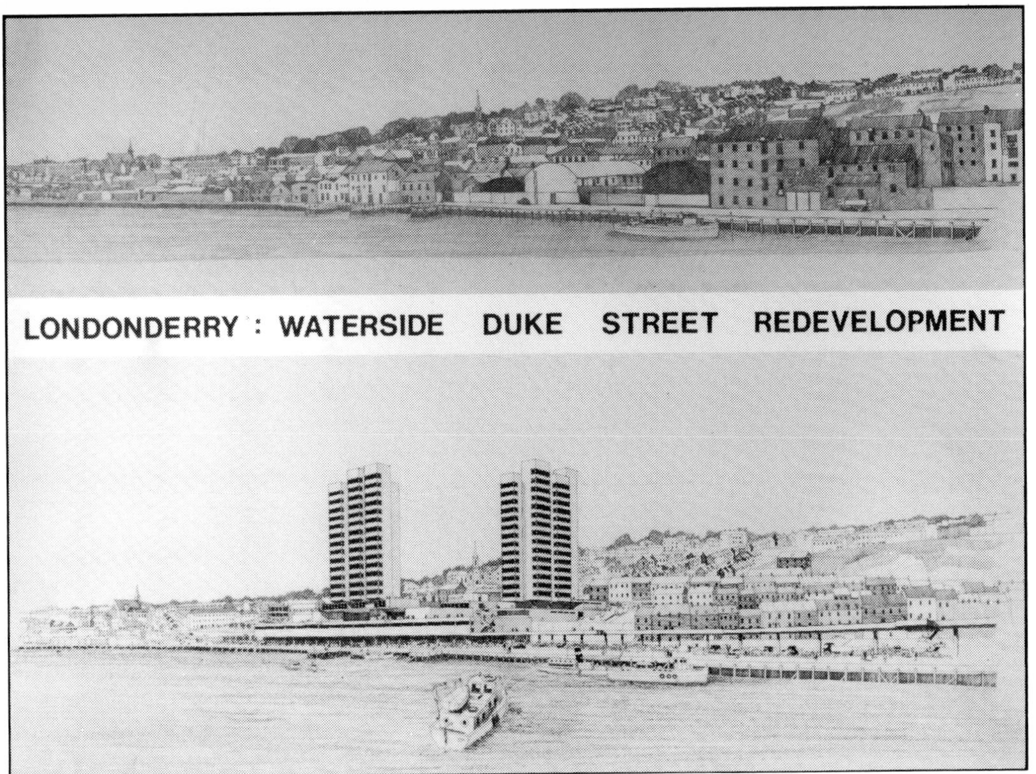

Proposals in the late 1960s for the development of the Waterside were never implemented (Derry City Council)

figure for Northern Ireland as a whole and almost ten times that for Great Britain.

By late 1966 evidence of Derry's problems had begun to surface all over the place. There were no Catholics working in the Guildhall. The British government's Cameron Commission discovered, at the outbreak of the Troubles, that only 30 per cent of all white-collar administrative, clerical and technical employees of the corporation were Catholic, although the bulk of the manual staff, and the majority of the total staff, were Catholic. The political impossibility of the Unionists' altering the electoral boundaries or the city's limits, without destroying their existing artificial majority, prevented them from introducing improvements in the appalling housing situation. Paul Kingsley, however, argues that reforms in all these areas were being contemplated. Planning consultants employed by the corporation in 1966 recommended radical changes:

> If Waterside, and Londonderry, are to be permitted to expand logically and economically, it will be essential that some reassessment of the City Boundaries take place. The development of Londonderry must not be inhibited by the Existing City boundaries. There are many methods whereby this problem can be overcome, ranging from extension of the City boundaries, to the setting up of a Federation of all authorities concerned. Action to overcome this problem should take place as soon as possible.

But action of this kind was extremely difficult, if not actually impossible, for the Unionist councillors if, in the short term, they were to prevent their world from falling apart. As one of the leading Protestant politicians in the city, Councillor Albert Anderson, claimed, 'We are front-line Unionists.'

OUTSIDE ATTENTION

Increasingly, outside political and media attention was being focused on Derry. Political excitement also began to mount in the city itself, reflected by the fact that the previously empty public gallery at corporation meetings was now, quite often, filled to capacity. In November 1966 the Nationalist Party launched a petition against the gerrymander. British politicians began to visit the city to examine the situation for themselves and the London *Times* printed an indictment of the system:

> Segregation amounting to discrimination is widely prevalent in the allocation of houses; and the Catholics are discriminated against . . . in any senior government appointments and private firms . . . In Londonderry the Nationalists are greatly in the majority of the population yet are greatly in the minority in the City Corporation. The Unionists' defence of this extraordinary under-representation is that when wards were decided in 1936, the rateable value in the Unionist wards was relatively higher than in the single Roman Catholic ward . . . Being given the 'Londonderry Air' is part of every investigator's education.

That same year the Derry Housing Association applied for planning approval to build houses on land that it owned at Pennyburn. Because most of the houses were likely to be given to Catholics, and as the land was in the sensitive Unionist North ward, the corporation refused permission and before the end of the year it confirmed its decision. Frank Curran has remarked, in *Derry: Countdown to Disaster*, that despite deep political differences, people of opposite religious traditions in Derry were still able to remain firm friends. He describes how, on the night of the second Pennyburn vote, he accompanied Nationalist councillor Paddy Friel (father of playwright Brian Friel) and Unionist councillor Alex McGowan, as they walked up Shipquay Street after the meeting:

> Their mutual respect had so far survived all the political clashes, but that day there was a strained and unusual silence . . . Friel could contain himself no longer. 'Alex,' he said, 'how do you, the decent man I know you to be, sit there and listen to arguments for the building of those badly needed houses, and vote against what you know to be right? How do you feel about it?' . . . McGowan looked at us as he replied, and his retort was so quick it was almost as if he had anticipated the question and rehearsed the answer. 'Ah, Paddy, how do you think I feel, with my hand up and my head down?'

Events in Derry now seemed to be heading inexorably towards confrontation. On 24 April 1968 BBC network television broadcast a major critical report on the city's peculiar electoral system and the nationalist complaints about various local problems. Nineteen sixty-eight was a year of protest, in Northern Ireland as elsewhere. In March members of the Derry Labour Party and the James Connolly Republican Club formed themselves into the Derry Housing Action Committee (DHAC) 'with the conscious intention of disrupting public life in the city to draw attention to the housing problem'. The committee caused uproar at corporation meetings throughout the spring of that year, attracting huge amounts of publicity. Although it was criticised by more moderate nationalists in the city, its tactics became increasingly dramatic. In June DHAC members were successful in obtaining the allocation of a house, by blocking a road with the caravan previously used as a home by the family in question.

End of an era – an official luncheon for the Duke and Duchess of Kent was held in the Guildhall in May 1968. The corporation, which hosted the royal couple on that occasion, was abolished later that year on 22 November.

On Saturday 24 August 1968 the relatively moderate Northern Ireland Civil Rights Association (NICRA) organised a march from Coalisland to Dungannon to highlight housing discrimination against Catholics in Dungannon. This was the first civil rights march held in Northern Ireland in imitation of similar demonstrations against racial discrimination in the United States. About two thousand people took part in the march and an additional crowd joined the protest at Dungannon. Although 1,500 loyalist demonstrators turned up in opposition, the RUC kept the two groups apart. Confrontation was avoided and after a public meeting the crowds dispersed peaceably, but with raised emotions. The DHAC – in particular, Eamonn McCann and Eamonn Melaugh – now decided to invite NICRA to hold a similar march in Derry. They chose 5 October as the date.

12

THE TROUBLES
UNFINISHED HISTORY

Derry has often been described as the 'cockpit of the Troubles', with many of the seminal incidents of the last two decades having taken place there, of which the civil rights march on 5 October 1968 was the first. William Craig, Northern Ireland Minister of Home Affairs, banned the demonstration on the grounds that 'it would be provocative' and because it would clash with a separate march, subsequently announced, by the Apprentice Boys of Derry for the same time and over the same route. At first the moderate elements in NICRA felt that the prohibition should be complied with. However, when the more radical DHAC organisers in Derry said that they intended to hold the march in any case, the decision was taken to go ahead with the rally, banned or not.

Eamonn McCann, one of the principal organisers of the 5 October 1968 civil rights march (Derry City Council)

5 OCTOBER 1968

Despite a public campaign of encouragement to participate in the march, most Derry people ignored it. The fact that Derry City football team was playing at its home ground in the Brandywell on the same day may well have deterred some potential demonstrators. Eamonn McCann, the most prominent member of the organising group, estimated that about four hundred marchers gathered at the rendezvous at the Waterside railway station, while another two hundred stood by and looked on. As the marchers formed up, the RUC arrested the three occupants of a Derry Labour Party loudspeaker van, charging them with incitement to break the prohibition. The march was led by, among others, Eddie McAteer, Gerry Fitt, Republican Labour MP at Westminster, Austin Currie, Nationalist MP at Stormont, and Ivan Cooper, a civil rights activist and member of the NILP. There were also three British Labour MPs, Russell Kerr, Ann Kerr and John Ryan, who had come directly from their annual party conference at Blackpool.

An article in the Belfast political periodical *Fortnight* recalls the dramatic events of that day, events which subsequently acquired unprecedented significance in the history of Northern Ireland:

> The marchers set off along Duke Street towards the lower tier [of Craigavon Bridge]. A cordon was thrown across the end of Duke Street

The Derry Citizens' Action Committee march of 16 November 1968 (at least fifteen thousand strong, John Hume centre right) approaching the police lines on the city side of Craigavon Bridge. This demonstration passed off peacefully and is thought to have been a major factor in the decision by the Northern Ireland government in the following week to dissolve Londonderry Corporation. (Larry Doherty, *Derry Journal*)

> and the first clashes occurred when the march reached the police line. Fred Heatley, a member of the NICRA executive, believes he was the first to be arrested. He had arrived late with other NICRA leaders from Belfast. Seeing the march moving off he ran to its head, where he was kneed in the groin by a policeman, dragged behind RUC lines and ordered into a black maria. Fergus Pyle of the *Irish Times* saw a Young Socialist hit on the head by a baton. He also observed a 'girl in a mini-skirt carrying the Plough and the Stars wrestling with a constable and a few men grabbing and fighting with policemen'.

It was at this point that Fitt, McAteer and Currie were injured. A Republican Labour councillor, Paddy Kennedy, who was also hurt, said Fitt appeared to be on his knees when hit with a baton.

There was a brief sit-down in front of police lines and a ragged snatch of 'We shall overcome'. An impromptu meeting was held. Michael Farrell of the Young Socialists said: 'We are met by police batons . . . Is that democracy?' Betty Sinclair, a veteran Communist and chairwoman of NICRA, said that the association was not anti-constitutional and had Craig consulted its members they would have changed the day of the march: 'There may be people here who think you have to spill blood . . . That would mean you are playing Mr Craig's game.' McAteer repeated the plea for restraint and advised the demonstrators to 'make [their] way in a wee walk to the Diamond'. But Eamonn McCann of the DHAC said: 'I don't advise anyone to charge that barricade. I also want to make it clear as a private individual that I can do nothing to stop them.' Violence broke out again almost immediately. Some of the crowd attempted to strike up 'We shall overcome' again. But they were interrupted by a police loudspeaker announcement, which was shouted down but was probably an order to disperse that few could have heard. Some Young Socialists threw their placards at the police, who advanced with batons drawn. Retreat for the fleeing demonstrators was blocked by a cordon at the other end of Duke Street, where the RUC also charged them. After a few minutes County Inspector William Meharg ordered: 'The police will hold their hands, please.' But the police carried on down Duke Street, methodically clearing the crowd as demonstrators screamed hysterically. Detachments of police chased and batoned individuals and when the street was nearly clear, water cannon were brought in.

More baton charges were made by the police as some of the marchers made their way back to the city centre. Rioting by young people from the Bogside, who had not taken part in the earlier events, now broke out and continued, accompanied by several police charges, until late that evening. About one hundred people had been injured by the police in Duke Street. Teams of journalists had witnessed these incidents and within twenty-four hours a particularly graphic film, taken by an RTE cameraman, Gay O'Brien, had been transmitted all over the world. Derry was now an international news story. This in itself was of major significance; incidents similar to those in Duke Street had occurred in Derry before, but apart from local coverage they rarely made headlines elsewhere. From now on, and particularly during the first few years of the crisis, Derry's problems were to be the subject of massive media reportage.

The official Cameron Commission which investigated the events of 5 October discussed the ministerial decision to impose a ban on the march:

> Whether to impose the prohibition was a wise action or not, and in the circumstances we are of the opinion that it was not, the results of the imposition were undoubted and unfortunate. As already noted . . . there was widespread resentment, particularly among the Catholic section of the population in Londonderry, at the Minister's action, and a large number of responsible persons who otherwise would have taken no part in the demonstration did in fact take part in it as a token of indignation and protest. The confrontation between the police and the demonstrators afforded certain extreme left-wing revolutionary elements among them an opportunity of provoking the police into a display of force which so far as it appeared excessive and unnecessary, produced an even more serious and widespread reaction against both Minister and police. The extensive press, radio and television coverage which was given of the day markedly enlarged both the field and extent of their reaction. All this stemmed directly from the Minister's order . . . If the objective of this operation was to drive the Civil Rights movement into the ground by a display of force and firmness in the enforcement of the ministerial order,

On 4 January 1969 a group of People's Democracy marchers, en route from Belfast to Derry, was viciously attacked at Burntollet Bridge by hostile loyalists; there were allegations of involvement of members of the B Specials and collusion with elements in the RUC.
(Belfast Telegraph)

it signally failed. The principal result of the operation, widely publicised at the time, was the opposite.

THE IMMEDIATE AFTERMATH

In the weeks following 5 October further meetings and demonstrations were held in the city and a moderate Derry Citizens' Action Committee was established. Despite another government ban, this body organised protests and sit-downs, culminating in a fifteen-thousand-strong march on 16 November, more or less along the same route that should have been taken by the original march. Local Unionists immediately began to make minor concessions but on 22 November, Londonderry Corporation was abolished as part of a Northern Ireland government five-point programme of reforms – a points system for housing allocations, an ombudsman, the ending of the company vote in council elections, a review of the Special Powers Act, and the setting up of the Londonderry Development Commission to replace the corporation. Vociferous loyalist protest began to be heard and the prime minister, Captain Terence O'Neill, made the famous television broadcast, pleading with the people of Northern Ireland to step back from the brink of disaster.

A truce and a cessation of marches was called for but on New Year's Day 1969 a group from the People's Democracy, a radical leftist organisation set up at Queen's University Belfast in the aftermath of 5 October, began a four-day march from Belfast to Derry. The march, which was joined by Bernadette Devlin, Michael Farrell and Eamonn McCann, went ahead despite opposition from moderate nationalists. En route the marchers were constantly harassed by loyalists. On 4 January, as they set off on the last few miles into Derry, the marchers were viciously attacked at Burntollet Bridge by a hostile crowd, some of whom, it was claimed, were members of the B Specials. The attack had been well prepared and well organised and there were immediate allegations of collusion between the attackers and the RUC. The depleted remains of the march finally made its way to a rally in the city centre, where the marchers told their story. Shortly afterwards, rioting against the police began. At 2 a.m. the following morning a group of policemen invaded the Bogside and wreaked havoc there. A Bogside resident was reporting the disturbance to the RUC by phone when he realised that it was members of the police force itself who were causing it. The Cameron Commission found

> with regret that our investigations have led us to the unhesitating conclusion that on the night of 4th/5th January a number of policemen were guilty of misconduct which involved assault and battery, malicious damage to property in streets in the predominantly Catholic Bogside area, giving reasonable cause for apprehension of personal injury among innocent inhabitants, and the use of provocative sectarian and political slogans . . . We are afraid that not only do we find the allegations of misconduct substantial, but that for such conduct among members of a disciplined and well-led force there can be no acceptable justification or excuse.

On the following day vigilante squads were set up in the Bogside area and the now famous graffiti, 'You are now entering Free Derry', was painted on a gable wall.

Tension eased for a while. In the February 1969 Stormont general

The famous graffiti, 'You are now entering Free Derry', was painted on a gable wall in the Bogside on 5 January 1969. Free Derry corner became a focal point for political meetings in the following years. Although the adjoining houses have now been demolished the inscribed gable itself has been preserved as a monument. (Camerawork)

election, John Hume, standing as an Independent, took the safe nationalist Foyle seat from the long-serving Eddie McAteer. The Londonderry Development Commission started to tackle some of the city's long-standing problems, particularly in housing. That Easter there was a huge turnout in the city for the 1916 commemorative parade, but fortunately there was no trouble. Riots flared again during the weekend of 18–20 April when the Government banned another civil rights march. Bernadette Devlin went to Derry on Saturday 19 April, the day after she had been elected Westminster MP for Mid-Ulster. In *The Price of my Soul* she recounts:

> I arrived about ten o'clock in the evening, Derry was a battlefield. It was like coming into beleaguered Budapest: you had to negotiate the car around piles of bricks and rubble and broken glass which were cluttering the roads. Every family in the Bogside . . . had left its home and was roaming the streets seeking whom it could devour. The police had arrived in their hundreds and pitched battles between the police and the Catholics were in progress . . .
>
> High above us the city wall was lined with a great silent mass of black figures. Slowly the mass started to move, down through the walls, into the two roads still not barricaded, and when the two battalions of police met, they joined forces and started a stomp towards us, beating their shields with their batons and howling dreadfully . . .
>
> The next day, Sunday, with the police still occupying the Bogside, I left for Belfast. John Hume and Ivan Cooper . . . got the whole population of the Bogside to evacuate, took this crowd of several thousand people up Creggan Hill, and told the police they had two hours to get out. If they weren't clear of the Bogside by then, the people were coming back in, and the police would be responsible for the consequences. The police stuck it out until about fifteen minutes before the end of the ultimatum. They then left.

The funeral of Samuel Devenny, on 21 July 1969, was attended by about twenty thousand people. Mr Devenny's death on 17 July was blamed on the savage beating he had sustained from members of the RUC at his home in the Bogside on 19 April. (Harry Bryson)

Left
The Battle of the Bogside, Little James Street, Derry, 12–14 August 1969 (Frank McFadden)

Right
Preparations for the Battle of the Bogside, 12–14 August 1969 (Magee College)

In the Bogside that Saturday night seven or eight uniformed policemen entered the home of Samuel Devenny and severely beat him in front of his family and some friends, who were also batoned. When he died of a heart condition three months later, it was claimed that Devenny's illness had been brought on by the assault. There were widespread allegations of murder, and a crowd of about twenty thousand people attended his funeral. No charges have ever been brought arising from the incident. An investigation in 1970 by Sir Arthur Young, chief constable of the RUC, revealed a 'conspiracy of silence' among the policemen involved.

There were more riots that summer and barricades were erected as tension in the city mounted in the lead-up to the annual Apprentice Boys parade on 12 August. Other preparations were made in anticipation of a major confrontation on the day of the march; supplies for the manufacture of petrol bombs and other home-made weapons were hoarded in the Bogside – a typical note left for the milkman is said to have read 'no milk, but leave 200 bottles'. A local community activist, Paddy Doherty, travelled to Dublin and passed a message to the Irish government via civil servants that official southern intervention was expected in the event of 'an attack on the Bogside'. Attempts to have the march prohibited failed. Sir Patrick Macrory, in a footnote to the concluding chapter of his epic book on the Siege of Derry, has written:

> On the eve of the march in August, 1969, I asked an Orangeman of my acquaintance, the kindest and most decent of men, why it was necessary

to keep up these obviously provocative celebrations. He looked at me in mild surprise and then said grimly: 'We have to show them who's master, that's why.'

THE BATTLE OF THE BOGSIDE

On the day of the march the inevitable rioting began in the early afternoon and continued into the night. Catholic youths began firing petrol bombs and the police responded with CS gas. The 'Battle of the Bogside' had started and it would last for three days. On the evening of Wednesday 13 August, Taoiseach Jack Lynch announced that the Dublin government 'could not stand by'. The *Sunday Times* Insight Team claimed that there was an Irish army plan, backed by a number of southern government ministers, to occupy Derry and other places in Northern Ireland. This would be put into operation following a proposed staged attack on an ambulance sent from Donegal in response to an emergency request from a Derry doctor. However, apart from establishing some border field hospitals and a certain amount of overseas diplomatic activity, the southern government did not intervene. It sent first-aid supplies to the Bogside but refused a request for gas masks. Bernadette Devlin was back in Derry during those days:

> What was happening there was that ordinary, peaceful people, who had no desire to spend fifty hours throwing stones and petrol bombs, had realized the harm that had been done to them for half a century and were learning how to fight in self-defence. We threw up barricades of rubble, pipe, and paving stones – anything we could get our hands on – to prevent the police coming straight into the area . . .
>
> We got medical supplies from the South, but gas-masks we had to go without. So we made do with wet blankets, with cotton wool steeped in vinegar, with handkerchiefs soaked in sodium bicarbonate, and we fought on through the night, all through the next day and the following night, and into the third day . . .
>
> We had an influx of foreign revolutionary journalists searching for illumination on the Theory of Petrol Bomb Fighting. The people of the Bogside thought it was fantastic: they didn't know how to spell revolution, never mind work it out, but they were really delighted with themselves, that people should come from the Sorbonne to ask the unemployed of Bogside where they learned to fight so well.

After three days the police were exhausted. The Northern Ireland government requested the assistance of the army from the British government and this was agreed to by Home Secretary James Callaghan. Previous to this, a number of leaders on the nationalist side, including John Hume and Bernadette Devlin, had called for the deployment of British soldiers. At 5 p.m. on Thursday 14 August a company of the Prince of Wales Own Regiment took over security control from the police in the city centre. Twenty-one years later the

The army arrives – 5.00 p.m., 14 August 1969. A British soldier takes up position in Guildhall Square in the centre of Derry. (Larry Doherty, *Derry Journal*)

army is still there. As the fighting raged in Derry, violence had flared in other parts of Northern Ireland, especially in Belfast. The Troubles had begun.

For some confused residents who saw the troops march into the Bogside on that first day it was not clear initially if they belonged to the British or Irish army. Frank Curran, a reporter for the *Derry Journal*, witnessed the extraordinary scenes on William Street. Twenty years later he described them in an anniversary supplement to the *Derry Journal*:

> A platoon of soldiers led by a young officer, probably a captain, was standing opposite Bradley's Bar and on the opposite side of the road, Eddie McAteer was at the head of a group of about 60 or 70 men.
>
> There was a period of silent, watchful indecision on both sides. The young officer said – 'We are here to keep the peace. We have no quarrel with you.' McAteer replied – 'If you are here as impartial peacekeepers we will not have any argument with you.'
>
> The officer asked if there was anything his soldiers could do to improve the situation immediately. 'Yes,' replied McAteer, 'remove the police from Derry Walls.' The officer didn't know where the walls were, but agreed to accompany the crowd there. At Magazine Gate the officer requested the police on duty to move off. They were reluctant, but he made it clear he intended his wish obeyed. The police moved away sullenly, and the now genial crowd proceeded to the Butcher Gate where a larger force of police commanded the Walls. Again there was some argument but the officer's will prevailed and as the police withdrew someone shouted, 'three cheers for the British army', and the proposal was loudly endorsed.

British Army barbed-wire barricades at the bottom of William Street, August 1969 (Frank McFadden)

THE HONEYMOON GOES SOUR

In those honeymoon days, relations between the army and most local people were good. The Derry Citizens' Defence Association, set up at the end of July 1969, became the principal body representing the Catholics of the Bogside area. At the end of August James Callaghan toured Derry and, somewhat patronisingly, promised to promote justice and solve the people's problems. In his book *A House Divided*, Callaghan describes his visit to the city:

> I did not know what to expect at the Bogside but an overwhelming reception awaited me . . . The main impression I had was of being at the centre of a whirlpool of humanity bowling down the street, in which I was swept up and carried along . . . We went on stumbling over barricades and rubble and broken glass and Hume and Cooper kept calling to the crowds to let us through, but it was near impossible. It could have become a very ugly scene because, like all crowds, this one would be impossible to control if something went wrong . . . It was a rare experience in a politician's life, a great and dramatic moment which brought home the awful responsibility I carried for their hopes and fears . . . I told the sea of upturned faces . . . 'You have engaged my sympathies and my energies. I will try and ensure that there is justice and equality, absence of fear and discrimination . . .'
>
> I scarcely had time to disengage from the Bogside and refocus my mind before I was walking among the Protestants in their part of the city. Fifty yards on the other side of the city walls stood a Protestant barricade. A group of men and women were standing around it waving Union Jacks and as soon as they saw me they started singing 'God save the Queen'.

As Callaghan walked up Fountain Street, Unionist MP Albert Anderson claimed that there was 'a revolver stuffed in nearly every house'.

In the following twelve months some reforms were introduced. On

Clearing up after the civi disturbances in Derry (Frank McFadden)

22 September 1969 all remaining barricades in the city were removed and white lines were painted on the roads in their place as a demarcation point beyond which the RUC was not permitted to patrol. However, it was not long before problems arose. On 24 September a Protestant man, William King from the Fountain area, died from a heart attack, having been beaten by a group of Catholics when rival gangs clashed. In January 1970 the republican movement split, and the Provisional IRA was established. There were more riots in Derry throughout that year and numbers of young people were given jail sentences. Increasingly, civil rights slogans were giving way to more traditional republican demands. In *Londonderry Revisited*, Paul Kingsley argues that these had been the underlying hidden agenda all along. The army began to use tougher tactics, which in turn further inflamed the situation.

On 8 July 1971 two young men, Seamus Cusack and Desmond Beattie, became the first persons in Derry to be killed by the army. The security forces claimed that the two men had been armed, but this was strongly denied by local people. Recruitment to the Provisional IRA soared in the weeks which followed. The one-year-old Social Democratic and Labour Party (SDLP), which had been founded by a group of nationalists and civil rights activists, including Fitt, Hume, Cooper, Currie and Paddy Devlin, subsuming the existing nationalist parties, announced that it would withdraw from the Stormont parliament unless an impartial public inquiry was set up to investigate the two deaths. As no such inquiry was instituted, the boycott began on Friday 16 July and continued until Stormont was prorogued in March 1972. The violence escalated and on 9 August 1971 the Government introduced internment without trial. As men were taken away, the violence intensified and barricades were re-erected all over Catholic Derry. The Provisional IRA bombing campaign against 'economic targets' began, with the result that some of the best-known landmarks in the city disappeared, such as the City Hotel in Foyle Street, and the Ulster Bank in Waterloo Place. Dr Raymond McClean recalls in *The Road to Bloody Sunday* how one day he set out to buy a pair of sports shoes:

> I passed the shop on my way up the town, and thought that rather than carry the shoes with me, I would get them on the way back. While in Gailey's buying some books, I heard a loud explosion, wondered where it was and carried on. On my way down the Strand Road again, I was stunned to find that the sports shop had disappeared while I had been up the town. I didn't get my training shoes that day, and the general advice was: 'If you really want to get something up the town, be sure to shop early.'

A well-known piece of graffiti read 'shop now, while shops last'. The sharp Derry wit struggled to cope with the extraordinary incidents taking place in the city, although the situation was far from being humorous.

BLOODY SUNDAY

On Sunday 30 January 1972, Bloody Sunday, troops from the 1st Battalion of the Parachute Regiment opened fire in the Bogside during a prohibited anti-internment march and rally organised by NICRA and attended by about twenty thousand people. One hundred and eight live rounds were fired by the soldiers, and thirteen men, seven of them under nineteen years of age, were killed. Fourteen people were seriously wounded and another man died later; armed civilians were said to have been seen in the area and the army claimed that it had been shot at first. The government Widgery Tribunal, set up to investigate the events of Bloody Sunday, commented on these allegations:

> The army case is that each of these shots was an aimed shot fired at a civilian holding or using a bomb or firearm. On the other side it was argued that none of the deceased was using a bomb or firearm and that the soldiers fired without justification and either deliberately or recklessly . . . Although a number of soldiers spoke of actually seeing firearms or bombs in the hands of civilians none was recovered by the Army. None of the many photographs shows a civilian holding an object that can with certainty be identified as a firearm or bomb. No casualties were suffered by the soldiers from firearms or gelignite bombs. In relation to every one of the deceased there were eye witnesses who said that they saw no bomb or firearm in his hands.

Nevertheless, the report surprisingly concluded:

> Soldiers who identified armed gunmen fired upon them in accordance with the standing orders in the Yellow Card. Each soldier was his own judge of whether he had identified a gunman. Their training made them aggressive and quick in decision and some showed more restraint in

Confrontation between John Hume and a British Army officer at Magilligan Strand, County Derry, on 22 January 1972, as demonstrators are blocked from proceeding towards the nearby internment camp (*Derry Journal*)

> opening fire than others. At one end of the scale some soldiers showed a high degree of responsibility; at the other . . . firing bordered on the reckless . . .
>
> None of the deceased or wounded is proved to have been shot whilst holding a firearm or bomb. Some are wholly acquitted of complicity in such action; but there is a strong suspicion that some others had been firing weapons or handling bombs in the course of the afternoon and yet others had been closely supporting them.

Following the incident, newspaper headlines spoke of 'massacre' and 'butchery'. In Dublin, Taoiseach Jack Lynch said that he was

> appalled and stunned that British soldiers should indiscriminately shoot into a crowd of civilians, who were peacefully demonstrating . . . Even if they were in technical breach of the recently imposed ban on demonstrations, this action by the British troops was unbelievably savage and inhuman.

Television film of what had happened was shown all over the world and, incidentally, brought to outside attention a local priest seen pathetically waving a white handkerchief as he helped move one of the casualties from the line of fire. Two years later that priest, Father Edward Daly, was appointed Catholic bishop of Derry. Following the killings, a wave of protest swept throughout all of nationalist Ireland. An official day of national mourning was observed in the Irish Republic to coincide with the funerals and late on the same day the British Embassy in Dublin was burned down as a vast crowd demonstrated outside.

It is now widely believed that the events and consequences of Bloody

Civil rights marchers in William Street on 30 January 1972 – Bloody Sunday (Camerawork)

Sunday were instrumental in the British government's decision of 24 March, when Prime Minister Edward Heath announced that he was suspending the Stormont parliament and instituting the system of direct rule from Westminster which is still in operation.

When the report of the official investigating tribunal under Lord Widgery into the events of Bloody Sunday was published in April 1972, it was totally rejected by the nationalist community as a whitewash. For a while the word 'widgery' found its way into the vocabulary of Irish political discourse with a definition that was less than honourable. When asked on a BBC 2 television programme in mid-1989 about the behaviour of the paratroopers on Bloody Sunday, Lieutenant General Sir Harry Tuzo (General Officer Commanding, Northern Ireland, at the time of the killings) answered, 'They went over the top – without any doubt!'

Violence was returned with more violence. After Bloody Sunday it was said that the IRA was under instruction to kill 'every British soldier [it] could'. On Sunday 21 May the Official IRA shot dead Corporal William Best. 'Ranger' Best was a young native of the Creggan area who had ignored warnings to leave the city after he had returned home on leave from Germany where he was stationed with the British Army's Irish Rangers. The killing provoked a massive wave of sympathy but an

Damage to the Guildhall caused by two separate bombs, June 1972 (Magee College)

attempt, particularly by groups of women, to bring an end to the violence in the city was not successful.

OPERATION MOTORMAN

Following Bloody Sunday, the Provisional IRA bombing campaign took off in earnest. Twice in the same week in June 1972 the Guildhall was badly damaged by bombs deposited inside the building. (Ironically, Gerry Doherty, one of the five elected Sinn Féin members of the 1985–9 city council, meeting once again in the restored Guildhall, had previously served a term of imprisonment, convicted of taking part in the planting of those explosives.) At 4.30 a.m. on the morning of Monday 31 July 1972, Operation Motorman was mounted by the British Army in Derry. Heavy bulldozing machines and military vehicles were brought in and used to tear down barricades which delimited the previous security force 'no go' areas of the Bogside and Creggan. In *War and an Irish Town*, Eamonn McCann describes the dramatic scenes:

> They came . . . unceasing lines of them in convoy, Ferrets, Whippets and APCs, Land Rovers, Saladins and bulldozers coming up Rossville Street past the High Flats and into Lecky Road, searchlights playing down from the city walls, bulldozers and earth movers beginning to grapple with the barricades, men shouting, machinery screaming, noise everywhere. 'Jesus Christ,' said Tommy McCourt, watching from Westland Street and getting his military parallels slightly crossed in his awe, 'it's like bloody Dunkirk.' All over the area volunteers were melting into the darkness and short back-and-sides. In McCafferty's in Beechwood Street Tommy, the American writer Jack McKinney and I made tea and discussed the theoretical implications of the changed situation. 'Are you three going to sit there,' asked Mrs McCafferty, 'and let those tanks come right into our street?' Ten minutes later an unmolested APC rolled round the corner from Elmwood Road and roared up the hill towards the barricade at the

top. 'Annie, Annie,' shouted Mrs McCafferty across the street to a neighbour, 'would you come out and see what they are doing. They're taking down our barricade.'

In the course of this operation throughout the Catholic areas of the city, two civilians were killed. Later that same morning the little County Derry village of Claudy, ten miles from the city, was devastated by three IRA car bombs. Six local people were killed instantly and three more died shortly afterwards. The horrific incident is remembered in the poignant song 'Claudy' by Derry-born James Simmons.

YEARS OF CHANGE AND VIOLENCE

Local government reform was introduced throughout Northern Ireland in 1973. Londonderry City Council was set up, restoring a municipal assembly to the city. Like all elected councils in Northern Ireland, it had a very restricted range of powers and responsibilities. At the elections in May the SDLP was returned as the largest party on the council, a position it has retained ever since. The office of mayor of the first council went to Dr Raymond McClean. The new council established a local powersharing arrangement for the positions of mayor, deputy mayor and committee chairs and, with some interruptions, this has continued to the present. The violence also continued.

A member of the Provisional IRA demonstrates an M60 machine gun in Derry, *c.* 1980 (Magee College)

In 1981 the mass hunger strike begun by Bobby Sands at the Maze Prison brought further tragedy to the city, as to other places in Northern Ireland. Two Derry men, Patsy O'Hara and Mickey Devine – both members of the Irish National Liberation Army – died from that dreadful protest as rioting continued in the city. Many controversial deaths, in particular of children – Paul Whitters, aged fifteen, in 1981 and Stephen McConomy, aged eleven, in 1982 – have resulted from the use of plastic bullets by the security forces, as well as from other equally disturbing incidents. Soldiers, policemen, paramilitaries, businessmen, tradesmen, even a woman census enumerator – 'innocent civilians', men, women and children have been killed as a result of the Troubles in the city. Fortunately there have been relatively few deaths from bomb blasts and purely sectarian tit-for-tat killing has also been relatively unknown.

Of a total of 2,810 people killed by violence associated with the crisis in Northern Ireland up to 14 August 1990, the twenty-first anniversary of the deployment of the troops, some 230 persons (roughly 8 per cent) have died in Derry. Many more have been injured and bereaved, and destruction of property has been enormous. An article in the *Guardian* on 24 May 1974, entitled 'Tumbledown Derry', claimed that in the previous three years 5,200 houses in the city had either been destroyed or badly damaged, 124 business premises, including shops and offices, had been destroyed and another 1,800 damaged. Over ten thousand separate claims for damage and injury amounting to £30 million had been submitted to the Government. That was the tally at the end of the first five of the twenty-two years of the Troubles. Thankfully, in recent years there was been a dramatic reduction in the incidents of violence in the city.

One sad consequence of the years of violence in Derry is that there has been a massive movement of Protestants from the west bank of the river to the Waterside. Although incidents of overt intimidation have been relatively few, and those that have occurred have affected both Catholics and Protestants almost equally, nevertheless there has been an overwhelming drift of those with a Unionist background away from the 'cityside'. No official figures for the extent of this migration (fuelled by the fear of what *might* happen) are available. Published estimates suggest a figure of around 12,500 to 14,500. The 'Scotch' Presbyterian Church, one of the great monuments to the early-nineteenth-century expansion of the city and its Protestant confidence, was converted to a public library, following the removal of its congregation to the Waterside. The elegant First Derry Presbyterian Church in Magazine Street has been damaged by petrol bombs on several occasions, and many local Catholics have contributed to its restoration. However, the building is now protected by massive fences and other twentieth-

century fortifications. Interestingly, the father of the mid-nineteenth-century Young Irelander, John Mitchel, was once minister at this church and the young John, later to become a father-figure of Irish revolutionary nationalism, lived for a while at its manse.

St Columb's Cathedral and its deanery, a nearby Church of Ireland rectory, and the homes of Protestant families were badly damaged by three bomb attacks on the adjacent courthouse in 1988 and 1989. The beautiful St Augustine's chapel-of-ease, itself almost certainly on the site of the ancient Columban monastery, was also damaged and its minister forced to leave his home. Not surprisingly, many Protestants who do remain on the west bank, particularly in the ugly, rebuilt Fountain Estate, believe themselves to be still in a state of siege.

THE MEDIA AND THE TROUBLES

When the Foyle Film Festival was established in Derry in 1987, it was claimed that no comparable-sized city in these islands had generated so much media coverage during the past nineteen years. Like the Vietnam War, the Troubles have been something of a media event. Television cameras have been present to record many of the historic incidents and international coverage has been massive and continuous.

Security force saturation of the Bogside during the funeral of IRA volunteer, Gerard Logue, on 24 March 1987 (Camerawork)

Martin McGuinness addressing a rally at the republican plot in the City Cemetery, Derry (Camerawork)

The degree to which this amount and type of attention has actually contributed to the evolution of the events themselves has been much debated. Certainly a number of well-known news-film sequences shot in Derry have acquired the status of 'images' of the Northern Ireland problem. Many years later, these pictures can still evoke strong emotional reactions. One response to this outside coverage, some of it fairly clichéd, has been the emergence of a number of local award-winning video and film production projects determined to present a truer, although not necessarily prettier, portrayal of the city. Derry Film and Video's *Hush A Bye Baby* has been lauded at several film festivals and it won the best drama award at the Celtic Film Festival in March 1990.

Occasionally, media coverage of the Troubles in Derry has become a news story itself. There have been a number of much-publicised conflicts involving the reporting and broadcasting of material related to the ongoing crisis. For example, in 1985 BBC network television made a series entitled *Real Lives*. One programme, 'At the edge of the Union', dealt with two men from Derry, Martin McGuinness, a well-known republican, and Gregory Campbell, a loyalist politican, both 'young, working-class, teetotal and church-going; both elected representatives of their communities'. The proposal to broadcast the programme, including an interview with Martin McGuinness, caused a furore.

(McGuinness was one of the IRA representatives who had taken part in the secret London talks with Secretary of State for Northern Ireland William Whitelaw on 7 July 1972.) Prime Minister Margaret Thatcher 'utterly condemned' the proposed broadcast and Home Secretary Leon Brittan pressurised the BBC board of governors until the programme was withdrawn. This action generated a storm of criticism: Brittan was described by the establishment figure Lord Annan as behaving 'like a demented poodle or a charging rhinoceros'; the National Union of Journalists, and the Association of British Editors condemned the decision, as did many bodies concerned with press freedom and civil rights. A leading article in *The Times* commented: 'Both the Prime Minister and the Home Secretary have emphasized the absence of censorship, though Mr Brittan's quasi-diktat is scarcely distinguishable from it. The inhibition he seeks to achieve is not derived from any law.' Defiantly, on 8 August the programme was shown by striking journalists outside Broadcasting House in Belfast for passers-by to see.

On 19 October 1988 the British government introduced a series of broadcasting restrictions, designed to keep spokespersons for a number of republican and loyalist organisations off the air. The first major casualty of these changes was a film documentary, *Mother Ireland*, produced for Channel 4 by Derry Film and Video. The film could not be broadcast in the United Kingdom as it included interviews with a number of women who had taken part in the 1916 Easter Rising and the War of Independence. (The programme also included an interview with a Belfast woman, Mairead Farrell. On 6 March, just a few days after the completion of the programme, Mairead Farrell, who, it was alleged, was taking part in an IRA action, was shot dead along with two men by British security forces in Gibraltar.) *Mother Ireland* went on to win a number of film awards, including the Femme Cathodique 1988 in Paris.

THE PRESENT AND THE FUTURE

Despite the appalling losses in Derry over the past twenty-two years, there have been some gains. The city's chronic housing problems have been reduced to manageable proportions. There has been a massive expansion of new public and private estates on the outskirts of the city as a result of the removal of the old constraints imposed by the gerrymander. If anything, the principal shortage in this respect nowadays is of suitable building land. The city centre is being redeveloped with relative sensitivity through a combination of government-sponsored projects, such as the busy, if architecturally uninspiring, Richmond shopping and office centre (since sold to the private sector), and the award-winning work of the Inner City Trust. This body, whose origins only go back to 1978, has made a huge impact on the physical fabric of the old walled city under the leadership of its director, the redoubtable and enigmatic Paddy 'Bogside' Doherty. Proclaiming that the city's troubled heritage, metaphorically represented by the seventeenth-century plantation walls, can be seen as either 'a noose or a necklace', Doherty has aggressively developed the trust into a multi-million-pound development project, based on a variety of imaginative unemployment relief schemes. While the trust has been responsible for the erection and restoration of many buildings in the city, it is possibly best known for the O'Doherty Tower, although this replica castle (suggested by Paddy Doherty) was actually built by the city council with the aid of funds from the European Community. In the early summer of 1990 a BBC Northern Ireland television programme levelled serious criticisms against the trust, which were immediately vigorously rebutted.

Smaller but similar schemes have been developed by others, such as the Maydown Youth Training Project run by Glen Barr, who figured prominently as a loyalist leader in the earlier years of the Troubles. However, despite all the changes of the past twenty-two years, actual unemployment figures for the city remain not much below 30 per cent. In fact, the official figures are worse now than they were in the late 1960s. Various attempts at alleviating unemployment have been made, such as the government tax-concessionary 'enterprise zones', and more recently the Derry–Boston venture, which seeks to develop transatlantic trade links. So far, however, these measures have had little success. More recently the Government has promised other employment schemes and the transfer to the city of several hundred public-sector jobs. Following a public inquiry in the spring of 1990, a Boston-based development company, O'Connell Brothers, was given permission to proceed with its intention to build a £65-million shopping and office complex in the city centre. When completed, it will be the largest single investment ever in the city.

In the European context, the infamous nearby frontier with the Irish Republic has, paradoxically, begun to make some sort of contribution to

The Foyle Bridge, the longest in Ireland, built in 1984 (Department of Environment for Northern Ireland)

the city. Money from the border area programmes of the European Regional Development Fund has helped finance some of the city's important development projects, such as the Foyle Bridge, built near the site of the boom of 1689, and is promised for the proposed new harbour facilities at Lisahally. Various road and telecommunications projects as well as several heritage initiatives have also been supported by funds from the European Community. Money from the International Fund for Ireland, set up after the signing of the Anglo-Irish agreement in 1985, is also beginning to be invested in the city, though as yet not on the scale that had been expected. The city's MP and Member of the European Parliament, John Hume, who was closely involved with the formulation of the Anglo-Irish agreement and who started his public career dealing with some of the city's apparently insoluble problems, is now leader of the SDLP and as a statesman he has won international acclaim, especially in Europe and in the United States.

Derry's long-standing tradition for versatility in all kinds of music has been extended and strengthened. At the height of the Troubles, in March 1970, the young Rosemary Brown – Dana – from Derry won the Eurovision Song Contest, singing for Ireland. She subsequently went on to establish a highly successful career as a popular singer. Phil Coulter, another native of Derry with Eurovision successes, has made an enormous impact both as a songwriter and a producer on the British pop-music industry. In more recent years he has carved out a separate career for himself as an internationally popular performer and orchestra conductor. His nostalgic song about Derry, 'The town I loved so well', has become something of an unofficial anthem of the city. The Derry punk group the Undertones also attracted international attention in the 1970s and one of its members, Feargal Sharkey, is now a well-known solo singer.

Feargal Sharkey of the Undertones (Orchard Gallery)

Despite the absence of a school of music in the city, a young generation of Derry performers is also attracting attention in the classical fields: Kevin O'Connell, composer; Mary Bergin, cellist; Gerard McChrystal, saxophonist; and Brian O'Doherty, classical guitarist, as well as several others, seem destined to make very successful careers in the years ahead. Other musicians, entertainers, artists and writers from the city have also been making an impression during these years. Although not from Derry, novelist Jennifer Johnston now lives on the outskirts of the city and some of her work has been set there. The outstanding Derry-born traditional musician and composer, Tomás Ó Canainn, has also written a novel about his native city, *Home to Derry*, while other novels have attempted to describe the background to the amazing events making the headlines, including Hugo Meenan's *No Time for Love* and Walter Hegarty's *The Price of Chips*. Two of Ireland's best-known journalists, Nell McCafferty and Eamonn McCann, have brought the distinctive, intelligent wit of their native city to bear on a

Sculpture by Anthony Gormley on the city walls overlooking the Bogside, with the bomb-damaged plinth of the Walker Pillar (blown up in 1973) in the background and St Eugene's Cathedral in the distance (Orchard Gallery)

host of local, national and international issues.

The Orchard Gallery, run since 1978 by the city council with the support of the Arts Council of Northern Ireland, has been in the vanguard of innovation in the contemporary visual arts. The gallery has won international recognition, while at the same time making an enormous contribution to various fields of community service in the city. Through an extensive programme of public exhibition, using venues and locations as diverse as the city walls and streets, billboards, shop windows and local discos, the Orchard Gallery has been able to expand opportunities for aesthetic enjoyment, extending them to audiences who would never venture into a formal gallery. In mid-1990 it was announced that its former organiser, Declan McGonagle, had been appointed as the first director of the newly established Irish Museum of Modern Art in Dublin. The opening by the city council as an arts facility of the recently restored old Foyle College – whose past pupils include John Lawrence (Viceroy of India, 1864–9), John Mitchel, and the songwriter Percy French, will further enhance the opportunities for cultural and artistic expression in the city.

In 1980 the distinguished Field Day Theatre Company was founded, with its base in Derry, and with a board of directors of outstanding distinction, including poets Seamus Deane, Seamus Heaney and Tom Paulin, playwrights Brian Friel and Thomas Kilroy, actor Stephen Rea and film-maker and musician David Hammond. As well as producing new dramatic works, the company has been involved in stimulating cultural reassessment throughout Ireland with the publication of a series of challenging pamphlets on many aspects of Irish intellectual debate. In 1981, Garret FitzGerald, then Taoiseach of the Irish Republic, spoke of the new company:

> Derry people, as I well know, take their talent in their stride. This talent is something which does not surprise them in the least. I hope they will allow the rest of us to mingle some of the amazement with the delight we feel that a city so troubled for so long should have the resources to produce Field Day.

In the 1970s the City of Derry Sub-Aqua Club discovered and excavated the remains of the Spanish Armada ship, *La Trinidad Valencera*. During 1988 the objects brought to light by this notable example of underwater archaeology played a key role in the international exhibitions marking the four-hundredth anniversary of the Armada.

The city is acquiring a reputation for self-help and imaginative innovation. There are many examples in Derry of successful local initiatives in various forms of community action. Despite its own relative poverty, the city's generous spirit is well recognised in terms of charitable donations, featuring high, if not highest, in both British and Irish league tables. BBC Radio Foyle has been an outstanding success since its foundation in 1979: in 1985 it moved into brand-new custom-built studios from which its programmes are broadcast locally, and it also contributes to the wider networks; it won the Sony award for the best local radio station in the United Kingdom in both 1988 and 1989. One of the station's best-known broadcasters, Gerry Anderson, has gone on to achieve a much wider audience. Although not to everyone's taste, his 'Stroke City' catchphrase, used to describe the Derry/Londonderry quandary, has caught the imagination of many.

In 1985, after a long absence, a Derry City football team began taking part in senior soccer again, playing significantly in the southern League of Ireland rather than the north's Irish League. In the early 1970s it had withdrawn from the Irish League after being issued with a directive to play its home matches in Coleraine rather than at the local Brandywell ground. The team's efforts to rejoin the northern league in the early 1980s were unsuccessful. Football enthusiasm on an unprecedented scale has become part of popular culture in the city, and Derry City supporters have won much respect for their loyalty, humour and good behaviour. In the 1988–9 season the team repaid this devotion by winning all three competitions in the south's professional football leagues. Unfortunately the celebrations were marred by sectarian, Burntollet-like attacks on the supporters as they returned from their final victory in Dublin on 7 May 1989.

Derry City Council has made huge strides in local sporting, cultural and community developments. Despite limited resources, the council's

The Ulster Orchestra, giving the first performance of the *Relief of Derry* symphony by Shaun Davey, specially commissioned by Derry City Council, in the Guildhall on 5 May 1990, as part of an overall pageant commemorating the tercentenary of the Siege of Derry (Tom Russell)

amenities section has developed a series of seasonal festivals and special events, among which the annual Halloween street carnival ranks as one of the best free shows in Ireland. In 1984, in adherence with general usage by the vast majority of local people and despite continuing opposition from Unionists, the council voted to change its name to Derry City Council, leaving the official name of the city itself, Londonderry, unchanged. However, nomenclature is still a thorny issue for the city. A spokesperson for the BBC recently admitted that its policy of always using the name Londonderry on first mention (sometimes actually misquoting its sources in the process) is without parallel.

The local district council elections in 1989 saw the return of an only slightly changed assembly. Most commentators agreed that the politics of municipal co-operation had been endorsed by the electorate.In 1989 the city council took a lead in commemorating the tercentenary of the Siege of Derry and an appropriate civic programme won widespread approval, even from among traditional opponents of the council. The weekend of 12–14 August 1989 saw two significant commemorations in the city – the three-hundredth anniversary of the end of the siege, and the twentieth anniversary of the arrival of British troops on the streets.

Each occasion was marked separately by parades and other community events, and both commemorations went off relatively peacefully.

In 1985, *Country Life* published a series of articles about Derry. The distinguished author John Cornforth lamented the fact that because of the Troubles, such a historic and visually important city had missed out on the European revival of interest in architecture and urban environment. Cornforth was optimistic, however, that Derry, aspects of which he found 'unexpectedly thrilling', was worthy and capable of regeneration. Three years later the Civic Trust in London, on the basis of a stated list of criteria, nominated Derry as 'one of the ten best places to live in, in the United Kingdom'. This was little consolation to Derry's 9,000 unemployed people, but it was a powerful recognition of the vitality of a city which is at least 1,400 years old. I have lived in Derry for the past sixteen years and during that time there have been many changes, good and bad. In recent years, however, a spirit has emerged determined to give the ninety thousand people of this historic and beautiful city, half of whom are under twenty-five years of age, a positive and hopeful future. Derry's problems are far from being solved, but there is no shortage of ideas about how to cope with them. In a recent article analysing the current state of the city and its prospects, the community activist Eamonn Deane quoted from the Gospel According to Saint Matthew, chapter 5, verse 14: 'A city set on a hill cannot be hid.'

SELECT BIBLIOGRAPHY

GENERAL

Annals of the Kingdom of Ireland by the Four Masters, from the earliest period to the year 1616, 7 vols, edited by J. O'Donovan, Dublin, Hodges and Smith, 1856

Annals of Ulster, 4 vols, edited by W. Hennessy and B. McCarthy, Dublin, HMSO, 1887–1901

Bonner, Brian. *Derry: An Outline History of the Diocese*, Dublin, Foilseacháin Náisiúnta Teoranta, 1982

Calender of the state papers relating to Ireland, 1509–1670, 24 vols, London, HMSO, 1860–1912

Colby, Thomas. *Ordnance Survey [Memoir] of Ireland: County of Londonderry*, vol. 1, Dublin, Hodges and Smith, 1837; reprint, Limavady, North-West Books, 1990

Gallagher, Charles. *Acorns and Oak Leaves: A Derry Childhood*, Derry, Dubh Regles Books, n.d.

Hamlin, Ann and Chris Lynn. *Pieces of the Past: Archaeological Excavations . . . Northern Ireland 1970–1986*, Belfast, HMSO, 1988

Hughes, Sam. *City on the Foyle*, Derry, Ogmios Press, 1984

Mullin, T.H. *Ulster's Historic City: Derry, Londonderry*, Coleraine, Coleraine Bookshop, 1986

Simpson, Robert. *The Annals of Derry*, Londonderry, Hempton, 1847; reprint, Limavady, North-West Books, 1987

CHAPTER 1

Brannon, Nick. 'Two historic sites at Enagh Lough', *Templemore*, vol. 2 (1987)

Byrne, Francis John. *Irish Kings and High Kings*, London, Batsford, 1973

Charlesworth, J. Kaye. 'The glacial geology of the north-west of Ireland', *Proceedings of the Royal Irish Academy*, vol. 36B (1924)

Lacy, Brian. 'The Grianan of Aileach', *Donegal Annual*, no. 36 (1984)

Lacy, Brian et al. *Archaeological Survey of County Donegal*, Lifford, Donegal County Council, 1983

Mitchell, Frank. *Shell Guide to Reading the Irish Landscape*, Dublin, Country House, 1986

O'Doherty, J.K. *Derriana*, Dublin, Gill and Son, 1902

Ross, Ann. *Pagan Celtic Britain*, London, Routledge and Kegan Paul, 1967

Rynne, Etienne. 'Celtic stone idols in Ireland', in *The Iron Age in the Irish Sea Province*, edited by Charles Thomas, London, Council for British Archaeology, 1972

Warner, Richard. 'The Broighter Hoard: a reappraisal, and the iconography of the collar', in *Studies on Early Ireland*, edited by B.G. Scott, Belfast, Association of Young Irish Archaeologists, 1980–1
Williams, B.B. 'A prehistoric complex at Ballygroll and Mullaboy, County Londonderry', *Ulster Journal of Archaeology*, vols 44–5 (1981–2)

CHAPTER 2

Anderson, A.O. and M.O. *Adomnan's Life of Columba*, London, Thomas Nelson, 1961
Herbert, Maire. *Iona, Kells and Derry*, Oxford, Clarendon Press, 1988
Hughes, Kathleen and Ann Hamlin. *The Modern Traveller to the Early Irish Church*, London, SPCK, 1977
Lacy, Brian. 'The Uí Meic Cairthinn of Lough Foyle', *Derriana* (1979)
Lacy, Brian. 'The development of Derry *c.* 600 to 1600', in *Kemelia*, edited by G. Mac Niocaill and P.F. Wallace, Galway, Galway University Press, 1988
Lacy, Brian and Michael McGuinness. 'The Creggan rath', *Templemore*, vol. 1 (1984–5)
Mac Niocaill, Gearóid. *Ireland before the Vikings*, Dublin, Gill and Macmillan, 1972
O'Kelleher, A. and G. Schoepperle. *Betha Colaim Chille: Life of Columcille*, Urbana, Illinois, University of Illinois, 1918
O'Meara, J. (trans.). *Topography of Ireland by Giraldus Cambrensis*, Dundalk, Dundalgan Press, 1951
The Story of the Long Tower Church 546–1946, Derry, Derry Journal, 1946

CHAPTER 3

Doherty, Charles. 'Exchange and trade in early medieval Ireland', *Journal of the Royal Society of Antiquaries of Ireland*, vol 110 (1980)
Mac Niocaill, Gearóid. *The Medieval Irish Annals*, Dublin, Dublin Historical Association, 1975
McNeill, T.E. *Anglo-Norman Ulster*, Edinburgh, Donald, 1980

CHAPTER 4

Bradshaw, Brendan. 'Manus the Magnificent: O'Donnell as Renaissance prince', in *Studies in Irish History*, edited by Art Cosgrove and Donal McCartney, Dublin, University College Dublin, 1979
Gwynn, Aubrey. *The Medieval Province of Armagh*, Dundalk, Dundalgan Press, 1946
Nicholls, Kenneth. *Gaelic and Gaelicised Ireland in the Middle Ages*, Dublin, Gill and Macmillan, 1972

Porter, J. Scott. 'The metropolitan visitation of the diocese of Derry', *Ulster Journal of Archaeology*, vol. 1 (1853)
Reeves, W. *Acts of Archbishop Colton in his Metropolitan Visitation of the Diocese of Derry*, Dublin, Irish Archaeological Society, 1850
Watt, J.A. 'John Colton, Justiciar of Ireland (1382) and Archbishop of Armagh (1383–1404)', in *Ireland in the Later Middle Ages*, edited by J.F.M. Lydon, Dublin, Gill and Macmillan, 1973

CHAPTER 5

Bonner, Brian. *That Audacious Traitor*, Dublin, Foilseacháin Náisiúnta Teoranta, 1975
Dowcra, Henry. 'Narration of the services done . . . Lough Foyle', in *Miscellany of the Celtic Society*, Dublin, The Celtic Society, 1849
Mac Curtain, Margaret. *Tudor and Stuart Ireland*, Dublin, Gill and Macmillan, 1972
Martin, F.X. 'Derry in 1590 – a Catholic demonstration', *Clogher Record*, vol. 6 (1968)

CHAPTER 6

Curl, James Steven. *The Londonderry Plantation 1609–1914*, Chichester, Phillimore, 1986
Gillespie, Raymond. *Conspiracy*, Belfast, Ulster Society for Irish Historical Studies, 1987
Hill, George. *The Plantation in Ulster 1606–1620*, Belfast, McCaw, Stevenson and Orr, 1877
Lacy, Brian. 'Two seventeenth-century houses in Linenhall St, Londonderry', *Ulster Folklife*, vol. 27 (1981)
Londonderry and the London Companies 1609–1629, Belfast, HMSO, 1928
Milligan, C.D. *The Walls of Derry*, Londonderry, Londonderry Sentinel, 1948
Moody, T.W. *The Londonderry Plantation 1609–41*, Belfast, William Mullan and Son, 1939
Moody, T.W. and J.G. Simms. *The Bishopric of Derry and the Irish Society of London 1602–1705*, 2 vols, Dublin, Irish Manuscripts Commission, 1968 and 1983
Reid, James Seaton. *The History of the Presbyterian Church in Ireland*, 3 vols, Belfast, William Mullan, 1853
Reps, John. *Tidewater Towns*, Williamsburg, Colonial Williamsburg Foundation, 1972

CHAPTER 7

Burnside, Sam. 'No temporizing with the foe', *Linen Hall Review*, vol. 5, no. 3 (Autumn 1988)

Macrory, Patrick. *The Siege of Derry*, Oxford, Oxford University Press, 1988
Maguire, W.A. (ed.). *Kings in Conflict*, Belfast, Blackstaff Press, 1990
Simms, J.G. *The Siege of Derry*, Dublin, APCK, 1966
Simms, J.G. *Jacobite Ireland 1685–91*, London, Routledge and Kegan Paul, 1969

CHAPTER 8

Dickson, R.J. *Ulster Emigration to Colonial America 1718–1775*, Belfast, Ulster Historical Foundation, 1988
Dwyer, Philip. *The Siege of Derry in 1689*, London, Elliot Stock, 1893
Fothergill, Brian. *The Mitred Earl*, London, Faber and Faber, 1974
Graham, John. *A History of the Siege of Londonderry*, Dublin, William Curry Junior and Company, 1829
Parker, Edward L. *History of Londonderry*, Boston, Perkins and Whipple, 1851; reprint, Town of Londonderry, New Hampshire, n.p. 1974

CHAPTER 9

Boyd, Andrew. *The Rise of Irish Trade Unions 1729–1970*, Tralee, Anvil, 1972
Murphy, Desmond. *Derry, Donegal and Modern Ulster 1790–1921*, Londonderry, Aileach Press, 1981
The Shirt Industry of the North-West of Ireland, Londonderry, Londonderry Teachers' Centre, n.d.

CHAPTER 10

Anderson, Ernest B. *Sailing Ships of Ireland*, Dublin, Morris and Company, 1951
Brooke, Peter. *Ulster Presbyterianism*, Dublin, Gill and Macmillan, 1987
Cooke, Sholto. *The Maiden City and the Western Ocean*, Dublin, Morris and Company, n.d.
Doherty, William. *Derry Columbkille*, Derry, n.p., 1899
Holmes, R.F.G. *Magee 1865–1965*, Belfast, BNL Printing, 1965
McNeill, D.B. *Irish Passenger Steamship Services*, vol. 1, Newton Abbot, David and Charles, 1969
O'Farrell, Patrick. *Letters from Irish Australia 1825–1929*, Belfast, Ulster Historical Foundation, 1984
Report of the . . . Riots and Disturbances in the City of Londonderry (1869), Dublin, HMSO, 1869
Stewart, A.T.Q. *The Narrow Ground*, London, Faber and Faber, 1977

CHAPTER 11

Blake, John W. *Northern Ireland in the Second World War*, Belfast, HMSO, 1956
Curran, Frank. *Derry: Countdown to Disaster*, Dublin, Gill and Macmillan, 1986
Derry: The War Years, Londonderry, Heritage Library, n.d.
Farrell, Michael. *Northern Ireland: The Orange State*, London, Pluto Press, 1980
Kingsley, Paul. *Londonderry Revisited*, Belfast, Belfast Publications, 1989
McCann, Eamonn. *War and an Irish Town*, London, Pluto Press, 1984
Report of the Irish Boundary Commission 1925, with an introduction by Geoffrey J. Hand, Shannon, Irish University Press, 1969
White, Barry. *John Hume: Statesman of the Troubles*, Belfast, Blackstaff Press, 1984

CHAPTER 12

Asmal, Kader. *Shoot to Kill: International Lawyers' Inquiry into the Lethal Use of Firearms by the Security Forces in Northern Ireland*, Cork, Mercier Press, 1985
Callaghan, James. *A House Divided: The Dilemma of Northern Ireland*, London, Collins, 1973
Cameron Report. *Disturbances in Northern Ireland*, Belfast, HMSO, Cmd 532, 1969
Deutsch, Richard and Vivien Magowan. *Northern Ireland 1968–74: A Chronology of Events*, 3 vols, Belfast, Blackstaff Press, 1973–5
Devlin, Bernadette. *The Price of my Soul*, London, Pan, 1969
Egan, Bowes and Vincent McCormack. *Burntollet*, London, LRS Publishers, 1969
Fortnight, no. 266 (October 1988)
McClean, Raymond. *The Road to Bloody Sunday*, Swords, Ward River Press, 1983
Martin, Colin. *Full Fathom Five*, London, Chatto and Windus, 1975
Sunday Times Insight Team. *Ulster*, Harmondsworth, Penguin, 1972
Widgery Tribunal. *Report of the Tribunal . . . into the events on Sunday 30th January 1972 . . .*, London, HMSO, 1972

INDEX